Cross Narratives

Princeton Theological Monograph Series

K. C. Hanson, Charles M. Collier, and D. Christopher Spinks,
Series Editors

Recent volumes in the series:

Philip Ruge-Jones
Cross in Tensions:
Luther's Theology of the Cross as Theologico-social Critique

Paul S. Chung
Martin Luther and Buddhism, 2nd ed.

Christian T. Collins Winn
"Jesus Is Victor!"
The Significance of the Blumhardts for the Theology of Karl Barth

Ryan A. Neal
Theology as Hope:
On the Ground and Implications of Jürgen Moltmann's Doctrine of Hope

Poul F. Guttesen
Leaning into the Future:
The Kingdom of God in the Theology of Jürgen Moltmann and the Book of Revelation

Jeff B. Pool
God's Wounds:
Hermeneutic of the Christian Symbol of Divine Suffering

Chris Budden
Following Jesus in Invaded Space:
Doing Theology on Aboriginal Land

Cross Narratives
Martin Luther's Christology and the Location of Redemption

NEAL J. ANTHONY

☙PICKWICK *Publications* • Eugene, Oregon

CROSS NARRATIVES
Martin Luther's Christology and the Location of Redemption

Princeton Theological Monograph Series 135

Copyright © 2010 Neal J. Anthony. All rights reserved. Except for brief quotations in critical articles or reviews, no part of this book may be reproduced in any manner without prior written permission from the publisher. Write: Permissions, Wipf and Stock Publishers, 199 W. 8th Ave., Suite 3, Eugene, OR 97401.

Pickwick Publications
An Imprint of Wipf and Stock Publishers
199 W. 8th Ave., Suite 3
Eugene, OR 97401

ISBN 13: 978-1-60608-654-4

Cataloging-in-Publication data:

Anthony, Neal J.

Cross narratives : Martin Luther's Christology and the location of redemption / Neal J. Anthony.

Princeton Theological Monograph Series 135

xxii + 300 p. ; 23 cm. Includes bibliographical references and indexes.

ISBN 13: 978-1-60608-654-4

1. Theology of the cross. 2. Jesus Christ—Person and offices. 3. Jesus Christ—Crucifixion. 4. Redemption. 5. Luther, Martin, 1483–1546. 6. Barth, Karl, 1886–1968. 7. Hall, Douglas John, 1928–. I. Title. II. Series.

BR333.5 C72 A55 2010

Manufactured in the U.S.A.

Dedicated to

Vítor Westhelle,
Doktor-Vater,
Friend,
Theologian of the Cross

Beatus auctor saeculi
servile corpus induit,
Ut carne carnem liberans
ne perderet quos condidit.

—Cajus Caelius Sedulius of Achaia,
WA 35:150, 431–34

Contents

Foreword / ix

Acknowledgments / xiii

Abbreviations / xvi

Introduction / xvii

1. Locating the Conversation: *Theologia Crucis* and "Within-Redemption" / 1
2. Luther's *Theologia Crucis*: An Outline / 52
3. *Communicatio Idiomatum*: The *Radix* of Luther's *Theologia Crucis* / 106
4. *Larvae Dei*: Wrappings of the Presence of "Within-Redemption" / 154
5. Countering a "High-Pitched" Anthropology: Barth's *Communicatio Gratiarum* / 197

Conclusion / 263

Appendix: Douglas John Hall and Complete "Within-Redemption" / 275

Bibliography / 281

Name Index / 293

Subject Index / 297

Scripture Index / 299

Foreword

Vítor Westhelle

THE FORMULA OF THE ECUMENICAL COUNCIL OF CHALCEDON (451) has been one of the most dazzling ecumenical accomplishments of the early church. And yet whilst being a celebrated doctrine it was simultaneously a tortuous one to be interpreted and baffling regarding the implementation of its pastoral implications. This book by Neal Anthony goes to the works of Martin Luther to establish a case for a radical interpretation of the formula of the Fourth Ecumenical Council that affirms the two natures of Christ in one person, without confusion, without change, without division, and without separation. This has been hailed as the *communicatio idiomatum*, the mutual exchange of essential properties of the divine and the human natures in one person. In this study the author presents a rereading of Luther's theology of the cross taking into account the importance of the Reformer's notion of the "third mode" of Christ's presence and its personal and cosmological implications.

The Lutheran reading of Chalcedon finds in Luther himself many anecdotal expressions and unexpected rhetorical tropes. The *locus classicus* for the definition of what came to be known in Lutheran Orthodoxy, as to the different genres entailed in the *communicatio idiomatum*, finds its basis in the Reformer's *Confession Concerning Christ's Supper* of 1528, extensively quoted (over 10 paragraphs) by the authors of the "Formula of Concord." In this text Luther distinguishes "three modes of [Christ] being at any given place" according to his *human* (!) nature. The first is the corporeal mode of presence, namely the historical Jesus of Nazareth. The second is the "incomprehensible, spiritual mode of presence," which is exemplified by Christ's presence at the Lord's Supper, in, with, and under the bread and the cup. But this mode of presence is still located in a recognizable "place," which is the Eucharistic community sharing the meal. Then Luther adds a distinct third mode of presence "according to which all created things are indeed much more permeable and present to him than they are according to the second mode." And he continues: "You must place this existence of Christ, which constitutes him as one person with God, far, far beyond things created, as far as God transcends them; and, on the other hand, place it as deep in and as near to all created things as God is in them." This includes even the dead, in whom Christ is also present according to his human nature.

It is this third mode of presence that allowed for the confection of the peculiarly and radical Lutheran understanding of the *communicatio idiomatum*. This third mode of communication between the natures in the person was described later in the confessional debates as entailing two genres. One is the *genus majestaticum* (the impartation of the majestic attributes of God to created things, e.g., "Jesus of Nazareth is the creator of the world"). The other mirrors the former and is known as the *genus tapeinoticum* (the impartation of the humble attributes of created realities to the divine nature, e.g., "God died"). They are, in fact, not two different genres, but only the mutual sides of the same communication between the natures.

The Lutheran reading of Chalcedon was further and more explicitly developed in *On the Councils and the Church* (1539). While maintaining the communication between the natures in the person, the Reformer insisted that the communication is not only about ascribing attributes and operations of either of the natures to the person but also that it is true communication. For it to be a true communication there needs to be a communication from the person, in whom the natures abide, to the natures, or more precisely, it needs to be a communication between the natures *in* the person, which for Luther, is indeed the case, for the natures, though unconfused, cannot be divided. By this mode of communication both the divine attributes can be ascribed to created reality (*finitum capax infiniti*—the finite is capable of the infinite) as much as attributes of creation can also be ascribed to the divine reality (*infinitus ferat finem*—the infinite suffers the finite).

The Lutheran insistence that God died according to the human nature is the final expression of the consequences of this interpretation. The implication of such reading is that wherever God is present there is also Christ according to the *human* nature for they cannot be separated. The Lutheran *est* already affirms this in Luther's second mode of presence in the bread and cup, as is known from the disputes over the Lord's Supper. But the third mode of presence carries this to its logical and radical end, for the Spirit (that is the energy working the *communio et unio*) blows wherever it wills and the person cannot be divided. This is the reason for the creedal affirmation that the "seated at right hand of the Father" means everywhere. Or to phrase it more rhetorically, using Luther's words: "Thus it is right and truthfully said that God is born, appeased or breast-fed, lays in a crib, feels cold, walks, stays, falls, wanders, awakes, eats, drinks, suffers, dies, etc." Yet it goes even further, for it applies not only to Jesus, but to whole of creation.

Luther's reading of the *communicatio* has been an issue in Luther research since the "Formula of Concord" has endorsed Luther's reading even if not elaborating on its far-reaching implications. Recent scholarship has revisited the debate. This book is an indispensible voice that significantly and provocatively furthers this conversation and adds to it new dimensions. A significant contribution of Anthony's study is to offer new lenses for assessing modern and contemporary theological discussions and criticisms of Luther from Schleiermacher to Barth, and conversely placing Luther as a critic ahead of our times pointing out new paths in the theological maze we often find ourselves. Yet, even more relevantly, this book, in a tour de force, unveils the pastoral and hopeful promises of presence "within-redemption" for a culture that invests in the festive Easter's encroachment into Good Friday, while the officially sanctioned optimism anesthetizes the daily pain of the cross we carry and conceals the graves we daily inhabit and in which we finally will lie.

The boldness of the argument makes it simple and compelling, however polemical it may be. Bringing to the fore Luther's third mode of presence allows the identification of creation and redemption through one Word. And such word inhabits the depth of all creation. It reaches even to the "within-locations" of humanity's tombs and indeed to the whole of creation groaning in labor pains.

This book is a Christological inquiry into the theology of the Cross, which Luther called his only theology (*sola crux est nostra theologia*). But, accordingly and unavoidably, this study unfolds the necessary theological implications of such theology for an array of *loci* (justification, revelation, faith, creation, the sacraments, anthropology, and pastoral care), while leaving for the reader guidelines, and ellipses to be filled in for numerous other loci.

The entire book is a sustained discussion of original sources, presenting a carefully argued thesis. As much as it touches a controversial topic, it is even more persuasive in its unfolding, remarkable in its conclusions, and promising in its function for the work of ministry.

Acknowledgments

THIS WORK BEARS THE FINGERPRINTS OF THE PERSONALITIES THAT have ushered it through the process of formation. But precisely when and where that process of formation began, one can never decisively discern. So I shall name the owners of those fingerprints in no precise, logical order. And, in the listing of the owners of those fingerprints, let it be known: implicit within the naming of these names is the acknowledgment—the confession!—that the writer of this work merely "stands on the shoulders of giants," that he lives and works by grace alone.

So a word of gratitude is extended to those whose wisdom provided inspiration and navigation through graduate school, thus in some manner galvanizing the thought process that resulted in this work: Ted Jennings, Bob Cathey, Ken Sawyer, Bill Wright, and Mark Thomsen.

I especially want to lift up Thandeka. It was Thandeka who, early in my course of graduate studies not only received this "honorary U.U." warmly (inviting me back for a second seminar on Schleiermacher), but taught me to embrace the "human" in the widest, most profound sense of the term. Her fingerprints are all over this dissertation.

And Antje Jackelén: Antje not only accompanied me through two graduate seminars as a prolific influence, but she accompanied me through two sets of graduate exams (qualifying and fields) and a colloquy. Her friendship, along with that of her husband Heinz, is a cherished gift. Antje's fingerprints—through a gaze that encompasses the universe—are also all over this work.

And Vítor. My "Doktor-Vater," teacher, advisor . . . "friend." It was Vítor who both opened a new perspective on Lutheran theology and the *theologia crucis*, and affirmed and inspired my theological vocation with his passion and kindness. Vítor's fingerprints are unmistakably clear: not only was it he who turned me in the direction of the oft-neglected "third mode," reminding me that it is a quintessential expression of Luther's *theologia crucis*, but it was Vítor who instilled in this pupil the need to fire his theological efforts with *imagination*. Perhaps this may be one of the most important, fundamental elements of the vocation of theologian.

And to my colloquy readers: Vítor, Antje, and Kurt Hendel: thank you for your work and spirit of accommodation.

And there are other "fingerprints" amassed at various points during the formation of this dissertation: those of Bud Christenson, Ed Roleder, Al Schwandt, Mike Ostrom, John Valentine, Gerhard Forde, Steven Paulson, Arland Hultgren, Gracia Grindal, Walter Sundberg; those of graduate school colleagues: John Nunes, Rebecca Proefrock, Joe Gaston, Anthony Biddings; those of the congregation in which I grew-up: Sheridan Lutheran, Lincoln, Nebraska; those of the congregations in which I have officially served: Trinity Lutheran, Victorville, California (as a vicar); St. Paul Lutheran, Blue Hill, Nebraska; and Salem Lutheran, Ponca, Nebraska. To Troy Koeppe: your support and assistance with my manuscript and your friendship have been immeasurable. To Bob and Cindy Anderson: your lives are an embodiment of your faith confession, "lights shining in the darkness."

And to K. C. Hanson and his incredible, patient staff at Wipf and Stock: Your input has been invaluable. Valuing the reality that the thoughts, movements and conclusions of this work will be strongly contested by some and received warmly by some (hopefully spawning a fuller conversation regarding an essential, yet oft-neglected aspect of Luther's *theologia crucis*), I cherish the opportunity for this work to be received by a larger audience. For this I am indebted to K. C. and his fine staff.

To my father-in-law Jim: your support during this process are cherished and will never be forgotten.

To my parents, Jim and Carmy: there are ways in which you have inspired and influenced me by your grace and love and support—*larvae Dei!*—that I'll continue to discover up until the day of my own death. I embrace the attributes of yours that I continually discover in my own self. It is beautiful to know that I am your child. My accomplishments are an expression in so many ways of everything you have given me. Only God can measure my gratitude for the two of you.

To our son Owen: someday, when you are old enough to understand, I'll explain to you why we uprooted you so many times during your young life. When the season is right, I pray for your understanding and forgiveness. You are an incredible, precocious child; "apples don't fall far from the tree." And you are a testament to the reality that children really do survive their parents!

To my wife Kim: not only did you resign your post from a great teaching job in Hastings, Nebraska (in a part of the world in which we were completely comfortable and happy!) in order to move to Chicago, but you helped to shoulder the burden of my insecurities, anxieties, and personality flaws (all of which were exacerbated at one point or another by the graduate school process!) during my graduate program. I am a weakling of wisdom and strength and endurance compared to you. No words can express the gratitude for what you have endured for my sake, for the sake of our family.

Abbreviations

BC   *The Book of Concord: The Confessions of the Evangelical Lutheran Church*, translated and edited by Theodore G. Tappert in collaboration with Jaroslav Pelikan, Robert H. Fischer, and Arthur C. Piepkorn. Philadelphia: Fortress, 1959.

CD   *Church Dogmatics* I/1—IV/4, edited by Geoffrey W. Bromiley and T. F. Torrance. Edinburgh: T. & T. Clark, 1936–1977.

LW   *Luther's Works*, edited by Jaroslav Pelikan and Helmut T. Lehman, 55 vols. Philadelphia: Fortress; St. Louis: Concordia, 1955–1986.

WA   *D. Martin Luthers Werke*, Kritische Gesamtausgabe. Weimar: Böhlaus, 1883–1957.

WA TR   *D. Martin Luthers Werke*, Kritische Gesamtausgabe, Tischreden.

Introduction

The theology of the Incarnation is and remains a theology of the cross, for it proclaims a God whose will is to be with us where we are (Emmanuel). To get Jesus off the cross has never been a difficult problem for the theology of glory. However, to get us off the cross—which is, after all, Christ's own work—is another matter. Least of all can it be achieved by reiterating the confession that Jesus has risen. When that is done (as it so often is) with a certain fanfare and with Easter Sunday gusto that behaves as if now everything were entirely put to rights, it is ironic and sometimes repulsive. The cross of the world and of humanity remains after all the Easter sermons have been preached and all the hallelujahs sung ... Christ has traversed the infinite abyss between cross and resurrection, decisively but not as yet finally. Were it final, we should have been left behind, nailed to our crosses, doubly forsaken.[1]

THE *THEOLOGIA CRUCIS* IS A THEOLOGY THAT ARTICULATES REDEMPtion from within (hereafter "within-redemption"). More precisely, the *theologia crucis* is a theology of *complete* "within-redemption." That is, the *theologian* of the cross does not rest after articulating a *completed*, "once-for-all," *in illo tempore* narrative of "within-redemption" which subsequently need only be applied to individual, embodied human narratives as merely things "signified." To operate as if the work of "within-redemption" is already accomplished, needing simply to be applied to the individual, embodied narratives of humanity as things "signified," not only errs by "rounding-off" and collapsing the manifold narratives of humanity into a meta-narrative of completed redemption,[2] but

---

1. Hall, *Lighten Our Darkness*, 115.
2. As we speak of the narrative of Christ's redemption and its relationship to the manifold narratives of humanity, and certainly their irreducible, individual, embodied integrity, let us be mindful of David Tracy's diagnosis of the present context in which theology is done, one that is, to say the least, cognizant of the particularity and "otherness" of narrative both with reference to God and humanity. In his "The Hidden God: The Divine Other of Liberation," 5, he states, "The real face of our period, as Emmanuel

indeed robs Emmanuel's work of "within-redemption" of his profound, ongoing involvement in the life of creation as its creating and redeeming Word. But, the *theologian* of the cross recognizes that the work of delineating "within-redemption"—honoring the significance and created integrity of all individual, embodied human narratives—is not complete until she is able to articulate a "within-redemption" which "takes place" "within" the manifold *loci* of all individual, embodied human narratives.

This project contends that *complete* "within-redemption" can only be accomplished through the explication of that which is foundational to Martin Luther's *theologia crucis*, or his radical interpretation of the *communicatio idiomatum*. Specifically, this project will develop the point that it is only through what Luther coined the exalted "third mode" of Christ's presence—the ultimate expression of his *theologia crucis*—that the theologian of the cross is able to locate the ongoing work, and thus presence, of redemption within all individual, embodied human narratives. If in Jesus Christ God is revealed to be Emmanuel, then it is only through the "third mode" that God is completely Emmanuel. In order to unpack this claim, this project will move through five stages—chapters—of development.

Chapter one, drawing upon the signal contributions of theologians of the cross Douglas John Hall and Alan E. Lewis, will be devoted to a development of the dynamics and implications—within the framework of the *theologia crucis*—of "within-redemption." But if chapter one is to be devoted to a development of the dynamics and implications of "within-redemption," it will also have to be involved with a development of *what* necessitates "within-redemption." It will become clear

---

Levinas saw with such clarity, is the face of the other: the face that commands, 'Do not kill me.' The face insists: do not reduce me or anyone else to your narrative. Each of us can accept evolutionary theory in understanding nature, as well as understanding ourselves as part of nature. But natural evolutionary theory is not useful for understanding myself as a subject active in history. There, I, like you, am other and different. No one should be viewed as simply more of the same, merely a moment in the grand social-evolutionary, teleological schema of modernity. Genuine thought today begins in ethical resistance; it begins by trying to think the unthought of modernity. Beyond the early modern turn to the purely autonomous, self-grounding subject, lies the quintessential turn of much contemporary thought—the turn to the other." He adds, "God's shattering otherness, the neighbor's irreducible otherness, the othering reality of 'revelation' (not the consoling modern notion of 'religion'): all these expressions of genuine otherness demand the serious attention of all thoughtful persons" (ibid., 6).

from the outset of this project that the *theologia crucis*, reflected by its corresponding dynamic of "within-redemption," is a theology *for* creation; a theology fired by a profound concern for affirming the integrity of creation, an integrity manifested especially through the narratives of individual, embodied humans. Chapter one, then, will begin with a delineation of what it is to be a "thorough-going psychosomatic" entity, or a "human." It is the integrity of this "human" that is addressed and affirmed by the "within-redemption" of the *theologia crucis*.

But if chapter one is devoted to an explication of "within-redemption" through the assistance of Hall and Lewis, it will also be concerned with delineating the shortcomings of their respective explications of "within-redemption" (see also Appendix). It will be contended that they fail to articulate *complete* "within-redemption" in relation to the individual, embodied narratives of humanity. As "within-redemption" is an *expression* of the *theologia crucis*, it will be asserted that Martin Luther's ultimate expression of the *theologia crucis* best assists the theologian of the cross in explicating complete "within-redemption." Chapter two, then, will develop by means of a fundamental, four-part outline Luther's *theologia crucis* in such a manner as to provide the conceptual framework for articulating the *ultimate, foundational* expression of his *theologia crucis* in chapter three. Chapter two is the building block for chapter three.

Not only will it be asserted in chapter three that Luther's radical interpretation of the *communicatio idiomatum* is foundational to his *theologia crucis*, but that the "third mode" of Christ's presence—a necessary expression of his *communicatio idiomatum*—most adequately assists us in delineating complete "within-redemption" within the parameters of the *theologia crucis*. But if it is the "third mode" of Christ's presence that most adequately allows us to extend Christ's "within-redeeming" presence to the locations of all individual, embodied narratives, and thus ultimately their tombs, then chapter four will develop the manner by which that presence of "within-redemption" is localized *per* all individual, embodied human narratives. This will be conducted through a delineation of what Luther refers to as the *larvae Dei* (and related terminology). As we will discover, the *larvae Dei* will not only allow us to articulate a localization of the "third mode" of Christ's presence regarding all human narratives, but will indeed afford us the opportunity of viewing all of creation through the lens of the *modus operandi* of the cross. It is through a delineation of the *larvae Dei* that we will be able to comprehend, ultimately, the individual human tomb as a *larva* of Christ's ongoing, "within-redeeming" presence, and thus his presence of complete "within-redemption."

But for all of Luther's help in assisting us in the articulation of complete "within-redemption" through his radical interpretation of the *communicatio idiomatum*, we must also be reminded that some of the greatest exponents of theology's discipline detest just such a formulation. Luther's radical interpretation of the *communicatio idiomatum* is not without its vehement detractors! Karl Barth was, perhaps, one of the most vociferous opponents to the "Lutheran" *communicatio idiomatum*. Chapter five will develop Barth's counter to the "Lutheran" *communicatio idiomatum*, or the *communicatio gratiarum*. The development of Barth's *communicatio gratiarum* will be conducted against the canvas of his reaction to both "absolute man" of the eighteenth century (represented most poignantly, he feels, by F. D. E. Schleiermacher in the nineteenth century), and "apotheosized man" of the nineteenth century (represented most acutely by Ludwig Feuerbach). Essentially, as we will see, it is Luther's *communicatio idiomatum* that provides both fertile soil and "opens the door" to the "apotheosized man" of Feuerbach and his ilk. We will also investigate the ramifications of such a Christological proposal by Barth, or his *communicatio gratiarum*.

If, as Douglas John Hall has pointed-out, the *theologia crucis* is represented by a "thin tradition"[3] of theological practitioners, then it will be revealed that the "third mode" of Christ's presence, a necessary expression of Luther's *theologia crucis*, can best be described as represented by an even "thinner tradition" of practitioners. We might say that it is "trickle tradition."

But whether it is represented by a "thick," "thin," or even "trickle" tradition, as this project will develop and contend, it is the "third mode" of Christ's presence that not only best assists us in articulating complete "within-redemption," but indeed reinforces the reality—especially with regard to questions of eschatology—that we cannot move beyond—for now—being a people—through Christ—of hope. The "third mode" of Christ's presence indeed offers a hope that is not only borne of "calling a thing what it is," but allows us to confess the human tomb (the ultimate

---

3. Hall, *Lighten Our Darkness*, 108.

"thing" we would rather not "call ... what it is") as a *larva* of the Creator's presence of "within-redemption."

Indeed, it will be argued, it is the "third mode" of Christ's presence that best fits the bill for the hope for which Hall searches: "I, too, am searching for a theology of hope but only a hope which emerges in the confrontation with the data of despair can be authentic—at least for this time and place. Hope that protects men from encounter with hopelessness is not Christian hope. All hopes, therefore, all dreams and visions, all 'positive thoughts' which are designed to preserve men from the meeting with death must be rejected, for in the end they only preserve men from meeting with life."[4] May this project reward that search.

---

4. Hall, *Hope against Hope*, 27.

1

Locating the Conversation
Theologia Crucis *and* "Within-Redemption"

Redeeming the Body

Celebrating the Creature

THE ASSERTION AMONG THEOLOGIANS THAT HUMANS ARE IN THEIR essence "thorough-going psychosomatic" entities,[1] or exist essentially as embodied beings, is certainly no recent, modish theological development. It is perhaps one of the fundamental trajectories of theological thought in both the twentieth and present centuries. Indeed, the corresponding idea of the goodness of creaturely embodiment, that we are permitted to be human beings, "nothing more and nothing less," has been such a significant development that Douglas John Hall could comment in the second volume of his three volume *magnum opus* in systematic theology, written in the last decade of the twentieth century, concerning this trajectory and its application with regard to the Gospel, that "Today, the most appropriate articulation of the meaning of gospel ... might be: You are free to be a creature. You are liberated for creaturehood. You do not have to be a god or a demigod or a superman/woman, a Prometheus."[2]

---

1. Polkinghorne, *God of Hope and the End of the World*, 104. Having analyzed the contributions of science, he adds "human beings look much more like animated bodies than like incarnated souls" (ibid., 105).

2. Hall, *Professing the Faith*, 340. Addressing the idea that ultimate human redemption, a topic which will be discussed in a more developed context below, is a "deliverance from creaturehood." Hall remarks, "The biblical God does not respond to this cry, because the God of Abraham and Sarah, of Mary Magdalene and John the beloved disciple and Judas Iscariot, does not want to save us *from* creaturehood but *for* it.

And, as it certainly must be pointed-out, a generation of theologians of the statures and influences of Rudolf Bultmann,[3] Karl Barth,[4] Dietrich Bonhoeffer,[5] and Reinhold Niebuhr,[6] to give just a sampling,

---

Redemption is redemption from our fear, distaste, and rejection of creaturehood, our fall. Sanctification is the sanctifying of creaturely life. Prayer in the name of Jesus Christ is a way in to the world, not out of it. The baptism of water quenches the false spirituality of the ecstatic, fiery baptism that is our soul's vain attempt at flight from earth, from the body" (ibid.). He adds, "Creaturehood is so very good that the biblical God intends not only to save it, provide for it, clothe it—but to repeat it. *Da capo*: Go back to the beginning!" (ibid.).

3. For instance, in his *Theology of the New Testament*, vol. 1, 192, Bultmann, asserts that, "The only human existence that there is—even in the sphere of the Spirit—is somatic existence . . ." He adds, ". . . it is clear that the *soma* is not a something that outwardly clings to a man's real self (to his soul, for instance), but belongs to its very essence, so that we can say man does not *have* a *soma*; he *is soma* . . ." (ibid., 194). And when applied to human redemption, the reality of *soma* remains. *Ergo*, "That *soma* belongs inseparably, constitutively, to human existence is most clearly evident from the fact that Paul cannot conceive even of a future human existence after death 'when that which is perfect come' as an existence without *soma* . . ." (ibid., 192).

4. Cf. his seldomly cited passage on embodiment, especially with reference to the "religious" attempt to apprehend God through direct communication, in *The Epistle to the Romans*, 268–69. I also refer the reader to his 1924/5 lectures on I Corinthians 15 entitled *The Resurrection of the Dead*, 197, in which Barth declares, that "To wish to be God's without the body is rebellion against God's will, is secret denial of God; it is, indeed, the body which suffers, sins, dies. We are waiting for our Body's redemption; if the body is not redeemed to obedience, to health, to life, then there is no God; then what may be called God does not deserve this name. The truth of God requires and establishes the Resurrection of the Dead, the Resurrection of the Body." Ultimately, and certainly as an expression of his Christology, noting the traditional emphasis of the soul over and against the body, Barth asserts, "Man's being exists, and is therefore soul; and it exists in a certain form, and is therefore body. This is the simplest description of the being of soul and body and their relationship. Man is soul and body—this is in brief the constitution of his being" (III/2: 325).

5. In his 1932/3 lectures on Genesis, translated into English as *Creation and Fall*, and appearing in *Creation and Fall / Temptation: Two Biblical Studies*, 50–51, Bonhoeffer asserts that the human's "body belongs to this essential being. Man's body is not his prison, his shell his exterior, but man himself. Man does not 'have' a body; he does not 'have' a soul; rather, he 'is' body and soul. Man in the beginning is really his body. He is one." Thus, "The man who renounces his body renounces his existence before God the Creator . . . he does not come to the earthly world from above, driven and enslaved by a cruel fate . . . he is called out by the Word of God the Almighty, in himself a piece of earth, but earth called into human being by God" (ibid., 51).

6. Essentially for Niebuhr as he develops in the first volume of his 1939 Gifford Lectures, published as *The Nature and Destiny of Man*, 3, the doctrine of justification is the Christian culmination of the question "What does it mean to be human?" Justification is thus the answer to the human attempt to transcend, or give unconditioned

made the claim of the essential psychosomatic unity of the human, as well as the corresponding goodness of creaturely embodiment, fundamental to the development of their own theological constructs. Indeed, representing the next generation of theologians, Oscar Cullmann, as well a pupil of Bultmann, after having examined the biblical sources, presented in 1955 a signal and influential series of lectures[7] in which Socrates' body/soul dualism, with its attendant expectation of the soul surviving bodily death, was thrown into relief by, and contrasted with, biblical orientations towards death and, certainly, its articulation of the resurrection of the body. And, as Nancey Murphy has observed, after surveying the production of both theological and biblical studies in the twentieth century, there has been a "gradual displacement of a dualistic account of the person, with its correlative emphasis on the afterlife conceived in terms of the immortality of the soul."[8] But, as we will see, the story is not so simple.

Having underscored the fundamental significance of the essential psychosomatic unity of the human for theology through the last century, as well as the corresponding goodness of its creaturely embodiment, to be sure, "immortal souls" do not simply go away. Regardless of what has been said up to this point, we must take the—what *prima facie* may seem to be an incredibly simple—observation of James McClendon with the utmost of seriousness. In McClendon's monumental task of planting Christian ethics deeply in the soil of "embodied selfhood," simultaneously observing that Scripture's witness regarding this same "embodied selfhood" is not so much an emphasis, but rather an assumption, he both recognizes the alien nature of this scriptural assumption by contemporaries, and diagnoses this malaise by declaring, "[P]erhaps our latter-day difficulty can be described this way: we simply do not believe

---

status to, its creaturely embodiedness which consists of nature—or being "subject to its vicissitudes, compelled by its necessities, driven by its impulses, and confined within the brevity of years," and spirit—as one whose self-transcendence expresses itself as one "who stands outside of nature, life, himself, his reason and the world" (ibid.)—and thus a restoration to the reality that these two irreducible facts of humanity—nature and spirit—reside within an irreducible unity called the human, or the "essential nature of man" (ibid., 270).

7. Cullmann, *Immortality of the Soul or Resurrection of the Dead?*

8. Murphy, *Bodies and Souls, or Spirited Bodies?*, 10. See ibid., 11–22, in which Murphy provides a thumbnail sketch regarding how the "soul" has been articulated from Plato and Aristotle through to the twentieth century.

the Scriptures, do not believe that God will have to do with *things*."[9] Again, especially with regard to talk of human redemption, "immortal souls" die hard. But let us ask: why? We might say the influences themselves display a timeless-ly attractive quality.

A Timeless Attraction

In other words, the dualistic anthropologies expressed in such philosophical writings as those of Plato, with his tripartite and hierarchically organized soul imprisoned in a mortal body,[10] and Descartes, with his

---

9. McClendon, *Ethics*, 97. Polkinghorne also states in his essay "Eschatological Credibility," 49, that "The message seems clear. In Christ there is a destiny for matter as well as for men and women. I believe that a downplaying of the empty tomb and of the bodily resurrection, evident in a good deal of contemporary theological discussion, is a severe impoverishment of our eschatological understanding."

10. In his "Phaedo," 48, Plato, having developed a framework for the philosopher's quest to attain truth, asserts, "Surely the soul can best reflect when it is free of all distractions . . . when it ignores the body and becomes as far as possible independent, avoiding all physical contacts and associations as much as it can, in its search for reality [read: ultimate truth]." Therefore, "Then . . . in despising the body and avoiding it, and endeavoring to become independent—the philosopher's soul is ahead of all the rest" (ibid.). But, note well, ultimately in the philosopher's quest for truth, she will recognize the body to be dispensable with regard to that same quest. Therefore, "So long as we keep to the body and our soul is contaminated with this imperfection, there is no chance of our ever attaining satisfactorily to our object, which we assert to be truth. In the first place, the body provides us with innumerable distractions in the pursuit of our necessary sustenance, and any diseases which attack us hinder our quest for reality. Besides, the body fills us with loves and desires and fears and all sorts of fancies and a great deal of nonsense, with the result that we literally never get an opportunity to think at all about anything" (ibid., 49). Ultimately, for Plato, the quest for truth requires deliverance from the body: "If no pure knowledge is possible in the company of the body, then either it is totally impossible to acquire knowledge, or it is only possible after death, because it is only then that the soul will be separate and independent of the body. It seems that so long as we are alive, we shall continue closest to knowledge if we avoid as much as we can all contact and association with the body, except when they are absolutely necessary, and instead of allowing ourselves to become infected with its nature, purify ourselves from it until God himself gives us deliverance. In this way, by keeping ourselves uncontaminate by the follies of the body, we shall probably reach the company of others like ourselves and gain direct knowledge of all that is pure and uncontaminated—that is . . . of truth" (ibid.).

mind[11] (nonphysical and disembodied)/body distinction,[12] and in such theological writings as those of G. E. Lessing,[13] in which that which is temporal/material exists merely at the disposal of discovering the timeless, eternal truths of reason, still influence. Their voices still speak.[14]

11. It is important note, as Murphy points out in her *Bodies and Souls or Spirited Bodies?* that, as Descartes distinguishes between two types of created substances, extended substance (*res extensa*) and thinking substance (*res cogitans*), there becomes for Descartes a "linguistic shift" from "souls" to "minds." According to Murphy, though earlier translations of Descartes's work employed "soul," as this term began to take on religious connotations, translators came to prefer the word "mind." The point being: "Either term is a fair translation of Descartes's Latin or French" (ibid.).

12. Though we could turn to the sixth meditation in his "Meditations on First Philosophy In Which The Existence of God And the Distinction of the Soul from the Body Are Demonstrated," for a delineation of Descartes' understanding of the soul's ("soul" appearing to be used interchangeably with "mind" in his writings) relation to the body in the context of attempting to provide a sure foundation for truth [*Discourse on Method and Meditations on First Philosophy*, 89–100], one can find a more concise articulation of the soul's relation to the human body in Article 30 of his *The Passions of the Soul*. In this latter book, in explaining "That the soul is jointly untied to all the parts of the body," Descartes explains that "[I]t is necessary to know that the soul is truly joined to the whole body, and that one cannot properly say that it is in any one of its parts to the exclusion of the others, because [the body] is one, and in a way indivisible, in proportion to the disposition of its organs, which are all so related to one another that when any of them is removed this renders the whole body defective; and because [the soul] is of a nature which has no relation to extension, or to the dimensions or other properties of the stuff the body is composed of, but only to the whole collection of its organs—as becomes apparent from the fact that one cannot in any way conceive of a half or a third of a soul, or of what extension it occupies, and from the fact that [the soul] does not become smaller from some part of the body being cut off, but separates from it entirely when the collection of its organs is dissolved" (ibid., 35). Essentially, for Descartes, though the soul is integral to its function, when the body is dissolved, the soul is ultimately revealed to be a distinct entity requiring no extension for its life!

13. By asserting in his "On the Proof of the Spirit and of Power," 53, that the "*accidental truths of history can never become the proof of necessary truths of reason*," one may already discern Lessing's attitude toward the significance of that which is material. But it is in his "The Education of the Human Race," that he articulates religions in their historical expressions as material "primers" (ibid., 91) preparing civilization for the ultimate, rational, abstract truth, no longer merely addressed to the senses, of the "immortality of the soul" (ibid., 92). For Lessing duty that emanates from this starting point, or the immortality of the soul, will no longer be fixated on the "concerns [of] our bodily needs" (ibid., 96). It will "love virtue for its own sake alone" (ibid.).

14. Cf. Schwarz, *Eschatology*, especially 261–80; and Schwarz, *On the Way to the Future*, especially 195–239. Also, with regard to popular employment of the "soul," Owen Flanagan in his book *The Problem of the Soul*, 164, notes, "The belief in souls—or at least in some permanent and abiding part of myself that makes me, and which in addition may survive my death—is widespread. According to a host of polls in the

Indeed, their influence is both perennial and, perhaps, even comforting for many, especially when the topic of discussion turns on the continuity of self-identity with regard to the after-life.[15] And let us not forget that a philosopher of the stature of Immanuel Kant, acknowledging the encumbering nature of the sensual, material world in relation to the fulfillment of the moral law's "highest good," could declare the immortality of the soul to be a postulate of unconditioned, legislative, or practical reason.[16] Without an "immortal soul" Kant's moral law would find no fulfillment. At the same time, the arena of philosophy is not the only arena projecting dualism's influence. A Church historian of such profile as Adolf von Harnack could assert that "In the combination of these ideas—God the Father, Providence, the position of men as God's children, the infinite value of the human soul—the whole Gospel is expressed."[17] But when this dualism, and its attendant "immortal soul," is applied to matters of ultimate human redemption, the material creation surrounding the "immortal soul" becomes seemingly insignificant. Essentially, the sensual human becomes nothing other than a dispensable "husk" enfolding the "kernel," or the essential, non-material, "immortal soul." How so?

In applying a dualistic anthropological framework, with its attendant "immortal soul" to his interpretation of the biblical category of the kingdom of God, Harnack asserts regarding the kingdom of God that "[It] comes by coming to the individual, by entering into his soul and

---

last decade, somewhere between 70 and 96 percent of Americans believe humans possess nonphysical souls, and they believe that this soul continues to exist forever after the body dies. These numbers are roughly the same as they were a century ago." Flanagan also notes that this belief is not an "idiosyncrasy of Westerners," for "The belief in a nonphysical soul that comprises an individual's essence, that is not physical, and that survives bodily death is a feature of virtually all of the world's great religions" (ibid., 168).

15. Polkinghorne touches upon this issue when, in his book *The God of Hope and the End of the World*, 105, having broached the observation that "human beings look much more like animated bodies than like incarnated souls," he asserts, "We must ask whether, in consequence of this anti-dualist conclusion, one has lost the possibility of speaking of the human soul altogether, so that there is no longer a way in which we may frame an understanding of a destiny beyond death, expressed in terms of the soul's provision of the necessary element of continuity required to make such a belief meaningful." In short, it is comforting to imagine that self-continuity with regard to the after life is endogenous.

16. See Kant's *Critique of Practical Reason*, especially 155–56.

17. Harnack, *What Is Christianity?* 68.

laying hold of it. True, the kingdom of God is the rule of God; but it is the rule of the holy God in the hearts of individuals[.]" Ultimately, "From this point of view everything that is dramatic in the external and historical sense has vanished; and gone, too, are all the external hopes for the future."[18] Again: when Harnack applies his dualism and its accompanying "immortal soul" to the kingdom of God, though everything external, material, and historical may vanish, the "immortal soul" remains alone into eternity with its God! And certainly a theologian of such enduring influence, hailing from the influential *Religionsgeschichtlicheschule*, as Ernst Troeltsch, could remark, also applying a dualistic conceptuality of the human to matters eschatological, or to ultimate redemption in Jesus Christ, that, "Redemption is simply faith; it is the gaining of certainty in God through the impact of the image of Christ. It is not a divine intervention that took place once for all time, but always a newly achieved, purely inward interaction between God and the soul. God speaks to the soul what no one else can hear!"[19] Essentially, regardless of what may occur in the material, sensual world, redemption, for Troeltsch, within a dualistic anthropological framework, remains located in an eternally isolated realm, *sans* all sensual and material diversion, between God and the non-material soul.

The Scope of Material Hope

Whether we are discussing the dualistic body/soul anthropologies of Kant, Harnack, or Troeltsch, to name just a few, with regard to matters of ultimate redemption in Jesus Christ, the Irish theologian Dermot Lane may, perhaps, provide the most apt observation of the consequences. Lane observes regarding these body/soul (or even spirit/matter) anthropological frameworks, and the general resultant tendencies of these anthropologies with regard to their eschatological application, that "[T]hey run the risk of being understood dualistically." He elaborates, "When this happens, the focus is reduced to the purely spiritual dimen-

---

18. Ibid., 56. Indeed, Harnack could declare, "To our modern way of thinking and feeling, Christ's message appears in the clearest and most direct light when grasped in connexion with the idea of God the Father and the infinite value of the human soul" (ibid., 63).

19. Troeltsch, *Christian Faith*, 283.

sion and an emphasis is placed simply on spiritual survival."[20] And, as Lane points out, there could be nothing further from the core of the Christian witness. He adds,

> Christian eschatology, however, is grounded in the hope of the resurrection of the body. An anthropology that emphasizes the self as an embodied self is much more available to an eschatology of the bodily resurrection. The primary eschatological symbols of Christianity, namely the New Creation, the new heaven and new earth, the heavenly Jerusalem, the reign of God, and bodily resurrection are all in one way or another corporeal and embodied. What is distinctive and central about Christian eschatology is its inclusive reference to material creation and embodied existence. The arrival of the Eschaton is not about the survival of disembodied souls and spirits, but the transformation of enfleshed beings into a New Creation.[21]

But it is Jewish scholar Neil Gillman who, perhaps, places the detrimental impact of thinking regarding body/soul dualism, and its corresponding "immortal soul," in the most salient perspective with regard to both the integrity of creaturehood, and the redemption of that same creaturehood (not to mention the ability of God to restore what has been created!). According to Gillman, "[T]he notion of immortality tends to deny the reality of death, of God's power to take my life and restore it; because the doctrine of immortality implies that my body is less precious, unimportant, even 'pure,' while resurrection [of the body] affirms that my body is no less God's creation and is both necessary and good . . ."[22]

But, if God will have to do with *things*, as McClendon points out, and not simply "immortal souls," and these *things*, according to Gillman, are *necessary* and *good*, as evidenced by the resurrection of the body, we will have to attend, as McClendon asserts, to the Scriptures, and especially as they relate to matters of human redemption, or the

---

20. Lane, *Keeping Hope Alive*, 40.

21. Ibid. Distinguishing the differing scope of hopes regarding those who subscribe to the immortality of the soul versus those who confess the resurrection of the body, Cullmann, in his *Immortality of the Soul or Resurrection of the Dead?*, 59, observes, "Even those who believe in the immortality of the soul do not have the hope of which Paul speaks, the hope which expresses the belief of a divine miracle of new creation which will embrace everything, every part of the world created by God."

22. Gillman, *Death of Death*, 238, also quoted in Murphy, *Bodies and Souls, Spirited Bodies?* 29.

redemption of "embodied selfhood." And, having already cited the likes of Bultmann, Barth, Bonhoeffer, Niebuhr, and Hall with reference to the essential nature of human embodiment for theological thinking throughout the course of the twentieth century, it will serve us well, taking McClendon's cue, to fund our project with *at least* a brief summary of analysis regarding the essential psychosomatic unity, and thus identity, of the human with particular reference to the question of redemption. If, as Murphy has observed, there has been a "gradual displacement of the dualistic account of the person" in biblical studies, especially in reference to the issue of redemption, then how is the ultimate redemption of this anthropological monism articulated by Scripture? As we pointed-out above, though Cullmann, as early as 1955, having analyzed the Scriptures and presenting his results in a signal series of lectures, revealed the importance of bodily resurrection for the biblical witness, in contradistinction to a Socratic expectation of the soul surviving bodily death, we still must ask: What does Scripture say directly on the issue of the location of the redemption of the embodied human? More importantly, if Scripture articulates a human whose essence is a psychosomatic unity, then where is this unity's continuity of self-identity located? But, let us note, because a survey of the results of even recent exegesis on the matter of a scripture's articulation of what is essential to the human would be a massive project unto itself, we will restrict our discussion to recent contributions which have applied themselves to this specific conversation as it has been carried-on between science and theology.[23]

An Exegetical Foundation

As we noted above, if Murphy has observed a "gradual displacement of the dualistic account of the person" with reference to the results of biblical studies through the twentieth century, then, according to Murphy this "dualistic displacement" has been perpetuated for at least two reasons. First, according to Murphy, this "dualistic displacement"

23. Both because the material covering both this area and its various nuances is massive in scope, and because the nature of this sub-section is to simply provide a context for the subject of "within-redemption," I have restricted our focus to the recent, signal contributions contained in *Resurrection: Theological and Scientific Assessments*; *Whatever Happened to the Soul? Scientific and Theological Portraits of Human Nature*; and *The End of the World and the Ends of God: Science and Theology on Eschatology.*

has been engendered "by a recognition of the holistic character of biblical conceptions of the person, often while still presupposing temporarily separable "parts," and then by a holistic but also physicalist account of the person."[24] Indeed, according to Murphy, observing the trend of twentieth century biblical exegesis—in relation to both the Old and New Testaments, but with particular attention to the New Testament—on just this issue, "[T]he dominant view of the person in the New Testament is that of ontological monism, with such notions as 'escape from the body' or 'disembodied soul' falling outside the parameters of New Testament thought."[25] Murphy presses her analysis farther by adding that "The central concern of these New Testament writers is the concept of soteriological wholism; in their portraits of human nature they place a premium on the person's relatedness to God and others. Furthermore, the emphasis on anthropological monism in the New Testament underscores the cosmic repercussions of reconciliation; the fate of the human family cannot be dissociated from that of the cosmos."[26] But if "anthropological monism" stands at the core of Scripture's delineation of the human, then how may we speak of the continuity of human identity with regard to redemption? Additionally, we may ask, what is the location of redemption with regard to this "anthropological monism"?

In applying his exegesis of Scripture, particularly with reference to the Pauline corpus, and with reference to both the issue of human self-identity as it relates to death, and particularly with reference to that same self-identity and its continuity in relation to ultimate human redemption through Christ, biblical scholar Joel Green concludes that a "profound continuity" does exist between this present life and "life everlasting with God."[27] But if this "profound continuity" between this life and "life everlasting with God" was, perhaps, thought to be located within a dualistic framework, thus locating the essence of enduring human self-identity, and thus what is essentially human, in a non-material "immortal soul," according to Green we having else coming. In short, Green's conclusion contains dramatic implications for dualistic conceptualizations of the human, as well as their subsequent application with regard to the self's continuity with reference to redemption located—

24. Murphy, "Human Nature: Historical, Scientific, and Religious Issues," 21.
25. Ibid., 28.
26. Ibid.
27. Green, "Bodies—That Is, Human Lives," 170.

apart from embodiment—in an "immortal soul." So Green states, "For human beings this continuity has do with bodily existence ... Paul cannot think in terms of a free-floating soul separate from a body ... [and thus] does not here think of "immortality of the soul." Neither does he proclaim a resuscitation of dead bodies that might serve as receptacles for souls that had escaped the body in death. Instead, he sets before his audience the promise of the transformation of their bodies into glorified bodies (cf. Phil. 3:21)."[28] In short, according Green, since the human is a psychosomatic unity (a body!), according to Scripture, then "continuity" as it pertains to redemption cannot be articulated through a reference to a dualistic framework and an accompanying "immortal soul" (denoting both endogenous and non-material continuity), and is thus not expressed apart from its location in "bodily existence." It is *this body* that is both the location of redemption and is glorified through redemption.

Building upon Green's observations and his own exegesis of Scripture, Ray Anderson, acknowledging that humans are not essentially an "immortal substance encased in a mortal body," but created by God as "personal, embodied, mortal creatures," thus knowing no existence *sans* the one that coincides "simultaneously with the bodily form of human existence,"[29] notes that human self-identity, especially as it pertains to death and redemption, is not endogenous. For, according to Anderson, not only is "Self-identity ... both determined by the Spirit of God within each person and acquired by the person through experience and interaction with the physical, social, and spiritual environment of life,"[30] but, according to Scripture, when that same self-identity is related, in particular, to death, "The identity of the self as a [material] unity is now dependent upon a source and power beyond its own capacity for survival. Even as the 'person' was present in the unborn state through divine perception and determination (Ps. 139), so the person can survive death by the same divine knowledge and power."[31] And, according to Anderson, where Scripture does point to the "stability and continuity" of self-identity with reference to death, again, the foundation of such a continuous self-identity, according to Scripture,

28. Ibid.
29. Anderson, "On Being Human: The Spiritual Saga of a Creaturely Soul," 189.
30. Ibid.
31. Ibid.

has no traffic with an "indestructible soul," but with *extra nos* agency, or faithfulness. He adds, applying the exegetical results of various portions of Pauline material, "The assurance that self-identity will survive death is not based on some nonphysical aspect of the person but on the bond between the risen Jesus Christ and the [human] through the Holy Spirit."[32] Anderson asserts, in conclusion to the essay from which we have already cited, "I have presented biblical evidence for the view that death is the end of human life in its totality, except for the sovereign power and determination of God, and that only through the death and resurrection of Jesus Christ do we have assurance of our own resurrection and continuing identity following death."[33]

Locating Extra Nos

If we could draw from Green's conclusion that human self continuity with reference to redemption could not be articulated through reference to a non-material "immortal soul" (for it is *this* "bodily existence" that is the location of redemption), then this is complemented by Anderson's emphasis that the continuity of embodied human self-identity is an *extra nos* matter of "sovereign power and determination of God" revealed through the death and resurrection of Jesus Christ. Restated: As the body remains the locus of redemption *sans* appeal to a non-material soul, so the agency of redemption *within* this location is also *extra nos*. Thus Polkinghorne can resonate "[T]here is indeed the Christian hope of a destiny beyond death, but it resides not in the presumed immortality of a spiritual soul, but in the divinely guaranteed eschatological sequence of death and resurrection. Only a hope conceived of in this way can do full justice to human psychosomatic unity . . . The only ground for this hope . . . lies in the faithfulness of the Creator, in the unrelenting divine love for all creatures."[34] As Polkinghorne and Anderson make clear with regard to the Scripture's articulation of ultimate redemption and its location, the human does not need a "soul" to account for what is *extra nos* at that same location. At the same time, according to Hall, acknowledging that that which is *extra nos* regarding the hope of bodily redemption is only granted to the eyes of faith and not sight, "What we

32. Ibid., 192.
33. Ibid., 194.
34. Polkinghorne, *God of Hope and the End of the World*, 108.

have to accustom ourselves to is that, in history," especially now as we speak of history with respect to human embodiment and it's redemption, "nothing is 'necessary.' There is not necessarily a new beginning in every ending, an alpha in every omega. We must live as Christians under the cross without assuming a resurrection [read: immortality!] that is either logically or existentially necessary."[35] In short, not only do "immortal souls" contribute to a triumphalistic "theology of glory"[36] which can offer security and continuity of essential identity with regard to death, albeit in their own disembodied fashion, but they also make human redemption *necessary*. What was once a matter of hope for all things material, now is reduced to "sight" regarding disembodied redemption. A bad bargain, indeed!

To sum matters up, if the only human of which we may speak is both the one whose essential identity—especially with regard to redemption—is *not* predicated upon a disembodied and non-material soul, and whose bodily continuity with regard to redemption is maintained in *extra nos* fashion at the location of embodiment, then two assertions may be made. First, essential humanity can be described completely from an embodied, creaturely standpoint ("conditioned by [a] contemporary understanding of the nature of present reality").[37] Second, essential humanity may be described in such a way that the description of essential humanity must incorporate every aspect of that same essence. *More pointedly: ultimately, this description of essential humanity and its ultimate redemption cannot circumvent this same essential humanity as it lies decomposing in the tomb. The location of human redemption in Christ entails a description of that same human which is conditioned by all we know of what comprises the human, even when the "human" is not recognizable.* Perhaps here, in order to draw this sub-section to a conclusion, it would be wise to learn a lesson from the Church Fathers on just this matter, that is, of sticking with the integrity of the body and bodily identity with respect to redemption and its location, no matter how "unrecognizable" the human may become.

---

35. Hall, *Lighten Our Darkness*, 145.
36. This term will receive elaboration in the following chapter.
37. Polkinghorne, "Eschatological Credibility," 47.

Body Hope

Noting the *sine qua non* nature of the bodily resurrection for Christian confession (counter to a hope merely borne on the wings of an "immortality of the disembodied soul"), and with specific reference to such second century theologians as Polycarp of Smyrna and Justin Martyr,[38] Brian Daley observes that, at its core, Christian theological debate turns on eschatology. With this being the case, Dailey asserts that "Eschatology . . . then as now, never stands alone: it is rooted in an understanding of the provident and saving God and the person of the Savior . . . just as it is rooted in a vision of God's relationship to the world of intelligent and material creatures and in a Christian sense of the natural identity and the transformed status of the human person before God. [Eschatology] belongs to a theological whole."[39] But, according to Daley, as the question of eschatology, and specifically the resurrection of the body is grounded in "God's relationship to the world of . . . material creatures," then we must also be aware of regnant thinking in reference to eschatological matters within, as we noted above, the influential Platonist trajectory of thought; thinking which takes offense at just this "relationship" with matter.

Specifically, the hope that bodies are raised from the dead, according to the Middle Platonist Celsus, is nothing more than "the hope for worms. For what sort of human soul would have any further desire for a body that has rotted . . . For God is not the author of sinful desire or of disorderly confusion, but of what is naturally just and right. For the soul he might be able to provide an everlasting life: but as Heraclitus says, 'corpses ought to be thrown away as worse than dung.'"[40] But, having noted this scandal for Platonists, Daley examines the various manners in which Christian hope for bodies is not only rooted, for the most part, in God's relationship to the world, but conditioned by contemporary understandings of the nature of present reality.[41]

---

38. Daley, "Hope for Worms: Early Christian Hope," 136.

39. Ibid., 137. See Polkinghorne's essay in the same volume, entitled "Eschatological Credibility," 47, in which he, alluding to this essay, states, "The expression Christian hope for an ultimate redeemed reality has always been conditioned by its contemporary understanding of the nature of present reality."

40. Daley, "Hope for Worms: Early Christian Hope," 138.

41. Ibid., 147. Cf. Polkinghorne's essay "Eschatological Credibility" in this same volume, especially 47.

Having analyzed signal expressions of the resurrection of the body in the Church's first four centuries, Daley categorizes these resurrection articulations under four main headings:[42] 1) resurrection as the completion of human potential; 2) resurrection as a noncorporeal reinterpretation of material existence; 3) resurrection as God's creative reassembling of the scattered particles of human decomposition; and 4) "resurrection as the adaption by the soul of its continuing bodily vehicle . . . to suit the more transparently spiritual conditions of life with God."[43] But, for the purpose of this sub-section and the development of this project, we shall focus on the third category developed by Daley.

According to Daley, whether we are dealing with Athenagoras, Justin, Tertullian, or even Augustine,[44] the point these theologians emphasize in their relating of human identity, and thus the body, to ultimate redemption, "is that it is *this present flesh*, this visible and recognizable body, that will rise again."[45] Daley adds that, for all of these theologians and their strenuous attempts to account for human particles *post-mortem*, "the goodness and dignity of the flesh, the material beauty of the body created by God as integral to the human person, appeared to be at stake, as well as the crucial role played by the flesh in our way to God."[46]

But if Daley, in his study of the Church Fathers, has identified the importance of *this present flesh* for the understandings of redemption by such theologians as Athenagoras, Justin, Tertullian, Augustine, et al., then Caroline Walker Bynum's study,[47] in which she examines both the early and middle Church's recognition that the body is integral to the self, and thus its perpetual attempts to locate the material continuity of the human with regard to bodily resurrection, also reveals the sobering context in which the body is allowed to be the locus of the self's identity

---

42. Cf. Daley, "Hope for Worms: Early Christian Hope," 140–60.
43. Ibid., 140.
44. Cf. ibid., 147–51.
45. Ibid., 150.
46. Ibid., 151.
47. Bynum, *Resurrection of the Body in Western Christianity*. I also refer the reader to Brown, *Body and Society*, for an enlightening development of the attitudes—implicit within the expression of complete sexual renunciation—expressed by signal Christian writers during the first five centuries of the Church toward the human body. This book is an essential read with regard to understanding early Christian attitudes towards the human body.

from beginning to end. In other words, if the body is the irreducible, integral locus the self,[48] and not simply with regard to an articulation of redemption, then that locus must embrace not only the vitalities of life, but the decomposing stench of death and the tomb.

According to Bynum's analysis, around the second and third centuries not only did resurrection guarantee "that it is *these very corpses* that achieve salvation,"[49] but ultimately, according to Bynum, Christianity—with its stress on the essential role of the human body with regard to redemption—"spread among peoples for whom bodily change was theoretically inexplicable and to whom corpses were horrifying."[50] She adds, "For the Romans and Jews (although in different ways), the cadaver that lay rotting in the grave was in some sense the locus of the person; its putrefaction was both terrifying and polluting. Moreover, decay was merely the final permutation in a body that was forever changing (eating, growing, giving birth, sickening, aging) [.]"[51] Even into the twelfth and thirteenth centuries, with such writers as Bernard and Hildegard emphasizing the psychosomatic unity of the human as the locus of personal identity with regard to redemption,[52] the horrifying ramifications of identifying the "necessity of body for personhood"[53] were not soft-pedaled. For these writers, according to Bynum, "The basic model of bodily process is putrefaction; to live is to rot."[54] Redemption was thus understood by these writers in such a way as to conquer "the decay to which matter is all too prone."[55] If ultimately the body was the locus of self, and could thus be identified with the cadaver and decomposition, then

> The resurrection body was a recast vessel, a temple reconstructed from its scattered stones, a golden statue reforged from its original metal; it was flesh and bones reassembled from the particles and pieces of itself earlier dispersed by the four winds or by marauding beasts. Its resurrection and glorification at the

---

48. Bynum, *Resurrection of the Body in Western Christianity*, 225.
49. Ibid., 46.
50. Ibid., 56.
51. Ibid.
52. Ibid., 156–66.
53. Ibid., 175.
54. Ibid., 174.
55. Ibid.

end of time were guaranteed by divine power, which was strong enough not only to reconstitute it and reunite it with its soul when the trumpet blew but also to preserve it, during all the intervening years, from the decay or digestion that might threaten its being.[56]

Although Bynum's work reveals the "tortuous attempts" of "[reconciling] the resurrection with material continuity,"[57] attempts taken with the utmost of theological rigor and intensity and argument, it also reveals that however it may be that the redemption of the body is articulated, the location of Christian redemption *is* the body, no matter what form that body may be in, no matter how unrecognizable that body may be as "human." Bynum concludes that the "notion of bodily resurrection itself

> is a concept of sublime courage and optimism. It locates redemption there where ultimate horror also resides—in pain, mutilation, death, and decay. Whether or not any of the images and answers . . . [still carry] conviction, those who articulated them faced without flinching the most negative of all the consequences of embodiment: the fragmentation, slime, and stench of the grave. It was this stench and fragmentation they saw lifted to glory in resurrection. To make body crucial to personhood is to court the possibility that . . . victory is swallowed up in death.[58]

Conclusion

If the core of Christian redemption is the resurrection of the body, and "Humans *are* their bodies,"[59] "however [they] may change,"[60] then, as we noted above, the location of human redemption in Christ cannot avoid a description of that same human identity, indeed of all that comprises the human, even when that which has been popularly recognized as "human" is no longer recognizably "human." But now the question

---

56. Ibid., 176.

57. Murphy, *Bodies and Souls, or Spirited Bodies?* 141. For Murphy's counter to these "tortuous attempts" of reconciling resurrection with material continuity, see 141ff.

58. Bynum, *Resurrection of the Body in Western Christianity*, 343.

59. Murphy, "Resurrection and Personal Identity," 207.

60. Murphy, *Bodies and Souls, or Spirited Bodies?* 132.

becomes—indeed the question that frames our entire project: acknowledging with folks like Douglas John Hall that embodiment is good, that we are created to be humans, "nothing more, nothing less," then how shall we speak of a redemption that encounters us precisely at this location of human embodiment, even when that which is human is no longer recognized as such, but perhaps recognized under such phrases as "dust and ashes," "particles," "decomposition," and "putrefaction"?

As will be developed, to speak of a redemption at this location means first and foremost to speak of a God who must be present *within* this same location. If this is the case, then the scandal that God "has to do with *things*" will pale in comparison to the scandal of a God who manifests a redeeming presence *within* those same things, whether they be alive or rotting. We need a theology which can fund these needs.

Excursus: Neuroscience's Contributions to the Reification of the Soul

If, as our brief recourse to biblical analysis has demonstrated, ultimate redemption of the human need not require a disembodied, non-material soul in order to account for what is *extra nos* at that same embodied location, then, regarding this claim's relationship to the wider realm of scientific investigation, as Murphy points out, "biblical studies and neuroscience are both pointing in the same direction: toward a physicalist account of the person. Humans are not hybrids of matter and something else, they are purely physical organisms."[61] Murphy both demonstrates[62] and argues that "[A]ll of the human capacities once attributed to the [non-material] mind or soul are now being fruitfully studied as brain processes—or, more accurately . . . processes involving the brain, the rest of the nervous system and other bodily systems, all interacting with the socio-cultural world."[63]

Complementing this analysis, noted neurologist Antonio Damasio, also developing the idea that the mind is derived "from the entire organism as an ensemble,"[64] and not "out of a disembodied brain,"[65] places the

---

61. Murphy, *Bodies and Souls, or Spirited Bodies?* 69.

62. See ibid., 40–47.

63. Ibid., 56.

64. Damasio, *Descartes' Error*, 225.

65. Ibid., 229. For Damasio's development of the "primacy of the body" with regard to mind processes, see ibid., 205–44.

reification of the mind, or the "primacy of the body," in articulating mind processes in its widest possible context by concluding: "The primacy of the body as a theme applies to evolution: from simple to complex, for millions of years, brains have been first about the organism that owns them. To a lesser extent it applies also to the development of each of us as individuals so that at our beginning, there were first representations of the body proper, and only later were there representations related to the outside world; and to an even smaller but not negligible extent, to the now, as we construct the mind of the moment."[66] Ultimately, according to Murphy, the soul, whose presence was necessitated through capacities which were once scientifically inexplicable, has been shown to be unnecessary.[67] Elaborating on this point, Murphy explains that a "physicalist thesis" means "... *that as we go up the hierarchy of increasingly complex organisms, all of the other capacities once attributed to the soul will also turn out to be products of complex organization, rather than as properties of a non-material entity.*"[68] And perhaps the great irony regarding this "complex organization," as we will see, is that, far from placing the human crown jewel of intellection within the airy realm of "timeless ideas," its "life" is funded by the pulsating, throbbing mass of flesh, blood, and nerves moving around with the *Sturm und Drang* of a creation whose encroaching stimuli are anything but orderly and clean.

Essentially, this "complex organization" of the now-reified soul—as developed here in drastically simplified fashion employing noted psychiatrist Michael Franz Basch's "self-system" (a "collective term encompassing the hierarchy of neurologically encoded, goal-directed feedback cycles whose activity constitutes behavior and governs behavior."),[69] but also similarly, and certainly much more technical in its employment of physiology, in Jaak Panksepp's SELF, or Simple Ego-type Life Form[70]—can be traced to the body's fundamental affective reactions (visceral/

---

66. Damasio, *Descartes' Error*, 229.

67. Murphy, *Bodies and Souls, or Spirited Bodies?* 69.

68. Ibid., 57. Italics are Murphy's. Murphy labels this a "nonreductive physicalist" view which is to be differentiated from a "reductive physicalist" view which "would be to say that if there is no soul then people must not be truly rational, moral, or religious" (ibid., 69).

69. Basch, *Understanding Psychotherapy*, 105–6.

70. Panksepp, *Affective Neuroscience*, see especially 47–54, 308–11.

vascular reactions stimulated by the body's innate reflex-action[71]) which are formed by the rise and fall of stimuli on the nervous system.[72] At the same time, this affective reaction becomes tied to particular behaviors,[73] and thus bound to particular patterns of expectation with regard to behavior and its consequences. Intellection, then—whose capacities were once attributed to the soul, then to the disembodied mind—is the product of "pattern-matching" (whose "purpose is to establish meaningful order among the many stimuli impinging on the brain . . .")[74] which itself is the process of attempting to match incoming environmental stimuli with prior expectations (laid-down in memory and thus associated with affective states) in order to generate information to guide decision-making and its subsequent behavior.[75] Thus, as Basch declares, "Affect is the Gateway to Action!"[76] But, with the reification of the soul/mind based within a "complex organization" of visceral/vascular, or affective, reactions to the rise and fall of environmental stimuli, what, let us ask, are the implications of this "physicalist thesis" for our discussion of human redemption?

As Murphy notes, if Christians have regularly taught that God's relation to the cosmos was both transcendent and immanent "in *all* of creation, including the physical, acting at least to sustain its existence and . . . govern its processes,"[77] then the physicalist confesses that "God must have to do with bodies, particularly our neural systems."[78] Indeed, touching upon the widely accepted view of God's immanence with Christianity, Murphy asks, "Why, then, the resistance to assuming that God makes us aware of the divine presence, speaks to us, heals our emotions, by acting on the neural and other bodily processes that give rise to consciousness?"[79] And, if it is the case that "*capacities once attributed to the soul [have turned out] to be products of complex organization,*

---

71. Basch, *Understanding Psychotherapy*, 78.
72. Ibid., 73.
73. Ibid., 63, 65, 67.
74. Ibid., 64.
75. Ibid., 52, 80.
76. Ibid., 65.
77. Murphy, *Bodies and Souls, or Spirited Bodies?*, 124.
78. Ibid.
79. Ibid.

rather than as properties of a non-material entity,"[80] then Bonhoeffer's famous words, penned in mid-1944 not only seem prophetic, but both diagnose the "religious" rationale for such a "resistance," and broaden-out the space, or location, of God's redemptive activity and presence. So I quote his signal words at length:

> Religious people speak of God when human knowledge . . . has come to an end . . . in fact it is always the *deus ex machina* that they bring on to the scene, *either for the apparent solution of insoluable problems* [read: "complex organization" of the mind], or as strength in human failure—always, is to say, exploiting human weakness or human boundaries. Of necessity, that can go on only till people can by their own strength push these boundaries somewhat further out, so that God becomes superfluous as a *deus ex machina*. I've come to be doubtful of talking about any human boundaries . . . *It always seems to me that we are trying anxiously in this way to reserve some space for God*; I should like to speak of God not on the boundaries (read: the once unknown "complex organization" of the mind) but at the centre, not in weaknesses but in strength; and therefore not in death and guilt but in man's life and goodness. As to the boundaries, it seems to me better to be silent and leave the insoluble unsolved. Belief in the resurrection is *not* the "solution" of the problem of death. *God's "beyond" is not the beyond of our cognitive faculties.* The transcendence of epistemological theory has nothing to do with the transcendence of God. God is beyond in the midst of our life. *The church stands, not at the boundaries where human powers give out,* but in the middle of the village.[81]

And does not, according to Murphy, certainly resonating with Bonhoeffer's observation of a half a century earlier, the "physicalist thesis" "emphasize[s] our unity with the rest of nature, and [suggest] that we are not saved *out of* the cosmos, but as part of it? That is, it leads us to expect that the entire cosmos will be transformed or re-created in the same way as we humans are."[82]

Essentially, as theology and neuroscience have pointed-out, thus converging on this point, if human identity is bound to the body "however it may change,"[83] even if that change renders the human un-

---

80. Ibid., 57.
81. Bonhoeffer, *Letters and Papers from Prison*, 281–82; italics added for emphasis.
82. N. Murphy, "Resurrection and Personal Identity, 203–4.
83. Murphy, *Bodies and Souls, or Spirited Bodies?* 132.

recognizable with reference to what humans are comfortable labeling "human," then to speak of redemption can only mean that we speak of an *extra nos* redemption only within the location of that same body, no matter what form it may take, even when it appears "inhuman."

Theologia Crucis and "Within-Redemption"

Why "Within"?

Robert Kolb, at the beginning of an essay in which he seeks to interpret for the contemporary context the theology of the cross, particularly as it is articulated through the writings of Martin Luther, identifies the mysterious nature of a theology whose foundation and conceptual framework is provided through crucifixion and the tomb by averring that, "Of all the places to search for God, the last place most people would think to look is the gallows. Luther confessed that there, in the shadows cast by death, God does indeed meet his straying, rebellious human creatures. *There God reveals who he is; there he reveals who they are.*"[84] Indeed, according to Kolb, Luther locates God "precisely where theologians of glory are horrified to find him: as a kid in a crib, as a criminal on a cross, as a corpse in a crypt. God reveals himself by hiding right in the middle of a [sinful] human existence."[85] And it is here, in the midst of sinful human existence—amid sin, death, and the tomb—that God gives humanity its "best view of the nature of God, for it reveals his *modus operandi*, his way of dealing with evil and reclaiming humanity for himself."[86] For it is through God's "still, small voice," "a seemingly foolish and impotent Word from the cross, in the Word made flesh, come to dwell among his people,"[87] that God comes to redeem his people.

But if this is the case, that it is the location of the gallows and its subsequent death and tomb at which it is revealed both who God and humanity are, and thus God's *modus operandi* for redeeming his people, then, according to Douglas John Hall, "The change for which faith hopes, which it believes possible . . . cannot be effected through power, might, majesty, dominion, and the like, but only through a divine *modus*

---

84. Kolb, "Luther on the Theology of the Cross," 443; italics added for emphasis.
85. Ibid., 449.
86. Kolb, "Luther on the Theology of the Cross," 451.
87. Ibid., 450.

operandi that stands all such preconceptions of God's way of working in the world on their head."[88] But the crucial question becomes: Why? Why the transformation of such attributes with regard to God's *modus operandi*? Here, as we speak of the theology of the cross in the tradition of Luther, according to Hall, especially as it applies to the issue of redemption, we must keep at least two realities at the forefront of our thinking.

First, according to Hall, "the theology of the cross, at base, is about *God's abiding commitment to the world.*"[89] Hall elaborates, "Over against and in opposition to every 'religious' temptation to abandon creation and to seek security and hope in a supramundane denouement to the riddles of existence, the representatives of this tradition insist that it is the world that the biblical God loves and wills to redeem."[90] This "abiding commitment," then, according to Hall, is expressed by the theology of the cross as a complete, unqualified solidarity by Emmanuel[91] which then allows the theologian of the cross to "[place her] hope in God's transformative solidarity with fallen creation, with the world in its brokenness."[92]

But, second, if it is *this* world that the God of Scripture "loves and wills to redeem" in his "abiding commitment," then, according to Hall, we must also simultaneously recognize that "Creaturehood is so very good that the biblical God intends not only to save it, provide for it, clothe it—but to repeat it."[93] Indeed, then, not only is the creation "very good,"[94] but redemption is expressed not as a redemption *from* creaturehood but *for* it.[95] Therefore, according to Hall, not only does redemption—according to the theology of the cross—*not* involve an abrogation or annihilation of the creation and its creatures to whom God is committed in Christ as Emmanuel,[96] but he adds that "this commitment would be questionable from the start if it were not understood as the determination to see

88. Hall, *God and Human Suffering*, 104.
89. Hall, *Thinking the Faith*, 25.
90. Ibid., 25–26.
91. Hall, *Professing the Faith*, 158.
92. Hall, *Thinking the Faith*, 28.
93. Hall, *Professing the Faith*, 340.
94. Ibid., 342, 190–91.
95. Ibid., 340.
96. Hall, *Professing the Faith*, 358.

the cosmos through to the 'very good' omega that is already implicit in the 'very good' alpha."[97] But, having identified through the theology of the cross with Hall both God's "abiding commitment" as Emmanuel to the creation and creatures God loves, and the reality that redemption involves not the abrogation or annihilation of a "very good" creation, but an affirmation of its created goodness, then the reality of God as Emmanuel must be farther developed as we discuss the transformation of the divine attributes regarding God's *modus operandi* in the world, especially as it relates to the redemption of humans.

According to Hall, when speaking of Emmanuel's commitment to a "very good" creation, especially on the issue of the redemption of that creation, then Emmanuel's "With presses on toward 'within.'"[98] Hall thus elaborates, "When therefore that which God loves, the creation, exists under conditions of radical disjunction and alienation, the loving God 'must' participate in these incongruities of creaturely existence; *for only from within can the destructive, annihilating power of creaturely ambiguity and estrangement be overcome without destroying creation as such*."[99] If what God desires is unqualified "proximity to the creature," especially in such a manner that it is the "fulfillment of the divine determination to ... participate unconditionally in the creaturely condition, to the end that it may be healed *from within*,"[100] then God's attributes are revealed to be accommodated to just that end.[101] On this point Hall elaborates:

> Power, even God's power, cannot behave powerfully when its object is loving proximity to that which is weaker. All-knowingness, even God's omniscience, cannot act all-knowingly when its object is fellowship with beings whose knowledge is strictly circumscribed. Ubiquity of being, even when it refers to the divine omnipresence, can only hope to communicate with creatures of time and space if it focuses itself in particu-

---

97. Ibid., 359; see also ibid., 191.

98. Ibid., 159.

99. Ibid., 67; italics added for emphasis. Polkinghorne resonates by asserting in his essay "Eschatological Credibility," 55, "The patient and subtle God who works through unfolding process in this world of the old creation may be expected to bring about eschatological fulfillment in a correspondingly gentle and developmental manner. In fact, there surely can be no other way in which finite creatures can adequately encounter the infinite reality of their Creator in a nondestructive fashion."

100. Hall, *Cross in Our Context*, 40.

101. Hall, *Professing the Faith*, 149.

larity—in being-*there*. Likewise must eternality subject itself to temporality, immutability to change, simplicity to complexity, incomprehensibility to comprehension, spirituality to materiality, holiness to the ordinary, and infinity to finitude . . . if [the] object is to be "with us" . . .¹⁰²

or, shall we say, if the object is to redeem us "from within." Ultimately the theology of the cross not only confesses a God whose loving participation in the conditions of creaturely existence forces that same God "to follow the creature through to that nonbeing 'toward' which all creaturely being moves,"¹⁰³ but in all cases to pass the Creator's transcendent attributes "'through the eye of the needle of the properly understood concept of the death of God.'"¹⁰⁴ "[T]hat is," Hall elaborates, with reference to God's attributes, we are "to speak historically and concretely, through the humiliation and crucifixion of the Word."¹⁰⁵ With this said, perhaps the most salient divine attribute transformed by a theology of the cross, especially with regard to the *modus operandi* of human redemption, is that of power. Although we have already touched upon this attribute above, let us further elaborate this attribute, especially with regard to its important role with reference to redemption "from within."

Far from employing the logic of a theological triumphalism whose essential metaphor is that of power, but at the same time, far from simply discarding the metaphor of power, as has already been outlined

---

102. Ibid., 149.

103. Hall, *Cross in Our Context*, 38. Cf. Balthasar's *Mysterium Paschale*, 174–75, in which he states, "That the Redeemer is solidary with the dead, or, better, with this death which makes of the dead, for the first time, dead human beings in all reality—this is the final consequence of the redemptive mission he has received from the Father. His being with the dead is an existence at the utmost pitch of obedience, and because the One thus obedient is the dead Christ, it constitutes the 'obedience of a corpse' . . . of a theologically unique kind. By it Christ takes the existential measure of everything that is sheerly contrary to God, of the entire object of the divine eschatological judgment, which here is grasped in that event in which it is 'cast down' . . . But at the same time, this happening gives the measure of the Father's mission in all its amplitude: the 'exploration' of Hell is an event of the . . . Trinity." Ultimately, ". . . when [the Father] sends the Son into the world to save it instead of judging it, and, to equip him for this function, gives 'all judgment to the Son' . . . then he must also introduce the Son *made man into* 'Hell' . . . But the Son cannot really be introduced into Hell save as a dead man, on Holy Saturday" (ibid., 175).

104. Hall, *Professing the Faith*, 153, quoted by Hall from Jüngel's *God as the Mystery of the World*, 63.

105. Hall, *Professing the Faith*, 153.

above, the theology of the cross transforms such a concept by allowing the revelation of God through the "humiliation and crucifixion of the Word," a revelation *sub contraria specie*, to provide its content.[106] Thus, keeping in mind—especially as our project relates to the work of "within-redemption"—the avoidance of the annihilation of the creature in her embodiment, no matter what form that creatureliness may take, and the transforming of the divine attribute of power through the cross, especially with regard to the process of "within-redemption," God's involvement is a "mysterious internal and intentional involvement in history; a God . . . who is obliged by his own love to exercise his power quietly, subtly[.]"[107] For, indeed, at their core the causes of human suffering and death are "inseparable from our very selves."[108] Therefore "the conquest of them *must* be an intensely subtle one—a conquest *from within*."[109] Anything *more* would annihilate the "very good" creature in the process of redeeming it.

Not only does the *sub contraria specie* incarnation of Jesus Christ transform traditional conceptualizations of "power" while providing a demonstration of a God who "has entered effectively and without reserve into the life of the world"[110]—indeed demonstrating "transformative solidarity"[111] with that same world—thus indicating creation's "capacity for being changed [redeemed!] from within,"[112] but it also reveals that the only "believable" answer to the question of human suffering and death is the presence of an Answerer. I again quote Hall at length on just this dynamic:

> The only satisfying answer [given to suffering and death] is the answer given to Job—*the answer that is no answer but is the presence of an Answerer*. It does not matter that the Answerer brings more questions than answers; *for the answer is not the words as such but the living Word—the Presence itself*. The answer is the permission that is given in this Presence to be what one is, to express the dereliction that belongs to one's age and place, to

---

106. Hall, *God and Human Suffering*, 105–6.
107. Hall, *Cross in Our Context*, 87.
108. Hall, *God and Human Suffering*, 107.
109. Ibid., 107.
110. Ibid., 109.
111. Hall, *Thinking the Faith*, 28.
112. Hall, *God and Human Suffering*, 109, 111.

share all of it with this Other ... Faith is the communion of the spirit with this fellow sufferer, this One whose otherness lies in the fact that he will not turn away in the face of one's failure, or the failure of one's world.[113]

The answer to the question of suffering and death of a humanity that is essentially both embodied, and embodied in its particularity—and ultimately entombed in its embodied particularities—is the presence of an Answerer who is both "fellow sufferer" in his "abiding commitment" to a humanity created "very good," and Redeemer "from within" through his "transformative solidarity" with that same embodied humanity.

Redemption "from within," not Certainty "from within"

Although, according to Alan Lewis, it is important that the Word of redemption be heard within history's narratives of suffering and death, this Word of "within-redemption" must not become an "overbearing interpretative instrument which forces rationality onto events of obvious absurdity ... [insisting] that they be recognized despite their negativity as inducements to confidence and joy in the future of history and history's God." He adds, "The gospel certainly makes hope possible; but never *necessary*."[114] The transformation of the Word of "within-redemption" into an "overbearing interpretive instrument" ultimately results in the de-dignification of particular, embodied human narratives of suffering and death for the sake of 1) historical certainty; 2) cosmological certainty; or 3) mythological certainty. Briefly, let us develop Lewis' points.

The first device of creating an "overbearing interpretive instrument" of "within redemption," according to Lewis, is to imagine that the Church's "memory of Christ's victory beyond the defeat and death of Easter Saturday ... provides some *historical* assurance that subsequent triumphs in human history of death or unrighteousness are at worst penultimate and must themselves yield, visibly if slowly, to the sway of grace and godliness."[115] At worst this interpretive device, through its penultimate-izing of particular, embodied human narratives, renders the horrors and atrocities of human history as merely

---

113. Ibid., 118.
114. Lewis, *Between Cross and Resurrection*, 291.
115. Ibid.

"one station along the way"; horrors and atrocities which we apparently no longer have to "look at" due to their penultimacy within a larger, "most real" history which is abstracted from the one of particular, embodied human narratives. At its best, this "interpretive device" relies upon "sight" and not "faith."

Second, Lewis adduces the interpretive device that fosters the reality of timeless, ahistorical, cosmological certainties in which "creativity must prevail and justice always vindicates life's victims in the end."[116] He elaborates—regarding this second interpretive device—that it reduces an understanding of the Word's redemption "to a species of a universal genus: the innate capacity of the cosmos for resumption and regeneration as nature's rhythmic cycles turn day by day, season by season . . ."[117] Not only does this interpretive device domesticate Saturday's tomb and Sunday's resurrection, relating them as if they were a part of an "immanent evolution,"[118] but it creates a "naturalistic hermeneutic" which ultimately "suppresses the novelty, unexpectedness, and inconceivability of hope grounded in the raising of the crucified and buried God."[119] Hope is domesticated to a time-less rhythm. Again, human horror and death become penultimate to a larger, "most real," overriding cosomological a-history.

---

116. Ibid., 291–92.

117. Ibid., 292.

118. Cf. Balthasar, *Mysterium Paschale*, 56. Balthasar notes, "If theology is to be Christian, then it can only be a theology which understands in dynamic fashion the unsurpassable scandal of the Cross. Certainly, such a theology will understand the Cross as a 'crisis,' but it will see the crisis in question as a turning-point between the old aeon and the new, in the tension between the 'world's situation' and the 'world's goal.' What ensures the connexion between these two is no immanent evolution, but that inconceivable moment between Holy Saturday and Easter" (ibid.). Ultimately, "What . . . theology must do is to discern whether the kind of universality which confronts it belongs to the unique historical fact of the Crucifixion and Resurrection of Christ, or to a general idea. In the latter case, emphasis may fall either on the symbolic, imagistic form, or on upon the concept, conceived as a law of history or of existence, but in any of these versions the Cross of Christ is regarded as a particular instance of something, if perhaps a remarkable one. That is theologically unacceptable" (ibid., 60). Ultimately, this theme, which, as we will be developing, is the question of what comprises a *theologia crucis naturalis*, as opposed to a *theologia crucis*, has severe implications with reference to maintaining the integrity of particular, embodied human narratives in relation to the work of redemption. This will be developed below.

119. Lewis, *Between Cross and Resurrection*, 292.

Finally, Lewis articulates a "mythological" hermeneutic regarding redemption in which "the events of salvation history are pressed into service as components of a religious myth, one among a profusion of cultural variants, all of which exhibit the ultimate resolution of the timeless, universal struggle between good and evil, eternity and time."[120] Lewis notes that this hermeneutic of redemption "seeks to abstract universal religious *a prioris* from the concrete nonsubstitutable affirmations and veridical claims of particular theological traditions and communities of faith."[121] This hermeneutic betrays the idea that the only "answers to historical despair lie beyond history in timelessness, outside the very sequence of events which causes our grief and woe."[122] The ground of hope, and thus its object, is abstracted from the very particular, embodied narratives it is called to redeem "from within." "Redemption" is located outside of particular, embodied human narratives.

Ultimately, the God who redeems, according to these three "interpretive instruments," is a "god" who is unable to be present to "redeem" "from within" creation and the concrete, particular embodied narratives and their histories which live in that "very good" creation. Again, echoing Hall's point, above, that it is only within history that answers to history's suffering and death can be credible answers, Lewis asserts that "History's redemption must be grounded, if anywhere, within the sphere of history itself and its own brokenness, and certainly not in any cyclic or mythic dehistoricization. That is why all attempts to detemporalize the narrative of the cross and of the occupied and empty grave must be resisted."[123] Essentially what is at stake regarding a proper articulation of "within-redemption" is both the Lordship of a God—and his presence—who can redeem the particular, embodied narratives he has created, and indeed the created dignity of those same narratives; historical narratives whose redemption must also come "from within" and not be sought elsewhere, such as in a time-less a-history. Additionally, as Gerhard Forde asserted, "If we can *see through* the cross to what is supposed to be behind it [so that] we don't have to *look at* it,"[124] then none of these hermeneutics of redemption has to look *at* history either

---

120. Ibid.
121. Ibid., 293.
122. Ibid.
123. Lewis, *Between Cross and Resurrection*, 293.
124. Forde, *On Being a Theologian of the Cross*, 97.

regarding the question of suffering and death (and ultimately entombment), or for the "solution" to such matters; all for the sake of a much more real, time-less, a-history of redemption.

But it is precisely at this point—the point of finding an answer (Answerer!) to the human question of suffering and death—that we encounter even greater difficulties with regard to maintaining the integrity of the particular, embodied suffering and death of particular, embodied human beings. How so?

The Cordon Sanitaire

The Gospel, the narrative of the "within-redemption" by the presence of an Answerer, or Jesus Christ, according to Lewis, "pivots on the axis of Easter Saturday, that boundary between the cross and the empty tomb which reveals the even greater presence of God in the midst of a great absence."[125] But if "it is not without, but through, the cross, that newness of life and death's defeat are accomplished—that God uses what is weak to overcome what is powerful,"[126] then this "word of the cross," or "positing resumption beyond rupture and hope beyond despair,"[127] also runs the risk—both on account of our knowledge of its *telos* with reference to Jesus Christ, or his bodily resurrection from the tomb, and our tendency to let this *telos* retrospectively encroach upon the prior narrative—of mitigating and even abrogating the infernal horror of Good Friday and the decomposing flesh, darkness, and hope-lessness of Saturday's tomb. Might we ask whether or not our reality and vision with regard to the narrative of "within-redemption" with regard to Jesus Christ is so infused with the resurrection of Jesus Christ—so coloring all the rest of the reality we see even with regard to our own memories—that the possibility of even conjuring up the hellish horror of Good Friday or the eternal silence of Holy Saturday is an avenue barricaded to us? To concede this reality as being the case, according to Lewis, "is to abandon *all* history, is so to eternalize the resurrection of the incarnate one, gathering up all time in that event or its *kerygma*, that temporality is not fulfilled but rescinded."[128]

---

125. Lewis, *Between Cross and Resurrection*, 163.
126. Ibid., 40.
127. Ibid., 291.
128. Lewis, "Burial of God," 344–45.

He quickly adds, "Then not only one day of history but all of them, including those of Exodus and Auschwitz, have lost their *created* integrity and are rendered out of bounds to memory and faith."[129] And not only is the created integrity of a humanity—which is only manifested in its embodied particularity—abrogated (that is, embodied, particular human narratives are abstracted for the sake of a universal, already redeemed humanity), but, more than this, the tendency to obliterate the narrative of history, and ultimately its created integrity, for the sake of a triumphant Easter Sunday only plays into the hands of the triumphal God of classical, Christian theism who writes history from the vantage point of the conqueror. This "God" will not be identified with anything but progress and triumph, as the cultures which have espoused this depiction have mirrored all too well.[130]

---

129. Ibid., 345.

130. With reference to this God of triumphant, classical Christian theism, and its development, Lewis asserts, "Both the liberal and the Marxist philosophies of history were essentially medieval in construction: secularized but optimistic teleologies fixed upon the 'heavenly city' lying in humanity's lost valley beyond the intervening peaks of evolution or revolution. But neither rationalism nor dialectics has been able to sustain the classical myth of progress in this century, as they did in the 19th and 18th, confronted now respectively with the inhumanness of the enlightened and with the stagnation of the process" (ibid., 338), Lewis adds, though, with reference to this genealogy of the "classical myth of progress" which is associated with classical theism, that, "If . . . it is secular versions of a Christian *Heilsgeschichte* which have at last succumbed to the historical realities of termination, the heavenly city itself was the Christianised version of a secular myth: the Greek cycle of decline and restoration. Of course," Lewis observes, "Augustine gave that cyclic rhythm a powerful and fecund reinterpretation, under the influence of Hebraic categories. The circle opened up into a horizontal, purposive progression, from an absolute beginning to an absolute end, when time's ambiguous intertwining of the two cities would be triumphantly resolved. Whether the undeviating rectilinearity of this history, and the irresistible sovereignty of this history's God, are recognizable as the Bible's history and the Bible's God is questionable—as is the more recent attempt to impose upon Scripture a straight and upward-moving line of 'salvation history'. And it is clear that Augustine's doctrine of providence, with its incitement to Christian triumphalism, and the accompanying classical doctrine of God, with its divinization of absolute power, stand together in the dock of contemporary affairs, accused of fostering attitudes and conditions which made Holocaust and Hiroshima possible. However fair that *causal* argument might be, the converse relation of *effect* is obvious: that in consequence of 20th- century history, of World War II in particular, and above all of the expected end to which our recent cataclysms have been mere prelude, society has lost its last shreds of secularized faith in the all-providing and powerfully-presiding God of medieval Christendom. That causal deity, though scathed, survived the Reformation, and even the Enlightenment; but now is discredited and dead. For the history he ruled has terminated, its progress halted, its process ruptured." (Lewis, *Between Cross and Resurrection*, 338–39)

Countering this tendency, Lewis observes that the Christian faith has always insisted on the memory—in its Scripture and creeds—that God the Son, the one in whom the Creator tabernacled with us, was buried, that there was a "2nd Day." He adds, "In all these modes of telling, the story throws a *cordon sanitaire* around the cross, against the premature encroachment of Easter."[131] The Church has always insisted that the death and burial of God the Son—indeed his very presence in Saturday's tomb—be given "space and time" to be itself, to be termination, unabbreviated in its malignancy and infernal horror; that the Resurrection must not seep back through Friday and Saturday. Thus, according to Lewis, taking his cue from the "narrated-ness" of both the Gospel story and the Church's creeds, "[I]f we adopt a second-day vantage point which takes time to regard the death of Christ in all its unabbreviated malignancy and infernal horror, we both protect the cross itself and throw into sharpest relief the resurrection Gospel; that out of just such a cross as this, and the occupied grave that followed it, come life and joy and hope."[132] He adds, and I quote at length, "And whereas the interval of the second day forces us to hear the first day and the third in orderly, narrative sequence, we are thereafter able to hear the drama again in such a way that 'the day between the days' unites what it first separated, and allows us to understand the Good Friday story with the pre-knowledge of its sequel, and the Easter tale in light of its preamble."[133] Holy Saturday becomes, in this fashion, a concrete boundary, a *cordon sanitaire* which refuses to allow the Resurrection to prematurely encroach on the eternal silence of Saturday's tomb. And so by confronting the boundary of the "2nd Day" "head-on," by allowing it to stand on its own, the entire story—both in the direction of the "1st Day" and the "3rd Day"—both receives sharper clarity, and is allowed to define (with reference to the mode of God's agency) its own undomesticable nature. As Lewis eloquently illustrates, "The no man's land disjoining cross and resurrection is just what clarifies the antithetical newness of the Easter victory, the life-restoring resumption of the ruptured. Falsifying from the start every analogy with the rhythmic continuities of death and life, it is the burial at the centre of the Christian story which safeguards the unprepared-for novelty of the raising of the crucified, and determines

---

131. Lewis, "Burial of God," 344.
132. Lewis, *Between Cross and Resurrection*, 40.
133. Ibid., 40–41.

the divine agency in that restoration."[134] When this "2nd Day" boundary is put in place, the presence of God is revealed as a crisis of human wisdom and language, a crisis that provides the point of departure for what a theology of the cross, at its core, is commissioned to proclaim. As Lewis observes, this is a crisis which contains two "ruptures." In what manner? Again, let us listen to Lewis:

> God's absence from Jesus [the first rupture], when the godlessness of the grave appeared to prove that it did not contain the Son of God, is a rupture yet more radical when Easter exaltation confirms that the Son of God is precisely whom the grave contains. The victory of nothingness and evil, whose silence loudly trumpets God's absence and defeat, is now the locus of his presence and the precondition of his victory. God is identified with his antithesis, and makes his way to the world's salvation and his self-fulfillment only by colluding in his own defeat, the surrender of his world and of himself to negativity.[135]

Lewis calls this theo-logic of the cross (and presence within Saturday's tomb!) the "expansive creativity of loving self-limitation,"[136] a logic which allows for the resumption of life beyond rupture. It is this unity with death and decomposing flesh (that which was once recognizably human and has now become "unrecognizable"!), this divine presence deep within Saturday's stone-sealed sepulcher, that both ultimately

---

134. Lewis, "Burial of God," 347.

135. Lewis, "Burial of God," 351. Cf. Balthasar's *Mysterium Paschale*, 52, in which he states—a logic which funds Lewis' own thinking—"the real object of a theology of Holy Saturday does not consist in the completed state which follows on the last act in the self-surrender of the incarnate Son to his Father—something which the structure of every human death, more or less ratified by the individual person, would entail. Rather dos that object consist in something unique, expressed in the 'realisation' of all Godlessness, of all the sins of the world, now experienced as agony and a sinking down into the 'second death' or 'second chaos', outside of the world ordained from the beginning by God. And so it is really God who assumes what is radically contrary to the divine, what is eternally reprobated by God, in the form of the supreme obedience of the Son towards the Father, and, thereby, in Luther's words, *sub contrario* discloses himself in the very act of his self-concealment. It is precisely the unsurpassable radicalness of this concealment which turns our gaze to it, and makes the eyes of faith take notice. It now becomes extraordinarily difficult to keep together in our sights the 'absolute paradox' which lies in the hiatus, and the continuity of the Risen One with the One who died, having previously lived. And yet this is asked of us, and it presses the paradox further still."

136. Lewis, "Burial of God," 355.

reveals the cross as a judgment on human sin (indeed also an indictment on human cruelty and indifference), and exposes sinners' original expectations as to the location and *modus operandi* of God's work of redemption.

Ultimately, when the entire narrative regarding Christ's *triduum* is allowed to speak, indeed with the full awareness of Saturday's irremovable *cordon sanitaire*, we discover, as Lewis has demonstrated, that the very place of God's quiescence and defeat is also the place where God is still more triumphantly engaged with the world's powers, yet on God's own terms, according to God's own wisdom and power. And it is precisely here, far from neglecting Friday and Saturday in favor of a classically theistic, triumphant God of the Resurrection who fails to be identified with the concrete narrative of suffering, death, and the tomb, along with the integrity and memory of that narrative, that we discover a radical God in Jesus Christ. For this is a God who is found beyond the farthest limits of human knowledge and language, who has descended among, and resides with—even at the farthest limits of their sinfulness revealed both in their perpetrators and victims—God's children in all their concrete Holy Saturday's, as well (even when that Saturday is opaque to everything except the product and memory of the "hells" of human self-assertion, power, violence, retribution, depravity, and death). Lewis can ultimately declare that "Crossing the gulf of alienation, [God] comes closer to the far off than they are distant from him, more reconciled with the unreconciled than they are hostile to him."[137] Again, when the narrative is allowed to speak—and the *cordon sanitaire* is allowed to stand—we discover a God whose redemptive presence will not be separated from our own narratives no matter how deep our Friday's descend, nor how long our Saturday's last, nor even when that which is recognizable as human becomes unrecognizable.

Redemption via Signification?

But for all of Lewis' ability to let the *cordon sanitaire* of Jesus' Saturday stand in order that we may more fully comprehend the mystery of God's "expansive creativity of loving self-limitation"[138] which articu-

---

137. Ibid., 358.
138. Ibid., 355.

lates a God in Jesus Christ who, "crossing the gulf of alienation,"[139] redeems humanity "from within," Lewis ultimately winds up abstracting the presence of "within-redemption" (the presence of the Answerer!) from the very particular, embodied human lives for whom he has so eloquently and exhaustively articulated *the same* God's presence of "within-redemption." He manages to do so by locating this presence of "within-redemption" outside of the particular histories this very presence is intended to redeem "from within." How so?

Although Lewis can assert that "The Gospel hope of everlasting life does not negate our temporal finitude, nor evaporate earthly time between a mist of heavenly timelessness," he can qualify this by adding (and here we must think of what was said above regarding the resurrection of Christ and its tendency in our articulations of it to color all of history, thereby abandoning *all* of history), "Rather, the raising of God's eternal Son, who entered time for us and lived his life of glory for forty days upon the earth, *signifies* the redeeming of our time."[140] Again, not only has all "time . . . been redeemed and sanctified"[141] in Jesus Christ, thus "signifying" the redemption and sanctification of all particular, embodied narratives, but "Christ's aloneness in the grave on Easter Saturday actually and savingly contradicts the contention that in our deaths we die alone." He adds, "In his aloneness of that day, the Son of God keeps company with us in our terminal aloneness, joins us in the solitude of death and judgment, so that we are solitary no longer, and do not have to die alone. In fact, if death means aloneness, and we are not alone after all, then, in the most real sense, because of Christ's own death we do not have to die at all."[142] Thus, "This is the mystery of Easter Saturday, of presence-in-absence, applied to me: my new self is present precisely where my old self is absent and replaced by Christ."[143]

But let us restate this essential matter: Although Lewis is right to contend for the *triduum's cordon sanitaire* which allows us to identify a God who resides within the Friday/Saturday narrative of Jesus Christ in order to redeem his life "from within," in the process of doing so he unfortunately removes the narrative of humanity—which is only mani-

139. Ibid., 358.
140. Lewis, *Between Cross and Resurrection*, 435; italics added for emphasis.
141. Ibid., 435.
142. Ibid., 439.
143. Ibid., 439.

fested in its irreducible, particular, embodied narratives (which as of yet awaits on this side of the *cordon sanitaire* a bodily resurrection, and thus full redemption "from within")—from the presence of "within-redemption" by articulating God's first century presence in Jesus' Saturday sepulcher as a signifier for his presence in all subsequent (and perhaps prior!) tombs. Ultimately, although this God may be able to redeem "from within" Jesus' tomb, his "within-redemption" extends to particular, embodied tombs only as things "signified." Embodied, particular humans are essentially removed from the location of God's redeeming presence in Jesus Christ. But now we must ask: is "redemption through signification" even a viable substitute for the redemptive presence of the Redeemer within our very own particular, embodied narratives? Were we to say that my "old self" (an irreducibly particular, embodied self) "is absent and replaced by Christ," we would be acknowledging that not only is redemption not "within" my particular narrative, but does not involve the full redemption of the tomb's contents. Shall we "throw down the gauntlet" and declare that either God in Christ is present as a redeeming presence—a Real Presence!—in our particular tombs, or he is not the "within Redeemer" of any human lives? Can a "signification" of a once-for-all redeeming presence be a substitute either for his presence, or our material redemption, the redemption of that which was created both as a "psychosomatic unity," and called "very good"? Not only—it appears—has Lewis reduced the created, "very good" integrity of particular, embodied human narratives to "things signified" by the "signifier" of a "most real" narrative (i.e., of Christ's *triduum*), but ultimately he has done the very thing he has set out not to do: He has allowed the narrative of Jesus Christ so to color *all* of history that *all* particular histories are abandoned!

If, as we have developed, we are created "very good" as particular, embodied humans, "nothing more, nothing less," and thus to speak of the redemption of particular, embodied humans entails both an affirmation—not an abrogation—of this "psychosomatic unity," and thus an articulation of Emmanuel's redemption "from within" particular, embodied human narratives is not to circumvent this same essential humanity in all of its manifestations, even when that which is recognized as human lies "unrecognizable" in the tomb, then does Lewis' "redemption via signification" do justice to "within-redemption"? Could it be that an understanding of Christ's resurrection in which his resurrection "signifies the redeeming of our time" performs the same dynamic with regard to particular, embodied human narratives which Lewis tried to avoid with regard to Christ's narrative? That is, it makes redemption *necessary*?

Although Lewis has deftly allowed us to extend "within-redemption" all the way into the deepest darkness of Jesus' Saturday sepulcher, does not his rendering of "within-redemption" become, when applied to particular, embodied human narratives, an "overbearing interpretive instrument" which creates the *certainty* of redemption? As will be developed, though Lewis extends the discussion of "within-redemption" by positive strides, his "redemption via signification" (which is, as we will see, a redemption of "finality" and "sufficiency")—and certainly articulations of redemption similar to it—creates more problems than promises when that redemption is extended to humans in their particular, embodied narratives.[144]

---

144. To give another example of this thinking, except in modified form, I refer the reader to Fiddes' *Past Event and Present Salvation*. Fiddes—and I present him in simplified fashion—details a God who, in the cross, comes to both forgive and absorb the sins of sinners. For it is God's "twofold journey of forgiveness" in Jesus Christ—*in illo tempore*—"through the stages of awakening awareness and absorbing hostility, [that] the forgiver [Jesus] is learning how best to win the offender to himself. The fruit of this agonizing journey is the ability to draw . . . hostile and stubborn heart[s] into forgiving love" (ibid., 178). Thus, "In this one past event the God who was and is always willing to forgive gains through the cross that experience of the human heart that gives him a way into our hearts. There is an objective 'change' in God, not with the effect of moving him from wrath to love, but rather with the subjective effect of moving us from rebellion to fellowship . . . Looked at from the human perspective, we experience God as the one who sympathises with us, and so we are enabled to face up both to judgement and to acceptance" (ibid., 178–79). Ultimately, the past event of the cross "is to have a creative power upon human lives" (ibid. 214) in that it both "evokes resentment" (ibid., 177) from sinners (regarding their destructive ways), and it gives meaning to present human suffering in that, in the cross, now viewed through the lens of the resurrection, the Christian sees that God has "expose[d] his being to the alienating power of death, he overcomes it through life. He absorbs it sting into is being and makes it serve his purpose" (ibid., 211). Knowledge of this exposure overcomes "all loss of meaning" accrued by contemporary suffers (ibid., 220). But does not the narrative of the *in illo tempore* work of atonement, for Fiddes, render particular human narratives as sub-themes? And how does this atonement extend to the contents of my tomb? Is not my tomb still a chapter in my narrative that cannot be reduced to "forgiveness" and "meaning"? Questions abound!

Redeeming *This* Body

Emmanuel's Commitment to Context

As Douglas John Hall observes, though getting Jesus off the cross has never been a problem for triumphalistic theologies, "to get *us* off the cross—which is, after all, Christ's own work—is another matter."[145] Hall elaborates his point by asserting, "Least of all can it be achieved by reiterating the confession that Jesus has risen. When that is done . . . with a certain fanfare and with Easter Sunday gusto that behaves as if now everything were entirely put to rights, it is ironic and sometimes repulsive."[146] He adds, "The cross of the world and of humanity remains after all the Easter sermons have been preached and all the hallelujah's sung."[147] If, as Hall points out, the theology of the cross is committed to "calling a thing what it really is" (as will be developed in the subsequent chapter), then its statements must "correspond with reality."[148] But here, as we must develop, according to Hall, a third important dynamic regarding the theology of the cross manifests itself. In addition to articulating both God's commitment to the world, and the goodness of creation and embodied creaturehood, as well as redemption's affirmation—not abrogation—of that creation and creaturehood, the theology of the cross will not surrender context.

According to Hall, the theology of the cross which stakes its claim on Emmanuel and his "transformative solidarity" with the world is also a theology committed to being a contextual theology.[149] Essentially, according to Hall, the "Emmanuel formula" insists upon "*not* a generalization but a radical particularization of God's gracious *mitsein* . . ."[150] or the "scandal of particularity."[151] Emmanuel is not called to be in "transformative solidarity" with a "theoretical humanity,"[152] for "such an abstraction robs God of God's real involvement in the life of the

---

145. Hall, *Lighten Our Darkness*, 115.
146. Ibid.
147. Ibid.
148. Ibid.
149. Hall, *Thinking the Faith*, 29.
150. Ibid., 100.
151. Ibid., 238.
152. Hall, *Professing the Faith*, 529.

world,"¹⁵³ but indeed by speaking of this Emmanuel's commitment to human context, all such ideas of contextuality with regard to God-talk are radicalized in such a manner that "there can be no God-talk which is not at the same time the most explicit sort of us-talk."¹⁵⁴ Thus the humanity to which Emmanuel is unqualifiedly committed in "transformative solidarity" "from within" is "an existing, living, breathing, interacting humanity, alive within the web of the universe—in fact, not even "humanity" at all, since no such universal actually exists, but human beings in their private and social reality, generation after generation; male and female human beings; adults and children; healthy, sick, dying, and dead people. In short, the actual condition of humankind describes and determines the condition under which God may be 'with' it."¹⁵⁵ In short, if Emmanuel is committed to this level of contextuality according to the theology of the cross, then it becomes vital that the theology of the cross express the "ongoingness"¹⁵⁶ nature of God's commitment to the world, especially, again, as that commitment relates to the discussion of redemption, and in our case, "within-redemption."

Logically, then, we must be careful when applying Christ's resurrection to talk of human redemption, especially if humans—and the redemption of humans—are to be identified according to their full contextuality. For, when speaking of a "triumph" with regard to Christ's resurrection which need only be applied (via signification!) to humanity in general for the sake of the *finality* of that same triumph, and certainly at the expense of the "ongoingness" of human contextuality, Hall asserts, "Surely it is a victory of Marcionism in the church when the [New] Testament is made to suppress that ongoingness in favor of a theoretical finality that permits no novelty, no surprises."¹⁵⁷ Hall elaborates this point by averring, "Surely the burden of the [New] Testament's witness is not that the song has ended, that the last great chapter has been written, but rather that an obstacle to the continuation of the epic tale of creation has been removed . . . [thus] The message of Easter is not that the tale has ended, so that the people of God . . . could sing of what once

---

153. Hall, *Thinking the Faith*, 101.
154. Ibid., 100.
155. Hall, *Professing the Faith*, 529.
156. Hall, *Thinking the Faith*, 101.
157. Ibid., 102.

occurred and pronounce upon its eternal import."[158] Were this to be the case, that the Gospel was merely the pronouncement of the final chapter of redemption that had already been written, we would have here nothing more than a "realized eschatology ... in which the divine work [was] truly finished already and [remained] only to be displayed to full view and acknowledged universally."[159] Ultimately, Hall asserts, "*Unless God's act in Christ is a credible participation in our very mundane lives, the redemptive import of it is lost to us.*"[160]

Thus, for Hall, when finality is attributed to the resurrection of Christ, especially with reference to—and at the expense of—the "ongoingness" of human existence in its profound contextuality, "God emerges from the tussle with death and hell as one who is above it. But we are not above it ... and the [commitment] ... that led the loving God toward solidarity with us is exchanged in this Theology for the kind of transcendence that simply displaces everything intended by the incarnation and humiliation of the divine Word."[161] Hall calls this "resurrectionism."[162] For not only does this "resurrectionism" fail to allow for a transformation of the divine attributes—especially as they relate to "power"—through the "humiliation and crucifixion of the Word," but it "achieves the ultimate coup of triumphalistic religion: it permits deity to seem, for a moment, to have been overcome—and therefore it makes the triumph of power and glory all the more impressive."[163] In the end, though, this "resurrectionism" is nothing more than an "effective nullification of the incarnation,"[164] or a denial of God's abiding commitment in Jesus Christ to be with his creation and creatures without reservation in "transformative solidarity" in their profound, ongoing contextuality.[165] If, according to Hall, triumphalistic religion's attempt at finality in regard to articulating Christ's resurrection and its relation to humans, or "resurrectionism," "removes the cross from

---

158. Hall, *Thinking the Faith*, 102.
159. Hall, *Professing the Faith*, 99.
160. Hall, *Thinking the Faith*, 330–31; italics original.
161. Hall, *Professing the Faith*, 96.
162. Ibid., 96, 528–30.
163. Ibid., 528.
164. Ibid.
165. Ibid., 528.

the heart of God,"[166] then we have also observed that all human crosses (and their eventual tombs!) are removed from the heart of Christ. But perhaps here Dorothee Sölle may have the most penetrating analysis of triumphalistic religion's attempt at finality with regard to applying Christ's resurrection to individual, human narratives and their redemption, especially with reference to how that "finality" relates to particular, embodied human suffering and, ultimately, death.

According to Sölle, addressing the position that declares "that what Christ has done for us is sufficient"[167] in such a manner—in our case—that it now need be only applied within a signifier-signified framework, that indeed, "Christ has indeed done everything for us, so that everything has been paid in full,"[168] God is not only revealed to be an "apathetic God,"[169] but individual human narratives are rendered insignificant. She elaborates, "What one suffers now still, in the history after the fact, history's postlude, so to speak, is to be particularly endowed as insignificant."[170] Ultimately, for Sölle, this "means an end to the worth that human suffering had as an extension . . . of Christ's sufferings. The assertion that in Christ everything has been fulfilled remains in that case completely without content, an ideal of lordship that excludes us."[171] In this scheme, human suffering is blessed by a triumphalistic theology that attempts to guarantee the certainty of redemption through the avoidance of the very reality for which it has articulated "redemption." Ultimately, "We are stuck in a world where suffering knows no end, where the poor are always with us, where it seems for all the world that God has abandoned us completely and forever."[172] In this case, according to Timothy Wengert, suffering is no longer made penultimate through the hope of the Easter proclamation, but, ironically, theology's attempt

166. Ibid., 96.
167. Sölle, *Suffering*, 128.
168. Ibid., 130.
169. Ibid., 129.
170. Ibid., 130. Cf. Sanders, *Tenebrae*, xv, in which she, resonating with Sölle, "What is too often lost in the celebration of Easter is precisely [the] sense of risk. In the hermeneutics of salvation, Easter is often seen as the happy ending to a well-worn tale that is enjoyable precisely and only because it all happened far away and long ago, and no one nee be too concerned about it anymore. Suffering here and now, in other words, is insignificant because it has already been overcome by the glory of the resurrection."
171. Sölle, *Suffering*, 131.
172. Wengert, "'PEACE, PEACE . . . CROSS, CROSS,'" 203.

at certainty, and thus finality, has made suffering and death ultimate and essential to the very religious pursuit which tries to avoid them.[173] The certainty of victory, according to Theresa Sanders, may also lead, ironically, to a "morbid fascination" with Christ and his suffering. She elaborates, "Because a happy ending has already been accomplished, there is leisure to linger over the details of the Passion. The thorns, the whips, the bloody cloak, and broken limbs—these would be unbearable if [Jesus'] story ended with his naked and rotting body being dumped unceremoniously into a mass grave. Tradition can afford to present and re-present the details only because it deems them, in the end, insignificant in light of the resurrection."[174]

No Theologia Crucis Naturalis

Ultimately, in our attempt to construct an articulation of "within-redemption" on the basis of the theology of the cross, a theology which takes seriously and factors into the mix the realities of 1) God's unreserved commitment to the world as Emmanuel; 2) the goodness of creaturehood, and the affirmation—not abrogation—of that creaturehood especially with regard to "within-redemption"; and 3) the commitment to the profound contextuality, or "ongoingness," of the world and the particular, embodied human narratives in that world, we must return to the issue which Lewis both addressed—and then circumvented—through his delineation of redemption "from within."

Let us recall that, at the core of his attempt to articulate "within-redemption," Lewis wanted to avoid permitting the Word of redemption to become an "overbearing interpretive instrument which forces rationality onto events of obvious absurdity . . . [insisting] that they be recognized despite their negativity as inducements to confidence and joy in the future of history and history's God. . . [for] The Gospel certainly makes hope possible; but never *necessary*."[175] Thus stated, this Word of redemption, even "within-redemption," according to Lewis, easily devolves into an "overbearing interpretive instrument," resulting in the dedignification of particular, embodied human narratives for the sake of delineating that redemption as 1) historical certainty; 2) cosmological

173. See ibid., 190–205.
174. Sanders, *Tenebrae*, 90.
175. Lewis, *Between Cross and Resurrection*, 291.

certainty; or 3) mythological certainty. In each case, whether historical, cosmological, or mythological, the assurance of redemption is achieved apart from the narrative of Christ's *triduum* in what amounts to be either a cyclic, or time-less, a-history of redemption which is part of the grain of the cosmos. This, essentially, is a natural theology of glory.

But, what is interesting here, and important to underscore for our project, is that in Lewis' attempt to circumvent a natural theology of glory that sidesteps the integral narrative of Christ's *triduum*, he meanders right into the middle of a *theologia crucis naturalis* by sidestepping the integral narratives of particular, embodied humans. Restated: when theology stresses simply the *necessity* of redemption above all else, it becomes a natural theology of glory in which our gaze is directed either to the location of an inherently cyclic, or inherently time-less "most-real" realm of the cosmos where "redemption" is effected, in either case normally at the expense of the integrity of materiality (think here, for our purposes, of the "immortality of the soul"). When theology stresses Christ's *triduum* above all else with regard to redemption, especially at the expense of the co-central importance of particular, embodied human narratives, it becomes a *theologia crucis naturalis* in which our gaze is directed to the location of a "most-real" narrative of Christ's redemption which rounds off the created integrity (profound contextuality!) of individual human narratives (think here, for our purposes, of redemption articulated within the "signifier/signified" framework). A *theologia crucis* in the tradition Luther, especially as it pertains to "within-redemption," will stress both the vital, ongoing significance of Christ's *triduum*, and the ongoing importance and integrity of the particular, embodied human *triduum* in its manifold manifestations. Never one at the expense of the other! But, as Oswald Bayer points out, the ability to create a *theologia crucis naturalis*, especially as we have witnessed with Lewis' articulation of "within-redemption," is only "natural" for the "old Adam/Eve." How so?

In his project to relate justification, and thus the passive righteousness of faith, to the old Adam/Eve and their attempts to locate ultimate meaning in the world, the pretext for such a project is the old Adam/Eve who, above all else, are "concerned to assure [themselves] about the meaning of the whole."[176] This attempt to concern oneself with the

---

176. Bayer, *Living By Faith*, 35.

"meaning of the whole,"[177] manifests itself in one of two ways: either through "justifying thinking" (metaphysics), or through "justifying doing" (morality). Either way, both seek to impose unity of meaning upon existence, while, in the process, attempting to justify human existence.[178] For the purpose of this project, especially as it relates to a development of unreserved "within-redemption," and specifically counter to a "redemption via signification," it is "justifying thinking" upon which we will further elaborate.

According to Bayer, "justifying thinking" attempts, with its own powers, to "harmonize reality in the concept of unity,"[179] to round all of reality off "under the concept of the one, the true, and the good[.]"[180] In this attempt it drives to attest that everything concrete and particular has the "general as its basis."[181] This "justifying thinking" not only attempts to vindicate the existence of the thinker (the confessor), but the existence of God, as well (the confessed). So Bayer observes that, "The individual in one's particularity and sensitivity is left on the garbage heap of history; the individual is refuse. Only in that the individual is a moment within the general is one's existence justified. Thus, the misery and suffering of this world are ultimately regarded as irrelevant. This contemplative theodicy supposes the painful difference between the promise of life and all that contradicts it to be already resolved."[182]

But Bayer counters this "justifying thinking" with the passive righteousness of faith—delineated from the theology of Luther—whose significance lies in what it does *not* attempt to do. The one who is justified by faith, who lives by the passive righteousness of faith, "advance[s] no claim to totality in what they do,"[183] whether it be in seeking totality—and thus finality—through metaphysical or moralistic constructs. In short, the passive righteousness of faith lets "'God alone work in us and that in all our powers we do nothing of our own.'"[184] Ultimately, Bayer notes, as nature and history are not segregated for the one who is

---

177. Ibid., 35.
178. Ibid., 20.
179. Ibid., 79.
180. Ibid., 23.
181. Ibid., 22.
182. Ibid., 75.
183. Ibid., 38.
184. Ibid., 19, quoted by Bayer from LW 44:72.

justified by the passive righteousness of faith, that indeed both wrath and grace are the works of the one God,[185] *lament*—and not metaphysics or morality—becomes the quintessential manner of perceiving and expressing one's world. "For [lament] never surrenders the faith that the creation is 'very good,' nor does it make evil and suffering harmless, regarding them as nothing."[186] With this said, Bayer observes, "Our most profound testing is that God, who has promised us life and eternal communion . . . is still the God who does not lament death or destroy it, but who is at work in life and death and all things."[187] It is the passive righteousness of faith that grasps God—amid this testing—precisely where he lets himself be found, that is, in the Word of the cross and its proclamation.[188] Regardless, as the passive righteousness of faith does not resolve the conundrums of existence by appealing to a natural theology of glory which ignores Christ's *triduum* for the sake of a non-material redemption (again, read: "the immortality of the soul"), certainly will it neither seek ultimate meaning, and thus finality for the word of redemption, by appealing to Christ's *triduum* at the expense of both the individual *triduum* of the particular, embodied human being, and the God who is present—in "transformative solidarity"—within the *triduum* of the human whose existence is only manifested as particular and embodied. Perhaps it is Gerhard Sauter who has best articulated this "passive righteousness" of faith as it manifests itself in a hope that defies finality-seeking, when he asserts regarding faith's perception that it is one "of the living God who by his promises discloses a way that we can go without being clear about where it may lead us and without being given any means to measure distances."[189] Again, it is the latter route—Christ's *triduum* at the expense of the human *triduum*—that Lewis has taken in his delineation of "within redemption" via significa-

---

185. Ibid., 30.
186. Ibid., 71.
187. Ibid.
188. Ibid., 72.

189. Sauter, "Our Reasons for Hope," 213. He adds, "Hope, then, is more like the day-to-day life-saver which is given to us according to our present needs; it is more the extent of clarity that emerges when the fog is lifting. In hope God gives us glimpses of his will and purpose, yet he withholds from us that overview-perspective that we as human beings wish to acquire: the intimate knowledge and control of what God intends to do, perform, and fulfill" (ibid.).

tion as he has rightly countered the various manifestations of a natural theology of glory.

An Apocalyptic Horizon and Epistemology of the Cross

As we have developed, to speak on matters of Christian eschatology, and specifically with regard to matters of ultimate human redemption, is to speak of a hope not only for creation in its materialty, but of a hope for humans in their particular, embodied, or "psychosomatic" essence. Indeed, as we must also point out, biblical studies through the course of the twentieth century have not only revealed the centrality of the apocalyptic perspective for Scripture, especially with reference to the Pauline corpus of writings, with signal motifs identified as "the idea of two aeons, the embattled sovereignty of God over time and history, [and] the revelation of an imminent *eschaton*,"[190] but specific attention has been paid to the apocalyptic's general emphasis upon the cosmic scope of God's sovereign, saving activity.[191]

But, by acknowledging both the fact that Christian redemption, especially with reference to humans, is a hope—founded upon the resurrection of the body—for particular, embodied humans, and that the apocalyptic emphasis involves the cosmic scope of God's saving activity, then the riddle becomes, as J. Louis Martyn points out, "How can the best of news be proclaimed in the midst of an unchanged world? How can the resurrection be proclaimed in the midst of the cross?"[192] Especially in the midst of the crosses of human narratives that continue to be lined-up *anno Domini*? And what are Christians to say who, in their own bodies, "live existentially the tension of their present incompleted existence in solidarity with an unredeemed creation . . . [in which] they must . . . yearn for the consummation of the resurrection, which is nothing but God's triumph over the power of death that poisons his creation[?]"[193] Do we not hope for a "completion" in which

---

190. Brown, *Cross and Human Transformation*, 3; quoted by Brown from Richard E. Sturm, "Defining the Word 'Apocalyptic,'" 24.
191. Ibid., 5.
192. Martyn, "Epistemology at the Turn of the Ages," 108–9.
193. Beker, *Paul the Apostle*, 179.

the "last enemy," or "death, [will] be swallowed up ... by life and by the triumph of God[?]"[194]

Addressing just this question raised by the emerging emphasis upon apocalyptic thought, Ernst Käsemann identified a "direct connection between apocalyptic and the theology of the cross."[195] The first connection which Käsemann raised between apocalyptic and the theology of the cross was through his noted assertion that "apocalyptic ... [is] the mother of Christian theology."[196] Second, Käsemann asserts that, at the core of Paul's thinking lies the "righteousness of faith" whose foundation lies in Jesus' crucifixion for sinners. For if

> The cross shows that the true God is the Creator who acts to bring existence out of nothing ... [who] since the beginning of the world proves himself to be the one who raises the dead ... [then] Likewise the cross also shows, in the perspective of salvation, that the true man is always the sinner, cannot at all help himself, is unable by his activity to overcome his infinite distance from God ... [and] exposes man's illusion that he can transcend himself, work out his own salvation, and exalt himself against God by his own capabilities, whether of strength, wisdom, piety, or self-love.[197]

And so ultimately, according to Käsemann,

> The coming of the God who humbles himself means the end for the man who tries to transcend himself, and not even a Christian mask can protect him in this divine presence. The dying Son of God does not make alive without putting to death, pardons as judge, glorifies by deeply humiliating, enlightens by confronting with the inescapable truth about ourselves, makes us whole by including us among those to whom the first Beatitude is addressed. For he calls us out of our fancied maturity into childlikeness as the only possibility for genuine life.[198]

---

194. Ibid.

195. Brown, *Cross and Human Transformation*, 6. Here my observations are heavily indebted to Brown's outline and delineation. For a presentation of the particular contributions of Käsemann, Beker, and Martyn to the recovery and development of apocalyptic thinking with regard to the Pauline writings, see ibid., 4–10.

196. Käsemann, "On the Subject of Primitive Christian Apocalyptic," 134; also quoted in Brown, *Cross and Human Transformation*, 6.

197. Käsemann, "Pauline Theology of the Cross," 159.

198. Ibid., 164.

Essentially, according to Käsemann, "All this can be reduced to the one common denominator: The justification of the godless [which] is for Paul the consequence of the death of Jesus, nothing else. This means, however, the *Regnum Dei* on earth."[199] With regard to this *Regnum Dei*, then, discipleship within this cosmic lordship of the crucified also bears the appropriate marks and obedience. For, according to Käsemann, "The token which distinguishes his lordship from the lordship of other religious founders is undoubtedly the cross and the cross alone . . . Following Jesus means, uniquely and unmistakably, becoming a disciple of the one who was crucified."[200] The disciple must never forget that the cross of Christ did not simply become "just the way to lordship or the price paid for it. Rather, it remains the signature of the risen Lord. He possesses no other visage except the countenance of the Crucified, and only under this countenance can we take our stand."[201] Essentially, as Alexandra Brown observes in analysis of Käsemann's program, the world's sovereignty belongs to the Crucified Jesus who "became Lord by virtue of his death for the sake of the ungodly, thus ending the power of sin and freeing humanity for the *nova oboedientia*."[202]

Thus, if we keep in mind Martyn's question ("How can the best of news be proclaimed in the midst of an unchanged world?"), we discover that his answer is predicated upon Käsemann's apocalyptic insights, but now with specific focus upon apocalyptic as epistemology. For not only is "Epistemology . . . a central concern in all apocalyptic,"[203] with the cross becoming the "absolute epistemological watershed,"[204] but "The cross is the epistemological crisis for the simple reason that while it

---

199. Ibid., 165.

200. Käsemann, "Saving Significance of the Death of Jesus," 42; also quoted in Brown, *Cross and Human Transformation*, 6.

201. Käsemann, "Pauline Theology of the Cross," 174.

202. Brown, *Cross and Human Transformation*, 6.

203. Martyn, "Apocalyptic Antinomies in Paul's Letter to the Galatians," 424 n. 28, also quoted in Brown, *Cross and Human Transformation*, 9. Martyn adds, "because the genesis of apocalyptic involves a) developments that have rendered the human story hopelessly enigmatic, when perceived in human terms, b) the conviction that God has now given to the elect true perception both of present developments (the real world) and of a wondrous transformation in the near future, c) the birth of anew way of knowing both present and future, and d) the certainty that neither the future transformation, nor the new way of seeing both it and present developments, can be thought to grow out of conditions in the human race" (ibid.).

204. Martyn, "Epistemology at the Turn of the Ages," 108.

is in one sense followed by the resurrection, it is not replaced by the resurrection."[205] Essentially, according to Martyn, "*Christ* defines the difference between the two ways of knowing, doing that precisely in his cross. The cross of Christ means that the marks of the new age are at present hidden in the old age . . . Thus, at the juncture of the ages the marks of the resurrection are hidden and revealed *in* the cross of the disciple's daily death, and only there."[206] If, asking with Martyn, "How can the best of news be proclaimed in an unchanged world?" we discovered—with Martyn—that the "marks of the resurrection are hidden and revealed in the cross of the disciple's daily death, and only there," let us also extend this epistemology of the cross in order to declare that the presence of Christ's work of redemption may not only extend all the way into all particular, embodied human narratives, but indeed extend into their very tombs; even tombs whose contents which were once recognizably "human" are now unrecognizably so. It is here that the "marks of the resurrection are hidden," as well, according to an epistemology of the cross.

"Within-Redemption": Where We Stand. What We Need

Thinking back to Lewis' proposal for an articulation of "within redemption," let us acknowledge that he is certainly to be lauded for such a delineation of "within-redemption," especially in contradistinction to the various manifestations of a natural theology of glory. But let us also be constructively critical.

Although Lewis rightly contends for the *triduum's cordon sanitaire* which allows us to identify a God who resides within the Friday/Saturday narrative of Jesus Christ in order to redeem *his* life "from within," in the process of doing so he removes the particular, embodied narratives of humanity from the presence of this same "within-redemption" by articulating God's first century presence in Jesus' Saturday Sepulcher as a signifier for his presence in all subsequent (and perhaps prior) tombs. Ultimately, although this God may be able to redeem "from within" Jesus' tomb, his "within-redemption" extends to the location of our particular tombs only as "things signified." But let us ask: Is "redemption via signification" even a viable substitute for his redeem-

---

205. Ibid., 109.
206. Ibid., 110.

ing presence—the "expansive creativity of self-limitation"!—within our very own particular, embodied narratives? Would it not be proper to conclude that if my "old self" "is absent and replaced by Christ," then we would be acknowledging that not only does redemption *not* "take place" "within" particular, human narratives, but does not involve the material redemption of those tombs' contents? Either God is the Real Presence of redemption "from within" human tombs, or he is not the "within-Redeemer" of lives which will only be articulated psychosomatically. And no signification of a once-for-all, *in illo tempore* presence can be a substitute either for his redeeming presence, or our material, corporeal redemption. Not only has Lewis reduced the created, "very good" integrity of particular, embodied narratives to "things signified" by the "signifier" of a "most real" narrative (i.e., Christ's *triduum*), but ultimately he has accomplished the very thing which he set out not to do: he has allowed the narrative of Jesus Christ so to color all of history that all particular histories are either abandoned or rendered superfluous in relation to a "most real" narrative of redemption. As of this writing, the tombs of our ancestors and loved ones are still sealed.

But how, we ask with Hall, "in view of [Christ's] indisputably biblical affirmation of triumph, is it possible to prevent the Bible's equally indisputable acknowledgment of the reality of evil, death, and decay from being swallowed up and rendered unreal or illusory by the triumph?"[207] No matter how loud and confidently we shout "Hallelujah, Christ is Risen!" the Saturday tombs of our loves remain sealed. And ours, too, one day.

So, culling what we have developed from our discussion regarding 1) the integrity of embodied humanity, 2) the necessity for redemption "from within," especially within the tradition of Luther's theology of the cross, 3) the importance of the "passive righteousness" of faith, 4) Scripture's emphasis upon the apocalyptic and its conceptualization of God's cosmic, sovereign lordship, and 5) the apocalyptic's accompanying "epistemology of the cross," especially developed by Käsemann and Martyn, *let us ask*: Can the Real Presence of redemption "from within" extend, ultimately, to the location of our own particular, material tombs? If the Word of redemption "from within" is a Word "within" all of creation and history, is it not a Word which extends, in its redeeming activity and presence, from *in illo tempore* to *in hoc tempore*, as well

---

207. Hall, *Lighten Our Darkness*, 137.

as *in hoc locus*?[208] If so, then how may this Real Presence of a "within-Redeemer" be articulated?

As we have worked within the tradition of Luther's theology of the cross up to this point, the next chapter will outline Luther's *theologia crucis* with an eye to laying the foundation for not only the core of that same *theologia crucis*, but also to developing a satisfactory answer to our question of complete redemption "from within."

---

208. With regard to the eclipse of "place" in modern theological discussion, and the rationale for this eclipse, I refer the reader to Inge, *Christian Theology of Place*; and Giddens, *Modernity and Self-Identity*, 10–21.

2

Luther's *Theologia Crucis*
An Outline

Introductory Matters

THOUGH, ACCORDING TO JÜRGEN MOLTMANN, "THE CROSS IS NOT AND cannot be loved,"¹ there seems to exist an inverse correlation between the cross' "unlovability" and scholarly output regarding that same cross, especially with reference to, for the purpose of our project, Luther's *theologia crucis*.

At the same time, we cannot fail to notice another inverse correlation. Simply, though Luther is known to have employed the phrase "theology of the cross" on only three occasions—in his *Lectures on the Hebrews* (early, 1518), the *Asterisci Lutheri adversus Obeliscos Eckii* (March, 1518), and the *Explanations to the 95 Theses* (August, 1518)—other than in his quintessential and most explicit use and development of it in his *Heidelberg Disputation* (April, 1518),² the theology of the cross, for Luther, was no "mere momentary concern or characteristic of the young Luther,"³ or a stage simply to be left behind on the way to a more mature, developed and systematic theology. No, the expression "theology of the cross," according to Gerhard Ebeling, "serves as an indication of the object of his constant concern, the fundamental orientation of

---

1. Moltmann, *Crucified God*, 1. We will return to Moltmann in chapter three, below, with reference to the conceptual flaws he attributes to the *communicatio idiomatum*, especially as articulated by Luther.

2. For a recent articulation of the context and content of these writings, see Madsen's *Theology of the Cross in Historical Perspective*, 77–80.

3. Ebeling, *Luther*, 229.

theological thought."⁴ The *theologia crucis*, for Luther, was not only the "criterion and subject of all true theology,"⁵ but, more importantly, as will be developed and as can be evidenced explicitly in the *Heidelberg Disputation*, it was—and is—the description of "how a *theologian* of the cross operates in the world in response to the transforming power of the cross."⁶ Far from being a doctrine, the *theologia crucis* is a "vision of reality"⁷ describing what it means "to live [as a *theologian*] *coram Deo* before a crucified God."⁸ Thus, for the theologian of the cross, the cross becomes a "paradigm of God's working,"⁹ the location in which God most profoundly "reveals his *modus operandi*"¹⁰ that "God does not operate in another way with men today than he did with Christ."¹¹

With this being said, for the theologian of the cross, not only is the subject matter of the *theologia crucis* simultaneously *Deus theologicus* and *homo theologicus*, neither ever considered *in abstractu*,¹² but, as Mary Solberg so eloquently asserts, Luther's articulation of *theologia crucis* reveals that "Theology is not about God; it is about how it is with *us*—in the presence of God-in-relation-to-us in the person of Jesus Christ."¹³ And, as this project's trajectory unfolds, after Luther's *theologia crucis* has been outlined, this dynamic will be pressed to its farthest conceivable limits with regard to "how it is with us": to the tombs of decomposing humans themselves and the dynamic of "within-redemption."

But, as this chapter unfolds, and perhaps as has already been detected, the reader will note the primary thrust of Luther's *theologia crucis* as one centered around the cross as "cognitive principle,"¹⁴ and

4. Ibid.

5. Ibid., 226.

6. Thompson, *Crossing the Divide*, 16; italics added for emphasis.

7. Ibid., 21.

8. Ibid., 16.

9. Vercruysse, "Luther's Theology of the Cross at the Time of the Heidelberg Disputation," 542.

10. Kolb, "Luther on the Theology of the Cross," 451.

11. Ibid., 542.

12. Ebeling, *Luther*, 226.

13. Solberg, "All That Matters," 148.

14. Hinkson, "Luther and Kierkegaard: Theologians of the Cross," 31. Although his presentation of Luther's theology of the cross is concisely placed within the context of a positive comparison with Kierkegaard's theology of the cross, Hinkson may have one the finer recent presentations in print.

thus as an "epistemology of the cross."[15] This should come as no surprise though, for the reader need only bear in mind theses 19–21 in Luther's *Heidelberg Disputation* in which he asserts

> 19. That person does not deserve to be called a theologian who looks upon the invisible things of God as though they were clearly perceptible in those things which have actually happened.
>
> 20. He deserves to be called a theologian, however, who comprehends the visible and manifest things of God seen through suffering and the cross.
>
> 21. A theologian of glory calls evil good and good evil. A theologian of the cross calls the thing what it actually is.[16]

In one way or another, then, each locus in this chapter's thematic outline of Luther's *theologia crucis* will be developed against this epistemological turn in Luther's thinking as a theologian, or the habit of comprehending "the visible and manifest things of God seen through suffering and the cross."[17]

What will become crucial for our purposes—and here we are "jumping the gun" a bit in order to survey the entire field of this project—is that we come to understand that the cross as "cognitive principle" entails by no means the whole presentation of Luther's *theologia crucis*. As I will develop, Luther's *theologia crucis*, understood within the parameters of an "epistemology of the cross" developed in this chapter, allows us to both situate and comprehend—*sola fide, sola gratia*—the *radix* of Luther's *theologia crucis*, or his radical interpretation of the *communicatio idiomatum*, or, stated for our purposes, the articulation of Christ's redemption of all particular, embodied human narratives "from within." Thus it becomes so very important, when speaking of this divine presence of redemption "from within," that we "nail down" the *modus operandi* of this same redeeming presence. Therefore the "outline" comes before the foundation—or *crux*!—of Luther's *theologia crucis*. The manner in which this outline is developed, then, is essential for laying the groundwork for the subsequent chapter.

---

15. For an elaboration of Luther's theology of the cross employed explicitly in the funding of an "epistemology of the cross," see Solberg's "All That Matters," 144–48. I also refer the reader to her *Compelling Knowledge*.

16. LW 31: 52.

17. Ibid.

In order to develop an outline of Luther's *theologia crucis* several options are open to us. On the one hand, Luther's *theologia crucis* could be developed against the background of his historical context, in addition to its development within that context. This would certainly involve, at the very least, a study of not only Luther's historical context in general, but obviously a study of the various contours of humanism, the Nominalism of the *via Moderna*, late-Medieval mysticism, and the air of the Augustinian order, especially its *humilitas*-theology, from which Luther drank deeply. Additionally, we would also need to examine the various forces which elicited his theological productivity, and thus this cross-centered "vision of reality,"[18] even after his famous *Heidelberg Disputation*. Excellent, exhaustive studies and outlines abound in both cases to fund such a project.[19] On the other hand, Luther's *theologia crucis*, because it "permeates all of Luther's theological thinking," and was "the standard by which all genuine theological knowledge [was] measured, whether of the reality of God, of his grace, of his salvation, of the Christian life, or of the church of Christ,"[20] can also be developed thematically according to *loci* deemed constitutive within Luther's entire corpus. Exemplar studies, no doubt, could fund a project conducted in this fashion.[21] And certainly we must not ignore, were we to treat

---

18. Thompson, *Crossing the Divide*, 21.

19. For instance, to give just a thumbnail sketch, in relation to material covering the historical context leading up to Luther's articulation of the theology of the cross, thus covering such *loci* as the influences of humanism, Nominalism, mysticism, and the tradition of the Augustinian order, one could turn to such volumes as Lohse, *Martin Luther's Theology*, esp. 3–184; McGrath, *Luther's Theology of the Cross*, esp. 7–92; Ngien, *Suffering of God according to Martin Luther's 'Theologia Crucis,'* esp. 19–42; Madsen, *Theology of the Cross in Historical Perspective*, esp. 65–167; Oberman, *Reformation: Roots and Ramifications*; Oberman, *Impact of the Reformation*, esp. 3–47; Oberman, *Dawn of the Reformation*, esp. 3–233; and certainly Oberman, *Harvest of Medieval Theology*; Hoffman's *Luther and the Mystics*, and his *Theology of the Heart*; and certainly at the least the first volume of Brecht's trilogy entitled *Martin Luther: His Road to Reformation 1483–1521*. With reference to the forces which elicited his productivity post-*Heidelberg Disputation*, I turn the reader to Hendrix, *Luther and the Papacy*; Edwards, *Luther and the False Brethren*, and *Luther's Last Battles, 1531–1546*.

20 Althaus, *The Theology of Martin Luther*, 30.

21. A sampling of these studies includes Lohse, *Martin Luther's Theology*, esp. 185–345; Ebeling, *Luther*; Althaus, *Theology of Martin Luther*; Pinomaa, *Faith Victorious*; Iwand, *Luther's Theologie*; Kolb, "Luther on the Theology of the Cross," 443–66; Loewenich, *Luther's Theology of the Cross*; and Hendel's concise "Luther's Theology of the Cross," 223–31.

the development of the *theologia crucis* solely within the parameters of the *Heidelberg Disputation* itself, the incredible studies devoted to the development and trajectory of the *Heidelberg Disputation*'s logic.[22]

But, since this outline will both serve to situate and prepare a conceptual framework and foundation for our discussion in the subsequent chapter regarding Luther's radical interpretation of the *communicatio idiomatum* (the foundation of his *theologia crucis!*) for the sake of funding an articulation of complete "within-redemption" (thus providing, in the process, an epistemological bridge between chapters one and three), our outline of Luther's *theologia crucis* will be developed in order to facilitate this end. In short, since the *theologia crucis* is the method by which, for Luther, the whole content of the Christian faith is articulated,[23] we will develop Luther's *theologia crucis* through a thematic outline—drawing its bearings from influential, thematic presentations of the *theologia crucis*[24] (providing modifications necessitated by the intended

---

22. A few examples include Forde, *On Being a Theologian of the Cross*; Vercruysse, "Luther's Theology of the Cross at the Time of the Heidelberg Disputation," 523–46; and Nestingen, "Luther's Heidelberg Disputation: An Analysis of the Argument," 147–53.

23. Cf. Ngien, *Suffering God*, 43.

24. McGrath, *Luther's Theology of the Cross*, 149–50, divides the constitutive principles of the *theologia crucis* into 1) *theologia crucis* as a theology of revelation; 2) *theologia crucis* as a theology of indirect revelation; 3) a theology recognized in the sufferings of Christ (as opposed to human morals or the created order); 4) *theologia crucis* as a theology of faith; and 5) a theology in which God is known through suffering. Loewenich, *Luther's Theology of the Cross*, 22, presents the constitutive principles of the *theologia crucis* as 1) in contrast to a theology of speculation, *theologia crucis* as a theology of revelation; 2) *theologia crucis* as theology of indirect revelation; 3) *theologia crucis* as a theology in which God's revelation, countering the claim that God's works are recognized in either the works of creation and human morals, is recognized in suffering; 4) *theologia crucis* as a theology of faith; and 5) *theologia crucis* as theology reflected in the theologian's concrete suffering. And Hendel, "Theology of the Cross," 223–31, distinguishes the constitutive principles of the *theologia crucis* as 1) *theologia crucis* as a theology of justification; 2) *theologia crucis* as a theology of revelation; 3) *theologia crucis* as a theology of faith; 4) *theologia crucis* as a theology of suffering; and 5) *theologia crucis* as a theology for the Christian life. As the reader will see, my presentation will mirror Hendel's first two loci while, recognizing the inseparable nature of faith/suffering in embodied human beings, drawing *loci* three and four together. The fourth *locus* in this presentation will provide a segue in chapter three. What is interesting, as well, is that both McGrath and von Loewenich present "revelation" and "indirect revelation" under separate *loci*. But one wonders: does Luther ever consider a revelation which is not concealed *sub contrario* and thus indirect? That I have placed "revelation" and "indirect revelation" in one locus as indistinguishable parts of the whole reflects my answer to this question.

ends of this project)—whose loci consist of traditionally identified constitutive principles, both grounded in the *Heidelberg Disputation* and maintained throughout the trajectory of Luther's *theologia crucis*. As the reader will discern, recourse to historical context, especially as it pertains to regnant thinking which Luther inherited, will be engaged where it is integral for the development of particular *loci*. With this being the case, when arriving at this chapter's final two *loci*, the reader will detect perhaps two significant modifications—when compared to existing influential outlines—in this thematic presentation of Luther's *theologia crucis*. In short, "faith" and "suffering" will be treated, cutting against the grain of traditional presentations, under one locus entitled "A Theology of Faith." "A Theology *for* Creation"—commensurate with our discussion in chapter one, above—will also be presented as a separate yet integral locus with the intention of widening the significance of Luther's *theologia crucis* beyond epistemologically-related concerns, and setting the framework for the following two chapters. This will be the shortest of the four *loci*. Ultimately, it may be added, though we will rely upon Luther as much as possible, certainly supplemented heavily with established, secondary voices, whoever submits a chapter on Luther's *theologia crucis*, be it only in outline, must always acknowledge that they stand on the shoulders of the giants who came before them.

With all of this said, this chapter will be developed under four headings: 1) *Theologia Crucis*: A Theology of Justification; 2) *Theologia Crucis*: A Theology of Revelation; 3) *Theologia Crucis*: A Theology of Faith; 4) *Theologia Crucis*: A Theology *for* Creation. Though no outline will ever be exhaustive, this one will set the stage for this project's constructive element, or the appropriation of Luther's radical interpretation of the *communicatio idiomatum* for the articulation of complete "within-redemption" in the subsequent chapter. But let us also say a few things regarding the first section of our outline of Luther's *theologia crucis*.

Commencing this thematic outline of Luther's *theologia crucis* with justification, we will do so with a relatively in depth interpretation of Luther's 1535 Galatians lectures wherein the doctrine of justification explicitly receives perhaps one of its most mature and sustained treatments by Luther. Reminding ourselves that, for Luther, "justification is the article by which the church stands and falls,"[25] it is in this writing

---

25. According to Bayer this particular expression originally appeared in Löscher,

that we see Luther's doctrine of justification developed in relation to his whole theology. So Oswald Bayer can assert: "*Justification is not a separate topic apart from which still other topics could be discussed. Justification is the starting point for all theology and it affects every other topic.*"[26] Indeed, according to Bayer, Luther

> ... understood the event of justification in its social and cosmic breadth just as profoundly as he perceived it in its existential depth. To him as biblical interpreter, particularly as the Old Testament scholar he primarily was, it was precisely the social and cosmic breadth of justification that was disclosed to him by its existential depth. Not only our relationship to God and ourselves is made new through justification by faith but at the same time our relationships with all creatures are renewed. Even a new perception of space and time is included in our new relationship to God and the world.[27]

Adding to this insight, we may assert, and will develop, that it is a doctrine which not only both manifests a reinterpretation, in light of the revelation of Jesus Christ, of the—what was for Luther the previously troublesome—word "righteousness," along with its proper mood, consequently placing "law" within its proper perspective, but also repositions the location of one's assurance regarding justification itself. Ultimately, this interpretation will both underscore the centrality of justification within Luther's *theologia crucis*, and lead us into a discussion regarding the reason it is intimately tied to his *theologia crucis*. Therefore, in order to underscore the centrality of justification for the *theologia crucis*, we will work both from Luther's later thought in his 1535 Galatians lectures, and from his struggles with *iustitia Dei* which culminated in his 1518 *Heidelberg Disputation*. As will be developed in two stages in this longest—by far—of the four *loci*, Luther's articulation of justification is developed upon, within the *theologia crucis*, "a radical critique of the analogical nature of theological language."[28]

According to Alistair McGrath, observing that—especially within the medieval trajectory of thought—the *iustitia Dei* had been developed

---

Vollständiger Timotheus Verinus, I:342–43, also quoted in Bayer, "Justification as Basis and Boundary of Theology," 288.

26. Bayer, "Justification as Basis and Boundary of Theology," 274.
27. Ibid.
28. McGrath, *Luther's Theology of the Cross*, 158.

in analogous fashion to human conceptions of *iustitia*, the *theologia crucis* not only represents a "programmatic critique of the analogical nature of theological language,"[29] but "represents the most radical critique of the principle of analogy in theological discourse yet known[.]"[30] Indeed the only human *iustitia* valid *coram Deo* is the one's recognition of their total deprivation of *iustitia*. As we will see, the confession of this deprivation is simultaneously the confession that God is Creator and thus alone our sole sufficiency.

Theologia Crucis: A Theology of Justification

The Heart of All Christian Doctrine

Echoing in adamantine fashion his confession from his "last theological will and testament,"[31] or the *Schmalkald Articles* (1537), that "[n]othing in this article [on justification] can be given up or compromised, even if heaven and earth and things temporal should be destroyed,"[32] Luther asserted in his famous Galatians lectures of 1535 that "If [the doctrine of justification] is lost and perishes, the whole knowledge of truth, life, and salvation is lost and perishes at the same time. But if it flourishes, everything good flourishes—religion, true worship, the glory of God, and the right knowledge of all things and of all social conditions."[33] Indeed, "if the doctrine of justification is lost, the whole of Christian doctrine is lost."[34]

At the same time, having placed the doctrine of justification as the central locus of Christian doctrine, the doctrine that determines the veracity of all other doctrinal assertions, Luther identifies an integral distinction within the doctrine of justification of itself. He elaborates,

---

29. Ibid.
30. Ibid., 159.
31. Russell, *Luther's Theological Testament*, 2.
32. BC: 292.
33. LW 26: 3.
34. Ibid., 9. Cf. LW 14:37 in which Luther states in his "Exposition of Psalm 117" (1530), that "If this one teaching [i.e. on justification] stands in its purity, then Christendom will also remain pure and good, undivided and unseparated; for this alone, and nothing else, makes and maintains Christendom. Everything else may be brilliantly counterfeited by false Christians and hypocrites; but where this falls, it is impossible to ward off any error or sectarian spirit."

"This is our theology, by which we teach a precise distinction between these two kinds of righteousness, the active and the passive, so that morality and faith, works and grace, secular society and religion may not be confused."[35] But now we must ask: What are "passive" and "active" righteousness? How are they related both to the doctrine of justification and each other? What happens when they are not properly distinguished? Ultimately, as will be developed, this distinction—like a "red thread"—will take us not only straight to the crux of Luther's *theologia crucis*, but to the fundamental—and for Luther problematic—contours of the regnant conceptualizations of human righteousness—and thus divine justice—as per the *via Moderna* of late-Medieval Nomimalism. But let us continue to develop Luther's doctrine of justification as it is presented in his 1535 Galatians lectures.

According to Luther, the "passive" righteousness, or the "righteousness of faith," is that righteousness "which God imputes to us through Christ without works"[36] and is received in such a manner that "we work nothing, render nothing to God; we only receive and permit someone else to work in us, namely God."[37] When Luther refers to the "active" righteousness of the Law, he has in mind quite specifically the "Human reason [which] has the Law as its object. It says to itself: 'This I have done; this I have not done.'"[38] And, according to Luther, this "reason and flesh work together against the hearing of faith, think [faith is] too easy, wants to use the Law for its own ends."[39] But, with "active" and "passive" righteousness delineated, the need for not confusing, but keeping these "necessary" realities "within their limits,"[40] must be addressed. It is here that we discover the reason that the "passive" righteousness of faith, the righteousness that permits God alone to work in us, plays the central role in Luther's theology. Ultimately, as we will see, it is contrasted with the speculative righteousness which provides one with no solid ground on which to stand.

If Luther's theology consists of a precise distinction between "active" and "passive" righteousness, the reason for this distinction takes

35. LW 26: 7.
36. Ibid., 4.
37. Ibid.
38. Ibid.
39. Ibid., 214–15.
40. Ibid., 7.

us to the *radix* of human concerns *coram Deo*: "[Passive righteousness] snatches us away from ourselves and places us outside ourselves, so that we do not depend on our own strength, conscience, experience, person, or works but depend on that which is outside ourselves [*extra nos*] ... on the promise and truth of God, which cannot deceive."[41] Thus, as will be developed, if "passive" righteousness is *extra nos*, depending on the "promise and truth of God," then God must reveal on his own terms both the shape and content of that same righteousness. But, what is even more pressing at this point, if this is the case, that the justification which comes by the "passive" righteousness of faith is the *extra nos* "truth" which *cannot* deceive, then what is the "truth" that *does* deceive?

If human reason—which has the law as its object, thereby saying to itself "This I have done; this I have not done,"[42] thus working in concert with the rest of the body (in a manner antithetical to the "passive," *extra nos* righteousness by which God works all things in us)—attempts "to use the Law for its own ends,"[43] then it becomes only a natural consequence that old Eve would elevate the active, outward righteousness of the law to a level transgressing both its intended function and the work of Christ himself. In short, the essential issue, for Luther, is this: "Is the Law necessary for justification, or is it not?"[44] If the answer to this question is a "yes," then, according to Luther, one conspicuous consequence arises: one attempts—through the "active" righteousness of the law—to become the author of one's own justification. It is the implications of this attempt that concerns Luther. And these implications are not theoretical.

If, as Luther notes, "To attribute glory to God is to believe in Him, to regard Him as truthful, wise, righteous, merciful, and almighty, in short, to acknowledge Him as the Author and Donor of every good,"[45] then human reason which attempts to justify itself through the "active" righteousness of the law becomes "God's bitterest enemy," an enemy associating with itself qualities which are attributed solely to divinity—manifested through the conquering of the world's sin, death, the curse, and wrath of God—and thus mark the One who is "true God by

41. Ibid., 387.
42. Ibid., 87.
43. Ibid., 215.
44. Ibid., 85.
45. Ibid., 227.

nature."[46] In short, reason attributes the qualities of the Creator to itself. But, following Luther, this is only one "side of the coin." The "flip side" of the "active" righteousness coin holds consequences as devastating for the conscience as it does for one's relationship to the "Author and Donor of every good," a relationship whose roles have now been flipped.

The one who answers "yes" to the question of whether the "active" righteousness of the law is necessary for justification will encounter a reality 180 degrees from the one whose "passive" righteousness creates "certainty" because "it snatches [them] away from [themselves] and places [them] outside [themselves]."[47] For the one whose righteousness is fed by the "active" righteousness of the will will inevitably begin to experience, according to Luther, that "[T]he conscience senses that it has not satisfied the Law; it cannot satisfy the Law or bear the wrath of God, which the Law reveals when it sets us into the sight of God this way, that is, when it terrifies us, accuses us, and shows us our sins."[48] One soon discovers that "the Law makes demands on us, and impossible ones at that."[49] Instead of ministering to righteousness *coram Deo*, the "active" righteousness of the law becomes a minister of sin. Luther declares regarding this "ministry" of the "active" righteousness of the law: "Thus if the Law is a ministry of sin, it follows that it is also a ministry of wrath and death. For just as the Law reveals sin, so it strikes the wrath of God into a man and threatens him with death. Thus the ministry of sin is necessarily the ministry of the wrath of God and death. For where there is sin, there the conscience soon declares: 'You have sinned; therefore God is angry with you. If He is angry, He will kill you and damn you eternally.'"[50] It is here that one discovers the "proper" use of the law. So Luther states in summation, "Let anyone who can understand . . . understand that in Christian theology and according to its proper description the Law does not justify but has exactly the opposite effect: It discloses us to ourselves; it shows a wrathful God; it manifests wrath; it terrifies us. It not only reveals sin but it causes it to abound, so that where there was small sin at first, it becomes large through the

---

46. Ibid., 282.
47. Ibid., 387.
48. Ibid., 150.
49. Ibid., 209.
50. Ibid., 150.

illumination of the law."⁵¹ But let us now, still remaining with Luther's exhaustive delineation of justification in his Galatians lectures of 1535, develop what Luther means by the "proper" use of the law. As we will discover, to understand the "proper" use of the law is to simultaneously understand its proper *telos*, and gain an insight into what Luther refers to as God's *opus alienum*.

If the one who grounds their *coram Deo* righteousness on the "active" righteousness of the law soon discovers that "the Law makes demands on us, and impossible ones at that,"⁵² and that indeed all attempts at righteousness through the law amount essentially to the disclosure of our sinful selves and a wrathful God, then the next logical step, according to Luther, is a contempt for both the law and its author. So Luther states, "[T]hen a man begins to hate the Law, to run away from it, and with a perfect hatred to hate God, the originator of the Law."⁵³ The attempt at righteousness *coram Deo* through the law backfires: sin has been disclosed, transgressions are magnified, and the wrath of God is revealed against sinners. So Luther concludes, "Therefore the true function and chief and proper use of the Law is to reveal man his sin, blindness, misery, wickedness, ignorance, hate and contempt of God, death, hell, judgment, and the well-deserved wrath of God."⁵⁴ So, we ask, who can end this wrath of God, the curse of the "active" righteousness of the law? Does this "proper" use have a "proper" *telos*?

If early in his 1535 Galatians lectures Luther could declare that "true Christian theology ... does not present God to us in His majesty ... but Christ born of the Virgin as our Mediator" so that we do not "stray into heaven with our idle speculations," and certainly that "we

---

51. Ibid., 326.

52. Ibid., 209.

53. Ibid., 326. It is crucial to point out here a distinction: God, being the originator of the law, for Luther, is the "user" of the law. Thus Forde, in his locus "Christian Life," in *Christian Dogmatics*, is right to state, "God is the author of the law; God, not we, is the user of the law. We cannot preside over the law's use in order to speak of a third use which neither restrains evil nor convicts of sin" (450). Indeed, to do this, for Luther, would be to act as if Christ not only was not the *telos* of the proper use of the law, but indeed that it was the law whose righteousness was eternal, and not the righteousness of Christ. On this matter I refer the reader to Haikola's discussion entitled "A Comparison of Melanchthon's and Luther's Doctrine of Justification."

54. LW 26:309.

must look at no other god than this incarnate and human God,"⁵⁵ then the reason has become clear: our attempt to locate righteousness apart from Jesus Christ, that is, through the "active" righteousness of the law, has only launched us into the wrath of God through the curse of the law. But, if we are not to speculatively seek God in his majesty—using the law as our ladder—but in "Christ born of the Virgin as our Mediator," then we must also see this incarnate One through to his end, as well. For it is here—crucified under the curse of the law's "proper" use—that God the Son becomes a "sinner of sinners."⁵⁶ And it is this "sinner of sinners" who becomes the *telos* of the "proper" use of the law. So Luther declares, "[Jesus Christ] is, of course, innocent, because he is the Lamb of God without spot or blemish. But because he bears the sins of the world, his innocence is pressed down with the sins and guilt of the entire world. Whatever sins I, you, and all of us have committed or may commit in the future, they are as much Christ's own as if He himself had committed them. In short, our sin must be Christ's own sin, or we shall perish eternally."⁵⁷

Essentially, for Luther, the deadly confrontation between the "proper" use of the law and Christ is a conflict between creature and incarnate, human Creator—whose "natural and proper work" is that he "makes everything out of nothing"⁵⁸—in which it is revealed that the "Law has sinned so horribly and wickedly against its God, [that] it is summoned to court and accused."⁵⁹ So Luther can point to the incarnate, human Creator "inside our mask"⁶⁰ who was crucified and declare, "Here the Law, which once condemned and killed all men, has nothing with which to defend or cleanse itself. Therefore it is condemned and killed in turn, so that it loses its jurisdiction not only over Christ . . . but also over all who believe in Him."⁶¹ So, in Christ, the "proper" use of the law has reached its limit and "proper" *telos*. Therefore, the one who lives by the "passive" righteousness of Christ not only is able to perceive

---

55. Ibid., 29.
56. Ibid., 278.
57. Ibid.
58. Ibid., 314.
59. Ibid., 370.
60. Ibid., 284.
61. Ibid., 370.

this "fortunate exchange"[62] between Christ and sinner, but indeed also comprehends *sola fide* both the "proper" use of the law in service of the gospel, and its duration.

Thus, regarding the duration of the law's "proper" use, Luther avers that [E]ven though it is permanent . . . [this] custody under the Law must not last any longer than until the arrival of faith [in Christ]; and when this comes, this theological prison of the Law comes to an end."[63] But, more than this, one is now able to understand how the "proper" use of the law actually works in service of the gospel, "driving" one to life, to the "passive" righteousness of Christ. Though the curse of the law is death, the one living by the "passive" righteousness of faith now understands that "God still uses this effect of the Law, this death, for a good use, namely, for life."[64] Luther can articulate the purpose of the "crushing" effect of the "proper" use of the law this way:

> But what is the value of this effect, this humiliation, this wounding and crushing by the hammer [of the "proper" use of the law]? It has this value, that grace can have access to us. Therefore the Law is a minister and preparation for grace. For God is the God of the humble, the miserable, the afflicted, the oppressed, the desperate, and of those who have been brought down to nothing at all. And it is the nature of God to exalt the humble, to feed the hungry, to enlighten the blind, to comfort the miserable and afflicted, to justify sinners, to give life to the dead, and to save those who are desperate and damned. For He is the almighty Creator, who makes everything out of nothing.[65]

Essentially, as the one who lives by the "passive" righteousness of faith perceives, it is God who employs the "proper" use of the law, or his "alien work,"[66] in order to drive the sinner to discern the God—whose *modus operandi* is revealed in the incarnate, human One—who is the only

62. Ibid., 284.
63. Ibid., 337.
64. Ibid., 335.
65. Ibid., 314.
66. See LW 13:135 in which Luther, regarding God's "alien work," asserts, "God's 'alien' works are these: to judge, to condemn, and to punish those who are impenitent and do not believe. God is compelled to resort to such 'alien' works and to call them His own because of our pride. By manifesting these works He aims to humble us that we might regard Him as our Lord and obey His will." For ultimately, "God permits evils to come to us; for it is His will that, when we have been chastened, we cast ourselves on His mercy" (ibid.).

active agent with regard not only to *coram Deo* righteousness, but life itself. Through justification one is now able to "break through" to the "proper" use of the law and confess it as a mask of God's redeeming work, the work of restoring sinners to life in him. But indeed let us point out, and let us never forget: it is by faith that one *may confess* a "proper" use of the law *in the first place*. The shear reality that one may confess the law's "proper" use means that they are already restored to the God of life. Thus Luther can assert regarding this "breakthrough" of faith to the "proper" use, that "Whoever knows how to bring these utterly contradictory things together amid temptation—that is, whoever knows that when the Law is most terrifying, then the end of the Law and the beginning of grace and the future faith are present—such a person uses the Law correctly."[67] But, let us point out, for Luther, that this life of "passive" righteousness is also death. How so?

When one lives by the "passive" righteousness of faith in Christ, for Luther, they have *actually* been crucified and have *actually* died with Jesus Christ to the "proper" use of the law. The "passive" righteousness of faith in Christ is the *telos* of the "proper" use of the law for the believer. Luther can thus declare,

> But Christ is the Lord of the Law, because He has been crucified and has died to the Law. Therefore I, too, am Lord of the Law. For I, too, have been crucified and have died to the Law, since I have been crucified and have died with Christ. How? Through grace and faith. When by this faith I am crucified and die to the Law, then the Law loses all its jurisdiction over me, as it lost over Christ. Thus, just as Christ Himself was crucified to the Law, sin, death, and the devil, so that they have no further jurisdiction over him, so through faith I, having been crucified with Christ in spirit, am crucified and die to the Law . . .[68]

When one has died to the law and sin through faith in Christ, according to Luther, one has died the eternal death to the damning voice of God's law. For Luther, then, justification is the beginning of eternal life; justification *is* death and resurrection.[69] Again, "To live to the Law . . .

67. Ibid., 338.

68. Ibid., 165.

69. Cf. Forde, *Justification By Faith*, 35. Regarding this reality, Iwand also states in *Luthers Theologie*, that "Luther distinguishes between two different types of death. One type is the death of the old person, it is the death of death, it is life from the Word, it is the great act of liberation. The other type is *das Tödlein*, the little death, the death, the

is to die to God; on the other hand, to die to the law [with Christ] is to live to God."[70] And, thus, ultimately we have come full circle. That is, to live with Christ by the "passive" righteousness of faith—and not the "active" righteousness of the law—is to understand, ultimately, that "we work nothing, render nothing to God . . . only receive and permit someone else to work in us, namely God."[71] In order to restore us to himself as a God whose "natural and proper work" is that of continually creating life *ex nihilo*, his law first must become a "hammer", and his works must become "strange." For [a]lthough He is the God of life and salvation and this is His proper work, yet, in order to accomplish this, He kills and destroys. These works are alien to Him, but through them He accomplishes his proper work. For He kills our will that His may be established in us. He subdues the flesh and its lusts that the spirit and his desires may come to life."[72]

But, as H. Jackson Forstman avers regarding the fundamental significance of Luther's doctrine of justification, recognizing that it is not *simply* one doctrine that relatively outranks all other Christian doctrines, but one which, "in the context of Christian faith . . . is *sui generis*, a conviction apart and different from all other beliefs and the foundation of them all,"[73] we must also pay heed to Dennis Ngien's observation regarding the framework in which Luther's doctrine of justification is caste. According to Ngien, "One must not identify the principle of justification by faith with Luther's theology of the cross, although the former is central to the latter. Luther's theology of the cross goes beyond any theological or doctrinal clarification."[74] He adds, "The doctrine of justification by faith is only the beginning in the development of Luther's

---

remainder; that which has parted with death, the flesh, which in the same way must be transformed, as I myself was transformed from a death-enslaved man into life by faith in the Word." (Ibid., 197) Translation mine.

70. LW 26:159.
71. Ibid., 4.
72. LW 14:335.
73. Forstman, "Beggar's Faith," 266. On this point Braaten, in *Justification: The Article by Which the Church Stands or Falls*, 28, also observes, "Luther regarded the article of justification as not merely a single article among many others, but as the foundational truth with generative power affecting the entire organism of Christian faith, life and thought. The relative importance of any Christian doctrine was determined by its proximity to this central article of faith. All doctrines, in fact, must somehow be corollaries of the vital principle of justification."
74. Ngien, *Suffering of God*, 47.

theology of the cross. It finds its concreteness there[.]"⁷⁵ Nevertheless, if, according to Luther, "*CRUX sola est nostra theologia*,"⁷⁶ and the *theologia crucis* served as the fundamental orientation of all of Luther's thought,⁷⁷ then we must square this with the central role Luther gives to justification. Although a contour of answers has become implicit thus far, we must ask "Why" and "How" justification is so intimately linked with the *theologia crucis*. The answer as to "Why" will lead us to "How." And here we must delve both into the trajectory of the conceptualization of the *iustitia Dei* which Luther inherited, along with the explicit reaction he developed to its manifestation through the *via Moderna* in the *Heidelberg Disputation* (1518). As we will see, the "How" is simply an explanation of the trajectory of the *Heidelberg Disputation* itself.

Divine Justice: Getting What You [Don't] Deserve

Though scholars are correct in developing Luther's *theologia crucis* against the background of the *via Moderna*,⁷⁸ the *via Moderna* itself needs to be developed against a fundamental concept of the *iustitia Dei* which we will, as concisely as possible, trace to both Aristotle and the trajectory of its eleventh century appropriation by Anselm. It is this development of the *iustitia Dei*, then, which will both further shed light on the *via Moderna's* fundamental conceptualization of divine justice with which Luther struggled, and thus more deeply explain what was for Luther the essential connection between justification and his *theologia crucis*, especially as it is developed in his *Heidelberg Disputation*. As is most often the case, the matter of justice will inevitably lead to questions of mercy.

Luther's project—as is widely known—was to locate a merciful God. That search led to what Luther regarded as the central matter of his angst, or simply: "What is the justice of God—*iustitia Dei*?"⁷⁹ But

---

75. Ibid.

76. See WA 5, 176, 32–33; also quoted by Forde, *On Being a Theologian of the Cross*, 3.

77. Ebeling, *Luther*, 229.

78. Cf. Solberg, *Compelling Knowledge*, 61ff.

79. Westhelle, *Scandalous God,* 38. It must be noted that this discussion of the *iustitia Dei* is deeply indebted to the insights of both Westhelle, *Scandalous God*, 35–59; and McGrath, *Luther's Theology of the Cross*, 55–147.

the question of the shape and content of divine justice can be traced-back to the eleventh century, at the very least, to one of its most famous answers which was provided by Anselm in his *Cur Deus Homo*. In sum, according to Anselm, if sin is attributed to the failure of giving God the honor that is due him, thus resulting in divine condemnation, yet the divine will is to "save" sinners from this same condemnation, then the question becomes this: "[H]ow is a just God to save . . . without infringing upon the principle of justice?"[80] But, since humans must make remuneration for this breach of divine justice, yet only God is able to give God the honor due him, it is Jesus Christ, true God and true Man, who contributes the divinely-desired deficit, suffering the full condemnation sinners had coming to them. Essentially, the foundation of Anselm's argument, as Vitor Westhelle points out, rests "on a fundamental juridical principle of old: The *suum cuique* (to each what to each is due)."[81] What this means is that if one owes a debt, only two options are available: either the satisfaction of the debt, or the punishment of the debtor. Given this framework for a conceptualization of the *iustitia Dei*, "Anselm's was . . . a convincing response."[82] At the same time, only a generation later, it was Abelard who carried the *suum cuique* principle to its logical outcome. If, according to Abelard, punishment was due to the one who committed the trifling sin of failing to render to God the honor due to him, then what was the punishment to be exacted—and who will make the payment?—for the ones who have executed the Son of God? Ultimately Abelard sidestepped the matter of *iustitia Dei* by affirming Christ's exemplar ability through his self-giving love to awaken the love of God within all humans. But evading the question of divine justice does not mean that it goes away. The larger issue though, as we will see, was that regnant concepts of *iustitia Dei* were simply accommodated, via analogy, to "established canons of rationality," "regimes of truth" or "economies" already operating in the world of trade, economics, philosophy, and politics.[83]

But as we move closer to the *via Moderna*, which directly shaped Luther's understanding of *iustitia Dei*, we notice that the *via Antiqua*, too, both represented in the theology of Thomas Aquinas and consid-

---

80. Westhelle, *Scandalous God*, 38.
81. Ibid.
82. Ibid., 39.
83. Ibid., 46.

ered the dominant theological model of Luther's day, involved a logic which revolved around Anselm's depiction of divine justice. "In God's economy," according to the *via Antiqua*, "a payment in the form of a punishment is devised in order to satisfy God's wrath by a vicarious substitution."[84] Thus it is God the Son—the true human without sin—whose payment, or sacrifice, vicariously makes satisfaction for the *iustitia Dei's* requirements. But, with this being the case, how are humans to "cash in" Christ's payment? If, according to the *via Antiqua*, Christ's sacrifice accomplished what humans never had in their power to do, then humans need only do that which is in them (*facere quod in se est*) to "cash" Christ's payment. As Westhelle notes, "The formula is similar to a matching fund: if we come up with our part, which we can and should, Christ pays the rest—a totally reasonable argument, congruent with the rules of the economy and jurisprudence of the time."[85] Christ may "pay the rest," but how, we may ask, can one be assured of matching their minimum "dues"? But, if ultimately Luther's conceptualization of *iustitia Dei* was shaped most directly by the *via Moderna*, as we have already noted, then here, too, we must consider the "canon of rationality," or "economy," which dictated by analogy its conception of *iustitia Dei*.

As Westhelle observes, the *via Antiqua*'s "economic-juridical model" was "shaken" in the thirteenth and fourteenth centuries by the burgeoning of the capitalist financial system.[86] Instead of basing itself upon coinage, or monetary, units bearing their own recognized, intrinsic value, such as gold, and recognized as such as the common currency through this intrinsic value, this new system utilized monetary units which contained only "negligible inherent value."[87] In essence, this new economic system utilized currency units that, possessing almost no intrinsic value in and of themselves—constituted perhaps of lead, were issued with the guarantee of being redeemed at a much higher, previously stipulated value. This system, then, attributed central significance to the ruler (or issuing bank) who thus both ascribed greater redemptive value to currency units that possessed little or no intrinsic worth, and thus also controlled the process of economic exchange.[88] Ultimately,

---

84. Ibid.
85. Ibid., 46–47.
86. Ibid., 47.
87. McGrath, *Luther's Theology of the Cross*, 59.
88. Cf. ibid., 59; and Westhelle, *Scandalous God*, 47.

then, this new economic system, or "canon of rationality," corresponded to a *pactum*-theology, or theology of covenantal causality, in which human merits (equated with lead coinage which contained little intrinsic value) were redeemed by God (equated with the ruler/issuing bank) at a value whose worth was previously guaranteed. It was this principle, as McGrath points out, "which govern[ed] the thinking of the theologians of the *via Moderna* on the causality of justification," or "covenantal causality."[89] Within this divinely ordained *pactum* between God and man, according to McGrath, the theologians of the *via Moderna* were able to maintain at least two important points. First, all human acts with regard to morality contained only negligible value (thus "the *moderni* were able to avoid exalting human works to Pelagian proportions").[90] Second, because God had committed himself in this contract to ascribe infinitely greater value to intrinsically worthless moral acts, humans were now able to merit God's justification *de congruo*. Essentially, according to McGrath, the whole medieval theological tradition regarding justification—from the twelfth century through the early sixteenth century—proceeded on the basic principle that, in God's commitment to justify humans, humans were also accountable for the fulfillment of a "certain minimum requirement."[91] This "basic principle," according to McGrath, "is that when man fulfils his obligations to God (by doing 'what lies within him,' *quod in se est*), God will respond by bestowing the gift of justifying grace."[92] Simply stated, justification becomes a matter in which God sets the minimal conditions of the *pactum* which humans are to fulfill in order for God to bestow justifying grace. But as McGrath observes, "The theology of the *via moderna* is most emphatically *not* Christocentric . . . [for] the entire discussion of man's justification before God on the part of the theologians of the *via moderna* proceeds without reference to the incarnation and death of the Son of God."[93] But, having established that Luther inherited and operated with a "covenantal concept of causality" with regard to justification, now, as McGrath points out, the main focus—especially for Luther—became the "minimum

---

89. McGrath, *Luther's Theology of the Cross*, 59.
90. Ibid., 60.
91. Ibid., 86.
92. Ibid.
93. Ibid., 61.

condition" required for justification, or simply: what is the content of "*quod in se est*"?[94]

Grafting "an essentially Augustinian emphasis upon humility on the covenant theology of the *via moderna*,"[95] the content of the "*quod in se est*," for Luther, was the Christian's acknowledgment and acceptance of "God's eye-opening judgment on one's own lame protestation of righteousness,"[96] which forced the Christian, recognizing their spiritual beggarliness and emptiness, to do nothing other than cry out for salvation. This condition, then, "produced sufficient contrition and humility to warrant God's forgiving grace."[97] But, though God had set the terms of the pact with the minimal condition of the "*quod in se est*," and thus one's recognition of their lack of righteousness *coram Deo*, or a complete humility which provided for the content of the "*quod in se est*," "humility" became precisely the problem. Or—shall we say—the active agent of the "humility" became the problem. How so?

No matter how little the Christian was forced to contribute to their own justification within the condition's of the *pactum*'s "*quod in se est*" (whose content was now reduced to one's recognition of their humiliation *coram Deo*), the fact of the matter remained, the *via Moderna*'s conceptualization was founded upon the claim that humans are capable of performing the "*quod in se est*" without the assistance of grace. Do we not still acquire scruples when we have even just one small line in the school's musical? Even if our part in the obtaining of justification still only requires the recognition of our total unworthiness, nonetheless, this *humilitas* is still acknowledged as a "*human* disposition towards grace."[98] But, more importantly, the content of this scheme's "*quod in se est*," or the humiliation of the Christian, simply employed Christ as the preeminent example of total humiliation *coram Deo*. The role of Christ, then, was nothing more than that of "lawgiver,"[99] or one who, within the *pactum*'s framework, simply provided the shape of humiliation that was required for justifying grace. But now the question became even more serious: if it is possible for Christians to do "*quod in se est*," with Christ

94. Ibid., 89.
95. Ibid., 91.
96. Solberg, *Compelling Knowledge*, 62.
97. Ibid.
98. McGrath, *Luther's Theology of the Cross*, 127.
99. Solberg, *Compelling Knowledge*, 63.

serving as the premier example of the shape of that *humilitas*, then how could one ever know for certain that they had achieved the proper content of even the minimal requirement of the "*quod in se est*"? In the case of the *via Moderna*, the discussion of justification and divine justice still revolved around the principle of *suum cuique* (to each what to each is due). Though the human contribution to the "*quod in se est*" was quantitatively miniscule, the stakes were qualitatively raised: How do I know that this *humilitas* is not simply a self-serving disposition? and not an authentic disposition of humility toward God? More sharply: How do I know for certain my minimal "dues" have been paid? Am I qualified to merit the "dues" stipulated by the pact? Reflecting upon the angst of this predicament, Luther, within his last year of life, stated that,

> Though I lived as a monk without reproach, I felt that I was a sinner before God with an extremely disturbed conscience. I could not believe that [God] was placated by my satisfaction. I did not love, yes, I hated the righteous God who punishes sinners, and secretly, if not blasphemously, certainly murmuring greatly, I was angry with God, and said, "As if, indeed, it is not enough, that miserable sinners, eternally lost through original sin, are crushed by every kind of calamity by the law of the Decalogue, without having God add pain to pain by the gospel and also by the gospel threatening us with his righteousness and wrath!" Thus I raged with a fierce and trouble conscience.[100]

At its core this was an issue regarding the *iustitia Dei*. But more than this, this was a question of what funded a theological conceptualization of the *iustitia Dei*. Is the *iustitia Dei* to be conceived of, and thus defined, via analogy to the "regimes of truth" and "economies" of this world? or somewhere else? somewhere "alien" to the truth regimes of this world?

Retrospectively ruminating in 1545 on the monumental shift in his thinking (which McGrath locates near the end of 1515)[101] regarding the "righteousness of God," and thus *iustitia Dei*, Luther states,

> At last, by the mercy of God, meditating day and night, I gave heed to the context of the words, namely, "In it the righteousness of God is revealed, as it is written, 'He who through faith is righteous shall live.'" There I began to understand that the righteousness of God is that by which the righteous lives by the

---

100. LW 34:336–37.
101. McGrath, *Luther's Theology of the Cross*, 132–33.

gift of God, namely by faith. And this is the meaning: the righteousness of God is revealed by the gospel, namely, the passive righteousness with which merciful God justifies us by faith, as it is written, "He who through faith is righteous shall live." Here I felt that I was altogether born again and had entered paradise itself through open gates. There a totally other face of the entire Scripture showed itself to me. Thereupon I ran through the Scriptures from memory. I also found in other terms an analogy, as, the work of God, that is, what God does in us, the power of God, with which he makes us strong, the wisdom of God with which he makes us wise, the strength of God, the salvation of God, the glory of God. And I extolled my sweetest word with a love as great as the hatred with which I had before hated the word "righteousness of God."[102]

If earlier we could speak of *iustitia Dei* within the context of the principle of *suum cuique* and its trajectory of theological appropriation from Anselm through the *via Moderna*'s conceptualization of justification with its "covenantal causality," or *pactum*-theology, then it must be noted that Luther's new definition of *iustitia Dei*, his monumental shift, attacks the very foundation of this principle of *iustitia*.

By asserting in theses 29–30 of his *Heidelberg Disputation* that "He who wishes to philosophize by using Aristotle without danger to his soul must first become thoroughly foolish in Christ. Just as a person does not use the evil of passion well unless he is a married man, so no person philosophizes well unless he is a fool, that is a Christian,"[103] Luther was doing nothing other than rejecting the concept of *iustitia* that was found in Book V of Aristotle's *Nicomachean Ethics*. This was a concept which had not only been employed by everyone from Anselm to medieval canonists and jurists, but had obviously found its way into the core of the *via Moderna*'s soteriology.[104] And not only did this ancient *suum cuique* principle also include the "*dictum* that a man becomes righteous by performing righteous deeds," but it manifested itself in a "common sense understanding of justice in terms of a *quid pro quo* morality, whose validity was immediately apparent to reason."[105] And it was this old definition of *iustitia*, grounded in Aristotle's *Ethics*,

---

102. LW 34:337.
103. LW 31:41, quoted in Westhelle, *Scandalous God*, 49.
104. McGrath, *Luther's Theology of the Cross*, 139.
105. Ibid.

and thus standing for what Luther "regarded as the dominant mode of reasoning, really any mode of reasoning that would norm theological discourse apart from faith,"[106] that Luther countered with a new definition of *iustitia* that emanated from the context of revelation and faith, and, specifically, from the faith created by *iustitia Christi aliena*.[107]

Opposing the sophists' *suum cuique* principle of *iustitia* which "is the fixed will to render to each his own," Luther, over ten years after his *Heidelberg Disputation*, could comment in his Isaiah lectures (53:11) that "righteousness is the knowledge of Christ . . . who bears our iniquities [and thus] [w]hoever will, therefore, know and believe in Christ as bearing his sins will be righteous."[108] And on this *iustitia Christi aliena* Luther could add, "You must therefore note this new definition of righteousness. Righteousness is the knowledge of Christ. What is Christ? He is the person who bears all our sins. These are unspeakable gifts and hidden and unutterable kinds of wisdom."[109] Or, as Westhelle asserts regarding this passage, "Such is the new concept of justice [according to Luther], the free gift of God surrendering Godself to us. Such is the meaning of Christ revealed ironically in his cross, the ultimate self-giving of God."[110] Citing Westhelle again, "[Luther's] radical rephrasing says, 'to us what is not due to us [but comes as a gift],' as well as "to others what is not due to them [but is freely given]."[111] Essentially, for Luther, if analogy operates "by the rule of correspondence, which allows one to know the unknown by the known,"[112] and, thus, the *iustitia Dei* was earlier defined analogically by the principle of *suum cuique*, or by an "[inference] from our finite standards of justice,"[113] then the *iustitia Christi aliena* was a radical subversion of all such attempts to define divine justice on the basis of established canons of reason.

---

106. Westhelle, *Scandalous God*, 50. Westhelle notes that Luther's point was that "as far as theology is concerned, as opposed to jurisprudence, politics, or economics, Aristotle could not be the norm. The distinction between the earthly and the spiritual regimes requires different semantic realms" (ibid., 51).

107. McGrath, *Luther's Theology of the Cross*, 133.

108. LW 17:229.

109. Ibid., 230, also quoted in Westhelle, *Scandalous God*, 39.

110. Westhelle, *Scandalous God*, 40.

111. Ibid.

112. Ibid., 45.

113. Ibid.

But if *iustitia Dei* was both now not only *not* funded by a mode of reasoning apart from faith,[114] and was subsequently considered to be a righteousness which was completely extrinsic to the human,[115] then God alone becomes the sole active agent with regard to every aspect of the human's justification, even working the human's complete *humilitas*.[116] And if this is the case, that God is the sole agent in every aspect of a person's justification, then, as can be discerned in his *Heidelberg Disputation*, all previous concepts in which the Christian was regarded as the active agent, such as the law, good works, and free will, are reformulated. But, before we observe how Luther's *Heidelberg Disputation* executes this "agency," let us first observe how Luther understands the human who is the object of this "sole agency" of God's.

If Luther's understanding of the *iustitia Christi aliena* afforded him the opportunity to perceive God as the sole active agent with regard to every aspect of one's justification, then this understanding also reinforced Luther's conceptualization of humans as "holistic creatures."[117] In particular, according to McGrath, Luther understood that "flesh" (*caro*) and "spirit" (*spiritus*) are not to be viewed "as man's lower and higher faculties respectively, but rather as descriptions of the whole person considered under different aspects."[118] *Caro* is understood as the whole person who exists in "radical alienation from God," while *spiritus* represents the whole person in their "openness to God and the divine promises."[119] Ultimately, then, through the *iustitia Christi aliena* the whole person is "righteous *coram Deo*." But, as this righteousness is "in no sense part of his person," that person remains a sinner. As *totus homo*, therefore, this is what Luther means by *simul iustis et peccator*.[120] Essentially, the *iustitia Christi aliena* is an affront to human conceptualizations as to who appears "righteous." With Luther's understanding of the *totus homo* in hand, we are now able to observe how the *Heidelberg Disputation* articulates God as the sole agent with regard to one's justification as a *totus homo*.

114. Ibid., 50.
115. McGrath, *Luther's Theology of the Cross*, 134.
116. Ibid., 128.
117. Solberg, *Compelling Knowledge*, 66.
118. McGrath, *Luther's Theology of the Cross*, 133.
119. Ibid.
120. Ibid., 134.

Through the first eighteen theses of the *Heidelberg Disputation*, culminating in the eighteenth thesis in which he asserts, "*It is certain that man must utterly despair of his own ability before he is prepared to receive the grace of Christ*,"[121] Luther, on the basis of the *iustitia Christi aliena* encountered at the cross (and keeping in mind his conceptualization of the human as *totus homo*), "peels way layer after layer of illusion, demonstrating how every possible avenue of human effort fails to achieve righteousness before God."[122] In Thompson's words again, "[Luther] begins by expressing how the sinful human being can never fulfill the law. Luther then shows how the law is based on the illusion of the effectiveness of good works, and he concludes that trust in good works springs from yet another illusion: a will free to choose good."[123] Or, again, as James Nestingen observes regarding the trajectory of the *Heidelberg Disputation*'s argument: "Considering the force of both [theses] 1 through 12 and 13 through 17—which attack individually the elements to which the sinful self turns attempting to define itself—and their overall effect, the first eighteen theses of the disputation could be spoken of as the cross side of the argument [in which the] sinful self, with all its evil deeds and desires to establish its hold by means of the law and its own will . . . is being crucified—not by the theologian but by the shape of daily life . . ."[124] And if it is at the location of the cross that the Christian understands that it is through the *iustitia Christi aliena* that we both come to understand that all theology and true knowledge of God begins with the crucified Christ (where God's "paradigm of

---

121. LW 31:51. Luther, in his explanation, states "The law wills that man despair of his own ability, for it leads him into hell and makes him a poor man and shows him that he is a sinner in all his works . . ." (ibid., 51–52).

122. Thompson, *Crossing the Divide*, 17.

123. Ibid., 17–18.

124. Nestingen, "Luther's Heidelberg Disputation: An Analysis of the Argument," 153. On this dynamic Vercruysse states in his "Luther's Theology of the Cross at the Time of the Heidelberg Disputation," 538, that "The first twenty-four theses of the Heidelberg Disputation aim at nothing else than to stimulate this process of extinction and retrogression towards the awareness of being frightened and despairing sinners and towards foolishness and nothingness." Though, for the most part, Vercruysse seems to mirror Nestingen's analaysis, Vercruysse appears to still leave room for ambiguity regarding the source of the agency of the "process of extinction and retrogression." In other words, how completely "passive" is his "righteousness" in his interpretation of Luther's passive righteousness?

working" in relation to the world is revealed *sub contraria specie*),[125] and that God is the sole agent in justification, then the theologian of the cross simply is able to confess that "God works on both sides of the street."[126] In other words,

> This is understood to mean that the Lord humbles and frightens us by means of the law and the sight of our sins so that we seem in the eyes of men, as in our own, as nothing, foolish, and wicked, for we are in truth that. Insofar as we acknowledge and confess this, there is no form or beauty in us, but our life is hidden in God (i.e. in the bare confidence in his mercy), finding in ourselves nothing but sin, foolishness, death, and hell, according to that verse of the Apostle in II Cor. 6[:9–10], "As sorrowful, yet always rejoicing; as dying, and behold we live." And that it is which Isa. 28 [:21] calls the alien work of God that he may do his work (that is, he humbles us thoroughly, making us despair, so that he may exalt us in his mercy, giving us hope) . . .[127]

If Luther, with his new definition of justice through the *iustitia Christi aliena* in tote, is able in the course of the first eighteen theses in his *Heidelberg Disputation* to "peel away layer after layer of illusion" with regard to the proper "user" of the law, good works, and the will (as they stand *coram Deo*), then what is ultimately revealed to the sinner is that "In every instance all loopholes are closed so that the believer will in the end simply be cast on that creative love of God, which makes the object of its love out of the nothing to which the sinner has been reduced."[128] For as the "alien work" of God drives humans to despair of their own ability—placing such things as law, good works, and the will in their proper perspective as gifts of the Creator (no longer employed in a "do it myself" fashion as a defense against the Giver)[129]—so its recognition also implies a confession that hidden *sub contraria specie* within that same "alien work" is God's "proper work," or that "love of God [which] creates precisely out of nothing."[130] Or, as Luther states in his *Magnificat*, God's "alien work" drives Christians to recognize that "our sufficiency

---

125. Vercruysse, "Luther's Theology of the Cross at the Time of the Heidelberg Disputation," 542.

126. Brueggaman, *Prophetic Imagination*, 23.

127. LW 31:44.

128. Forde, *On Being a Theologian of the Cross*, 12.

129. Ibid., 27.

130. Ibid., 9.

is from God. [Therefore] this is a most important article of faith, introducing many things; it completely puts down all pride, arrogance, blasphemy, fame, and false trust, and exalts God alone. It points out the reason why God alone is to be exalted—because He does all things."[131] As Luther declares, justification restores Christians to a God who is "an energetic power, a continuous activity, [Who] works and operates without ceasing."[132] Essentially, "Where man's strength ends, God's strength begins."[133]

Thus, if "the justification of man is located in the existential discovery of one's own nothingness,"[134] then the confession of one's "nothingness" is simultaneously the confession that "nothing" is the building block of "everything" a loving Creator needs in order to create and sustain life. For justification "is the application of a theology of creation from nothing upon one's personal existence. This is the way of the cross (*Kreuzweg*)."[135]

Ultimately then, whether one is comprehending Luther's doctrine of justification by faith through his 1535 Galatians lectures (in which central nature of justification is lifted up by Luther) or his 1518 *Heidelberg Disputation* (which is developed against the trajectory of Aristotle's *suum cuique* principle of justice), at the core of the doctrine stands a radical subversion of all concepts of *iustitia Dei* which both correspond to worldly calculations of *iustitia*, and take shape in a context apart from faith and God's cruciform revelation. For if *iustitia Dei* was once conceived in a logic corresponding to the old principle of *suum cuique*, through the cross and the revelation of *iustitia Christi aliena* we may now speak of a radical subversion of divine justice in which that same justice can be considered in a such a manner as "'to us what is not due to us [but comes as a gift],' as well as 'to others what is not due to them [but is freely given].'"[136] All life *coram Deo*, then, is both understood and transformed in light of this revelation of passive righteousness, a passive righteousness which restores one to her

131. LW 21:328.
132. Ibid.
133. Ibid., 340.
134. Vercruysse, "Luther's Theology of the Cross and its Ecclesiological and Ecumenical Implications," 78.
135. Ibid.
136. Westhelle, *Scandalous God*, 40.

Creator, and hence to creation.[137] But, according to Luther's *theologia crucis*, as has become obvious by now, we cannot speak of a subversion of *iustitia Dei* without speaking of a subversion of traditional manners of comprehending where and how that same God reveals himself.

Theologia Crucis: A Theology of Revelation

"At" or "Through"?

If, as has already been pointed out, previous definitions of *iustitia Dei* relied upon analogy, or the "rule of correspondence which allows one to know the unknown by the known"; of defining *iustitia Dei* by inferring from historically-conditioned standards of justice already established by the regnant canons of jurisprudence and rationality,[138] then the "new definition" of *iustitia Dei* articulated by Luther's *theologia crucis*, or the *iustitia Christi aliena*, was developed upon an understanding of divine revelation, or an "epistemological gesture"[139] that resulted in an ironic deconstruction of analogy: that which seems to be is in fact its opposite."[140] Or, as Ngien has stated, "*Theologia crucis* evinces the epistemological principle wherein like is known by unlike ... God's nature reveals itself in that the 'fullness of God's power' is seen not in the pompous, powerful, and the proud, but in the shameful, weak, and lowly,"[141] or *sub contraria specie*. But if the old principle of *iustitia Dei* which was based upon an analogy in which unknown is inferred by the known, and therefore "invisible things of God" are inferred by that which is visible and worldly, then this "new definition" of justice through Christ would mean, for Luther, a radical reorienting of both the theologian's *modus operandi*, and a repositioning and re-valuation of that which is visible and worldly. But this means that we must first reckon with the presuppositions of an "old" way of theologizing which corresponds to the "old" concept of *iustitia Dei*.

If, when Luther declares, "*That person does not deserve to be called a theologian who looks upon the invisible things of God as though they*

---

137. Bayer, *Living by Faith*, 62.
138. Westhelle, *Scandalous God*, 45.
139. Ibid., 50.
140. Ibid., 45.
141. Ngien, *Suffering of God*, 67.

were clearly perceptible in those things which have already happened,"[142] then, at a fundamental level, he is identifying and exposing a speculative mode of "doing" theology which presupposes a "privileged"[143] way of "knowing" and "seeing" God in this world.[144] Theologians of this stripe—"theologian[s] of glory"[145]—operate under the assumption—commensurate with what we have already identified with analogical reasoning—that there exists "an unbroken and direct communion with God"[146] which determines the essential subject matter of theology. In other words, the theologian of glory operates under the assumption that the "visible creation yields clues, if not directly at least by analogy, to what is invisible in God, to the nature and logic of God."[147] Ultimately, the assumption is that "creation and history are transparent to the human intellect, that one can *see through* what is made and what happens so as to peer into the 'invisible things of God.'"[148] But if the theologian presumes both that "creation and history are transparent to the human intellect," and that she is able to *see through* what is made in order to investigate the "invisible things of God," then not only has the theologian forgotten that both she and her knowledge are an "historically conditioned affair," and that theological knowledge can never be an "intuitive grasp of transcendental states of affairs,"[149] but—ultimately—the "invisible things" of God are concretized according to the theologian's wishes. In this case, ironically, the "invisible things of God" mirror, and become timeless abstractions of, that which is visibly held in high esteem in this world by theologians of glory: "virtue, godliness, wisdom, justice, goodness, and so forth."[150] But, paralleling what we have already said on the matter of justification, one encounters in the theologian of glory "only that human self-reliance and arbitrariness which insists on dealing with God on the basis of man's own ideas rather than obediently meeting

---

142. LW 31:52.
143. Williams, *Christian Spirituality*, 146.
144. Cf. Forde, *On Being a Theologian of the Cross*, 70.
145. LW 31:53.
146. Loewenich, *Luther's Theology of the Cross*, 20.
147. Forde, *On Being a Theologian of the Cross*, 73.
148. Ibid., 72.
149. Williams, *Christian Spirituality*, 146.
150. LW 31:52.

him at the place which he has appointed."[151] This is nothing more than to equate God with an idol.[152]

Ultimately, then, if human rationality is able to carry the Christian "speculatively into the invisible realm of divine truth,"[153] thus directing the theologian from that which is visible and worldly to that which is invisible and un-worldly, then the question of divine truth and its relation to that which is visible and worldly becomes an interesting matter.

If the quest for divine truth, "an attempt to perceive the invisible nature of God [analogically] from the works of creation . . . through reason,"[154] is conducted under the assumption—to quote Forde again—"that creation and history are transparent to the human intellect, that one can *see through* what is made and what happens so as to peer into the 'invisible things of God,'"[155] then creation in all of its visible, concrete particularity becomes nothing more than fodder for speculative flights into time-less, un-worldly divine truth. Whether creation, then, is viewed as a transparency or a ladder to divine truth, at least two things become clear: divine truth is both never timely and worldly, and that which is timely and worldly is purely dispensable in the quest for divine truth. But, again, this divine truth is nothing more than a mirror of the world's "regimes of truth" in which that which is "particular" is sacrificed on the altar of the "general"; that which is "individual" is sacrificed to the machinations of the "system."

But, to those theologians of glory who would still continue to partake in "lingering over the seductive portrait of the majestic God," and thus want to "reign with Christ"[156] in this speculative, un-worldly manner, ascending from visible to invisible via analogy, hearkening to Exodus 33:20, and reminding us that we must "refrain from speculation about the majesty of God, which is too much for the human body, and especially for the human mind, to bear,"[157] Luther simply re-asserts the importance of the visible realm when he declares:

---

151. Althaus, *Theology of Martin Luther*, 17.
152. Ibid., 23.
153. Williams, *Christian Spirituality*, 146.
154. Ebeling, *Luther*, 227.
155. Forde, *On Being a Theologian of the Cross*, 72.
156. Thompson, *Crossing the Divide*, 24.
157. LW 26:28.

> [T]rue theology ... does not present God to us in His majesty, as Moses and other teachings do ... [thus] ... [N]othing is more dangerous than to stray into heaven with our idle speculations, there to investigate God in His incomprehensible power, wisdom, and majesty ... If you attempt to comprehend God this way and want to make atonement to Him apart from Christ the Mediator ... you will inevitably fall ... and in horrible despair lose God and everything. For as in His own nature God is immense, incomprehensible, and infinite, so to man's nature He is intolerable. Therefore if you want to be safe and out of danger to your conscience and your salvation, put a check on this speculative spirit.[158]

For, in Christ, according to Luther, this is a God of things particular and visible, a God who "overthrows speculative theology by making himself a worldly reality."[159] So, Luther adds, in a fashion commensurate with his *theologia crucis* which "concerns itself only with the visible, the worldly,"[160] "Therefore begin where Christ began—in the Virgin's womb, in the manger, and at His mother's breasts. For this purpose He came down, was born, lived among men, suffered, was crucified, and died, so that in every possible way *He might present Himself to our sight*. He wanted us to fix the gaze of our hearts upon Himself and thus to prevent us from clambering into heaven and speculating about the Divine Majesty."[161] But, if this is the case, that divine truth is revealed in "down-to-earth" fashion,[162] then as that which is visible, particular, and worldly is no longer perceived as "fodder" for speculative flights of theological fancy into timeless, un-worldly divine truth, it also rejects out of hand "the idea of privileged authoritative propositions delivered from religious illumination."[163] But, more importantly, if "*He deserves to be called*

---

158. LW 26:28–29.
159. Williams, *Christian Spirituality*, 146.
160. Ibid., 147.
161. LW 26:29.
162. I take this phrase "down-to-earth" from Forde's little book *Where God Meets Man: Luther's Down-to-Earth Approach to the Gospel*.
163. Williams, *Christian Spirituality*, 146. Corresponding to this idea, Forstman in "Beggar's Faith," 270, observes that "The [theology of glory] is more ostentatious about the transference of divine truth and authority to this world. By means of knowledge of the divine mind, a guarantee of truth and finality is bequeathed to a human group: the church as the extension of the incarnation, infallible in faith and morals, the Bible as

a theologian ... who comprehends the visible and manifest things of God seen through suffering and the cross,"[164] then the theologian's occupation regarding the cross is not one of reducing historical, particular "visible things" to a cipher of time-less, "invisible things," always attempting to see "behind" it all for a glimpse of transcendent meaning, but of recognizing that we cannot see through the cross, and thus have to look at it.[165] Thus, if the theologian of the cross has to look at the cross, and not through it, then she has permission to call this visible, particular thing "*what it actually is*."[166] For "What is at stake" with reference to whether one conducts themselves as a theologian of the cross or as a theologian of glory, "is nothing less than an accurate representation of reality,"[167] or reality as it is. Ultimately, refusing to deal with an accurate representation of reality, for the theologian of glory, is to "end up denying God's alien activity."[168] To deny this activity is to deny God's activity as Creator. Therefore "Theologians of the cross are ... those whose eyes have been turned away from the quest for glory by the cross, who have eyes only for what is visible, what is actually there to be seen of God, the suffering and despised crucified Jesus."[169] Essentially, then, the theologian of the cross understands that there is no knowledge of God other than that which is found in the locus of the human Jesus. Thus, denied direct knowledge of God, and subsequently denying that God can be known analogically via "intelligent reflection upon the nature of man's moral sense or the pattern of the created order,"[170] the theologian of the cross is the one who—*sola fide*—discerns the presence of God hidden *sub contraria specie* in his revelation in Jesus Christ and his passion and cross.[171]

---

the law book of the New Israel, the divine light in the souls of those who are redeemed or who govern the redeemed. This theology creates distinctions among men, focuses on and reflects the glory of God and the higher world, and points and lifts men above the sphere of this life."

164. LW 31: 52.
165. Cf. Forde, *On Being a Theologian of the Cross*, 76–77.
166. LW 31: 53.
167. Thompson, *Crossing the Divide*, 23.
168. Ibid., 24.
169. Forde, *On Being a Theologian of the Cross*, 79.
170. Ngien, *Suffering of God*, 51.
171. Cf. McGrath, *Luther's Theology of the Cross*, 150.

But if "God is to be found precisely where theologians of glory are horrified to find him: as a kid in a crib, as criminal on a cross, as a corpse in a crypt . . . [thus revealing] himself by hiding right in the middle of human existence,"[172] then God's participation in our world must be underscored as fundamental. For the theologian of the cross not only is the divine realm united with the human in the man Jesus, but sacred is united with the secular, "the holy with the profane."[173] But now, for the theologian of the cross who has permission to focus squarely on the visible world as the arena of divine truth, the question becomes one of just how the Word relates to the visible realm within revelation. The dynamic of God's revelation *sub contraria specie* is just now what we need to clarify.

Relating Revelation

If Luther could both declare in his *Smalcald Articles* that "we should and must constantly maintain that God will not deal with us except through his external Word and sacrament,"[174] then this declaration must be augmented with his assertion that "true theology and recognition of God are in the crucified Christ."[175] Ultimately then, if the external, visible Word of the crucified Christ is "criterion and subject of all theology"[176] revealing the location in which God most profoundly "reveals his *modus operandi*,"[177] or "paradigm of working,"[178] then it is essential to understand how Luther relates the visible realm with God's Word with regard to Christ's revelation *sub contraria specie*.

According to Westhelle, appealing to Gustaf Törnvall's[179] "functional interpretation" of Luther's understanding of the "two kingdoms" in which the two governances or regimes are "fundamentally expressions of the Creator/creature theme in God's self-revelation, through

172. Kolb, "Luther on the Theology of the Cross," 449.
173. Madsen, *The Theology of the Cross in Historical Perspective*, 81.
174. BC: 313.
175. LW 31:53.
176. Ebeling, *Luther*, 226.
177. Kolb, "Luther on the Theology of the Cross," 451.
178. Vercruysse, "Luther's Theology of the Cross at the Time of the Heidelberg Disputation," 542.
179. Törnvall, *Geistliches und weltliches Regiment bei Luther*.

the masks of God (*larvae dei*), the invisible Word of God (*verbum dei*), and the visible world,"[180] the two kingdoms are functional dimensions of the "single act of God's creation and revelation": a "listening" kingdom (*Hörreich*) and a "seeing" kingdom (*Sehereich*).[181] Ultimately then, as Westhelle observes regarding Luther's thinking, the basic distinction—traced back to at least the *Heidelberg Disputation* (1518)—is the distinction "between the visible and the Word, between creature and Creator, the outer and the inner, between what the senses register and reason draws together and what grace reveals to the spirit."[182] But with this being the case, we must now ask how these two dimensions of God's one revelation within the matrix of creation are both related to one another, and distinguished within this same relationship.[183] Our answer will not only serve to clarify what is meant when Luther speaks of God's revelation *sub contraria specie*, but also lay the groundwork for our discussion in chapter four regarding the *larvae Dei* and their relationship to the *communicatio idiomatum*.

Between these two sets of categories, the visible world and the Word, according to Westhelle, exists a relationship consisting of paradox and asymmetry which is fundamental for Luther's conceptualization of revelation. On the one hand, this relationship between the visible world and the Word is "paradoxical" in the sense that that which is visible points to the Word, "but is thereby simultaneously negated or dissimulated."[184] Although Luther never completely jettisons the employment of analogy in his conceptualization of revelation, according to Westhelle, it is "analogical reasoning" that Luther rejects while "keeping open some room for analogical correspondence."[185] Even here, though, elements of irony constantly "disturb the tranquil realm of analogical correspondence."[186] On the other hand, according to Westhelle's analysis, the relationship between the visible world and the Word within revelation is "asym-

---

180. Westhelle, *Scandalous God*, 43. This section, relying heavily upon Westhelle's research, is absolutely essential in laying the conceptual framework for chapter four, below.

181. Ibid.

182. Ibid., 43–44.

183. Ibid., 44.

184. Ibid.

185. Ibid.

186. Ibid.

metrical" in the sense "that what appears to be the case in one set of categories that belong to one of the regimes (spiritual or earthly) is not simply reflected in the other, but is shaped by it in unexpected ways."[187] Thus, by continually moving between of the one set of categories to the other, and back (thus relating the Word to the World—or *larvae Dei*), Luther is able to avoid the method of analogical reasoning by keeping alive his "ironic destabilizing tone" between the two categories.[188] As we will see, in a manner reflecting Luther's conceptualization of the *communicatio idiomatum*, "Luther's theology is neither a total synthesis or a complete separation, yet simultaneously it is both; it is irony breaking into the realm of analogy. What the mask reveals is the very Word hidden in its cracks."[189]

If analogy operates on the assumption of direct correspondence which allows for the unknown to be inferred by the known, then irony—and Luther's employment of "ironic destabilization" between the two categories of Word and world in the dynamic of revelation—which is employed "to convey something by using concepts, ideas, and words that suggest the opposite of their literal meaning" is Luther's intention when he articulates the cross of Christ as a revelation *sub contraria specie*.[190] Indeed Luther's "epistemological gesture" is an "ironic deconstruction" of analogical reasoning with regard to revelation: "that which seems to be is in fact its opposite."[191] On a fundamental level, this dynamic manifests itself at every level of what we have to say regarding the *theologia crucis*.

For the theologian of the cross, then, *that* God is made known *sub contrario* to humans in Jesus' abandonment and death on the cross simultaneously means that the world in which we live "does not present God to us as simple fact."[192] Instead, and only here in what "negates and mocks" all human preconceptions about God, it means that to confess the Crucified Christ is to confess that God can only be apprehended "in circumstances and experiences where there are no signs of

---

187. Ibid.
188. Ibid.
189. Ibid.
190. Ibid., 45.
191. Ibid.
192. Williams, *Christian Spirituality*, 146.

transcendence, no religious clues."[193] These circumstances, obviously, include (but are not limited to) sin, death, suffering, hell, despair, and abandonment. With this in-breaking of irony, or "epistemological gesture," into the realm of the theologian's analogical reasoning, "the One who becomes present . . . is simultaneously manifested in God's most radical absence."[194] Ultimately, then, to confess the Crucified Christ, for the theologian of the cross, means not only to confess that "the *cloaca* . . . is the location of Christ's advent,"[195] or the location of the Advent of Christ's redemption,[196] but, though the Word is always manifested in this world as an external, bodily word, "What the eyes cannot see, faith brings to vision."[197] In other words, according to Westhelle, the theologian of the cross affirms that "faith is only possible when the evidences that point directly and unambiguously to the divine are not there, when analogy no longer rules, when all we see is the back side of God . . . or God's rear end, as Luther translated Exodus 33:23."[198]

But, with this said, that "faith brings to vision what the eyes cannot see" regarding the external, bodily Word of God revealed *sub contrario*, we have now arrived at our third section: Luther's theology of the cross is a theology of faith

Theologia Crucis: A Theology of Faith

A "Seamless Robe"

Although faith and suffering have traditionally been presented as separate but integral *loci* in Luther's *theologia crucis* by influential theologians,[199] this outline draws both *loci* together in order to treat

---

193. Ibid.

194. Westhelle, *Scandalous God*, 22.

195. Oberman, *Reformation: Roots and Ramifications*, 100, also quoted by Madsen, *Theology of the Cross in Historical Perspective*, 85. On this note, Westhelle asserts in his *Scandalous God*, 54, "[W]hat we call Epiphany is not an unequivocal manifestation of the divinity; it is indirect and even expressed in is reverse: glory lies in a manger, power in fragility, wisdom in foolishness." Thus, to speak of the revelation of God is to speak of the conversion of the categories of *humilitas* and *sublimitas*. See ibid., 24ff.

196. Madsen, *Theology of the Cross in Historical Perspective*, 85.

197. Westhelle, *Scandalous God*, 52.

198. Ibid.

199. Cf. McGrath, *Luther's Theology of the Cross*, 150–51; Loewenich, *Luther's Theology of the Cross*, 22; Hendel, "Theology of the Cross," 228–30.

them as a "seamless robe," each as indicators of the other's presence, and thus inseparable as a *locus* in Luther's *theologia crucis*. It is just this point that we will develop in this half of this section.

If, for Luther, knowledge of "God's working"[200] is revealed *sub contraria specie* under his "strange" or "alien work,"[201] or "hidden in suffering,"[202] then this reality has dramatic implications for the manner itself in which revelation apprehended. How so?

As Luther observes, "It is most difficult of all to recognize as King one who has died such a desperate and shameful death."[203] Because of this, Luther adds, "The senses are strongly repelled by such a notion, reason abhors it, experience denies it, and a precedent is lacking."[204] Accompanying this, according to Luther, is a second difficulty in that

> [T]hrough His reign the King teaches that all the things you hoped for in the Law should be condemned, and that all the things you feared should be loved. He offers cross and death. He advises contempt for the good that one sees, and likewise for the evil, since He will confer on you a much different good, namely, that which the eye has not seen, the ear has not heard, and has not entered into the heart of man ... [thus] You must die if you would live under this King ... You must not flee from ignominy, poverty, hunger, and thirst, in other words, all the evil that floods the earth.[205]

For one discovers that, when following such a "King," "this is the entrance into darkness, where everything that the feeling, reason, mind, and understanding of man is able to grasp will be dissolved."[206] Perhaps this dynamic of a hidden faith corresponding to a God who reveals and manifests his activity in this world *sub contraria specie* is no more famously articulated than when Luther declared in his 1525 *Bondage of the Will*, "Hence in order that there may be room for faith, it is necessary that everything which is believed should be hidden. It cannot, however,

---

200. Cf. Vercruysse, "Luther's Theology of the Cross at the Time of the Heidelberg Disputation," 542. Although we have already pointed this out, he indicates that the cross is a "paradigm of God's working."

201. LW 14:335.

202. LW 31:52.

203. LW 14:342.

204. Ibid.

205. LW 14:342.

206. Ibid., 343.

be more deeply hidden than under an object, perception, or experience which is contrary to it. Thus when God makes alive he does it by killing, when he justifies he does it by making men guilty, when he exalts to heaven he does it by bringing down to hell."[207] Essentially, then, as knowledge of God is manifested only through the revelation of God *sub contraria specie*, then faith itself, standing in permanent conflict with all human psychic functions and "proceeding in opposition to all appearance,"[208] is unable to judge its very own existence by empirical or quantifiable standards. It is just this point that Craig Hinkson observes when he avers that "Because faith is a hidden reality, the presence of which is compatible with the most palpably felt despair, Christians must maintain a resolute ingnorance of their own inner condition, placing their confidence not in some feeling that they may perchance find in themselves, but in God's promise alone. Faith is a clinging to God's Word, and in time of trial it does so blindly, against reason and experience."[209] Ultimately, then, as the apprehension of revelation cannot be "grasped by [the] pure contemplation"[210] of the cognitive faculties alone, or even of the affective faculties alone, nor can it strictly be an answer to, and thus employed for, a "crisis of meaning"[211] produced by those same faculties. To understand "faith" in this manner would both reduce it purely to a level of meaning (divested of material concerns) and also, most importantly, keep it focused squarely within the realm of analogical reasoning.

But, as we have seen, if faith "must not only live without experience . . . but even has experience against it . . . and must persevere . . . in opposition to experience,"[212] then, according to von Loewenich, if one wants to acknowledge this revelation seriously, she "must affirm it with [her] *whole existence*."[213] He elaborates this reality by stating,

---

207. LW 33: 62.

208. Loewenich, *Luther's Theology of the Cross*, 80.

209. Hinkson, "Luther and Kierkegaard," 33.

210. Loewenich, *Luther's Theology of the Cross*, 20.

211. Cf. Sobrino's *True Church and the Poor*, 10–18. Here Sobrino underscores the reality that theology done within the trajectory of the European Enlightenment tends to reduce theological crises to crises of meaning, whereas "third world" theological crises are addressed to concrete, practical realities of daily existence.

212. Althaus, *Theology of Martin Luther*, 36.

213. Loewenich, *Luther's Theology of the Cross*, 20; italics added for emphasis.

"That is to say, the cross of the Christian corresponds to the cross of Christ. To know God 'through suffering and cross' means that *the knowledge of God comes into being at the cross of Christ, the significance of which becomes evident only to the one who himself stands in cross and suffering.*"[214] Thus if God's activity in creation is revealed through the "strange" work of the cross' suffering and death, not only does the cross have less to do with *theology* than it does with *theologians* for whom "trial and temptation is not the exception but the rule,"[215] but the sheer dynamic of apprehending God's revelation itself *de facto* positions the human—theologian!—at the location of the cross. One cannot authentically speak *about* God's revelation, one can only speak *from the location of* revelation as one who is crucified with Christ to the life-dealing activity of God.[216] Luther describes this *location* eloquently in *The Maginficat* when he observes that

> You must feel the pinch of poverty in the midst of your hunger and learn by experience what hunger and poverty are, with no provision on hand and no help in yourself or any other man, but in God only; so that the work may be God's alone and impossible to be done by any other. You must not only think and speak of a low estate but actually come to be in a low state and caught in it, without any human aid, so that God alone may do the work. Or if it should not go to pass, you must at least desire it and not shrink from it.[217]

And it is this "pinch of poverty," or as Luther refers to it in his 15th thesis in his *Explanations to the 95 Theses* (1519), this tangible presence of suffering "the punishment of eternal destruction, separated from the presence of the Lord and from the glory of his might" in such a wise that one feels "stretched out with Christ so that all his bones may be counted, and every corner of the soul is filled with the greatest bitterness, dread, trembling, and sorrow in such a manner that all these last forever"[218] that Luther also calls *Anfechtung*. *Anfechtung*, though it is difficult to capture its meaning in English, can be defined as the tangible "*terror [one] feels in the moment he is confronted with some dark aspect*

---

214. Ibid; italics added for emphasis.
215. Althaus, *Theology of Martin Luther*, 56.
216. See Westhelle, *Scandalous God*, 113–24.
217. LW 21:173–74.
218. LW 31:129.

of God. God may [assail] man as judge, as enemy, as tempter, as the hidden one and as the arbitrary one."[219] But ultimately *Anfechtung* is nothing more, within the *theologia crucis*, than the theologian of the cross standing at the location of revelation and thus being restored by the living God to life.[220] *Anfechtung* means that one is being restored to God's sole sufficiency as the Creator. It is a concrete, tangible location.

So, explicitly, this "pinch of poverty," this *Anfechtung*, is nothing more than an affirmation of God's revelation with one's "whole existence." And this affirmation of God's revelation with one's whole bodily existence is nothing more than to "suffer" a God who, hidden within his "strange" work, manifests his "proper" work as "true Creator"[221] and thus demonstrates that "our sufficiency is from God."[222] And this "affirmation" is a confirmation of both the reality that "The theologian of the cross cannot speak *about* the cross from the standpoint of the cross itself . . . [but] can only speak *from* the cross in sheer faith without evidence,"[223] acknowledging that the only proper engagement with the cross is *in usus passionis*,[224] and the reality that faith involves a "flight" of one's whole existence. It is to this "flight" that we shall now turn.

From God to God

Hearkening back to the first locus of this chapter in which we developed both the dynamics and differences between "passive" and "active" righteousness, and, more importantly, the ultimate outcome of attempting to ground one's *coram Deo* righteousness in the "active" righteousness of the law, we soon discovered, according to Luther in *descriptive* fashion, that one's "conscience senses that it has not satisfied the Law; it cannot satisfy the Law or bear the wrath of God which the Law reveals when it sets us into the sight of God this way, that is, when it terrifies us, accuses us, and shows us our sins."[225] Ultimately, as we discovered,

---

219. Hovland, "Anfechtung in Luther's Biblical Exegesis," 46, also quoted in Madsen, *Theology of the Cross in Historical Perspective*, 108.

220. See McGrath, *Luther's Theology of the Cross*, 151–52.

221. LW 21:301.

222. Ibid., 328.

223. Westhelle, *Scandalous God*, 114.

224. Ibid., 124.

225. LW 26:150.

for Luther, the "active" righteousness of the law becomes a "ministry of sin" that "strikes the wrath of God into a man and threatens him with death."[226] With this said, though, Luther strangely declares this to be the "proper" use of the law in that it reveals to humans their "sin, blindness, misery, wickedness, ignorance, hate and contempt of God, death, hell, judgment, and the well-deserved wrath of God."[227] But the matter here is not so simple. For between the "striking of wrath" which is tangibly, corporeally apprehended with one's "whole existence" and the ability to name this as the "proper" use of the law, stands a "flight," a "breakthrough"—indeed "the greatest achievement which a human can reach"[228]—in which God's *opus proprium* of creating life is not simply perceived *sub contraria specie*, but that this wrath and death is confessed to exist only purely, "properly," and penultimately in service of this life. But, to honor this "flight" means, strangely, that we must honor the "wrath of God." But, ultimately, to honor the "wrath of God" is to honor a distinction, according to Luther, regarding the one Triune God who concretely, tangibly manifests himself as both God "not preached" and "preached." In what manner?

If, according to Luther, the one who pursues the "active" righteousness of the law soon discovers that "God, in his nature and majesty, is our enemy, because he demands that we fulfill the law . . . [and that] When his finger writes the law on Moses' tablet of stone, he appears in his majesty, accuses of sin, and terrifies our hearts . . . [thus revealing that he] always is the word of the eternal and almighty God,"[229] then Luther can also assert, according to the dictates of the ultimate manifestation of the law's "active" righteousness, that "God must therefore be left to himself in his own majesty, for in this regard we have nothing to do with him, nor does he will that we should have anything to do with him."[230] Thus a fundamental distinction—corresponding to his teaching on law and gospel[231]—must be made:

---

226. LW 26:150.

227. Ibid., 309.

228. Wingren, "Doctrine of Creation," 364.

229. WA 39, 1:370, 12–371, 1, also quoted in Lohse, *Martin Luther: An Introduction to His Life and Work*, 170.

230. LW 33:139.

231. Lohse, *Martin Luther: An Introduction to His Life and Work*, 171.

> But we have something to do with him insofar as he is clothed [*sub contraria specie*] and set forth in his Word, through which he offers himself to us and . . . In this regard we say, the good God does not deplore the death of his people which he works in them, but he deplores the death which he finds in his people and desires to remove from them. For it is this that God as he is preached is concerned with, namely, that sin and death should be taken away and we should be saved.[232]

But, regarding the second half of this distinction, the half associated with the horrifying ramifications of the "active" righteousness of the law which, on the basis of that same law, "attempts to stray into heaven with idle speculations," Luther declares, "God hidden in his majesty neither deplores nor takes away death, but works life, death, and all in all. For there he has not bound himself by his word, but has kept himself free over all things."[233] Luther adds, "God does many things that he does not disclose to us in his word; he also wills many things which he does not disclose himself as willing in his word. Thus he does not will the death of the sinner, according to his word; but he wills it according to that inscrutable will of his."[234] It is for this reason that we must be directed by the revelation of Jesus Christ *pro nobis, sub contraria specie* "and not by that inscrutable will."[235] For it is precisely the God of this "inscrutable will," this "God of fearsome abstraction,"[236] to whom Luther refers when he speaks of the *Deus nudus in sua maiestate*, the God above whom "nothing can be exalted, but [for whom] all things are under his mighty hand";[237] "the disposer of all things, by whose power and will all things come to be and not to be."[238]

If this is the case, then, that "God is God" and therefore works "all in all," and hence cannot simply be reduced to his Word of revelation (although there is an obvious temptation to embrace the God "in" revelation while shunning the God "behind"/"beyond" revelation),[239] then

---

232. LW 33:139–40.
233. Ibid., 140.
234. Ibid.
235. Ibid.
236. Forde, *Theology is for Proclamation*, 15.
237. LW 33:139.
238. Forde, *Theology is for Proclamation*, 15.
239. Westhelle, *Scandalous God*, 56.

we must acknowledge that as God is confessed to be "wise" within his Word of revelation, so he must also remain "wise" outside of his Word of Revelation, as well.[240] In short, the law which drives one to the gospel is as "wise" as the gospel itself, so to speak. Ultimately the wrath of God, the ultimate manifestation of the "active" righteousness of the law, cannot be reduced to a "placeholder,"[241] or a "figment of our imagination"[242] which is simply explained-away through a little theologizing,[243] but must be acknowledged as the "power of God at work in [all] life as well as history."[244] As Brian Gerrish observes, for Luther the *Deus nudus in sua maiestate* references the "'God' of everyday experience apart from Christ, what we encounter apart from the Word."[245] He adds, "When [Luther] looked directly at nature, apart from the Word, he was aware of an awesome, creative power quite other than the God he encountered in Jesus Christ."[246] Resonating on this point, David Tracy asserts that

> The central dilemma for Christian self-understanding is that Luther does speak . . . of a second sense of hiddenness. He even dares to speak of a second sense of hiddenness as behind or even "beyond" the word. At the very least, this literally awful, ambivalent sense of God's hiddenness can be so overwhelming that God is sometimes experienced as purely frightening, not tender, sometimes even as an impersonal reality—"it"—of sheer power and energy signified by such metaphors, such fragmentary metaphors as abyss, chasm, chaos, horror . . .[247]

But perhaps it is Gerhard Forde who provides the most trenchant interpretation of what is truly at stake both regarding the *Deus nudus in sua maiestate*, and how this irremovable "monkey on the back" of

---

240. Paulson, "Wrath of God," 249.

241. See Gregersen, "Ten Theses on the Future of Lutheran Theology," 1, in which he asserts that "Luther's doctrine of the hidden God is a necessary *placeholder* for an awareness of God's majestic being; but the identification of the reality of God can only be offered *via* the doctrine of the Trinity."

242. Lohse, *Martin Luther: An Introduction to His Life and Thought*, 171.

243. Cf. Forde, *Theology is for Proclamation*, 13–30.

244. Lohse, *Martin Luther: An Introduction to His Life and Thought*, 171.

245. Gerrish, "To the Unknown God," 138. Gerrish names *Deus nudus in sua maiestate* "Hiddenness II," while God revealed in Christ *sub contraria specie* is named "Hiddenness I" (ibid., 134).

246. Ibid., 139.

247. Tracy, *Form and Fragment*; also quoted by Westhelle, *Scandalous God*, 57.

theology defines and shapes—yet limits—the task of theology, when he asserts that,

> When Martin Luther issued his frightening dictum to Erasmus and stated that God, hidden in majesty, has not bound himself to his word but kept himself free over all things, he was, I think, insisting on the impossibility of simply collapsing God into Jesus. True, not many have followed Luther on this, but it is a critical point ultimately for soteriology and contemporary theology as well. For Luther it springs from his realization that it is simply impossible to bring the 'naked God' in his majesty to heel systematically. Indeed, God hidden in majesty actively removes or hides himself from the clutches of our control . . . There is no solution to this problem in systematic theology or kindred theological disciplines for that matter.[248]

But if systematic theology has no capacity to domesticate the *Deus nudus*, no ability to "round-off" the living God's fearsome edges in accordance with the canons of analogical reason, or to logically reconcile the God hidden *within* revelation with the *Deus nudus*, or the God *beyond* revelation, then Tracy observes that this theological inability can also be viewed as an opportunity for the retrieval a theological strand already present within the Christian tradition. So he states that "This Hiddenness allows for a new theological recovery of apocalyptic as a fragmenting form in our own period. Indeed, to 'let God be God again' is also to let that awesome and numinous strand of our common Christian heritage be heard again with the kind of clarity and courage that Luther found in his apocalyptic visions of history and nature alike, and, in his willingness to dare to speak of God's hiddenness in the full sense."[249] But, no matter how the issue of the *Deus nudus* is posed,

---

248. Forde, "Robert Jenson's Soteriology," 136.

249. Tracy, *Form and Fragment*, also quoted in Westhelle, *Scandalous God*, 57. Indeed Tracy in "Hidden God: The Divine Other of Liberation," 12, asserts, "I do not doubt that Luther's most theological—or, more exactly, most Christological—reflections on God's hiddenness may be found in the *theologia crucis* of Hiddenness I. And yet I agree with Gerrish that one should resist those interpreters who either try to harmonize (i.e., domesticate) Luther's two really different senses of God's ambivalent hiddenness or try simply to dismiss Hiddenness II as somehow unimportant (a "medieval fragment"—Ritschl) or somehow wrong ("destructive of God's unity"—Barth)." Tracy adds, "The theological justification, I believe, is best found along a path which Luther never explicitly gives but which he could have given. The justification is scriptural and, thereby, on Luther's terms, in principle, christological. Luther could appeal not only to Paul on predestination but the fuller dialectical implications of Christ Crucified (in

negatively or positively, what can be asserted without qualification on the matter is this: though God is *revealed* in concealment *sub contraria specie*, the *background of concealment* out of which the concealed God reveals himself *sub contraria specie*, and God's activity within that same background of concealment, still remain. With this being the case, then, the "idea of God's love" revealed in Jesus Christ "dare never become a general truth."[250] As—because this background of God's activity in concealment remains—"secrets remain" within the revealed God,[251] so, too, does faith become a matter of "urgency because the hidden God prevents faith from becoming complacent."[252]

Ultimately the problem for Luther, then, as Forde observes, was not one of justifying God's ways nor even proving God's existence, but how to get the *Deus nudus* of the majestical, terrifying abstractions "off our backs."[253] Yet, Forde adds, "Only God can deal with God."[254] Ultimately

---

extreme situations Hiddenness I itself becomes Hiddenness II): the most radical sense of the Crucified God. We can see today that hermeneutically (i.e., here, theologically and christologically) Paul's dialectic of Christ Crucified is deeply resonant with Mark's Gospel. Note how history, for Mark, is like Luther's (not Luke's) view of history: interruptive, apocalyptic, erupting often in awe and terror, constituted often by a conflict between Christ and Satan, open to both the Hidden God and the Hidden Satan. Note how Mark's Jesus prays, indeed cries out, the psalm which is also a lament and cry in his terrifying last words on the cross, 'My God, my God why have you forsaken me?'" (ibid., 12). Though an entire dissertation itself could be written on "hiddenness II," let us also be sure to note that it is certainly not unanimously accepted as part-and-parcel of the theological landscape. In his signal *Luther's Theology of the Cross*, 166, McGrath states on the matter of God "willing many things which he does not disclose in his Word" that, "Not only do such statements suggest that Luther has abandoned his earlier principle of deriving theology solely on the basis of the cross: they also suggest that the cross is not the final word of God on anything." On the argument that the God beyond revelation may actually will the death of the sinner, McGrath asserts, "This argument inevitably makes theology an irrelevancy, if any statements which can be made on the basis of divine revelation may be refuted by appealing to a hidden and inscrutable God, whose will probably contradicts that of the revealed God" (ibid., 167).

250. Loewenich, *Luther's Theology of the Cross*, 38. Westhelle, *Scandalous God*, 57, points out that "it is better to admit that there is an inscrutable shadow-side to God than the other options available to us. It would be simply a descriptive statement of our finite experience, and of the very finitude of our reason. But if it is blasphemy, it is the one of Job. This is the one God is great enough to take."

251. Loewenich, *Luther's Theology of the Cross*, 38.

252. Gerrish, "'To the Unknown God,'" 147.

253. Forde, *Theology is for Proclamation*, 22.

254. Ibid.

the "clothed God must conquer the naked God for us."[255] In other words, faith is the flight from wrath to mercy, from the hidden God to God revealed *sub contraria specie* in Jesus Christ, the clothed God. For though God's wrath continues to be active in this life, as the background of concealment from which God reveals himself constantly remains, faith—on the basis of the revelation of Jesus Christ *sub contraria specie*—presses on through this wrath to the "proper" work of God hidden within it, or the presence and activity of the life-giving Creator[256] who alone is our "sole sufficiency." Ultimately von Loewenich captures this dynamic of faith's movement—or "flight"—when he states regarding this faith, that it "presses through from the alien work to the proper work ... *Thus the turning point in the trial has clearly arrived when faith recognizes the trial as an alien work.*"[257] Indeed, to even recognize an "alien" work of God means that the "flight" has safely arrived, that one *is* the location of God's revelation. Thus faith is a "constant movement,"[258] or "flight," from God to God. But, having said this, we have now arrived full circle regarding our presentation of Luther's *theologia crucis*.

For it was just this reality that Luther articulated when, as we have already seen at the core of his understanding of justification, he asserted, "Whoever knows how to bring these utterly contradictory things together amid temptation—that is, whoever knows that when the Law is most terrifying, then the end of the Law and the beginning of grace and the future of faith are present—such a person uses the Law correctly."[259] Thus if all of this is the case when faith's "flight" safely "lands," then that background of concealment, or *Deus nudus in sua maiestate*, finally gets placed in its proper perspective. In Luther's theology, according to Forde, if all of those fearsome attributes of the *Deus nudus in sua maiestate*

---

255. Ibid. As Forde observes there is no solution to this problem of the hidden God in systematic theology, as the hidden God "actively removes or hides himself from the clutches of our control"; then, as he states in "Robert's Jenson's Soteriology," 137, "The only solution lies in the living proclamation in the present. Yet it must be a timely happening, an actual 'break through,' not just a systematic assertion that the faith it engenders will always live in the face of temptation." It is through proclamation that the "clothed God" conquers the "naked God" for us in the present.

256. Thus, for Luther there is never a human location in this life which is "*jenseits Gesetz und Evangelium*." Cf. Iwand "Um den rechten Glauben," 87–109.

257. Loewenich, *Luther's Theology of the Cross*, 137.

258. Thompson, *Crossing the Divide*, 63.

259. LW 26:338.

"such as divine necessity, immutability, timelessness, impassability, and so forth, function as masks of God in his hiddenness ... [thus functioning] on the one hand as wrath, as attack on human pretense," then, on the other hand, through faith they function "ultimately as comfort, as backup for the proclamation."[260] Thus, as Luther asks, "If God were not immutable, who can believe his promises?"[261]

Thus 'faith is the greatest achievement which the human can reach,"[262] according to Gustaf Wingren, in that amid all of the trials and evidences that empirically counter "the thesis that God is love," it is able to "*hold fast* to the certainty that we are loved by the Creator and that God's 'genuine work' ... is really life."[263] It is able to hold fast to the promise that death and suffering are only penultimate to the ultimate work of the Creator's love, and thus are ultimately in no need of an explanation, and thus justification, which would reverse the relationship between Creator and creature/creation.

But could it be that an even greater miracle of faith's "flight," according to Luther's *theologia crucis*, is what it leaves "on the ground"; that the only "flight" which faith necessitates is the one that shuttles the human from the speculation of *Deus nudus* to the *Deus revelatus* who reveals the life-giving Creator at the heart of it all? In other words, perhaps the greatest miracle of faith is that it restores humans to a Creator who creates and sustains particular, embodied creatures on this good earth, in this "very good" creation; a creation which need not be a "sign" or cipher for someplace else, or a *Heilsgeschichte* divested of all things profane and particular. Indeed the *theologia crucis* reveals that it is this creation in which God both reveals himself, and to which God is committed in love. Having said this, we will move to our final, and shortest locus of this chapter.

---

260. Forde, "Robert Jenson's Soteriology," 137.
261. LW 33:42, also quoted in Forde, "Robert Jenson's Soteriology," 137.
262. Wingren, "Doctrine of Creation," 364.
263. Ibid.

Theologia Crucis: A Theology for Creation

Getting Behind the Matter?

Corresponding with what we have already observed, above, regarding the fact that God refuses to deal with humans "except through his external Word,"[264] in his treatise countering Andreas Karlstadt von Bodenstein entitled *Against the Heavenly Prophets*[265] Luther—within the trajectory of his *theologia crucis*—both develops the nature of this "external Word," and observes the ramifications regarding the neglect of this "external Word" for the sake of another avenue to communion with God.

"Now when God sends forth his holy gospel," according to Luther, "he deals with us in a twofold manner, first outwardly, then inwardly."[266] Luther develops this dynamic of the Word by adding that "Outwardly he deals with us through the oral word of the gospel and through material signs, that is, baptism and the sacrament of the altar. Inwardly he deals with us through the Holy Spirit, faith, and other gifts . . . The inward experience follows and is effected by the outward. God has determined to give the inward to no one except through the outward."[267] But if the "inward" is always borne on the matter of that which is external, or "outward," then the urgency of this priority is quite clear.

In a fashion commensurate with the "theologian of glory" who believes that the cognitive faculties "can carry them speculatively into the invisible realm of divine truth,"[268] the theologian of Karldstadt's ilk not only "subordinate[s] God's outward order to an inner spiritual one . . . [thus] tear[ing] down the bridge, the path, the way, the ladder, and all the means by which the Spirit can come to you,"[269] but, most importantly, she "spiritualize[s] that which God has made to be bodily,"[270] "makes inward whatever God makes outward."[271] If ultimately this reversal of

---

264. BC: 313.
265. LW 40:79–223.
266. LW 40:146.
267. Ibid.
268. Williams, *Christian Spirituality*, 146.
269. LW 40:147.
270. Ibid., 181.
271. Ibid., 182.

priority regarding "outward" and "inward" grants to human memory and knowledge (all internal functions of the cognitive faculties)[272] only what the external, material presence of Jesus Christ himself can offer, thus reversing the direction of the relationship between God and humans,[273] then this reversal also presupposes, at a fundamental level, a diminished value placed on the material world, especially with reference to the material world as a realm for divine activity.

According to this "reversal" the sacred/spiritual and profane/material realms are inimicable. Thus, as William Hordern observes, the "theologian of glory" assumes a "dualistic view of reality" which is constituted, on the one hand, by the "material world" which is "evil or, at least, a very poor vehicle for the concerns of the spiritual world,"[274] and, on the other hand, a "spiritual world" which is "good and always intimately related to the divine."[275] According to this logic, then, as Hordern points out, "inner experience"—always equated with matters spiritual—"is held to be more pleasing to God and more God-filled"[276] than the material, visible realm. Essentially then, if the theologian of glory works with the presupposition that the visible creation is only essential for yielding "clues, if not directly at least by analogy, to what is invisible in God, to the nature and logic of God,"[277] then she truly never has to look at the visible, material world in all of its trials, accidents, tragedies, sufferings, troubles (and joys!), for these are "mere accidental problems to be solved by metaphysical adjustment."[278] The matter of creation then, this life, becomes a mere accident to a larger metaphysical narrative sought behind it all. We might say that the "inward" seeks the substance of all the accidents around us!

But if, as Luther asserts, "true theology and recognition of God are in the crucified Christ,"[279] then not only are we ultimately confessing that the speculative theology of inner experience has been rendered obsolete for the sake of a God who has revealed himself in Jesus Christ

272. Ibid., 213.
273. Ibid., 207.
274. Hordern, *Experience and Faith*, 101.
275. Ibid.
276. Ibid., 100.
277. Forde, *On Being a Theologian of the Cross*, 73.
278. Ibid., 13.
279. LW 31:53.

to be a "worldly reality,"[280] but we are also recognizing that through this revelation *sub contraria specie* (indirect, mediated revelation[281]) God limits himself within the "structures of creation, to what is historical, natural, human, finite."[282] So Luther observes, "[T]his is [God's] command (Matt. 17:5): 'This is My beloved Son; listen to him. There I descend to you on earth, so that you can see, hear, and touch Me.'"[283] And again, "[W]e must nestle and cuddle on the lap of Christ, like dear children on their mother's lap or in her arms, and close our eyes and ears to everything but Him and His words."[284] And with this being the case, that God limits himself to the "structures of creation," then we must also observe what *does not* transpire within this dynamic of God's self-revelation.

Far from mirroring "traditional religious systems" whose conceptualization of divine revelation relies upon a "direct supernatural epiphany" in which "the human partner is effectively overcome—taken by storm,"[285] according to Douglas John Hall the *theologia crucis* articulates a "God whose power subjects itself to, and is a function of, the divine love [which] will not overwhelm our humanity . . . God can be known only through God's own grace, God's approach to us in the humble form of the ordinary: ordinary events, ordinary creatures, ordinary people, ordinary thought and discourse."[286] For as the theologian of the cross perceives the visible, material world as a "garment of Christ,"[287] she thus perceives Christ "enveloped in an image, namely, in the Word and sacraments. These are His masks, or His garments . . . in which He conceals Himself . . . through works He performs . . . by means of the ministry and other offices."[288] For the theologian of the cross there is no narrative of the "things of God" which is either divorced from the things of this visible, material world, or divinely disabuses the "things of the world" for the sake of direct epiphany. For ultimately a Creator who

---

280. Williams, *Christian Spirituality*, 146.
281. See Hall, *Thinking the Faith*, 387.
282. Ibid.
283. LW 24:65.
284. Ibid., 64.
285. Hall, *Thinking the Faith*, 388.
286. Ibid.
287. Williams, *Christian Spirituality*, 147.
288. LW 24:67.

through love commits himself to participation in creation through the Incarnation "affirms and celebrates the great good and eternal worth of all creation—of all that is embodied, of all that is involved in its embodiment."[289]

As the theologian of the cross is not driven to *see through* this visible, material world to perceive the "real" "invisible things of God"[290] behind the matter, she thus recognizes through the "cross story"[291] that she is simply "cast on that creative love of God"[292] which operates *sub contraria specie* in this visible, material world. For ultimately, at its core, the *theologia crucis* does not prescribe a *modus operandi* for transcending this visible, material world's narrative in order to encounter the "invisible things of God" behind the accidents of it all. But what the *theologia crucis* does do is describe—on the basis of Christ alone—God's *modus operandi* (via God's *opus alienum/opus proprium*) in this visible, material world in all of its embodied particularity for restoring sinners to his sole-sufficiency as the Creator of a "very good" creation. For if the "cross story" drives us to the "creative love of God" in such a manner that we can "only die *with* [*Christ*] and await God's answer in him"[293] in this creation, then eternal communion with God, according to the *theologia crucis*, means that all human narratives in all their particular, embodied materiality can never be "closed," but must remain "ongoing"—"cast on that creative love of God"—and thus "open," even in death.

Conclusion and Segue

In the development of this chapter we have presented an outline of the Luther's *theologia crucis* according to four constitutive *loci* which have been categorized under the appellations of the *theologia crucis* as 1) "A Theology of Justification"; 2) "A Theology of Revelation"; 3) "A Theology of Faith"; and 4) "A Theology *for* Creation." In the course of the outline we have discovered the radical, transforming effects of Luther's *theologia crucis* with regard to articulating a new definition of *iustitia Dei*, a definition which then allowed us to understand the central role of

---

289. Hall, *Cross in Our Context*, 38.
290. LW 31:52.
291. Forde, *On Being a Theologian of the Cross*, 8.
292. Ibid., 12.
293. Ibid., 3.

justification as one grounded in God's sole-sufficiency as Creator, or "Author and Donor of every good." In addition to this, we have developed both the manner in which God, through the Word, relates himself to the world by means of his analogy-subverting revelation in Christ *sub contraria specie*, and the holistic human apprehension of that concealed revelation, or faith. Last, we have underscored the significance the *theologia crucis* places on the integrity of this visible, material world as the realm of God's revealing/creating activity. We are led to no other "narrative of God" than this one with us.

But having come this far in our outline of Luther's *theologia crucis*, we have only articulated a part of the whole, indeed a part that has tended to stress the epistemological trajectory of the "cross story." As will be developed, this is by no means the foundational part of the *theologia crucis*. For if "Luther observed that God is found precisely where theologians glory are horrified to find him: as a kid in a crib, as a criminal on a cross, as a corpse in a crypt,"[294] thus resulting in the ability of the *theologia crucis* to articulate redemption "from within" through God's "still, small voice," or the "impotent Word from the cross, in the Word made flesh, come to dwell among his people,"[295] then this "theology" and its object, or the Word, cannot be confined in its articulation to a "cognitive principle." If it is truly a Word of "within-redemption" regarding particular, visible, material, embodied creatures and their respective narratives (from which they can never be removed without destroying their created integrity), then this Word must "take place"; it must be a redemptive presence "within" those respective narratives which are irreducible from their created, material nature.

But, as we learned in the first chapter from Alan Lewis, this presence cannot simply be the "place" and "presence" of a first-century incarnation (which, then, "signifies" my "place," thus forcing every particular, embodied narrative which comes after this "most real" one to become merely a "thing signified"), but the "within-place" of all particular, material embodied narratives. And if it is a Word of "resumption beyond rupture" (Lewis), a resumptive Word and presence of redemption through and in the midst of death and the tomb, then it must be a presence in *my* material tomb.

---

294. Kolb, "Luther on the Theology of the Cross," 449.
295. Ibid., 450.

So now we must ask: How can this *sub contraria specie* Word "take place" in my tomb, thus fully becoming a Word of "within-redemption" for all particular, embodied human narratives? We now turn to the foundation of Luther's *theologia crucis*, or his radical articulation of the *communicatio idiomatum*. As we will see, at its core, this articulation not only involves a radical interpretation of Chalcedon's formulation of the "two-natures" of Christ in which Luther stresses the indivisibility of the Word's divine and human natures, but, more importantly, Luther's absolute refusal to deliberate on the Word of God apart from the man Jesus who is revealed *sub contraria specie* in the cross. Let us now turn to the communication of the Word's attributes.

3

Communicatio Idiomatum
The Radix *of Luther's* Theologia Crucis

Humanity *for* Us

BY THE TIME WE ARRIVED AT THE END OF THE PREVIOUS CHAPTER, WE were able to develop two significant consequences related to the humanity of Christ with regard to the integrity of creation. Let us briefly rehearse these two points for the sake of continuity and the development of this present chapter.

First, the point was developed that it was through the Word's incarnation in the man Jesus that God limits himself in his revelation within the "structures of creation." In the words of Douglas John Hall, again, the *theologia crucis* articulates a God, revealed in the man Jesus, "whose power subjects itself to, and is a function of, the divine love [which] will not overwhelm our humanity"[1] for the sake of a "direct supernatural epiphany." For as God's redemption is not revealed in a manner that would destroy "us earthly and sinful men"[2] in order to save us (Exodus 33:20), it is revealed in the man Jesus on "the lowest rung on the ladder to heaven which God has placed for us so that we may come to him."[3] Second, and correlative, we discovered that God's concealed revelation in the humanity of Jesus, far from perpetuating a dualism which diminishes the worth of all things material for the sake of things "spiritual," actually is a divine affirmation and celebration of all things

---

1. Hall, *Thinking the Faith*, 388.
2. Althaus, *Theology of Martin Luther*, 186.
3. Ibid.

material within this "very good" creation; an affirmation and celebration "of all that is embodied, of all that is involved in its embodiment."[4]

But, having adduced these two central *consequences* regarding the importance of the humanity of Christ, ultimately the significance of Christ's humanity is—as will be fully developed in this chapter—fundamentally grounded in soteriological soil. If, at a fundamental level, for Luther failing to acknowledge the absolute identification of Christ's divinity with his humanity within the unity of the incarnate Word not only reveals a Creator who is not *inextricably* tied to the work of redemption, then failing to absolutely identify the revealed Word's humanity with his divinity results in a Redeemer who is not completely identified with the Creator's Word and the totality of his agency through that same Word. As will be developed, the implications for this complete identification of humanity and divinity within the one Word of God, especially with regard to the latter articulation (i.e., completely identifying the Redeemer with the Creator's agency through the Word), are dramatic with regard to a full articulation of the "within-redemption" of the *theologia crucis*. This chapter will both unpack and develop this claim's grounding and implications in the process of outlining the *fundamentum* of Luther's *theologia crucis*, or his radical interpretation of Chalcedon's (451) *communicatio idiomatum*, an interpretation which will fund an articulation of complete "within-redemption." But first, let us identify the meat of the issue.

Luther in his 1518 *Heidelberg Disputation*, as we have already cited, could assert—in contradistinction to the attempt to comprehend the "invisible things of God"[5] analogically, or by inferring the unknown from the known, especially as this speculative theologizing pertains to matters of the *iustitia Dei* and human attempts at justification *coram Deo*—that "true theology and recognition of God are in the crucified Christ."[6] With this being the case, it was only a consistency prompted by the anti-speculative dictates of that same *theologia crucis* which impelled Luther in 1531, in an exposition of the 6th chapter of John, countering those who would refer to Christ's "divinity to the exclusion of his humanity,"[7] to assert that

4. Hall, *Cross in our Context*, 38.
5. LW 31:52.
6. Ibid., 52.
7. LW 23:101.

> We are not that smart; we must believe that our God sent His Son, Jesus Christ, who was born of the Virgin Mary, as we also confess in our Creed: "I believe in Jesus Christ, His only-begotten Son, our Lord, etc." In Him I believe; and I believe, therefore, in the Son of God without severing Him from the Son born of Mary. My faith adheres not only to the Son of God or to His divinity but also to Him who is called Mary's Son; for they are identical. I am determined to know nothing of a Son of God who is not also Mary's Son who suffered, the God enveloped in humanity who is one Person. *I dare not separate the one from the other and say that the humanity is of no use, but only the divinity.*[8]

To divorce the humanity from the divinity in Christ, for Luther, is to "tumble from the ladder that leads to Christ."[9] For ultimately, Luther adds, "If he is not the Man born of Mary, I will have nothing of him."[10]

Thus if, on the one hand, Luther's declaration that "apart from this man [Jesus] there is no God"[11] was both a fundamental elaboration of his refusal to conduct theology apart from where God reveals himself *sub contraria specie* in the incarnate One, and a confession of faith's epistemological point of departure for discerning God's *modus operandi* in *this* world, it was also, on the other hand, a manifestation of Luther's absolute refusal to identify—in any case—God apart from the location, or the humanity, in which redemption was accomplished on behalf of sinners, in which God is *pro nobis*. For, as Marc Lienhard points out, to think that one could encounter God outside of the man Jesus would not only move one in the direction of the naked God of speculation, but fail to acknowledge that it is in the humanity of Jesus Christ alone that God has come near to us.[12] As the dynamics of its manifestation will be more fully developed below, it is in the presence of the humanity of Christ alone that believers recognize that God the Creator is *pro nobis*.[13] And it was because of this point, ultimately, that Luther could assert "that we are not able to pull Christ deep enough

---

8. Ibid., 101–2; italics added for emphasis.
9. Ibid., 102.
10. Ibid.
11. LW 37:218.
12. Lienhard, *Luther: Witness to Jesus Christ*, 220.
13. Ibid., 222.

into the flesh."[14] But if, for Luther, "apart from this man there is no God," then we will continue to more fully, explicitly develop this confession's background and rationale.

If Luther exhorted sinners to "cleave to the humanity of Christ and to know no other God but this God incarnate and clothed with man's nature,"[15] then, as we have already touched upon, the reason—for the theologian of the cross—is obvious: it is only in the incarnate, crucified Jesus that God is—again—concretely encountered *pro nobis*.[16] In Luther's words, it is in no other location than "inside our mask"[17] that "[God] attached Himself to those who were accursed, assuming their flesh and blood . . . [thus interposing] Himself as the Mediator between God and men."[18] Or again,

> Thus He joined God and man in one Person. And being joined with us who were accursed, He became a curse for us; and He concealed His blessing in our sin, death, and curse, which condemned and killed Him. But because He was the Son of God, He could not be held by them. He conquered them and triumphed over them. He took along with Him whatever clung to the flesh that he had assumed for our sake. Therefore all who cling to this flesh are blessed and are delivered from the curse.[19]

Thus, commenting on the fundamental importance of Christ's humanity for the "fulfillment of his proper office" of justifying sinners, or restoring them to the "passive" righteousness of Christ, and thus articulating Christ's humanity as the sole location in which the curse of the law is conquered, Philip Watson notes, "Since the conflict between God and the Tyrants takes place in the human life, where God and His adversaries contend, as it were, for the mastery of Mansoul, it is in human life that the victory must be won, at any rate, if it is to effect man's salvation, and if God is to be truly God *for man*."[20] Complementing this observation, Lienhard asserts that the humanity of Christ "belongs to the so-called

---

14. "daß wir Christum nicht tief genug ins Fleisch ziehen können." Quoted in Iwand, *Luthers Theologie*, 118.
15. Watson, *Let God be God,* 127.
16. Lohse, *Martin Luther's Theology*, 173.
17. LW 26:284.
18. Ibid., 289.
19. LW 26:290.
20. Watson, *Let God Be God*, 127.

'historicity' (*Geschichtlichkeit*) of God."[21] For, in contradistinction to the impassible deity of the Greeks, it is through the humanity of Christ that "God 'puts on' humanity," and ultimately the whole of creation, and it is for this reason that Luther is able to express the extent to which God is able to be fully involved within both creation and human history.[22] And, ultimately, according to Lienhard, "The incarnation of the Son manifests this confrontation of the Trinity at the level of human history and allows God to be discovered precisely through the history of Jesus, confronted with the wrath of God and subject to human condition."[23] Ultimately, then, if the central question is one of how the sinner is justified by God, then the concrete *location*—here, completely at the level of creation and human history—of that revelation of "passive" righteousness is central to the answer: "Not independently of the man Jesus[.]"[24] At the same time, if the question of the justification of sinners is tied to the concrete location of that justification in the humanity of Christ, or the location in which God is revealed to sinners as *pro nobis*, then the concrete locations of particular, embodied sinners must also, for Luther, be factored into account. How so?

For if it is only the God "inside our mask" that is the location of a sinner's justification, and thus "guarantees the reality of our redemption,"[25] then, for Luther, thinking strictly on the basis of the incarnation, "there is no longer any valid relationship with God which is not also a relationship with the man Jesus."[26] Countering Andreas Bodenstein von Karlstadt, who (while maintaining with reference to the Sacrament of the Altar that the flesh of Christ is both "of no avail," and bound to one particular location) "spiritualized" that which "God made to be bodily,"[27] or our participation in the body of Christ, by emphasizing the role of human remembrance with regard to one's individual appropriation of the benefits of Christ,[28] Luther, in his *Against the Heavenly Prophets in the Matter of Images and Sacraments* (1525), could assert the opposite

---

21. Lienhard, *Luther: Witness to Christ*, 380.
22. Ibid.
23. Ibid., 229.
24. Lienhard, *Luther: Witness to Christ*, 229.
25. Ibid., 233.
26. Ibid., 342.
27. LW 40:181.
28. See ibid., 144–223.

point. Or, as Luther states, "Christ on the cross and all his suffering and his death do not avail, even if, as you teach, they are 'acknowledged and meditated upon' with the utmost 'passion, ardor, heartfeltness.' Something else must always be there. What is it? The Word, the Word, the Word."[29] Luther drives his point home by confessing,

> Even if Christ were given for us and crucified a thousand times, it would all be in vain if the Word of God were absent and were not distributed and given to me with the bidding, this is for you, take what is yours. Even if I followed the Karlstadtian teaching and preached the remembrance and knowledge of Christ with such passion and seriousness that I sweated blood and became feverish, it would be of no avail and all in vain. For it would be pure work and commandment, but no gift or Word of God offered and given to me in the body and blood of Christ.[30]

Ultimately then, because one's "passive righteousness" is bound to the presence of the whole Word, therefore—in keeping with the *modus operandi* of his *theologia crucis* which understands the true subject matter of all theology as consisting of both *Deus theologicus* and *homo theologicus*—Luther could treat the matter of the justification of sinners simultaneously in two ways (neither diminished for the sake of the other), or with regard to the two concrete locations regarding theology's true subject matter: "how it is achieved and won,"[31] or the "once-for-all" location of justification in the humanity of Christ, *and* how and where Christ's Word "is distributed and given to us,"[32] or the location of justification with regard to the narratives of individual sinners who live in *this* world. As the humanity of Christ is essential with regard to both material locations, or narratives according to Luther, "[Christ] has won it once for all on the cross. But the distribution takes places continuously, before and after, from the beginning to the end of the world."[33] Ultimately, then, if one's "passive" righteousness cannot be considered either objectively or subjectively apart from the presence of the humanity of Christ, and individual, embodied narratives of sinners fill this world, then, for Luther, "the gospel is and must be free in regard

---

29. Ibid., 212.
30. Ibid., 213.
31. Ibid.
32. Ibid.
33. Ibid., 214.

to all places and bound to no particular spot."[34] The "realm of Christ," according to Luther, "is in every place" and "fills all in all."[35] The presence of the humanity of Christ, for Luther, was absolutely essential for both narratives of justification: the narrative of the justification of sinners once-for-all, *in illo tempore*, and the narratives of the justification of individual, embodied sinners in their manifold locations. Without the presence of Christ's humanity, there is no justification of sinners, and hence no "passive" righteousness, or restoration of sinners to God's life-giving Word which works in us. Confirming this point, Lienhard states, "It is not enough for us to see that it is attested that God saves us, nor that we can be content to receive only the benefits of the redemptive work of Christ accomplished in the past. We must receive Christ himself, Christ with his flesh, because it was in his flesh that he accomplished redemption. Everything depends then on the identity between the historic Christ and Christ present, between Christ dead on the cross and Christ who now constitutes my righteousness before God."[36] Again, if the question began with the matter of the sinner's justification before God, and, consequently, Luther's *theologia crucis* impelled him to provide an answer based on an articulation of God strictly dictated by the incarnation, then wherever God reveals himself, there the humanity of Christ must also be present.

But if it is only through Christ's humanity that God is identified as *pro nobis*, and that, ultimately, wherever God's redemptive activity occurs, there his humanity must also be present (as, again, "there is "[no] valid relationship with God which is not also a relationship with the man Jesus"), then the matter of ubiquity regarding the Word's humanity necessarily lies not only at the "very heart of a theology of revelation,"[37] but is revealed to be of foundational importance for Luther's *theologia crucis*. If the justification of sinners necessarily involves the presence of the Word's humanity, the Word must literally, concretely "take place" regardless of where the sinner is located.

But, more than this, if, as we have contended, at its core the *theologia crucis* is a theology of "within-redemption" whose "passive" righteousness materially "takes place" (with regard to the particular,

---

34. Ibid., 220.
35. Ibid., 216.
36. Lienhard, *Luther: Witness to Christ*, 222.
37. Ibid., 229.

embodied narratives of all sinners)—at its farthest extreme—in the "within-locations" of all particular, material tombs, then what we mean by "humanity" and "flesh" as these terms pertain to Jesus Christ shatter all *a priori* conceptualizations of the terms. If Luther could declare that "I know not where to find God, either in heaven or on earth, except in the flesh of Christ,"[38] then could it be the case, perhaps, that this flesh fills "heaven and earth"?

So, we must ask, how is this essential "humanity"—at the core of Luther's *theologia crucis*—articulated? To answer this question it becomes necessary to communicate the *radix* of Luther's *theologia crucis*. In other words, we turn to the "very heart" of Luther's *theologia crucis*, or Luther's radical interpretation of Chalcedon's (451) formulation of the two natures of Christ, or his *communicatio idiomatum*. For it is just this interpretation which is able to express the reality that Christ's humanity is "bound to no particular spot," especially—and ultimately—as it "takes place" at "within-locations" of all human tombs.

The "Axle and Motor"[39] of Luther's *Theologia Crucis*: Communicatio Idiomatum

As will be developed, below, if Luther's articulation of the *communicatio idiomatum* is not only grounded in Chalcedon's (451) formulation of the two natures of Christ, but indeed in a radical interpretation of that formulation, then, before we present Luther's interpretation (in order to place his interpretation in a broader context of theology), we will need to both present the Chalcedonian formulation, and present, as well, a sampling of signal criticisms. For the purpose of this project, we will limit our presentation of criticisms to a sampling of signal perspectives representing a relatively broad spectrum of theological voices. Let us begin, though, with a presentation of the Chalcedonian formulation.

---

38. LW 23:123.

39. The phrase "axle and motor" is taken from Johan Anselm Steiger's piece "The *Communicatio Idiomatum* as the Axle and Motor of Luther's Theology." See also his *Fünf Zentralthemen der Theologie Luthers*, 3–51.

Chalcedon: Presentation and Criticisms

Though the *Creed of Nicaea* (325) elaborated an answer on the question as to whether the *Logos* was "true God," the question of the person of Jesus Christ remained. How was one to speak of the "unity" of his person? In what sense do we articulate this union while maintaining that he is "true man?" Involving three major schools of theology (Alexandria, Antioch, and Western Christianity),[40] and weaving its way between Apollinarianism (which diminished Christ's humanity for the sake of a divine soul), Nestorianism (which threatened the unity of the divine person for the sake of the integrity of the individual natures), and Eutychianism (whose articulation of Christ's unity absorbed the human nature into the divine nature),[41] the *Definition of Chalcedon* (451) confessed the person of Jesus Christ as such:

> Following, then the holy fathers, we unite in teaching all men to confess the one and only Son, our Lord Jesus Christ. This selfsame one is perfect [*teleion*] both in deity [*theotēti*] and also in human-ness [*anthrōpotēti*]; this selfsame one is also actually [*alēthōs*] God and actually man, with a rational soul [*psychēs logikēs*] and a body. He is of the same reality as God [*homoousion tō patri*] as far as his deity is concerned and of the same reality as we are ourselves [*homoousion hēmin*] as far as his human-ness is concerned; thus like us in all respects, sin only excepted. Before time began [*pro aiōnōn*] he was begotten of the Father, in respect of his deity, and now in these "last days," for us and on behalf of our salvation, this selfsame one was born of Mary the virgin, who is God-bearer [*theotokos*] in respect of his human-ness [*anthrōpotēta*].
>
> [We also teach] that we apprehend [*gnōridzomenon*] this one and only Christ-Son, Lord, only-begotten-in two natures [*duo physesin*]; [and we do this] without confusing the two natures [*asunkutōs*], without transmuting one nature into the other [*atreptōs*], without dividing them into two separate categories [*adiairetōs*], without contrasting them according to the area or function [*achōristōs*]. The distinction of each nature is not nul-

---

40. Leith, *Creeds of the Churches*, 34.

41. Though, for the purpose and space of this project, it is not necessary to present Chalcedon's historical/theological background, for concise delineations of the background of these schools of thought and their arguments, I refer the reader to Kelly, *Early Christian Doctrines*, 280–343, Pelikan, *The Emergence of the Catholic Tradition (100–600)*, 226–77; and Braaten's "Classical Christology and Its Subsequent Criticism."

lified by the unison. Instead, the "properties" [*idiotētos*] of each nature are conserved and both natures concern [*suntrechousēs*] in one "person" [*prosōpon*] and in one *hypostasis*. They are not divided or cut into two *prosōpa*, but are together the one and only and only-begotten Logos of God, the Lord Jesus Christ. Thus have the prophets of old testified; thus the Lord Jesus Christ himself taught us; thus the Symbol of the Father . . . has handed down [*paradedōke*] to us.[42]

But whether or not the fourth ecumenical *Council of Chalcedon* (451)—again, represented by the schools of Alexandria, Antioch, and Western Christianity—represents the pinnacle of ecumenical achievement in that it "was truly catholic in the very great degree in which it was the result of the shared theological wisdom of the Church,"[43] thus manifesting ecumenical energies "with a singleness of interest that is hard to duplicate,"[44] perhaps the recent criticisms of Chalcedon's doctrine overshadow its showcase of vigorous, single-minded ecumenism. For our purposes, a sampling of criticisms will suffice.

According to Douglas John Hall, the Chalcedonian doctrine of the two natures of Christ—with its "substantialistic language of the Greco-Roman,"[45] and thus betrayal of the "relational language" of Scripture—"assumes an ontology that is neither biblical nor contemporary."[46] Jon Sobrino asserts, with reference to the Chalcedonian formulation, that, seen from the lens of the contemporary situation, "[the Chalcedonian formulation] suffer[s] from a lack of concreteness, historicity, and relationality."[47] Not only does its "abstract manner"[48] betray the mindset that one knows *a priori* "who God is and what it means to be a human being,"[49] but that ultimately "it pays a price for this insofar as it says *less* than the New Testament does. For the [New Testament] tells us that the humanity of the eternal Son has a concrete, well-defined history; and that the reference-pole of that history is the Father and the kingdom of

---

42. "Definition of Chalcedon" (451), in Leith, *Creeds of the Churches*, 36.
43. Leith, *Creeds of the Churches*, 34.
44. Ibid., 35.
45. Hall, *Professing the Faith*, 399.
46. Ibid., 500.
47. Sobrino, *Christology at the Crossroads*, 329.
48. Ibid., 330.
49. Ibid., 329.

God."⁵⁰ In Leonardo Boff's words, the Chalcedonian formulation "runs the grave risk of placing God and humanity, the Infinite and the finite, the Creator and the creature, within the same horizon and on the same level."⁵¹ For ultimately, according to Boff, the formulation runs the risk of flattening-out, or domesticating God's transcendence through the mistaken attempt to interpret this doctrine as a "fusion of two essences and a unification of two dimensions."⁵² Isabel Carter Heyward asserts that, as the doctrine emphasizes Christ's personal unity "on the terms of, and at the initiative of, the divine, irrespective of the role of the human,"⁵³ it establishes a dominant motif—running headlong into her feminist critique—in which all life exists within an ontological structure of hierarchical dualism, in which the higher essence is the valuable essence."⁵⁴ Wolfhart Pannenberg, expounding upon what he calls the "impasse" created by every Christology which begins with the "incarnational concept,"⁵⁵ in addition to observing that the "concept of the incarnation" itself cannot explain the unity of God and man in Jesus Christ because the "incarnation" itself is an "expression of this unity,"⁵⁶ asserts that the problem with the two natures doctrine is that it speaks of the natures as if they were fundamentally on the "same plane."⁵⁷ Essentially, then, the real problem of the two natures doctrine is its attempt to conceive what happened in the incarnation as the "*synthesis* of the human and the divine nature in the same individual."⁵⁸ In the attempt to articulate this synthesis of natures, ultimately either the personal unity of Christ, or his "real humanity or true divinity [are] lost to view."⁵⁹

But if the recent "press" regarding the Chalcedonian formulation of the two natures of Christ is critical, to say the least, and Luther's interpretation of the *communicatio idiomatum* is obviously an interpreta-

---

50. Ibid., 332.
51. Boff, *Jesus Christ Liberator*, 194.
52. Ibid.
53. Heyward, *Redemption of God*, 192.
54. Ibid.
55. Pannenberg, *Jesus—God and Man*, 322.
56. Ibid.
57. Ibid.
58. Ibid.; italics added for emphasis.
59. Ibid.

tion of the Chalcedonian formulation,[60] then one perhaps may be able to predict the (critical!) theologial acclaim for Luther's "radical" interpretation of this same doctrine, a doctrine which he carries "to its peak and radicalizes ... as he makes it the hermeneutical motor of his whole theology[.]"[61] Again, for the purpose of our project, in order to place the *radix* of Luther's *theologia crucis*, or his *communicatio idiomatum*, in fuller theological context, only a sampling of signal criticisms will suffice.

Criticisms of Luther's Communicatio

Because chapter five, below, will be devoted to an elaboration of Karl Barth's Christology, a Christology constructed with a critical eye placed in the direction of Lutheran Christological endeavors, at this point it is enough to briefly touch upon Barth's criticism of Luther's *communicatio idomatum*. For now it is enough to know that Barth interpreted the major implication of Luther's *communicatio idiomatum*, especially with reference to the *genus maiestaticum* as it was articulated by Luther's successors, as nothing other than leading theology "smoothly and directly to anthropology ... a 'high-pitched' anthropology."[62] The result of Luther's Christology, for Barth, was nothing more than a "heaven-storming doctrine of the humanity of the Mediator" which did little more than lead to the "modern transition from theology to a speculative theology."[63] (See chapter five, below.) But if Barth could accuse Luther's doctrine of the *communicatio idiomatum*, especially with reference to the *genus maiestaticum*, of leading theology in the direction of talk that was "all too human," then, for Jürgen Moltmann, Luther's *communicatio idiomatum* betrays an opposite impulse. For if essentially the Chalcedonian formulation was conceived within the "Platonic axiom that God cannot suffer,"[64] and therefore within the "old axiom of divine immutability"[65] in which God is unable to suffer, and thus love ("Anyone who is able to love is able to suffer because he opens himself to the sufferings

60. Steiger, "*Communicatio Idiomatum*," 125.
61. Ibid.
62. CD IV/2:81–82.
63. Ibid., 83.
64. Moltmann, "The 'Crucified God,'" 287.
65. Ibid., 290.

that love brings"),⁶⁶ then for all of Luther's success in overcoming the Church's traditional "intellectual barrier against perceiving God in the death of Christ"⁶⁷ with regard to his *communicatio idiomatum*, it still "remains within the framework of the early church's doctrine of the two natures."⁶⁸ But what's more, according to Moltmann, Luther's *communicatio idiomatum* was never conceived of within a developed doctrine of the Trinity.⁶⁹ For it is the Trinity, according to Moltmann, which is both "God's essence,"⁷⁰ and helps us to more fully comprehend "God's inner-relationship to Jesus"⁷¹ in which Jesus' death becomes an event within the Godhead itself between Father and Son.⁷² According to Paul Althaus, although the core of Luther's "christological confession ... will always be significant"⁷³ in such a manner "that the Father's heart and will are present in Christ,"⁷⁴ its significance cannot keep theology from moving past it. In other words, as Althaus observes through a comparison of Luther's writings, though Luther is cited as positing the *genus tapeinoticon* as both complementing the *genus maiestaticum*, and being appropriately fundamental to his *communicatio idiomatum*,⁷⁵ because Luther vacillates on his articulation of whether or not (and if so, in what fashion) the deity suffered, "[Luther's] dogmatic theory which describes Christ as true God and true man is not unified within itself but displays contradictions. Theology had to go beyond it."⁷⁶ And though Ian Siggins' study⁷⁷ presents Luther's Christology in a positive light, he is able to observe that one's appropriation of Luther's *communicatio idiomatum* runs the risk of devolving them from their lived faith by replacing their lived faith with a dogmatic formula [the *communicatio idiomatum*] which thus "fails to clarify the faith [which it is] intended

66. Ibid., 288.
67. Moltmann, *Crucified God*, 234.
68. Ibid., 235.
69. Ibid.
70. Moltmann, "The 'Crucified God,'" 288.
71. Ibid.
72. Ibid., 295.
73. Althaus, *Theology of Martin Luther*, 198.
74. Ibid., 198.
75. Ibid., 197.
76. Ibid., 198.
77. Siggins, *Martin Luther's Doctrine of Christ*.

to express."⁷⁸ Additionally, Siggins also notes that Luther, for the sake of articulating his interpretation of the *communicatio idiomatum*, commandeers existing dogmatic formulations which "arose in the course of metaphysical analyses of the hypostatic union" and interprets them as functioning "merely as a descriptive grammar in the language of faith."⁷⁹ Ultimately, the "new wine" submits to the "old wineskins," or, according to Siggins, "remnants of a philosophical logic are imported unrecognized into what Luther intends to be biblical discourse."⁸⁰

But, having adduced various signal criticisms of both the Chalcedonian formulation of the two natures of Christ, and Luther's interpretation of the *communicatio idiomatum* itself, let us understand Luther's *communicatio idiomatum* on his own terms. For if, on account of the incarnation of Jesus Christ, there is both no relationship with God outside of the man Jesus, and, necessarily, Christ's humanity must be "bound to no particular spot," then we need to understand how Luther is able to conceptualize this man who "fills" heaven and earth to such an extent that he is the presence of "within-redemption" regarding all material, individual tombs.

Soteriologizing the Metaphysic

The fact that Luther was absolutely unwilling to identify God apart from the humanity of Christ was, as we have already stressed with top priority, no mere minor key of theological deliberation, but the unavoidable *Leitmotiv* of a thinking that was driven "aus *soteriologischem Interesse*";⁸¹ the motivation for such absolute identification was placed squarely on the shoulders of the question of who the sole author of one's justification is. Thus, in his 1535 lectures on Galatians 1:3, Luther asserted that "[W]henever you consider the doctrine of justification and wonder how or where or in what condition to find a God who justifies sinners, then you must know that there is no other God than this *Man* Jesus Christ."⁸² But indeed, as Oswald Bayer points out, even the basis for deliberating on the Trinity itself is subordinated, for Luther, to this

78. Siggins, *Martin Luther's Doctrine of Christ*, 222.
79. Ibid., 234.
80. Ibid.
81. Bayer, *Creator est Creatura:*, 22. Cf. Altmann's *Luther and Liberation*, 23–24.
82. LW 26:29; italics added for emphasis.

concrete, human starting point, or the humanity of Christ. For, according to Bayer, in contradistinction to the Scholastics who preceded him, Luther's thinking on the Trinity itself emanates not from categories of abstract "generalization" and "potentiality," but he "begins with the biblical witness to the fact of the incarnation. Accordingly, he does not open his disputation theses on the doctrine of the Trinity with a "prologue in heaven," but rather with that Word through which the Father presents the historical Son: "[This is my beloved Son with whom I am well pleased;] listen to him!" (Mt 17:5) The question about the possibility for thinking is put aside."[83]

But, as this is the case, that God is to be identified and deliberated on solely with reference to the concrete, particular man Jesus, and, since the incarnation, there is no valid relationship with God apart from the humanity of Christ, then *how* Luther is able to theologically articulate this absolute identification—in all locations of God's activity—between the "humanity" and "divinity" of God the Son becomes "the touchstone of true theology" and indeed the center of his exposition of theology.[84] As we will see, it is both Luther's "ignorant" starting point regarding all theological deliberation, and the expression of that "ignorant" starting point, or Luther's radical interpretation of Chalcedon's (451) doctrine of the two natures of Christ that is employed in expressing this absolute identification. Ultimately not only will we discover that Luther's "Christology is really the doctrine of the *communicatio idiomatum*,"[85]

83. "Setzt beim biblisch bezeugten Faktum der Inkarnation an; dementsprechend eröffnet er seine Disputationsthesen über die Trinitätslehre nicht mit einem 'Prolog im Himmel,' sondern mit jenem Word, durch das der Vater den Sohn geschichtlich präsentiert: '[Dies ist mein Lieber Sohn, an welchem ich Wohlgefallen habe;] den sollt ihr hören!' (Mt 17,5). Die Frage nach der Denkmöglichkeit wird von Luther zurückgestellt." Bayer, *Creator est Creatura*, 22.

84. Lienhard, Luther: *Witness to Christ*, 335.

85. "Christologie is geradezu *Idiomenkommunicationslehre* . . ." Bayer, *Creator est Creatura*, 23. At this point in our project a full delineation of both Luther's Christology and its development could certainly be warranted without much argument. But on account of both the focus of this chapter—a development of Luther's interpretation of the *communicatio idiomatum* as the *radix* of his *theologia crucis*—and the shear scope of such a project that included an in depth delineation of Luther's Christology—along with its development—in addition to the focus of this project, I simply give the reader a few concise overviews/outlines of Luther's Christology. These include Lohse, *Martin Luther's Theology*, 219–31, Altmann, *Luther and Liberation*, 213–25, and Braaten, "True Humanity of Christ" and "True Divinity of Christ" (see especially 507–8, 522, 533–34). Basing his observation on Luther's articulation of the second article of the Apostles'

but that indeed Luther's *Idiomenkommunicationslehre* is able to express a human Redeemer—absolutely identified with the Creator's Word—who not only "fills" heaven and earth with his redeeming presence, but becomes the presence of "within-redemption" with reference to all of humanity's individual tombs. But, first, what do we mean by his "ignorant" starting point? The answer to this question will lay the foundation for his interpretation of the two-natures doctrine, or the expression of his "ignorant" theological starting point.

Instead of first elaborating a theory with regard to God's "honour and majesty" and then thinking in the habit that God's majesty eludes us unless we seek to attain it "by cutting away what is human,"[86] rather, Luther deliberates in such a manner that he is "ignorant about God" and thus "unable by speculation to produce a single thought about God: for this reason he has nowhere else he can go but to the humanity of Christ when he wants to seize hold of God."[87] More specifically, according to Gustaf Wingren, "Apart from the Gospel [of the justification of sinners] Luther had no concept of God into which he could have fitted the revelation in Christ as a significant modification of our knowledge of God. Rather he starts by knowing nothing of God, then he stands before Christ's cross; and afterwards he seizes upon the words and expression that he has been able to find in the Gospel to state the fact that *here*, in this humiliation, *God dwells*."[88]

If this is the case, then, not only is Christ's humanity *not* a mere *provisional* vestibule simply to be jettisoned when God's revelation of himself is completed, but it is revealed that Christ *is* man, then his divinity is absolutely inseparable—at all times and all locations—from

---

Creed in his Small Catechism, Lohse points out—with reference to the peculiarity of Luther's Christology—that "The explanation thus affirms in most tightly concentrated form the ancient church's two-natures doctrine, the new Reformation emphasis on Jesus as Lord, and the doctrine of redemption. The three themes are fused here into a unity, without giving priority to one or the other" (ibid., 221). Further elaborating the peculiarities of Luther's Christology, Lohse also observes that Luther's Christology, additionally, is both grounded within—and moves beyond—the Alexandrian "Word became flesh" motif (ibid., 228), and sharpens the doctrine of the *enhypostasis* "to read that the human nature of Jesus Christ has no *hypostasis* . . . of its own but possesses it in the divine manner" (ibid., 229).

86. Wingren, *Living Word*, 208.
87. Ibid., 212.
88. Ibid., 205.

his humanity.[89] Thus, as the divine attributes are singly identified "with reference to *redemption* and were thus drawn from the actual *Gospel*,"[90] then, for Luther, "Majesty lies in the manger and hangs on the cross[.]"[91] But, if the incarnation alone defines both the *modus operandi* of theological deliberation, and allows the theologian to identify the divine attributes singly with reference to redemption, then, for Luther, this has dramatic implications for the language of theology itself. For, as Bayer points out, and as we will see developed, "Theology must speak a '*novis linguis*' from its center, from soteriology and Christology. In this fashion it determines anew concepts such as 'man,' 'God,' 'Creator,' 'creature,' and, because of that, it determines anew the relation between Creator and creation."[92] But now we must ask: how is this "ignorant" starting point which results in a theological "novis linguis"[93] expressed? We now turn to the expression of the "ignorant" starting which results in Luther's radical interpretation of Chalcedon's two-natures of Christ, or the foundation of his *theologia crucis*.

Theologians such as Oswald Bayer,[94] Kjell Ove Nilsson,[95] Gustaf Wingren,[96] Marc Lienhard,[97] and Johan Anselm Steiger[98] concur on the central role of Luther's radical interpretation of the Council of Chalcedon's (451) doctrine of the two natures of Christ, or his articulation of the *communicatio idiomatum*, for the delineation of his

89. Ibid., 210.

90. Ibid., 206.

91. Ibid.

92. "Die Theologie muß von ihrer Mitte, von der Soteriologie und Christologie, her 'novis linguis' sprechen. Auf diese Weise bestimmt sie Begriffe wie 'homo,' 'deus,' 'creator,' 'creatura' und damit das Verhältnis von Schöpfer und Geschöpf neu." Bayer, *Creator est Creatura*, 21.

93. For an explicit development of this "novis linguis" by Luther with regard to the *communicatio idiomatum*, see Tolpingrud's translation of Luther's *Disputatio de divinitate et humanitated Christi* (1540) or "Luther's Disputation Concerning the Divinity and the Humanity of Christ." See also Vind, "'Christus factus est peccatum metaphorice'"; and Hinlicky, "Luther's Anti-Docetism in the Disputatio de divinitate et humanitate Christi."

94. Bayer, *Creator est Creatura*, 10–34.

95. Nilsson, *Simul: Das Miteinander von Göttlichem und Menschlichem*.

96. Wingren, *Living Word*.

97. Lienhard, *Luther: Witness to Christ*.

98. Steiger, "*Communicatio Idiomatum* as the Axle and Motor of Luther's Theology," 125–58. See also his *Fünf Zentralthemen der Theologie Luthers*, 3–51.

entire theology. For, according to Steiger, "[Luther] carries this doctrine to its peak and radicalizes it as he makes it the hermeneutical motor of his whole theology, or an axle around which many other theological themes now begin to turn[.]"[99] Thus, as Steiger observes, not only Christology, but the doctrine of justification, the doctrine of the Lord's Supper, hermeneutics, rhetoric, pastoral care, the doctrine of creation, and theological anthropology are all *loci* which are informed, or woven-together, by Luther's interpretation of the *communicatio idiomatum*.[100] Citing the fact that *life* and *blessedness* itself rest, for Luther, upon the *communicatio idiomatum*, or the absolute unity of Christ's humanity and divinity, the centrality of Luther's *communicatio idiomatum*—not a consequence, but an expression of the redemptive unity of Christ's person—is perhaps expressed most poignantly by Nilsson who avers that

> Therefore Luther's entire theology stands and falls with the *communicatio idiomatum*. The *communicatio* is really—and this is an extremely important ascertainment—not more or less an immaterial, decorative accessory to Luther's theological construct. It is also not a completely unnecessary doctrine which one could derive through a particularly bold and risky conclusion from Luther's thought on a unity in Christ's person and work. The doctrine of the *communicatio idiomatum* is *not at all a mere consequence* of the unity in Christ, rather it is *an expression of this unity itself* and the whole basis on which, for Luther, life and happiness rests.[101]

But, let us ask, *why* is the *communicatio idiomatum* so foundational to Luther's theological program? Again we shall return to the fact that Luther's "christology is above all soteriology."[102]

99. Steiger, "*Communicatio Idiomatum*," 125.

100. Ibid.

101. "Deswegen steht und fällt mit der communication idiomatum Luthers ganzes theologisches Denken. Die communicatio ist wirklich—und das ist eine äußerst wichtige Feststellung—kein mehr oder weniger gleichgültiges, dekoratives Beiwerk auf Luthers theologischem Gebäude, sie ist auch keine eigentlich ganz überflüssige Lehre, die man durch besonders kühne und halsbrecherische Schlußfolgerung aus dem Gedanken an eine unitas in Christi Person und Werk ableiten könnte. Die Lehre von der communicatio idiomatum ist überhaupt *keine bloße Konsequenz* der Einheit in Christus, sondern *ein Ausdruck dieser Einheit selbst* und des ganzen Fundamentes, worauf für Luther Leben und Seligkeit ruhen." Nilsson, *Simul*, 228.

102. Lienhard, *Luther: Witness to Christ*, 372.

Regarding the unity of the person of Christ, as Wingren points out, soteriological rationale declares both that if Christ does not become human, humanity is lost, and if Christ is a human, Satan is lost.[103] This logic involves a strict, material unity between the divine and the human natures in the person of Christ with regard to the matter of human redemption. Commensurate with this rationale, and countering a merely nominal articulation of Christ's personal unity which would compromise the work of redemption and abrogate human assurance regarding that same redemption, Nilsson further elaborates this point by asserting that

> for Luther everything depends on the matter that Christ—who is truly the united, divine-human one—has accomplished the work of redemption *pro nobis*. And because the unity of the action itself is connected with the unity of the person, in which the *communicatio* doctrine is the center, therefore the *communicatio* comprises the core of Luther's theology. This means: when Luther's interpretation of the *communicatio* is not accepted, the unity becomes—as Luther puts it—a mere "manner of speaking." With that, the work of redemption in Christ would both be relinquished, and the dispensation of this work, for Luther, would also become a meaningless undertaking which in such a case could not be dispensed with assurance to humans.[104]

At the same time, for Luther, if the unity of Christ as expressed in the *communicatio idiomatum* insures an absolute material *unity* within the person of Christ with regard to the work of redemption, it also insures an inalterable material *identity* which guarantees that Christ cannot be employed either as a moralistic, urchristian "superman," or as a nightmarish "God-judge." Elaborating this point, Nilsson again avers regarding the fundamental importance of Luther's *communicatio idi-*

---

103. Wingren, *Living Word*, 210.

104. "... für Luther alles darauf ankommt, daß Christus wirklich das einheitliche, gottmenschliche Erlösungswerk pro nobis ausgeführt hat, und weil die Einheitlichkeit dieser Handlung ihrerseits mit der unitas der Person zusammenhängt, wobei die communicatio-Lehre das Zentrum bildet, deswegen macht die communicatio idiomatum das Herzstück der Theologie Luthers aus. Das heißt: wenn die communicatio in Luthers Deutung nicht gelten darf, wird die Einheit, wie Luther es ausdrücken kann, zu einer bloßen 'Redeweise'. Damit wäre auch das Erlösungswerk in Christus preisgegeben und damit würde für Luther auch die Austeilung dieses Werkes zu einem bedeutungslosen Unternehmen, den in solchem Fall könnte nichts mit Sicherheit an die Menschen ausgeteilt werden." Nilsson, *Simul*, 228.

omatum, that "it expresses the relation between divine and human, and for Luther, is unavoidable unless one wishes to make of Christ either a perfect 'super-human,' or a terrifying 'God-judge.' In both cases redemption is nullified."[105] But, ultimately, with all that we have already said with regard to the central significance of Luther's *communicatio idiomatum*, according to Lienhard's evaluation, the *communicatio idiomatum* can be identified under three central points of reference. According to Lienhard, in addition to Luther's ability to both implement the *communicatio idiomatum* in such a fashion as to make "room for the living God proclaimed by the Holy Scripture"[106] against traditional metaphysical conceptions of God, and delineate the peculiarity of this particular human Christ,[107] Lienhard first observes that the *communicatio idiomatum*, for Luther, underscores the centrality of the revelation of God in Jesus Christ. For "[t]he unity of God and humanity in Christ must be so strongly emphasized because from now on God wishes to be found no longer apart from the man Jesus."[108] Thus, Lienhard adds, the *communicatio idiomatum* emphasizes the rudimentary theme, for Luther, "that since the incarnation, there is no longer any valid relationship with God which is not also a relationship with the man Jesus. There where God reveals himself, the man must be present also."[109] Second, Luther's interpretation and employment of the *communicatio idiomatum* affords him the ability to elaborate the unity between God's work of creation and redemption. This is to say, according to Lienhard, that "no less than that from the beginning the creative activity of God, in the person of the Logos, did not occur independently of the man Jesus, but in union with him."[110] Therefore, if we are able to assert that not only does the incarnation lead us to the cross' work of redemption, but also back to the meaning of creation itself, then, through the *communicatio idiomatum*, we are able to reverse the logic and assert that it is the creating Word,

---

105. " . . . sie drückt das Verhältnis zwischen Göttlichem und Menschlichem aus und is für Luther unausweichlich, wenn nicht Christus entweder zum perfkten Übermenschen oder zum richtenden Schreckensgott werden soll. In beiden Fällen wird die Erlösung zunichte," ibid., 171.

106. Lienhard, *Luther: Witness to Christ*, 343.

107. Ibid., 343–44.

108. Ibid., 341.

109. Ibid., 342.

110. Ibid.

or God himself who effects the work of creation, who is crucified and dies. Thus, again, there is no "rift" between the Creator's work and the Redeemer's work.[111] This one, particular, concrete Word is completely identified with both. So Nilsson asserts, "He demonstrates the connection from the unity between creation and redemption, the first and second article. The same God who has created the world has been nailed to the cross of Golgotha in the man Jesus. And he, who lay in Bethlehem's trough, was, as well, at the creation of the world and sits at God's right hand."[112] Also, with regard to this point, Philip Watson observes that the *communicatio idiomatum* insures that "wheresoever and howsoever [God] acts, His activity springs from no other source than the love that is revealed in Christ."[113] And, third, Lienhard observes a soteriological dimension to Luther's interpretation of the *communicatio idiomatum*. For as redemption is understood through the indivisible union of the Word, thus, "For the believer, it is essential to know that the acts and exploits of the man Jesus are not those of some saint or superman, but that they are the acts and exploits of God. And, on the other hand, the God who saves me must not be sought anywhere except in the form of the man Jesus."[114] But what ultimately interests us here, for the purpose of this project, is the specific connection between Luther's interpretation of the *communicatio idiomatum* and his conceptualization—at a foundational level—of his *theologia crucis*. Here we discover the fundamental ontology of Chalcedon's two-natures doctrine radically reappropriated for the sake of the priority of soteriological concerns.

According to Steiger, the *communicatio idiomatum* forms the foundation of Luther's *theologia crucis*. Steiger asserts, and I quote him at length, "So Luther even calls this God naked in the manger the "diaper Lord and manger prince," and again and again it becomes clear: for Luther, the birth of Jesus is not only part of the humiliation, but also al-

---

111. Ibid., 343.

112. "Er zeigt den Zusammenhang von und die Einheit zwischen Schöpfung und Erlösung, erstem und zweeitem Artikel auf. Derselbe Gott, der die Welt geschaffen hat, ist im Menschen Jesus an das Kreuz von Golgath genagelt worden, und er, der in Bethlehems Krippe lag, war bei der Erschaffung der Welt mit dabei und sitzt zu Gottes rechter Seite." Nilsson, *Simul*, 245.

113. Watson, *Let God be God*, 136.

114. Lienhard, *Luther: Witness to Christ*, 343. Cf. Lars Thunberg, "The Cosmological and Anthropological Significance of Christ's Redeeming Work," 79; Nilsson, *Simul*, 228, 243ff.; and Bayer, *Creator est Creatura*, 22ff.

ready the beginning of the passion, and, of the suffering not only of the human nature in Christ, but of God himself, which has its high point in the deepest trouble in the Garden of Gethsemane and on the cross."[115] For Luther, as the *theologia crucis* finds its foundation already in the *communicatio idiomatum*'s radical exchange of the essential properties of the divine and human properties in the indivisible person of Jesus Christ, so he also applied "the metaphysical ontology of the early church's two-natures doctrine soteriologically and thus historicized the metaphysics, in this way furthering with consistency a process of historicization of metaphysics that had already begun in the early church."[116] In short, not only is the original metaphysical ontology of the two-nature doctrine now historicized and reappropriated with reference to a more radical interpretation of Christ's person and work "for us,"[117] but by doing so, Steiger points out, Luther is more radically able to illustrate the realization that "[b]y becoming human, God himself not only comes near to the human being, but becomes what human beings are, and is nearer to them than husband and wife are near to each other."[118] Thus, just as the two-natures "metaphysic" is "soteriologically historicized" for the sake of the *pro nobis*, so also all things which are stated with reference to the human nature of Christ may also be simultaneously referred to the one who is baptized into Christ, creating a perichoresis between Christ and human which is analogous to the perichoresis of natures in the person of Christ.[119] We are *simul iustus et peccator* through the incarnation of Christ.[120] Thus Steiger is able to observe regarding Luther's soteriological historicization of the *communicatio idiomatum*'s *pro nobis* that "By becoming a human, God takes on not only a human nature but also the whole of humanity and makes his own everything that constitutes this humanity: mortality, neediness, sin and corruption, yes, the whole judgment of God's anger over humans. But, in the opposite direction, everything that really belongs to God alone is made proper to the human: righteousness, eternal life and glory."[121]

115. Steiger, "*Communicatio Idiomatum*," 128.
116. Ibid., 128–29.
117. Ibid., 129.
118. Ibid., 130.
119. Ibid., 136.
120. See Nilsson, *Simul*, 313–15.
121. Steiger, "*Communicatio Idiomatum*," 138.

But, having articulated—perhaps at the very least outlined the fundamental dynamics—the point that the *communicatio idiomatum*, through its radical interpretation, is the foundation of Luther's *theologia crucis*, or articulation of "within-redemption" with regard to humanity, how can we be so sure that Luther is not repeating the mistake of Lewis? that redemption will "take place"—when the time so comes—within our particular tombs themselves? that the historicization of the two-natures metaphysic for soteriological purposes actually will involve the material redemption of our particular narratives within creation, within history, and thus within our same narratives without referring us to another "most real" narrative redemption of which our narratives are only "things signified"?

In order to answer these questions, the elaboration of our answer will require a concrete exposition of Luther's radical interpretation of the unity of Christ's person. This exposition, then, will both allow us to both bring Luther's *communicatio idiomatum* out of the stage of description (primarily through secondary sources), and lead us into a stage of application, or take us through the steps which allow us to place this same person—the real presence of the Word of "within-redemption"—within our very tombs. To accomplish this task, we will primarily appeal to Luther's *On the Councils and the Church* (1539). It is in this writing that Luther's radical interpretation of the two natures of Christ receives sustained, concrete application both with regard to an interpretation of Chalcedon and soteriological concerns. Ultimately, at the core of Luther's *theologia crucis*, we will discover Luther's articulation of the "third mode" of Christ's bodily presence. Our answer will be developed in two steps. But let us begin with Luther's concrete exposition of Chalcedon's two-natures doctrine, or his radical interpretation of the unity of the divine and human *idiomata* in Christ's person, as it is attested in his oft-neglected writing from 1539, or *On the Councils and the Church*.[122] And let us bear in mind: How does Luther express the communication of the divine and human attributes in such a manner as to insure that the Word of redemption revealed in Jesus Christ is the same real presence of "within-redemption" within, ultimately, my very tomb?

---

122. LW 41:9–178.

Advice on Communicating? Be Direct!

As God "does not wish that [we] seek him . . . apart from the Word,"[123] and indeed God "makes and does nothing except through his Word," then it is also essential that we place on equal footing Luther's assertion that "where you place God for me, you must also place the humanity for me. They simply will not let themselves be separated and divided from each other."[124] In other words, a Christian, for Luther, cannot speak of the presence and activity of the Word *sans* the divinity of Christ, for were she to do so, she would cease to be encountered by a Creator whose Word both everywhere and at all times "creates, effects, and preserves all things through his almighty power and right hand,"[125] and is "full of divinity . . . eternal good, life, and salvation." At the same time, a Christian cannot speak of the presence and activity of the Word *sans* the humanity of Christ, for were she to do so, she would not only be speaking of another word apart from the one by whom God has encountered sinners *pro nobis*, but she would be speaking of a "god" apart from the one who, sitting on the "scale" and becoming human, redeems "from within" the whole of humanity through his assumption of the flesh.[126] In short, the presence and activity of the Word without the flesh of humanity is the presence and activity of a God *other* than the One who reveals salvation, or "within-redemption," while the presence and activity of the Word without divinity would simply be a Word that left sinners to their own devices in the attainment of redemption. With this stated, we turn to Luther's *On the Councils and the Church* (1539) in which he explicitly exposits, in the course of radically interpreting the Chalcedonian formulation of the two-natures of Christ, both the indivisibility of the divine and human natures in the one Word of God, and delineates the nature of their communication within that Word. As we will see, Luther accomplishes this task while providing an interpretation of the Christological controversies pertaining to the "heresies" of Nestorius and Eutyches and their attempted resolution through the Church's ecumenical councils.

---

123. LW 36:342.
124. LW 37:219.
125. Ibid., 57–58.
126. LW 41:103.

Contrary to popular caricatures, according to Luther, Nestorius did not believe in two Christ's, or two persons, but only one Christ, and one person. Indeed, Nestorius subscribed to the belief that "Christ was true God born of the Father in eternity, as the Nicene council had defended, and afterward born of a true man of the Virgin Mary."[127] Thus "staunchly did he regard Christ as true God and man."[128] "Moreover," Luther adds, "he also conceded that Christ, God's Son, was born of the Virgin Mary into his humanity, not into his divinity, which we and all Christians also say."[129] But the problem arose for Nestorius in that "he did not want Mary to be called mother of God because of this, since Christ did not derive his divinity, or, to express it plainly, since Christ did not derive his divinity from her as he did his humanity."[130] So, according to Luther, we have arrived at the central "bone of contention" regarding the error of Nestorius' thinking: although "We too know very well that God did not derive his divinity from Mary ... [we know that] it does not follow that it is therefore wrong to say that God was born of Mary, that God is Mary's Son, and that Mary is God's mother."[131] For, essentially, Nestorius' error was not—Luther asserts against traditional caricatures—that "he believed Christ to be a pure man, or that he made two persons of him" but that "after he concedes that God and man are united and fused into one person, he can in no way deny [which he does, contradicting his original premise] that the *idiomata* of the two natures should also be united and fused. Otherwise, what could God and man united in one person be?"[132] For instead of defining the natures of Christ through the priority, or original premise, of their unity, Nestorius allows their individual attributes, conceptualized in *a priori* fashion, to determine his conceptualization of the unity of Christ's person. For how can we confess that God and man are united and fused in the one person of Christ and *not* declare that "Mary suckled God, rocked God to sleep, prepared broth and soup for God?"[133] Is this not the nullification of his own original confession of Christ's unity?

127. Ibid., 98.
128. Ibid.
129. Ibid.
130. Ibid.
131. Ibid., 99.
132. Ibid., 100.
133. Ibid., 101.

But, Luther observes, if it seems strange that God assumes human attributes, should not have Nestorius originally thought "it equally strange that God becomes man . . . [in the first place]?"[134] The *radix* of the problem, according to Luther, is that Nestorius will not allow for a *communicatio idiomatum*. For "This crude, unlearned man did not see that he was asserting the impossible when simultaneously he seriously took Christ to be God and man in one person and yet declined to ascribe the *idiomata* of the natures to the same person of Christ."[135] Elaborating this logic contra Nestorius, Luther avers that

> [I]f I were to say, "There goes God down the street, fetching water and bread so that he might eat and drink with his mother," Nestorius would not grant me this, but says, "To fetch water, buy bread, to have another, to eat and drink with her, are *idiomata* or attributes of human not of divine nature." And again, if I say "The carpenter Jesus was crucified by the Jews and the same Jesus is true God," Nestorius would agree that this is true. But if I say, "God was crucified by the Jews," he says, "No! For crucifixion and death are *idiomata* or attributes not of divine but of human nature.[136]

But if, ultimately for Nestorius, the *idiomata naturae humanae*, or those qualities which are inherent in the created nature of humanity ("such as dying, suffering, weeping, speaking, laughing, eating, drinking, sleeping, sorrowing, standing, working, sitting, lying down")[137] are not allowed to directly communicate with the *idiomata Dei*, or attributes inherent in the divine nature (immortality, omnipotence, infinity, unbegottenness and non-capability/necessity of eating, drinking, sleeping, standing, walking, sorrowing, weeping),[138] then "he means to say with this that Christ is indeed God, but God is not crucified."[139] For, ultimately, "He had in mind . . . that God and death are irreconcilable. It seemed terrible to him to hear that God should die. His meaning was that Christ, in his divinity, was immortal[.]"[140]

134. Ibid., 100.
135. Ibid., 102
136. Ibid., 101.
137. Ibid., 100.
138. Ibid., 101.
139. Ibid., 102.
140. Ibid.

The upshot of all of this is, according to Luther, stressing that Christians must, based upon the premise of Christ's unity, necessarily allow for a direct *communicatio idiomatum* within the one person of Christ—recognizing that whatever is said of Jesus as a man is simultaneously said of him as God (and vice-versa, but certainly emphasizing the former assertion as even more fundamental)—runs straight to the heart of Luther's articulation of the *theologia crucis* and its "within-redemption." For if we are tempted to trod the path of Nestorius, Luther reminds us that

> We Christians should know that if God is not in the scale to give it weight, we, on our side sink to the ground. I mean it this way: if it cannot be said that God died for us, but only a man, we are lost; but if God's death and a dead God lie in the balance, his side goes down and ours goes up like a light and empty scale. Yet he can also readily go up again, or leap out of the scale! But he could not sit on the scale unless he had become a man like us, so that it could be called God's dying, God's martyrdom, God's blood, and God's death. For God in is own nature cannot die; but now that God and man are united in one person, it is called God's death when the man dies who is one substance or one person with God.[141]

Ultimately, contra Nestorius, Mary is *Theotokos* and God was crucified. The *idiomata* of the human nature must be given directly to the divine nature if the Word is one.[142] But with this Christo-logic founded upon the priority of Christ's incarnation having been applied to Nestorius, Luther has now only to turn his cheek in the opposite direction in order to greet Eutyches with this same Christo-logic.

For, according to Luther, as "Nestorius does not want to give the *idiomata* of the humanity to the divinity in Christ, even though he maintains that Christ is God and man," Luther astutely observes regarding Eutyches, on the other hand, that he "does not want to give the *idiomata* of divinity to the humanity, though he also maintains that Christ is true God and true man."[143] Again, the issue, or logic, is the same. So Luther can aver with regard to Eutyches that "[I]f I continue and preach that this same man Christ is creator of heaven and earth, then Eutyches

---

141. Ibid., 103–4.
142. Ibid., 104.
143. Ibid., 109.

takes offense and is outraged at the words, 'A man created heaven and earth,' and says 'No! Such a divine *idioma* (as creating heaven) does not appertain to man.' But he forgets that he previously conceded that Christ is true God and man in one person and nevertheless refuses to admit the conclusion or 'the premise for a good conclusion.'"[144] Essentially, then, instead of allowing the unity of Christ's person in the incarnation (and, according to Luther, Eutyches never explicitly refuted the priority of this unity, but only denied it in his articulation of the relation of the two natures!) to determine the relation and function of the attributes of the divine and human natures in Christ, Eutyches allows *a priori*, abstract, conceptualizations of the individual natures to determine their interaction with one another within the person of Christ. Whereas Nestorius—because of his abstract Christo-logic—was unable to accept such realities as "Mary suckling God" or "God being crucified," Eutyches was unable to accept that "The man Jesus created the heavens and the earth," or "The man Jesus is omnipotent." For what both men had in common was the inability to allow the priority of the incarnation, and thus unity of Christ's person—thinking "ignorantly" (Wingren) from it alone—to destroy their *a priori*, "pure forms"[145] of both "humanity" and "divinity" as they are considered in the abstract, in isolation. For, ultimately, according to Luther, whoever confesses such a unity with reference to the person of Christ—thus allowing their theo-logic to be dictated by the incarnation alone—should necessarily be able to "unquestionably concede that this man Christ, born of Mary, is creator of heaven and earth; for he has become this one person, namely, God who

---

144. Ibid.

145. See Latour, *We Have Never Been Modern*, 76ff., for the development of this phrase within the context of conceptualizing "modernity." Employing Latour's discussion, Jesus Christ, far from being a "hybrid" consisting of two originally "pure forms," i.e., "divine nature" and "human nature," is a "mediator." A "mediator"—thinking "ignorantly" on the basis of the incarnation alone (Wingren)—"is an original event and creates what it translates as well as the entities between which it plays the mediating role" (ibid., 78). "Modernity," according to Latour, managed to cancel out such an understanding of a "mediator"—in our case applied to the incarnation of Christ—"*By conceiving every hybrid as a mixture of two pure forms*" (ibid.). The conversation regarding the "*novis linguis*" (Bayer) resulting from Luther's radical interpretation of the *communicatio idiomatum* may also be posed within Latour's framework of "pure forms." Latour's work has significant implications for Christology.

created heaven and earth."[146] Such a conclusion is unavoidable when the premise of unity is posited.[147]

Eventually, Luther concludes, "Eutyches' heresy must be regarded contradictory because he regards Christ God and man, but refuses to ascribe the *idiomata* of the divine nature to the human nature; just as Nestorius, on the other hand, would not ascribe the *idiomata* of the human nature to God in the one person of Christ."[148] Ultimately, as Luther asserts again and again, "whoever confesses the two natures in Christ, God and man, must also ascribe the *idiomata* of both to the person; for to be God and man means nothing if they do not share their *idiomata*."[149]

For if the Word is a unity consisting of a flesh by which God both encounters sinners *pro nobis* and sits on the "scale" in order to redeem humanity "from within," and a divinity which both "creates, effects, and preserves all things" and is "full of . . . eternal good, life, and salvation," then, for Luther—maintaining that apart from this Word there is no God—the priority of this unity must be maintained at all points of one's Christology: for as God does not wish to be known apart from his Word,[150] he also "makes and does nothing except through [that same] Word."[151] Ultimately Luther declares with regard to the unity of the humanity and divinity in Jesus Christ, and I quote him at length

> And if you could show me one place where God is and not the man, then the person is already divided and I could at once say truthfully, "Here is God who is not man and has never become man." But no God like that for me! For it would follow from this that space and place had separated the two natures from one another and thus had divided the person, even though death and all the devils had been unable to separate and tear them apart. This would leave me a poor sort of Christ, if he were present only at one single place, as a divine and human person, and if at all other places he had to be nothing more than a mere isolated God and a divine person without humanity. No, comrade, wherever you place God for me, you must also place the humanity

---

146. LW 41:109.
147. Ibid.
148. Ibid., 117–18.
149. Ibid., 118.
150. LW 36:342.
151. LW 37:61.

for me. They simply will not let themselves be separated and divided from each other.[152]

Thus, as the Word of the Creator is the Word of the Redeemer, so the Word of the Redeemer is the Word of the Creator; an absolute identification. *But let us underscore the implications of all that we have developed*: If the inability to "give" the human *idiomata* to the divine nature in the person of Christ (Nestorius' error) results in a God who has not entered the "scale" of "within-redemption," and thus for whom—as the Creator—an inviolable *pro nobis* commitment to and identification with sinners is *not* inextricable with his identity, then the inability to give the divine *idiomata* to the human nature in the person of Christ (Eutyches' error) results in a God for whom—as the Redeemer (and particularly as the "within-Redeemer")—a complete identification with the Creator's agency, and ultimately (based upon the immanence of that activity) creation itself, is *not* inextricable with his identity. But if the *idiomata* of both natures are directly, fully ascribed to one another within the person of Christ, then not only are Creator and Redeemer absolutely identified, but, ultimately, for our specific purpose, that identity's real presence, or the Word, necessarily extends all the way to the "within-locations" of humanity's tombs as the presence of God's "within-redemption." As we will see, Luther calls this the "third mode" of Christ's bodily presence. It is here, as we will develop, via the "third mode" of Christ's bodily presence that "within-redemption" becomes complete. And again, as we have already pointed out, the "third mode" of Christ's bodily presence is nothing other than a necessary expression of the complete identification between the agency of the Creator and the Redeemer in the one, indivisible Word of God revealed in the incarnation.

Summation and Segue

Earlier, above, we could commend Alan Lewis for his ability to articulate the *triduum* of Jesus Christ in such manner that God could not only be delineated as the presence of "within-redemption" in Jesus' Saturday sepulcher, but indeed the merit of his proposal consisted in the fact that Saturday—through a focus on the temporal narrative—became a *cordon sanitaire* preventing the encroachment of Easter Sunday back

---

152. Ibid., 218–19.

upon the events of Friday and Saturday. But for all the good this has accomplished with regard to maintaining the integrity of Jesus' own Friday/Saturday narrative, and of our ability to more clearly perceive the presence-amid-absence of God; indeed, of comprehending God's radical presence within the horrifying crucifixion and eternal silence of the respective days, in the process of his articulation, Lewis has removed the presence of "within-redemption" from the very intended object of that same redemption, or the concrete narratives of particular, embodied humans. In short, through his employment of Jesus' narrative as a "signifier" of our own particular, embodied narratives, Lewis has removed the very deaths and—ultimately—tombs from the presence of "within-redemption" for which his theology of Holy Saturday originally intended to articulate the "within-redemption" of "resumption beyond rupture." The particularity of created, embodied humans becomes nothing other than a "signified" reality of "within-redemption" which has already taken place in Jesus, the "signifier"; God's presence in Jesus' narrative signifies our own narratives. What good, we asked, is a "within-redemption" of "resumption beyond rupture" if it is not present and "within" our particular narratives? Ultimately, Lewis does the very thing with regard to all of humanity's narratives he intends not to do with reference to Jesus Christ's narrative: He allows "Sunday" so to color all of our "Fridays" and "Saturdays" that indeed all particular "Fridays" and "Saturdays" are abandoned. But, as of the writing of this project, people (in their irreducible, particular narratives) are still suffering, dying, and lying in their tombs awaiting a complete bodily redemption "from within." And nothing can be a substitute for this redemption; it must be a "within-redemption" within the particular narratives of all humanity lest the scope of the Word's *redemption* become reduced to something less than the material embodiment which was *created* and declared "very good" at the very beginning.[153]

Countering this quandary, we have been developing Luther's *theologia crucis* and, ultimately, his foundational articulation of "within-redemption" through his radical interpretation of the *communicatio idiomatum*. Ultimately, in our development of Luther's radical interpretation of the *communicatio idiomatum* (certainly countering the errors of Nestorius and Eutyches), we have discovered that when both natures are directly "given" to one another within the priority of the personal

---

153. Genesis 1:31.

union of Christ, then not only are the agency of Creator and Redeemer absolutely identified through the one Word, but indeed the Word necessarily extends all the way to the "within-locations" of humanity's tombs as the real presence of God's "within-redemption." Thus, again, as we will see, this is called the "third mode" of Christ's bodily presence, or Christ's redeeming presence within all particular tombs.

But now we must ask, understanding that God does not wish to be known apart from his Word, if the inability to the give the divine *idiomata* to the human nature in the person of Christ results in a God for whom—as the Redeemer—a complete identification with the Creator's agency is *not* inextricable with his identity, then how does Luther articulate that very agency of the Creator? The articulation of this agency will dictate how Luther is able to avoid the aforementioned pitfall of Lewis' articulation of "within-redemption." It is here, in the development of our answer, that we discover how, through Luther's interpretation of the *communicatio idiomatum*, "within-redemption" becomes completely "within." Ultimately the "third mode" of Christ's bodily presence is the absolute identification of Christ's humanity with the Creator's all-embracing agency.

The "Third Mode" of Christ's Presence

If—as will be more fully developed shortly—God's all-embracing activity, or omnipotence, is "an essential aspect of Luther's concept of God," coloring "everything that [he] says [with regard to God],"[154] then, essentially for Luther, being God and "working all in all"[155] are identical. Or, as Paul Althaus avers, "God is God because he and only he creates."[156]

Therefore it was no mere momentary modification employed in support of a preeminent sacramental system that allowed Luther, in the midst of debate regarding the Lord's Supper, countering Ulrich Zwingli's spatially circumscribed depiction of the "right hand of God" (based upon John 6:63 and a figurative interpretation of the Lord's Supper's *est*),[157] to assert that the "right hand of God' is not a specific place" but is indeed "the almighty power of God" which therefore "at one and the

154. Pinomaa, *Faith Victorious*, 16.
155. LW 33:140.
156. Althaus, *Theology of Martin Luther*, 105.
157. See especially LW 37:13–57.

same time can be nowhere and yet must be everywhere."[158] But if this is the case, then, according to Luther, "the power of God" must be unequivocally "present at all places, even in the tiniest tree leaf."[159] And the reason for this omnipresence of divine "power" lies in the preeminent position which Luther accords to God as the creator.[160] According to Luther: "It is God who creates, effects, and preserves all things through his almighty power and right hand . . . For he dispatches no officials or angels when he creates or preserves something, but all this is the work of his divine power itself. If he is to create or preserve it, however, he must be present and must make and preserve creation both in its innermost and outermost aspects."[161] And it is the necessity of the immanence of the Creator's presence which Luther elaborates by adding that:

> [God] himself must be present in every single creature in its innermost and outermost being, on all sides, through and through, below and above, before and behind, so that nothing can be more truly present and within all creatures than God himself with his power. For it is he who makes the skin and it is he who makes the bones; it is he who makes the hair on the skin, and it is he who makes the marrow in the bones; it is he who makes every bit of the hair, it is he who makes every bit of the marrow. Indeed, he must make everything, both the parts and the whole. Surely, then, his hand which makes all this must be present; that cannot be lacking.[162]

158. LW 37:57.

159. Ibid.

160. See Löfgren, *Die Theologie der Schöpfung bei Luther*, 21. "Schöpfung und Erlösung dürfen nach Luther nicht gleichgesetzt werden. Gott ist der Urheber alles übrigen; er schenkt also *allen Menschen* Leben und Bewahrung schon vor der Offenbarung des Evangeliums." Already this reality came to the foreground in the preceding section. Althaus, in his *Theology of Martin Luther*, 129, asserts, "Luther's doctrine of justification by faith alone is thus completely based on his principle that God alone is the creator. Only this understanding of justification treats the creaturliness of man with the full seriousness which Luther feels its demands. The justification of the godless is the most sublime of all the specific examples of the way in which God creates out of nothing and under a contrary form." Thus we might declare that the Gospel can be summed-up as "God is Creator."

161. LW 37:57–58.

162. Ibid., 58. With regard to the nature of this creating activity, who can forget, from Luther's *Large Catechism*, BC: 412, these words, "I hold and believe that I am a creature of God; that is, that he has given and constantly sustains my body, soul, and life, my members great and small, all the faculties of my mind, my reason and understanding, and so forth; my food and drink, clothing, means of support, wife and child,

Ultimately, then, if Luther's "decisive emphasis"[163] upon God's effective, immanent presence as Creator, or the "most active working of God" (*deus actuossimus*),[164] not only amounts to the reality that "Nothing *is* and nothing *continues to be* without his activity,"[165] but that creation—itself, according to Luther, coming into being from nothing (*ex nihilo*) and, hence, of itself, capable of nothing (*nihil . . . potest*)[166]—"cannot exist for even one moment unless God maintains it,"[167] then ultimately, for Luther, "We Christians know that with God creating and preserving are identical."[168] How so? And by what means?

If, as Paul Althaus points out, God's omnipotence not only "does *not* consist in having the power to do what he actually does not do, but in the ceaseless activity with which he works all in all,"[169] which is a "ceaseless activity" active in *this* concrete, existing world, then it also must be understood that the "instrument" or "means"[170] of that "ceaseless activity," or "most active working," is the Word. Indeed, for Luther, this Word is to be understood within the context of a communicative event within the Godhead himself. For as Luther avers, "What else is the entire creation than the Word of God uttered by God, or extended to the outside?"[171] Therefore "God reveals Himself to us as the Speaker

---

servants, house and home, etc. Besides, he makes all creation help provide the comforts and necessities of life—sun, moon, and stars in the heavens, day and night, air, fire, water, the earth and all that it brings forth, birds and fish, beasts, grain and all kinds of produce. Moreover, he gives all physical and temporal blessings—good government, peace, security. Thus we learn from this article that none of us has his life of himself, or anything else that has been mentioned here or can be mentioned, nor can he by himself preserve any of them, however small and unimportant. All this is comprehended in the word 'Creator.'" Logically Luther adds, "Therefore, this article would humble and terrify us all if we believed it" (ibid., 413).

163. Bayer, "I Believe that God Has Created Me with All that Exists," 147.

164. LW 33:233.

165. Althaus, *Theology of Martin Luther*, 105; italics added for emphasis.

166. LW 4:61.

167. Althaus, *Theology of Martin Luther*, 105.

168. LW 4:136.

169. Althaus, *Theology of Martin Luther*, 110; italics added for emphasis.

170. LW 1:18.

171. Ibid., 22. "This Word is God; it is the omnipotent Word, uttered in the divine essence. No one heard it spoken except God Himself, that is, God the Father, God the Son, and God the Holy Spirit. And when it was spoken, light was brought into existence, not out of the matter of the Word or from the nature of Him who spoke but out of the darkness itself. Thus the Father spoke inwardly; and outwardly light was made and

who has with Him the uncreated Word, through whom He created the world and all things with the greatest ease, namely, by speaking."¹⁷² With this being the case, then it is in the context of this communicated Word, then, that the doctrine of *creatio ex nihilo* is to be understood. "For," according to Luther, "God calls into existence the things which do not exist (Rom 4:17). He does not speak grammatical words; He speaks true and existent realities. Accordingly, that which among us has the sound of a word is a reality with God. Thus sun, moon, heaven, earth, Peter, Paul, I, you, etc.—we are all words of God[.]"¹⁷³ For Luther, the "divine rule of language" consists of the reality that "when He says: 'Sun, shine,' the sun is there at once and shines. Thus the words of God are realities, not bare words."¹⁷⁴ But may not one ask, "Is not the Sabbath rest, the 'seventh day,' an indicator that God is finished 'creating' through his Word?" Here, within the parameters of the communicated Word, and thus *creatio ex nihilo*, Luther maintains a distinction between "establishing" and "governing."

Though "the Sabbath rest," for Luther, may mean that God has ceased creating more heavens and earths, it does not mean that God has ceased sustaining the heaven and earth he already created.¹⁷⁵ For, according to Luther, "God works till now—if indeed He has not abandoned the world which was once established but governs and preserves it through the effectiveness of His Word. He has, therefore, ceased to establish; but He has not ceased to govern."¹⁷⁶ Luther adds that

> Until today there abides the Word which was pronounced over the human race: "Grow and multiply" ; there abides the Word: "Let the sea bring forth fish and birds of the heaven." Almighty, therefore, is the power and effectiveness of the Word which thus preserves and governs the entire creation . . . Thus Moses has clearly established that the Word was in the beginning. But because all things grow, multiply, and are preserved and governed until now in the same manner as from the beginning of the

---

came into existence immediately" (ibid., 19). On the matter of creation as communicative event through the Word, see also Schwanke, "Luther on Creation," 3–5, and Bayer, "Creation as History," 253.

172. LW 1:22.
173. Ibid., 21.
174. Ibid.
175. Ibid., 21.
176. Ibid.

world, it obviously follows that the Word still continues in force and is not dead.[177]

Therefore as God has "created the world and all creatures through the Word," and it is also through that same Word that "God still governs and preserves His creation and will govern and preserve it until the end of time,"[178] according to Luther, this also means that God

> is, however, not like a carpenter or architect who, after completing a house, ship, or the like, turns over the house to its owner for his residence or the ship to the boatmen or mariners for sailing, and then goes his way. Craftsmen are wont to do this; after doing a job or finishing a task, they leave without any concern for their work and enterprise and without any regard for its maintenance. God proceeds differently. God the Father initiated and executed the creation of all things through the Word; and now He continues to preserve His creation through the Word, and that forever and ever. He remains with His handiwork until he sees fit to terminate it.[179]

For as the sun rises and sets day after day, year after year; as parents beget children; as the earth produces manifold varieties of fruit; as the oceans yield fish for consumption,[180] all of this, for Luther, is not only created and preserved by the effective presence of the Word of God, but "If God were to withdraw His hand, this building and everything in it would collapse."[181]

Ultimately, then, according to David Löfgren, "Luther employs ... 'ex nihilo' as a safeguard against the aristotelian conception of the world, a safeguard which, in the end, expels all thoughts about unceasing creation."[182] What this means, explicitly, according to Löfgren, is that the *nihil* is not simply a reality of the past, but remains both an ever-present possibility, and the ever-present source of reality. In other words, Löfgren adds, "For Luther the world is not a ship that is

---

177. Ibid., 75–6.
178. LW 22:26.
179. Ibid.
180. Ibid., 26–27.
181. Ibid., 27.
182. "Luther setzt ... 'ex nihilo' als eine Sicherung gegen das aristotelische Weltbild ein, das jeden Gedanken an ein unablässiges Schaffen letzlich ausschließt." Löfgren, *Die Theologie der Schöpfung*, 25.

constructed in order to sail by itself. The "nothing" of the world, from which it has come, does not lie somewhere in the past, but rather is that from which every new creature, every new human appears at their birth, indeed every moment and every hour are constantly newly created by God."[183] But it is at a further point in his work that Löfgren is able to place this dynamic into starker relief, and thus more explicitly against "den soteriologischen Hintergrund"[184] of Luther's theological program—explicitly between the prospects of eternal life and death—by stating that: "In Luther's creation-faith the natural life is therefore seen as a journey through the Red Sea in which God holds back the forces of death and maintains the life of the creature through the tremendous power of his Word. The narrow wall, which holds back extermination and destruction, is, after the fall of creation, very thin. As the mass of water swept away the mighty army of Egyptians, so also the life of humans can be swept away if God withdraws his all-powerful Word."[185] But if the Creator's work of preservation—from the outset—

---

183. "Die Welt ist fur Luther kein Schiff, das gebaut ist, um dann von selbst zu fahren; das "nihil" der Welt, aus welchem sie hervorgegangen ist, liegt also nicht irgendwo in der Vergangenheit, sondern ist das, woraus jede neue Kreatur, jeder neue Mensch bei seiner Geburt hervortritt; ja sogar jeder Augenblick und jede Stunde warden von Gott stets neuem geschaffen" (ibid.). Holze, in his "Luther's Concept of Creation," 50, also asserts, "As we can see the world as creation is not a neutral reality but it is penetrated by the presence of God; it owes its being, order and permenance to this immanent presence of God. Creation is not a matter of a mythical past but an event that happens in our present and embraces all aspects of our life (*creatio continua*)."

184. Nilsson, *Simul*, 243.

185. "In Luthers Schöpfungsglauben wird deshalb das kreaturliche Leben als eine Wanderung durch das Rote Meer gesehen, wo Gott die Machte des Todes zurückhült, und das Leben der Kreatur durch die gewaltige Kraft seines Wortes erhält. Die schmale Wand, die Zerstörung and Vernichtung zurückhält, is nach dem Fall der Schöpfung sehr dünn. Wie die Wassermassen das machtige Heer der Ägypter wegschwemmten, so kann auch das Leben des Menschen weggeschwemmt warden, wenn Gott sein allmächtiges Wort zurückzieht." Löfgren, *Die Theologie der Schöpfung bei Luther*, 44. Further elaborating this point, Luther asserts, "Thus it happens through divine power that the waters do not pass over us, and until today and until the end of the world God performs for us the well-known miracle which He performed in the Red Sea for the people of Israel. At that time He displayed that might of His in a unique manner by an obvious miracle, in order that He might be worshiped with greater zeal by the small nation. For what is our entire life on this earth but a passage through the Red Sea, where on both sides the sea stood like high walls? Because it is very certain that the sea is far higher than the earth, God, up to the present time, commands the waters to remain in suspense and restrains them by His Word lest they burst upon us as they burst forth in the Deluge. But at times God gives providential signs, and entire islands perish by

is completely identified with his *ex nihilo* work of creation, then it is important to note that there is one more aspect of the Creator's work that Luther frames—from the beginning—within the context of the prevenient work of the Creator. It is the work of redemption. Let us briefly develop this point.

Commenting on Genesis 1: 26, Luther, hypothetically explicating the trajectory of *imago Dei*—sans the "fall"—through the Creator's Word states, "Moses . . . indicates to those who are spiritually minded that we were created for a better life in the future than this physical life would have been, even if our nature had remained unimpaired."[186] He elaborates: "Therefore the scholars put it well: "Even if Adam had not fallen through his sin, still . . . God would have translated [him] from this animal life to the spiritual life."[187] Elaborating on the intentions (present from the beginning) implied with the designation of "our image" (applied by the Creator) for humans, Luther comments that

> Adam was not to live without food, drink, and procreation. But at a predetermined time . . . these physical activities would have come to an end; and Adam, together with his descendents, would have been translated to the eternal and spiritual life . . . [for] Just as the beasts have need of food, drink, and rest to refresh their bodies, so Adam, even in his innocence, would make use of them. But what is added—that man was created for his physical life in such a way that he was nevertheless made according to the image and likeness of God—this is an indication of another and better life than the physical.[188]

Indeed the upshot of such an observation is the reality that redemption (articulated as "translation" in a "pre-fall" scenario), far from being merely a separate "fix-job" of creation, is a matter—a *telos*—already contained within the purpose of the Creator's Word from the beginning.[189] Not only is redemption articulated by Luther within the context of creation, but indeed "redemption" ultimately involves the restoration of the creature to the Creator's sole-sufficiency. Redemption *is* complete

---

water, to show that the sea is in His hand and that He can either hold it in check or release it against the ungrateful and the evil" (LW 1:35).

186. LW 1:56.

187. Ibid.

188. Ibid., 57.

189. For a fine explication of this dynamic—the necessity of articulating redemption within the context of creation—I point the reader to Alison, *Raising Abel*, 49–97.

restoration to the Creator, and the life which was originally intended by the Creator. (This point will be elaborated in chapter four, below.)

But it also needs to be added at this point—lest one still be tempted to subordinate the "right hand of God," or God's effective presence as Creator who creates/preserves *ex nihilo*, to some species of automatic mechanistic causality (no matter how immanent and personal)—that one must always bear in mind that, for Luther, the "power" of God, or his "right hand" at which the Word "sits," is preeminently the creating power of a sovereign personal presence who is not beholden either to or within the causality he works. Though God's effective presence is everywhere "and in all things to the innermost and outermost degree, through and through, as it must be if he is to make and preserve all things everywhere,"[190] Luther (perhaps in an oft-neglected sentence that speaks volumes more than its length!) is quick to remind us that '[God's] power is not an ax, hatchet, saw, or file with which he works, but is himself.'"[191] Thus, far from either being a "substratum which belongs to 'nature,'" or a concept which can be captured by philosophical descriptions of the world,[192] God's presence, again, is nothing other than the

---

190. LW 37:61.

191. Ibid.

192. Löfgren, *Die Theologie der Schöpfung bei Luther*, 43. Dalferth captures this dynamic well in his "Creation—Style of the World," 135, in which he notes, "If questions of actuality are the business of science, the concern of philosophy is questions of possibility. It is therefore the business of philosophy to nurture, cultivate and improve competence in perceiving the possible in the actual, and of understanding its truth against the background of the full range of possibility." But, Dalferth adds, and note the emphasis upon the "presence of God" with the "unanticipated," "The questions theology asks are different again. It is concerned with the possibility of the real in the light of the presence of God as the space (*Spielraum*) of the real that is owed to God. This space determines what a reality can be, and, in the face of what it in fact is, what else it might have been and could still be; but it also describes the open horizon where that which is surprising, new and unanticipated takes place. Nothing is only what it has become. Everything is an occasion for the new. Each new thing is owed to God's presence, without which it would not be what it is becoming, and without which nothing is what it can be. Theology approaches reality and possibility as God-given, as the gift of God. It describes them as something that reveals or conceals God's presence, and it enquires into what it means for human life that it can understand itself and the world as the gift of God, and how life can, should and must be lived in accordance with this insight. In short, theology does not add a further aspect to the picture of the reality and possibility of the world painted by the sciences and philosophy, rather it alters the entire frame of the discussion." Ultimately Dalferth, patterning his reflection upon Goethe's categories of "imitation," "manner," and "style" from a 1789 essay entitled "Simple imitations of na-

effective agency of his personal presence through the Word, an agency *who*, in every moment, decides upon the course and causality of his creation. This agency—with which the humanity of Christ is completely identified—as we will see, becomes the foundation for what Luther calls the "third mode" of Christ's presence.

Ultimately then, if we can both assert with Luther that "apart from this man [Jesus] there is no God,"[193] and indeed also that the "right hand" at which this man "sits," or God's effective presence, is "in all things to the innermost and outermost degree, through and through, as it must be if he is to make and preserve all things everywhere,"[194] then—as the Redeemer is inextricably identified with the Creator's agency through the *communicatio idiomatum*—all that we have said regarding God's effective presence as the Creator, or his "right hand," must also be said with regard to this same "man" who sits at God's "right hand." It is this absolute identification between the "right hand" of the Creator and the man who is the Redeemer which leads us to what Luther calls the "third mode" of Christ's presence.

Luther, in his 1528 *Confession Concerning Christ's Supper*,[195] was able to distinguish three modes of Christ's presence. The first mode of Christ's presence, according to Luther, is "the circumscribed corporeal mode of presence, as when he walked bodily on earth, when he occupied and yielded space according to his size."[196] As this "corporeal mode" refers to Jesus Christ in his first century existence, according to Luther, Jesus Christ "can still employ this mode of presence when he wills to do so, as he did after his resurrection and as he will do on the

---

ture, manner, style," avers that theology in its understanding of "reality" and subsequent treatment of the world as "creation" (in contradistinction to science and philosophy) emphasizes a the "third possibility" of "style," or "the creative grasp of the creative principle that bestows on reality its unity. Reality is not simply what it is; part of the essence of reality is the appearance of a newness that cannot be anticipated." As God's "power" is not, nor analogous to, an "ax, hatchet, saw, or file" (or any other type of mechanistic causality), but solely predicated of his immanent, personal, effective presence, so, too, theology is the voice of the Creator's unanticipated possibilities!

193. LW 37:218.

194. Ibid., 61.

195. Ibid., 151–372. This distinction also stands at the core of the Reformers' articulation of the Lord's Supper in Article 7 of the *Formula of Concord*. See BC: 586–87. See also Westhelle, *Scandalous God*, 28–29.

196. LW 37:222.

Last Day . . ."[197] The second mode of Christ's presence, according to Luther, is "the uncircumscribed, spiritual mode of presence according to which he neither occupies nor yields space but passes through everything created as he wills. This "spiritual mode" is also Christ's mode of presence in the elements—bread and wine—of the Lord's Supper "by which [the] real presence 'in, with, and under' the elements can be affirmed without appealing to a transformation of the substance of the elements, that is, without transubstantiation."[198] Essentially, then, this second mode of presence allows one to affirm the presence of Christ without abrogating the integrity of the creation in which Christ is present through a reference to "transubstantiation." Ultimately, "since [Jesus] is one person with God,"[199] Luther is able to articulate a third mode of presence—a "divine, heavenly mode, according to which all created things are indeed much more permeable and present to him than they are according to the second mode."[200] It is just this third mode of Christ's presence, in which the man Jesus partakes in God's "infinity and omnipresence,"[201] that we will now elaborate.

For, according to Luther, if Jesus, "By virtue of the incarnational unity between the infinite and finite"[202] "is a man who is supernaturally one person with God, and apart from this man there is no God, it must follow that according to the third supernatural mode, he is and can be wherever God is, and that everything is full of Christ through and through, even according to his humanity,"[203] then (for the sake of our

---

197. Ibid.
198. Westhelle, *Scandalous God*, 28.
199. LW 37:223.
200. Ibid.
201. Westhelle, *Scandalous God*, 28.
202. Ibid.

203. LW 37:218. Indeed P. Gennrich, *Die Christologie Luthers in Abendmahlsstreit*, quoted by Lienhard, *Luther: Witness to Jesus Christ*, 245, states, "The humanity of Christ is, for Luther, not only the man Jesus of Nazareth, but all that represents a concretization of the infinite in the finite and the bodily, such as the 'virgin's womb,' the 'manger,' the cross, over and above the Scripture and the Apostles. All these outward and material things are, like the man Jesus, bearers of the divine Word." And Nilsson observes that "On the one hand, the humanity (*Menschlichkeit*) of Christ appears to signify, not only the historical and biological being of the man Jesus, which took form in a human body, but all of what Luther calls *indumenta Dei*, the Word, Baptism, and the Eucharist, for it is in these human things that God shows himself and acts toward us. Wherever such *species Dei* appear, they rightly indicate the humanity of Christ. On the other hand,

project) the presence of the Word's "within-redemption"—now completely identified with the Creator's agency through the Word—knows no spatial/temporal limits with regard to the particular, embodied human narratives God has promised to redeem "from within." Again, quoting Luther at length on the reality of this third mode of the Redeemer's presence, or Luther's complete identification of the Redeemer with the Creator, Luther articulates this "third mode" in such a manner that

> [S]ince he is one person with God, the divine, heavenly mode, according to which all created things are indeed much more permeable and present to him than they are according to the second mode. For if according to the second mode he can be present in and with created things in such a way that they do no feel, touch, measure, or circumscribe him but where they are present to him so that he measures and circumscribes them. You must place this existence of Christ, which constitutes him as one person with God, far, far, beyond things created, as far as God transcends them; and on the other hand, place it as deep in and as near to all created things as God is in them. For he is one invisible person with God, and wherever God is, he must be also, otherwise our faith is false.[204]

At this point, though, let us be very careful to point out—especially in light of the preceding chapter's discussion of "revelation" solely within the context of the *theologia crucis*—Luther's caveat regarding the third mode of Christ's bodily presence. He states, "Although he is present in all creatures, and I might find him in stone, in fire, in water, or even in a rope, for he is certainly there, yet he does not wish that I seek him there apart from the Word, and cast myself into the fire or the water, or hang myself on the rope. He is present everywhere, but he does not wish that you grope for him everywhere. Grope rather where the Word is, and there you will lay hold of him in the right way."[205] In other words, the third mode of Christ's presence is not a speculative, *a priori* category of

---

Luther is never in any doubt of what he means by the humanity of Christ, even through the concept has a many-sided content and can refer to a multitude of *externa res*. In fact, all these have in common that they are a means of expression for the incarnation of the Word. It is only in the Word and by the Word that things and human signs can be called divine. In this way, it is possible for Luther to see all apparitions, all *species Dei*, included and summed up *in homine Christo*" (*Simul*, 155, quoted in Lienhard, *Luther: Witness to Jesus Christ*, 245).

204. LW 37:223.

205. LW 36:342.

the theologian of the glory, but an *a posteriori* confession of the theologian of the cross—justified by faith—who has discerned God's *modus operandi* through the cross where God has definitively chosen to reveal himself. Perhaps it is Regin Prenter, commenting on this third mode of Christ's presence, or his ubiquity, within the context in which Luther was forced to more fully elaborate the antispeculative, soteriological core of his theology, or the doctrine of the Lord's Supper, who best develops this distinction. Prenter asserts, and I quote him at length,

> By distinguishing between the absolute ubiquity outside of the Supper, which is not accessible to us, and Christ's gracious presence for us in the Supper by the Word, every way of speculation and worked toward the most high and omnipresent Christ is blocked. He is exalted, and he is omnipresent; for if this were not the case we should not meet the real God, when in the Supper he gives us himself. But he is not accessible to us in his absolute exaltation and omnipresence. We can only lay hold on him in his divinity when he clothes it in his earthly, human, and bodily form. It is no more possible to separate the human and the divine nature of Christ—for it is insolubly united in a divine-human person—than it is to separate the exalted, omnipresent Christ present in the bread and the wine. It is one and the same divine-human person. It is the omnipresent Christ we meet in the bread and the wine. If we take omnipresence away from the Christ we meet in the bread and the wine we make him another and a smaller one than he really is. We make him another instead of God himself and thereby we reduce the value of the gift of the Supper. On the contrary, if we attempt to understand or to meet the omnipresent Christ in some other way than hidden in his humble humanity, in the bread and the wine of the Supper, then we speculate on the *Deus nudus* and we do not meet the divine majesty as our God but as our enemy who puts us to death.[206]

Thus, as the theologian of the cross confesses on account of the *Deus incarnatus* that the fullness of God is only revealed *sub contraria specie* in the humanity of Christ, so any discussion of the third mode of Christ's presence can only be conducted within the confession that it is "only through the humble humanity of Christ … [that it is] possible to lay hold on the majesty of God,"[207] or his creation encompassing pres-

206. Prenter, *Spiritus Creator*, 271.
207. Ibid., 270–71.

ence. Any other method of deliberation reveals a species of speculation which betrays the inception of the third mode of Christ's presence in Luther's thought. But, ultimately, as Westhelle observes, it is because of this third mode of presence, always placed within the perspective of its inception, or the Cross and the *Deus incarnatus*, that "God's embodiment through Christ encompasses the world. That is true even in the midst of God's radical identification with the most deprived of the human condition."[208]

But, let us ask at this point: can we still possibly raise question marks by referring to this "third mode" as a "heavenly" mode? that is, as a mode of presence which is only present according to a resurrected, "triumphant," victory, a victory which supersedes the particular, individual narratives of suffering, death, and entombment for which Christ was initially intended to redeem "from within"? Could it still be the unavoidable case—regardless of how much we speak of Christ's presence (and a "humble" one at that!)—in Luther's articulation (thinking back to Lewis) that Christ's narrative of redemption "so colors all of our "Fridays" and "Saturdays" that indeed all particular, individual "Friday" and "Saturdays" of human suffering and death are abandoned for the sake of Christ's *in illo tempore* "metanarrative" of redemption? one that is simply made present? On the contrary. Steiger points out that this manifestation of the *communicatio idiomatum*—or the third mode of Christ's presence—receives a pastoral intensification which allows Luther to articulate Christ as "emptied," or in the state of humility, even after his ascension. Thus, Steiger observes, "Christ has gone into glory as the emptied one; he is still found sitting at the right hand of God in the state of humility."[209] Simply, the risen Christ only encounters us with his wounds as the Crucified Christ![210] Thus, as Steiger points out, the ascended, exalted Son of God continuously struggles against these forces of sin and death as they encounter God's children—in all particular, individual, embodied narratives—just as he did during his original presence on earth according to the first mode of presence.[211] Thus it

---

208. Westhelle, *Scandalous God*, 29.

209. Steiger, "*Communicatio Idiomatum*," 136.

210. "He is hidden to us and he remains hidden to us in the flesh as well as in his majesty," asserts Klaus Schwarzwäller, "Theology as Unfolding the Article of Justification," 41.

211. Ibid.

is within this frame of reference—the dialectical relationship between exaltation/humiliation with respect to Christ's ascension—regarding the third mode of Christ's presence of "within-redemption" that Luther is able to assert, "If Christ were not with me in dungeon, torture, and death, where would I be? He is present there through the Word, although not in the same way as . . . in the sacrament, where through the Word he binds his body and blood to bread and wine so that he is also received corporeally."[212] And, ultimately, according to Luther, it is on account of the third mode of Christ's presence—the complete identification of the Redeemer's presence with the Creator's "right hand"—that, according to Luther,

> [A] godly mind is not shocked to hear that God is present in death or hell, both of which are more horrible and foul than either a hole or a sewer. Indeed, since Scripture testifies that God is everywhere and fills all things [Jer. 23:24], a godly mind not only says that He is in those places, but must needs learn and know that he is there. Or are we to suppose that if I am captured by a tyrant and thrown into a prison or a sewer—as has happened to many saints—I am not to be allowed to call upon God there or to believe that he is present with me, but must wait until I come into some finely furnished church?[213]

Therefore, as Westhelle has already pointed out, if God's embodiment through the third mode of Christ's presence "encompasses the world" in such a fashion that this equates to a "radical identification with the most deprived of the human condition,"[214] a human condition still wallowing in the horror of its manifold "Fridays" and the interminable grief of its innumerable "Saturdays," then this reality "holds promise for understanding the connection between the passion of Christ and the passion of the world, it sharpens the paradox of the theology of the cross, because it follows that God's death . . . was a death then, is now, and will be in the future."[215] The *sub contraria specie* presence of Christ's redemption is an ongoing matter! Again, as Heinrich Holze observes, it

---

212. LW 36:342–43.
213. LW 33:47.
214. Westhelle, *Scandalous God*, 29.
215. Ibid.

is through the Word of the Cross that "God has disclosed himself to the world and has defined himself in his relationship to the world."[216]

But perhaps most importantly though, for the sake of this project, through a complete identification of the Redeemer with the Creator's agency, the third mode of Christ's presence—the *radix* of Luther's articulation of "within-redemption," or his *theologia crucis* (as we have contended in this chapter)—does not ask individual, embodied humans to look outside of their own narratives to another "most real" narrative of redemption in order to partake in that same redemption. That is, with regard to redemption, individual humans are not simply things "signified" by an *in illo tempore* "signifier." For, through the third mode of Christ's presence, the "still, small voice," a "seemingly foolish and impotent Word from the Cross,"[217] is also the omnipresent, ongoing Word of "within-redemption"; a presence of "within-redemption" who embodies himself within all particular, embodied human narratives—within their particular "Fridays" and "Saturdays"—asking not for those same narratives to become diminished for the sake of, and by sole reference to, a "most real" meta-narrative of redemption which has already occurred. Thus, as Bayer observes regarding the narrative of Jesus Christ, the one in whom Creator and creature are bound together through a direct communication of attributes, "This specific story . . . turns out to be the center and criterion of all other stories—yet without becoming a 'metanarrative' that would force all others to submit . . ."[218] The integrity of our "Fridays" and "Saturdays" remains. We remain "Friday" and "Saturday" people living by faith in hope. And through the third mode of Christ's presence, we are able to articulate Christ's redemption as a present, ongoing event within all particular, embodied human narratives. Ultimately, then, it is the real presence of this Word that allows us not only to speak (with Lewis) of "resumption beyond rupture" with regard to the presence of God's redeeming activity in the person of Jesus Christ in the first century, but indeed to speak of all individual human tombs themselves as the location of this same ongoinging presence "within-redemption."

But, if this is the case, that the third mode of Christ's presence allows us to confess the presence of God's "within-redemption" through-

---

216. Holze, "Luther's Concept of Creation," 52.
217. Kolb, "Luther on the Theology of the Cross," 450.
218. Bayer, "Creation as History," 260.

out all of creation, indeed even with regard to all particular human tombs themselves, then we must—again—remember the context for articulating the *modus operandi* of that same "within-redemption" according to the third mode of Christ's presence: the *theologia crucis*.

For as the crucified Christ is the "seal leading us back through his incarnation to the recognition of the [C]reator,"[219] so also "God's permanent relationship to the world became visible in the place where the Word manifested itself. Therefore, the fact that the world as creation can only be recognized and understood as such by God means that its very nature as creation discloses itself in the place of God's incarnation. Thus, understanding Christ is the theological prerequisite for understanding the entire creation."[220] Therefore, as Ingolf Dalferth points out, especially with regard to the ubiquitous nature of Christ's presence of "within-redemption" according to the *theologia crucis*, this presence is always—no matter the mode—in the form of God's hiddenness, his *sub contraria specie* presence.[221] Dalferth adds, "it is a presence tied to an absence, and it can only be apprehended by apprehending the present of the absent or the absence as sign of the present."[222] And, if we are to continue to conduct our discussion of the third mode of Christ's presence—his ubiquitous embodiment throughout all of creation—within the context of the *theologia crucis*, then we must remember Luther's assertions from theses 19–20 of his Heidelberg Disputation: "God is neither to be seen or sought behind creation, nor be inferred from it, but only recognized in and through it."[223] Westhelle adds with reference to the Word by whom God has "defined himself in his relationship to the world," commensurately with Dalferth, "This 'in and through' is misleading, however, if we do not understand that creation 'reveals' the concealment, the absence of God, our own blindness of the divine reality."[224]

Essentially, then, if we are to extend to the presence (amid absence) of "within-redemption" to the scope of all creation, and, specifically, with reference to a "within-redemption" that "takes place" within the particular, individual tombs of humanity according to the *modus*

---

219. WA 33/II, 340, 23, quoted in Holze, "Luther's Concept of Creation," 52.
220. Holze, "Luther's Concept of Creation," 52.
221. Dalferth, *Becoming Present*, 88.
222. Ibid.
223. Westhelle, *Scandalous God*, 100.
224. Ibid.

operandi of the *theologia crucis* (acknowledging that the nature of creation "discloses itself in the place of God's incarnation"), then ultimately we may refer to particular human tombs, in a fashion commensurate with Luther's *theologia crucis*, as "masks" of God's redeeming presence within creation. In other words—now in light of our development of the third mode of Christ's presence through our development of the *radix* of Luther's *theologia crucis*, or his *communicatio idiomatum*—as the theologian of the cross is not driven to *see through* this visible, material world in order to perceive the "real" "invisible things of God"[225] behind all matter, the theologian of the cross is also able to describe God's *modus operandi* of restoring sinners to his sole sufficiency as Creator of a "very good" creation within this same visible, material world. But with this said, it is to the justification for the employment of the term "mask" that we now turn in the subsequent chapter. As we will see, the concept of the "mask"—*larva(e) Dei*—is both an expression of Luther's *theologia crucis* and its description of God's *modus operandi* extended from Cross to Creation, and an essential expression of Luther's theology as a theologian of the cross. As we will see, if the "third mode" of Christ's presence afforded us the ability to extend the presence of "within-redemption" to the scope of creation, then the *larvae Dei* are the means by which that "within-redemption" is localized for the sake of individual, embodied narratives.

---

225. LW 31:52.

4

Larvae Dei

Wrappings of the Presence of "Within-Redemption"

Preliminary Remarks

WITHIN OUR DEVELOPMENT OF LUTHER'S *THEOLOGIA CRUCIS*, AND which has been argued to be foundational to the *theologia crucis*, we were able to fully develop in the previous chapter Luther's radical interpretation of the Church's doctrine of the *communicatio idiomatum*. Involving both an elaboration of the priority of the Redeemer's humanity and the all-encompassing purview of the Creator's agency, and thus delineating the complete identification of the two through Luther's interpretation of the *communicatio idiomatum*, we were able to arrive at what Luther termed the "third mode" of Christ's bodily presence. Essentially, as has been developed, the "third mode" of Christ's presence affords us the ability to extend the location of the presence of "within-redemption" in such a manner that it encompasses the whole of creation.[1] With this being said though, that all of creation provides

---

1. Let us note at this point in the discussion that it was Joseph Sittler who made this point abundantly clear—against the canvas of the twentieth century's technological/ecological concerns when he asserted in an address to the Third Assembly, World Council of Churches at New Delhi, India on November 21, 1961, published as "Called to Unity," 178—that "a doctrine of redemption is meaningful only when it swings within the larger orbit of a doctrine of creation. For God's creation of earth cannot be redeemed in any intelligible sense of the word apart from a doctrine of the cosmos which is his home, his definite place, the theatre of his selfhood under God, in corporation with his neighbour, and in caring-relationship with nature . . ." Sittler added, "Unless the reference and the power of the redemptive act includes the whole of man's

the scope, or location, for Christ's presence of "within-redemption," one must never fail to be cognizant of the theological framework for such an assertion regarding creation, or the *theologia crucis*. Therefore, it was necessarily noted at the end of our development of this "third mode" of Christ's presence—this "majestic" presence of Christ—that, reminding ourselves of its elaboration within the *theologia crucis*, Christ "is hidden to us and . . . remains hidden to us in the flesh as well as in his majesty."[2] It is just this dynamic that provides the foundation of what will be developed in this current chapter.

For, as has already been delineated in chapter two, above, not only does the *theologia crucis* provide for a "vision of reality"[3] in which the cross most profoundly manifests God's *modus operandi*,[4] that "God does not operate in another way with men today than he did with Christ,"[5] but does so in such a manner that the cross becomes the "paradigm" for comprehending all aspects of God's agency.[6] No aspect of creation is exempt from that agency, an agency which is most profoundly revealed at the cross. And, specifically with reference to this project as it relates to the integrity of individual, particular narratives of humanity, there is, ultimately, no tomb which is bereft of this agency, or presence of Christ's "within-redemption." The human tomb is itself a "mask" of Christ's presence of "within-redemption" within creation.

---

experience and environment, straight out to its farthest horizon, then the redemption is incomplete. There is and will always remain something of evil to be overcome. And more. The actual man in his existence will be tempted to reduce the redemption of man to what purgation, transformation, forgiveness and blessedness is available by an 'angelic' escape from the cosmos of natural and historical fact—and in that option accept some sort of dualism which is as offensive to biblical theology as it is beloved of all Gnosticism, then as now" (ibid., 179). This point is followed-up, and further elaborated, eleven years later in his essay "The Scope of Christological Reflection." For a similar focus I also point the reader to Sittler's essay, "A Christology of Function." For concise, informative discussions regarding the minimal attention which the subject of creation has received in theology near the end of the twentieth century, especially with reference to a doctrine of redemption, I point the reader to Hendry's "Eclipse of Creation," and Allen's "Theological Reflection on the Natural World."

2. Schwarzwäller, "Theology as Unfolding the Article of Justification," 41.

3. Thompson, *Crossing the Divide*, 21.

4. Kolb, "Luther on the Theology of the Cross," 451.

5. Vercruysse, "Luther's Theology of the Cross at the Time of the Heidelberg Disputation," 542.

6. Ibid.

In order to unfold this claim, with particular attention paid both to justification for the employment of the term "mask" (*larva*) and the role which Luther attributes to this term, this chapter will essentially consist of applying the *modus operandi*, and indeed the epistemology, of the *theologia crucis*—per Luther—to the scope of creation itself. Ultimately, as will be developed, "mask"—and associated terminology—is employed by Luther to express the essential role of the medium of creation with reference to the *modus operandi* of Christ's redeeming presence—a *modus operandi* revealed most profoundly at the cross—within that same creation. Essentially, for Luther, if the cross is the "material criterion"[7] by which one may perceive the agency of God within creation, then creation—within the *theologia crucis*—becomes the "formal criterion for the recognition of God's revelation as creation out of nothing[.]"[8] Concretely, for the sake of our project, the cross will provide the material criterion by which God's agency is perceived at the location of the human tomb, while, ultimately, the human tomb will provide the formal criterion which allows us to perceive God's creative, *ex nihilo* agency.

In order to arrive at this aforementioned claim, this chapter will be developed through the course of three sections. First, it will be demonstrated that the sheer employment of the word "creation" implies the *confession* of a specific "Creator." As will be developed, creation—as opposed to "nature" or "world"—is the confession of reality through the lens of one who is justified by the Creator. To confess creation means that one confesses the Creator, and thus the Creator's "effective presence," or the "unity of reality" (Dalferth) hidden within that same reality, or—as the Christian confesses—creation. Second, we will demonstrate that *this* creation alone is the medium for God's creating/redeeming agency. Creation is never, according to the *modus operandi* of the *theologia crucis*, transparent to a redemption which "takes place" elsewhere than this concrete location. It is in this section that we will develop both what Luther means by "mask" (*larva*)—and its associated terms—and how it is employed with regard to understanding creation as a "medium" of God's Word. Ultimately, then, drawing upon our development of the term "mask" (and related terminology), we will apply—in the final section—the *modus operandi* of the cross to the medium of creation in order to comprehend how creation may be comprehended

7. Westhelle, *Scandalous God*, 103.
8. Ibid., 103–4.

as the location of Christ's presence of "within-redemption." Finally, we will both reiterate Lewis' delineation of "within-redemption," again elaborating its inadequacies, and supplement it—through our development of Luther's "third mode"—with a fuller, more concrete articulation of Christ's presence of "within-redemption"; an articulation of "within-redemption"—without recourse to a "metanarrative" which "so colors all human narratives so as to render them obsolete"—within the scope of humanity's manifold, particular, embodied narratives. But first, let us articulate what it means that "creation" is "confessed."

Creation is Confessed!

Ingolf U. Dalferth simply notes that "When we take a good look at ourselves and our world, the fact that we live in God's good creation does not leap to our attention."[9] He elaborates this dilemma by observing,

> Whatever the phenomena we may name—the astounding orders and structures of the universe, the wonder of life, the sheer improbability of there being consciousness in the world—the opposite observation can always be made: the obvious disorder, the evil and wickedness, the avoidable or unavoidable destruction of life in the process of preserving it, the senseless natural catastrophes and the futility of human efforts in the face of the approaching end of the universe. How is it that Christians speak of a good creation in the face of all this? What do they mean by "creation"?[10]

Essentially, according to Dalferth, this dilemma is placed within the context of a larger discussion which is concerned with reconciling competing conceptions of world and nature, or competing "interpretations" of "reality"—and subsequent attempts at articulating a "unity of reality" from the perspective of these interpretations—as they are evidenced (in general) by the sciences, philosophy, and theology.[11] Thus if

---

9. Dalferth, "Creation—Style of the World," 129.

10. Ibid.

11. Dalferth, "Creation—Style of the World," 119, 128. "Interpretations," according to Dalferth, "are in the broadest sense descriptive movements, in which in a particular practical context something is thematized by someone through something from a particular vantage point as something, and is brought to speech or described, indicated, named, interpreted, set forth or defined . . ." (ibid., 120). "Reality," Dalferth explains, refers to "the sum total of that which is interpreted, and thus something which is not generated exclusively by our interpretations" (ibid.).

the sciences—on the whole—base their interpretations of reality within the realm of *actuality* in order to arrive at explanatory knowledge (description, analysis, and explanation of actuality), and philosophy—on the whole—grounds its interpretations of reality within the realm of *possibility*, or "nurture[ing], cultivat[ing], and improv[ing] competence in perceiving the possible in the actual, and of understanding its truth against the background of the full range of possibility,"[12] then the sum-total of such "interpretations" of "reality," or their resultant delineations of the underlying "unity of reality," when taken as a whole and placed within a historical perspective, only further reveals the provisional nature of such "interpretations." In what fashion?

As Edward Harrison observes, such attempts by the sciences and philosophy at "interpreting" "reality"—and thus attempting to construe an underlying "unity of reality"—ultimately has only provided for an endless catalogue of a succession of "universes," or "models," by which the sum of reality is comprehended, and thus accounted for as to "unity," or "ultimate meaning."[13] According to Harrison "The universes are our models of the Universe." He avers, "They are great schemes of intricate thought—grand belief systems—that rationalize the human experience. They harmonize and invest with meaning the rising and setting Sun, the waxing and waning Moon, the jeweled lights of the night sky, the landscapes of rocks and trees, and the tumult of everyday life. Each [universe] determines what is perceived and what constitutes valid knowledge, and the members of a society believe what they perceive and perceive what they believe."[14] Harrison then adds, "*A universe is a mask fitted on the face of the unknown Universe*."[15] It is the study of history, then, as Harrison observes, that betrays the ultimate impermanence of such "interpretations," or "universes."[16] Even putting aside Dalferth's observation that "good creation" does not immediately leap to one's attention (indeed, quite the opposite!), Harrison observes that not only does a historical cataloguing of such "interpretations," or "uni-

---

12. Ibid., 126.

13. Harrison, *Masks of the Universe*, 1–11.

14. Ibid., 1.

15. Ibid. As we will see, Harrison's employment of the term "mask" is far different than that of Luthers!

16. Ibid., 3.

verses," "regard the universes of earlier societies as pathetically unreal in comparison with our own," he adds that

> We cannot understand our universe and see it in full perspective without heeding the earlier universes from which it springs. Through the historian's eyes we see the past as a gallery of grand cosmic pictures, and we wonder, is our universe [read: "interpretation"] the final picture, have we arrived at last at the end of the gallery? We see the past as a procession of masks . . . and we wonder, will the procession continue endlessly into the future? And if there is no end in sight to the gallery of pictures, no end to the mockery of masks, what are we to make of the contemporary universe in which we live, or think we live?[17]

Ultimately, then, the attempt to perceive—with the sciences and philosophy—the underlying "unity of reality" on the basis of either actuality or possibility within the parameters of that same reality, not only reveals the provisionality—when the discussion is placed within the long view of historical perspective—of all such "interpretations," but brings one back to the Dalferth's starting point: How do we manage the observation—based upon the perceptions of the sciences and philosophy both with regard to the immediate observation of the surrounding world, and the long view afforded by the study of history—that "The unity of the world is not obvious?"[18] With regard to this dilemma—that of the various "interpretations" of "reality" and, thus, of the subsequent multitude of conceptualizations of an underlying "unity of reality"—Dalferth asserts that theology—in contradistinction to the methodologies of the sciences and philosophy—frames the dilemma in an entirely different manner, thus producing a manifestly different context for discussion regarding a proposed "unity of reality." How so?

Far from attempting to conceptualize a "unity of reality"—as per the sciences and philosophy—*coram mundo*, or solely "within the horizon of the world of reality or possibility,"[19] theology, according to Dalferth (and, as we will see, in a manner commensurate with Luther), speaks of reality *coram deo*. That is, "It is concerned with the possibility of the real in the light of the presence of God as the space (*Spielraum*) of the real that is owed to God." Dalferth elaborates, "This space deter-

17. Ibid., 3–4.
18. Dalferth, "Creation—Style of the World," 137.
19. Ibid., 127.

mines what a reality can be, and, in the face of what it in fact is, what else it might have been and could still be; but it also describes the open horizon where that which is surprising, new and unanticipated takes place."[20] Thus, if it is this *Spielraum*, or presence of God, that provides the "open horizon" by which all reality "takes place," then, ultimately, "Nothing is only what it has become. Everything is an occasion for the new. Each new thing is owed to God's presence without which it would not be what it is becoming, and without which nothing is what it can be."[21] Theology evaluates all reality *coram deo*, in the light of God's "effective presence,"[22] and thus as the "gift of God"[23] who, as the Creator, "is the bearer of what is new, and so is the One who brings all things to a unity."[24] Essentially, then, to speak of reality from the perspective of God's "effective presence" is to recognize that the "unity of reality" may only be *confessed*. More pointedly: to locate the "unity of reality" within the dynamic of God's "effective presence" is to confess reality (a term which, for our purposes, in its neutral sense, as employed by the sciences and philosophy, encompasses the terms "nature" and "world") as "creation"; a creation whose unity is perceived solely in light of its relationship to the Creator's "effective presence" and subsequent giftedness by that same Creator. As Luther asserts, "The sooner someone recognizes God, the better he understands created beings."[25] Reality, then, cannot be perceived as creation without acknowledging the Creator. To recognize the Creator and the Creator's agency means to simultaneously recognize both creation and the unity of that creation. Again, as Holze observes, "World and nature [read: "reality"] can only be recognized as creation as far as God is concerned."[26]

But if this is the case, then, that all talk of reality—for theology—is conducted from the perspective of the Creator's "effective presence," then one must also be cognizant of the fact that "creation," or reality perceived from the perspective of the "effective presence" of the Creator, is not a conclusion which can be gleaned, or read, from a general experi-

20. Ibid., 126.
21. Ibid.
22. Ibid., 130.
23. Ibid., 126.
24. Ibid., 136.
25. Quoted in Holze, "Luther's Concept of Creation," 50.
26. Ibid., 49.

ence of actuality or possibility located within reality,[27] or a "generalized experience of finitude"[28] acquired via our "native faculties."[29] In other words, to speak of "creation," according to Luther, is to confess a specific Creator. "Only faith can see creation."[30] But, what this entails for Luther is that there is no discussion of creation that is not the product of one's reflection upon one's own experience of salvation in relation to the Creator. As Dalferth points out, "Christian talk of creation is . . . universalized experience of salvation."[31] In what fashion, might we ask?

As Oswald Bayer, in his interpretation of Luther's theology of creation, observes, reinforcing what has already been said, "Within the context of the Christian faith, whoever speaks about the world as the creation must necessarily speak about the Creator of the world. Whoever speaks about the Creator, speaks about the one in relationship to whom nothing greater can be conceived (*quo maius cogitari non potest*)."[32] Observing that the one who utters such thoughts would "contradict himself" were he to speak of God beyond the "foundation of his faith,"[33] Bayer immediately asserts that, "While speaking in this manner, one is at the same time speaking about oneself."[34] Thus, for Luther, any deliberation regarding creation which emanates apart from reflection upon one's own existence is considered impossible.[35] For not only is the "relevance" of the Creator determined within a conceptualization of

---

27. Dalferth, "Creation—Style of the World," 135.
28. Ibid., 130.
29. Westhelle, *Scandalous God*, 97.
30. Ibid.
31. Dalferth, "Creation—Style of the World," 130.
32. Bayer, "I Believe that God Has Created Me with All that Exists," 129.
33. Ibid.
34. Ibid.. Thus Johannes Schwanke points out in his essay "Luther on Creation," 1–2, "God's creation is not a collective, abstract occurrence but something profoundly personal: The 'I' who speaks, the human being who is endowed with individuality, perceives its individuality to be created by God and praises God, according to this faith, as one's own Creator." He adds regarding Luther's doctrine of creation, that "it begins with the concretely created instance of *my own* person and world. The relevance of the Creator is ground in the relevance of this Creator to *me*." Thus, "From Luther's perspective . . . one must first grasp the personal existence of creation before the global aspect of the created world can come into view" (ibid., 2). Ultimately, "that God 'has created *me*' cannot be divorced from the '*together with* all that exists'" (bid.).
35. Holze, "Luther's Concept of Creation," 50.

the Creator's "relevance" to *me*,³⁶ but, as David Löfgren asserts, "Luther's theology of creation does not begin with an exposition of the Creator, but rather with the concretely created world."³⁷ More explicitly: "There is no abstract . . . neutral way of defining creation . . . [apart from] the experiences we have made in and with our lives."³⁸ But it must also be added, according to Dalferth, that to treat the world as creation is tantamount to comprehending "the principle of that which is creative in our reality, describing it in the light of a knowledge about God, which knows God to be good and to will what is best for us—a knowledge that comes not from the world, but from the particular experience of God gained from the death and resurrection of Jesus Christ."³⁹ The concrete, created world is viewed through the lens of one's concrete encounter with redemption. The question, then, we must ask is this: how does one "comprehend the principle" of that which is "creative in our reality"? More specifically, how does one perceive the "effective presence," or Creator, in such a manner that redemption receives epistemological priority?⁴⁰

Hearkening back to what we have already developed in chapter two, above, let us recall that, for Luther, it is through the doctrine of redemption, or justification by faith—situated within the framework of active and passive (*extra nos*) righteousness, law and gospel, *opus alienum* and *opus proprium*—that one perceives that their "sufficiency is from God [alone]."⁴¹ To be justified by faith, or to perceive that God is one's sole, *extra nos* sufficiency, is "a most important article of faith,

36. Schwanke, "Luther on Creation," 2.

37. "Luthers Theologie der Schöpfung beginnt nicht bei der Darstellung des Schöpfers, sonder beim konkret Geschaffenen." David Löfgren, *Die Theologie der Schöpfung bei Luther*, 21. He adds, "Hier nimmt der Mensch eine besondere Stellung ein. Ihm ist nicht nur das Leben, sondern auch die Offenbarung Gottes gegeben. Vom Schöpfer weiß der Mensch nur, weil sich Gott, indem er fortwährend schaft, in seinem Werk fortwährend kundtut. Vom Menschen kann man theologisch nur in Beziehung zu diesem Schaffen und Sich-Offenbaren Gottes sprechen, aus dem auch die Gerechtigkeit des Menschen entspringt" (ibid.).

38. Holze, "Luther's Concept of Creation," 50.

39. Dalferth, "Creation—Style of the World," 135.

40. Let the reader note precisely at this point: the development of the answer to this question is founded upon the results, and indeed is an application, of our discussion in chapter two regarding the dynamics of revelation, now applied to the scope of creation.

41. LW 21:328.

including many things; it completely puts down all pride, arrogance, blasphemy, fame, and false trust, and exalts God alone. It points out the reason why God alone is to be exalted—because he does all things."[42] It is through the justification of faith, or when one perceives that God has "imposed death on us all and laid the cross of Christ together with countless sufferings and afflictions upon his beloved children,"[43] that one perceives that God is an "energetic power, a continuous activity, that works and operates without ceasing";[44] that God reveals himself to be the "true Creator."[45] The flip side of this, for Luther, is the revelation, regarding what "constitutes humankind,"[46] that "[One is] as clay in the hand of the creator, equipped only with a passive and not an active capacity."[47] Or again, as Luther similarly points out, "[I]n those matters that pertain to God and are above us no human being has a free will; he is indeed like clay in the hand of the potter, in a state of merely passive potentiality, not active potentiality."[48] Thus, underscoring the fact that for Luther the Creator's creativity and the Redeemer's work of redemption—always conceptualized throught the lens of the *theologia crucis*—are intimately connected,[49] Luther elaborates upon

42. Ibid.
43. Ibid., 321.
44. Ibid., 328.
45. Ibid., 301.
46. Holze, "Luther's Concept of Creation," 50.
47. WA 42, 64, 33, quoted by Holze, "Luther's Concept of Creation," 50.
48. LW 1:85.
49. Cf. Regin Prenter, *Luther's Theology of the Cross*, especially 16–18. According to Prenter, "Luther's theology of the cross includes a theology of history and creation. Luther sees the creative work of God in close connection with his redemptive work in Jesus Christ the crucified. He knows nothing of the modern division between the theology of the first article and that of the second" (ibid., 16). Prenter asks, "How do we come to identify the cross in the creation as the cross of Jesus Christ? Can we go along with this at all? And if not, must we then not admit that Luther's theology of the cross is not relevant for us?" (ibid., 17). He answers: "I will not go so far as to say that Luther's theology of the cross is completely irrelevant to us. I do believe, however, that it will have no meaning for us unless we acquire a new understanding of our daily life and take it seriously as both the gift and the judgment of God. Then it will become something more than just edifying talk when we say that Jesus Christ bore the guilt and punishment for our sins upon the cross. As we in the course of our own lives experience the punishment for our fall into sin through suffering, through temptation, through death, it will become clear to us that—because he bore exactly the same on our behalf and because he, who possessed the power of divine love as no other human

the relationship between his doctrine of redemption and his doctrine of creation through his articulation of the doctrine of justification in his 1535 Galatians lectures by asserting that

> God is the God of the humble, the miserable, the afflicted, the oppressed, the desperate, and of those who have been brought down to nothing at [through the ministry of the proper function of the law]. And it is the nature of God to exalt the humble, to feed the hungry, to enlighten the blind, to comfort the miser-

---

person, lived and suffered for us—this all is no longer guilt and punishment for us, but the role of the children of God, which is permitted us through the gracious command of God in the gospel. But as long as we in our own conscience do not experience the guilt and death of life earnestly as the punishment of the Creator who gives us life, preaching about the reconciliation which was effected by the cross of Christ remains a statement whose meaning we do not really understand" (ibid.). Prenter adds, "But how shall we learn to take our earthly life seriously in such a way that the reality of guilt and death becomes a genuine experience of the Creator's wrath? I believe that we can in no way guarantee it; we possess no theological or homiletical method in order to bring this about. We can only do one thing: we must be concerned about both life and the word of God with equal honesty and determination, so that we neither play life against the word, as is the case in a theology of the cross without the word, nor play the word against life, as is the case in all sorts of thinking in terms of two realms such as occurs in the orthodoxy entrenched in the church. God is the trinitarian God. He is the God life, the Creator; he is the God of the word, the Safior; he is the God of faith, the Holy Ghost. This trinity as Father, in our common experience of life, as Son, in the preached word, and as Holy Ghost, in our personal convictions, teaches us in the last analysis what these words mean: *Omnia bona in cruce et sub cruce abscondita sunt* ("All good things are hidden in and under the cross"). Therefore they cannot be understood anywhere else except under the cross; 'under the cross' means under the cross on which Jesus, our Redeemer, bore our punishment, and under the cross which my Creator has laid upon me in my suffering and in my death. In both places we are talking about the same cross. But a cross which is either only objective . . . or only subjective . . . is not the cross of Christ which is the means of our salvation. The deep truth of Luther's theology of the cross is that it views the cross on Golgotha and the cross which is laid upon us as one and the same" (ibid., 18). Although much can be said regarding Prenter's complete identification of the cross of Christ with the crosses of humanity, on the point of the identification of the Creator with the Redeemer, the first and second article, it is the assertion of our present project that it is the "third mode" of Christ's presence that provides the concrete "identification" between both the first and second articles, and the cross of Christ and the crosses of humanity. Though Prenter can speak of "identitification" properly through trinitarian language, it is the presence of the humanity of Christ that he fails to connect between the two narratives—which would provide a concrete connection between the two narratives, or between Christ and humans. Luther's interpretation of the *communicatio idiomatum* is obviously absent in Prenter's presentation of the *theologia crucis* due to the reality, Prenter thinks, that it not only fails to express the core intention of Luther's Christology, but indeed it also "inevitably leads to docetism." See Prenter, *Creation and Redemption*, 341–47.

able and afflicted, to justify sinners, to give life to the dead, and to save those who are desperate and damned. For [here it is revealed that] He is the almighty Creator, who makes everything out of nothing [*ex nihilo*].[50]

At its core, then, Luther's doctrine of justification by faith—which articulates the "saving action of God"[51] through the Word, or Christ, alone—is the "principle" by which one perceives the "effective presence" of the Creator within the scope of creation (and thus the "unity" of reality).

Therefore, elaborating upon the point that, for Luther, it is through Christ alone—*sola fide*—that God has definitively "defined himself in his relationship to the world," Holze deftly summarizes the fact that "God's permanent relationship to the world became visible in the place where the Word manifested itself. Therefore, the fact that the world as creation can only be recognized and understood as such by God means that its very nature as creation discloses itself in the place of God's incarnation. Thus, understanding Christ is the theological prerequisite for understanding the entire creation."[52] Specifically, as Bayer avers, it is the doctrine of justification that provides the context for Luther's doctrine of creation.[53] But, to be sure, such a dynamic is echoed in Luther's Small Catechism explanation of the first article of the Apostles' Creed when he confesses that

> I believe that God has created me and all that exists; that he has given me and still sustains my body and soul, all my limbs and senses, my reason and all the faculties of my mind, together with food and clothing, house and home, family and property; that he provides me daily and abundantly with all the necessities of life, protects me from all danger, and preserves me from all evil. *All this he does out of his pure, fatherly, and divine goodness and mercy, without any merit or worthiness on my part.* For all of this I am bound to thank, praise, serve, and obey him. This is most certainly true.[54]

Essentially, then, as Luther elaborates his doctrine of creation with the employment of the language of justification, so he points up how the

---

50. LW 26:314.
51. Dalferth, "Creation—Style of the World," 135.
52. Holze, "Luther's Concept of Creation," 52.
53. Bayer, "Justification as the Basis and Boundary of Theology," 274–75.
54. BC: 344–45; italics added for emphasis.

fundamental, mundane aspects of human life are grounded in the active, *extra nos* Word whose agency, bound by absolutely no concepts of human merit, is motivated completely by "divine goodness and mercy." Therefore, according to Bayer, "My very being is faith, that is, my trusting that life and what is necessary for life is given to me."[55] Thus, as Bayer observes, the doctrine of *creatio ex nihilo*, derived through the doctrine of justification, refers to the confession that all reality—confessed as creation—exists purely out of God's creative goodness, God's "divine goodness and mercy": "The world was not called into being because of any this worldly necessity, but out of pure freedom and goodness."[56] So, again, the key to understanding Luther's theology of creation, of which *creatio ex nihilo* is the *radix*,[57] resides within the conceptual framework of his articulation of justification by faith.[58] For "only through the en-

---

55. Bayer, "Justification as the Basis and Boundary of Theology," 275. On this point see also Schwarzwäller's foreward in Mattes, *Role of Justification in Contemporary Theology*, xi, and his essay "Theology as Unfolding the Article of Justification," 39.

56. Bayer, "Justification as the Basis and Boundary of Theology," 277. See also Bayer's essay "I Believe that God Has Created Me with All that Exists,"155, in which he asserts, reflecting upon Luther's Small Catechism explanation of the first article of the Creed, and thus the fact that the divine goodness and mercy forms the framework of articulating the doctrine of *creatio ex nihilo*, "I am continually receiving God's giving goodness and saving mercy that are given without incurring debt, freely." He adds, "A second meaning of the formula is associated with its first meaning. This meaning emerges as the answer to the urgent question: What would happen if this giving goodness and this saving mercy, this God, did not exist? Then, everything would be nothing, all would be lost" (ibid.).

57. Cf. LW 1:16, "I have said that in the beginning there was created through the Word that unformed mass of earth and heaven . . . and that this must be assigned to the work of the first day, although this is the first time Moses speaks thus: 'God said, 'Let there be light!' However, this expression is indeed remarkable and unknown to the writers of all other languages, that through His speaking God makes something out of nothing. And so here for the first time Moses mentions the means and the instrument God used in doing His work, namely, the Word." Again: "For God calls into existence the things which do not exist . . . He does not speak grammatical words; He speaks true and existent realities" (ibid., 21).

58. Let us note again how the doctrine of *creatio ex nihilo* is tied with the doctrine of justification: "Therefore in the beginning and before every creature there is the Word, and it is such a powerful Word that it makes all things out of nothing." He thus adds, "These are difficult matters, and it is unsafe to go beyond the limit to which the Holy Spirit leads us. Let us, therefore, come to a halt with the knowledge that when the unformed heaven and the unformed earth, both of them marred by mist and darkness, had come into existence, light also came into existence out of nothing, that is, out of the very darkness. Paul cites this first work of the Creator as an extraordinary work . . . This, therefore, is sufficient for the confirmation of our faith: that Christ is true God,

counter with Christ, the Word that became flesh, through whom all things came into being . . . it becomes possible to recognize the world as creation."[59]

But here, again, precisely at this point, we must be careful: though *creatio ex nihilo*, articulated within a conceptualization of the doctrine of justification, sits at the root of Luther's theology of creation (thus identifying the *modus operandi* of God's "effective presence"), we must be sure to underscore—with Bayer—the Creator's commitment in his creativity to the creatures which he creates/preserves. In other words, *creatio ex nihilo* does not refer to a God who creates/preserves without the assistance of creation, without the mediation of creatures/creation. As will be developed, we may say that creation is the medium of the Creator's creating. This point becomes clear in Luther's fuller elaboration of the first article of the Apostles' Creed in his Large Catechism when he asserts, "Besides, *he makes all creation help provide* the comforts and necessities of life—sun, moon, and stars in the heavens, day and night, air, fire, water, the earth and all that it brings forth, birds and fish, beasts, grain and all kinds of produce. Moreover, he gives all physical and temporal blessings—good government, peace, security."[60] Ultimately, then, creation is the medium, and thus the "mask" of the redeeming and creating Word. Restated: if, as we have asserted, to confess reality, or the world, as *creation* is inextricably bound to the confession of its *Creator*, then—as will be developed below—to confess creation simultaneously means that one both perceives—by faith—the world in all of its manifestations as a *larva Dei*, while piercing through those masks to perceive the unity, or "substance,"[61] in, with, and under that same creation.

It is to the development of this dynamic—creation as the medium, or "mask," of the Word—to which we will now turn our attention.

---

who is with the Father from eternity, before the world was made, and that through Him, who is the wisdom and the Word of the Father, the Father made everything. But in the passage referred to this point should be noted: *that Paul regards the conversion of the wicked—something which is also brought about by the Word—as a new of work of creation*" (LW 1:17).

59. Holze, "Luther's Concept of Creation," 52.
60. BC: 412; italics added for emphasis.
61. LW 9:7.

Medium as Mask

Countering the Theologia Gloriae: The Proper "Use" and "Substance" of Creation

If it is sheer "folly to argue much about God outside and before time," for Luther, this is the case because "this is an effort to understand the Godhead without a covering, or the uncovered divine essence."[62] Elaborating upon this point, Luther adds that "outside [the] beginning of . . . creation there is nothing except the uncovered divine essence and the uncovered God. And, because He is incomprehensible, that, too, is incomprehensible which was before the world, because it is nothing except [God in his naked majesty]."[63] But what all of this means according to Luther, that is, with reference to the consequences for those who seek God beyond the realm of creation, is that "those who want to reach God apart from . . . [his] coverings exert themselves to ascend to heaven without ladders (that is, without the Word). Overwhelmed by His majesty, which they seek without a covering, they fall to their destruction."[64] The Creator, then, must "wear a 'mask' [*larva*] or 'veil' [*involucrum*][65] in all His dealing with men, to shield them from the unapproachable light of his [naked] majesty."[66] Or, as Vítor Westhelle points out, to appropriate another one of Luther's metaphors, "The *Deus vestitus*, the clothed God . . . protects us from the *Deus nudus*, the naked God, which is the irresistible abyss."[67] But essentially what this discussion points up, according to Philip Watson, is the reality that "God is not to be sought behind His creation by inference from it, but is rather to be apprehended in and through it."[68] The cardinal error of all theology, then, especially as it concerns a doctrine of creation, is when the veiled (*involuto*) God

---

62. LW 1:11.
63. Ibid., 17–18.
64. Ibid., 14.
65. See LW 26:95.
66. Watson, *Let God Be God*, 78. Sittler, *Doctrine of the Word in the Structure of Lutheran Theology*, 65, states, "Now Luther holds to the biblical principle that man cannot see God in his naked transcendence, and live. God, therefore, wears a mask (*larva*) or veil (*involucrum*) in all his dealings with men to shield them from his unapproachable brightness."
67. Westhelle, *Scandalous God*, 99.
68. Watson, *Let God Be God*, 78.

is bypassed for the sake of the *Deus nudus* who lies beyond the limits of the created world.[69] And, having stated this, we have reached the nub of the matter.

Ultimately, then, it may be asserted that if, acknowledging the "cruciform character of [Luther's] theology,"[70] Luther's doctrine of justification was grounded in his absolute refusal to seek the "invisible things of God" analogically (i.e., in such a manner that that which is unknown is inferred by the known), and thus apart from "this Man Jesus Christ,"[71] thus "spurn[ing] all speculation about the Divine Majesty,"[72] then his doctrine of creation is—as will be developed via his employment of the *larva*-terminology—a corresponding and commensurate application of the *theologia crucis* and its accompanying epistemology to his perception of the created world. The *larva*-language, or the application of Luther's cruciform epistemology, is the application of cross to the realm of creation. Therefore Luther can declare, "The whole creation is a face or mask of God."[73] Both this sub-section and the subsequent sub-section will unpack this claim from the perspective of both its negative significance (against the background of the methodology of the *theologia gloriae* and its "misuse" of the created world, as we have already initiated) and its positive significance (as a confession of both God's communion with, and presence within, creation) respectively.[74] But let us continue developing the negative significance of Luther's employment of the concept *larva(e) Dei*.

Watson observes that the root error of a theologian of glory "is not merely that [she] ignores the mediation of Christ [with regard to the matter of salvation],"[75] but, she "is equally at fault in [her] treatment of the created world."[76] Watson, pointing out the theologian of glory's employment of analogical thinking with reference to creation, elabo-

---

69. Ibid.
70. Sittler, *Doctrine of the Word*, 66.
71. LW 26:29.
72. Ibid.
73. Ibid., 95.
74. The phraseology "negative significance" and "positive significance" is adapted from Philip Watson who explicitly employs the phrase "negative significance." Cf. Watson, *Let God Be God*, 78ff.
75. Watson, *Let God Be God*, 78–79.
76. Ibid., 79.

rates: "If [she] begins with 'the things that are made,' [she] argues all too literally *from* them, for [she] seeks in fact to *pass beyond* them, so that they are left behind as knowledge of their Maker is gained."[77] Staying with Watson a bit further, he adds, "Luther refuses to regard the [created world] as a mere starting-point in the quest for God. He does so, moreover, not simply because he has no confidence in man's ability to find God by that method, but even more because he sets a different value on 'the things that are made.'"[78] For, essentially, as Watson observes, "the things that are made"—the created world—are interpreted by Luther as "masks of God" (*larvae Dei*), thus asserting that "'every creature is His mask (*larva*)' . . . insisting that, in this life at any rate, the mask (*larva*) can never be removed for us to see God 'face to face.'"[79] With this in mind, thus spurning speculation and the subsequent terror of encountering the *Deus nudus* as per the methodology of the *theologia gloriae*, Luther avers that (and observe how he involves the Trinity in his articulation in God's "covered" agency), "the works of God are set before us so that we can grasp them. Such works are: that He created the heaven and the earth, that He sent His son, that He speaks through His Son, that He baptizes, that He absolves from sin through the Word . . . [for] He who does not apprehend these facts will never apprehend God."[80] Again, God's presence (which is tied with his agency, as has been developed in chapter three, above) is only mediated to humanity, and thus perceived, "through the mediation of creatures,[81] or *larvae Dei*,

77. Ibid.
78. Ibid.
79. Ibid.

80. LW 1:15. See also LW 2:45 in which Luther asserts that, as God in his majesty is unknowable, so "It is for this reason that God lowers Himself to the level of our weak apprehension and presents Himself to us in images, in coverings, as it were, in simplicity adopted to a child, that in some measure it may be possible for Him to be known by us."

81. Schwanke, "Luther on Creation," 4. Again, I point the reader to Luther's assertion his "Schmalkald Articles," BC: 313, that "we should and must constantly maintain that God will not deal with us except through his external Word and sacrament." Indeed, as Gustaf Wingren points out, in his *Luther on Vocation*, 117, for Luther, the *larvae Dei*—countering the Enthusiasts—express the reality that "God does not come to man in thoughts and feelings which well up in him when he isolates himself from the world, but rather in what happens to man in the external and tangible events which take place about him." Thus: let always be careful to note that Luther's doctrine of creation is an extrapolation of his articulation of the sacraments, or the external Word!

in such a manner—according to Luther—that through such "veils" or "wrappers"[82] one may assuredly declare: "Look! Under this wrapper you will be sure to take hold of me."[83] Thus, countering the theologian of glory's analogical "use" of creation, according to Luther, "God does not act in the abstract, *nudum* (without means) . . . but rather binds his activity to creaturely events."[84] And, as will be more explicitly developed below, it is the "veil" or "wrapping" motif, as it is employed by Luther, that "reveals a presence while denying to our eyes' sight any evidence of its content."[85] Thus, "The visible things . . . do not allow for any direct or even indirect access to revelation . . . but they make [God's "effective agency" present] simultaneously directly and indirectly."[86] The presence of the Creator, thus, is understood as a "mediated immediacy."[87] But if Luther's *larva*-terminology—indeed as an expression of his *theologia crucis* now applied to his doctrine of creation—counters the theologian of glory's analogical "use" of creation by binding God's creating activity to creaturely covers, or *larvae*, then—also against the predilections of the *theologia gloriae*—we must acknowledge a second negative significance of Luther's *larva*-terminology. In short, if God's creating activity is bound to external, creaturely "wrappings," or *larvae*, then Luther also observes that this externally-mediated agency itself provides the opportunity for temptation for theologians of glory. How so?

"[E]ven if God creates, nourishes, preserves, and governs all the sons of men," as Luther asserts, "nevertheless He does not want any to be idle but gives them members with which they should bear, cherish, and govern one another, whereby God [has] given the occasion for creating, nourishing and ruling."[88] Thus, according to Luther, the "occasions" which God grants for creating, nourishing, and ruling consist of, but are certainly not limited to "the magistrate, the emperor, the king, the prince, the consul, the teacher, the preacher, the pupil, the father, the mother, the children, the master, the servant—all these are social positions or external masks. God wants us to respect and acknowledge them

82. LW 1:15.
83. Ibid.
84. Schwanke, "Luther on Creation," 4.
85. Westhelle, *Scandalous God*, 98.
86. Ibid., 98.
87. Ibid. Cf. Watson, *Let God Be God*, 103.
88. LW 9:40–41.

as His creatures, which are a necessity for this life."[89] But if these "social positions," and outward appearances in general, through which God creates, nourishes, and rules are a "necessity for this life" which "God wants us to respect," they also, as Luther observes, provide problems for humans who fixate on outward appearances, or "have the innate fault that [they] show great respect for the position of men and pay more attention to it than to the Word."[90] In other words, if these social positions are the covers by which "the power of God hidden under the human activity is seen by faith to do all things,"[91] then, for the "unbeliever," they also become nothing more than another opportunity to exhibit partiality to the "shell" as opposed to the "kernel,"[92] "to fear and respect [outward appearances] in such a way that we trust them and forget [the Creator]."[93] Simply, the *Deus vestitus* by which God's creating activity is concealed becomes a potential idol,[94] thus affirming the point that the "material world ... can be both an idol as well as ... the wrapping of the divine."[95]

Ultimately then, if, on the one hand, Luther understands the "covers" by which God conceals his creating agency to counter the attempts of theologians of glory to "use" creation analogically, then, on the other hand, he also recognizes the opportunity they provide for human self-aggrandizement by fixating on their outward appearance alone to the exclusion of the God who both "uses" them, and is their "substance." But, Luther also notes, if it is the "secular and unregenerate man"[96] who "attributes divinity"[97] to such outward appearances, then it is only the "spiritual man"[98]—justified by faith—who perceives "the stuff and substance behind the masks,"[99] or the Word. According to Luther, then, it is the "spiritual man" who "alone can distinguish the position from the

---

89. LW 26:95.
90. LW 26:94.
91. LW 9:41
92. LW 26:94.
93. Ibid., 95.
94. Westhelle, *Scandalous God*, 99.
95. Ibid. 100.
96. LW 26:94.
97. Ibid., 95.
98. Ibid.
99. LW 9:7.

Word, the divine mask from God Himself and the mask of God."[100] Or, as Wingren asserts, "[M]an must beware lest he place his faith and reliance in external things, which are only a garb for God, and not God himself ... [therefore] All creation is good, but it becomes evil if it is worshiped and substituted for God."[101]

Regarding Luther's implementation of the *larva*-terminology, if the *larvae Dei* are employed by Luther to counter the analogical "use" of creation by theologians of glory, they also are a confession (by faith!) of the reality—by the sheer employment of the terminology—that there is no human position, power, possession, or production which is not "a mask under which He blesses us and dispenses His gifts."[102] In other words, for Luther, to even acknowledge the *larvae Dei* is to confess that God alone is the "substance" of one's entire existence. For "if someone knows that the power and wisdom of God are of such a sort, he trusts wholly, not in the mask of God but in the Word behind the mask; and he can and does perform wonders, yes, everything, in the Lord."[103] To confess the *larvae Dei*, especially with reference to human social positions, and certainly to outward appearances in general, then, is to both properly distinguish—contra the theologian of glory—creature from Creator, and recognize the sole source and strength, or "substance," of the creature's existence. Indeed, we must add, to perceive the covers by which God conceals his creating agency through the Word as the *larvae Dei* is to acknowledge a sanctity the world is unable to recognize, or, that is, to "know that all things are sanctified by the Word."[104] For if one perceives by faith that God is the "substance" of all works, then "whether you see the sordidness [read: performance of mundane, domestic duties] or the gems of the saints and their works, yet they [both] are pleasing to God, who is the Author of trifling and noble works alike; for they are works of God, and God cooperates."[105]

---

100. LW 26:95.
101. Wingren, *Luther on Vocation*, 138.
102. LW 9:96.
103. Ibid., 41.
104. LW 5:275.
105. LW 5:277. Therefore, as Wingren thus points out in his *Luther on Vocation*, 138, "man must beware lest he place his faith and reliance in external things, which are only a garb for God and not God himself. Our equipment is only a 'costume' for God, behind which he hides to help us; but he expects us to give our hearts to him, not to his 'costume'; we must not pray to that."

But if, with reference to its negative significance, the *larva*-terminology, for Luther, is employed to counter the tendencies of theologians of glory who both "use" creation analogically, and attribute ultimacy to the social positions of humans—not to mention the outward appearance of creation in general—to the exclusion of the Creator, then we must certainly lift up the positive significance of Luther's *larva*-terminology, or that of articulating both the reality that creation itself is an expression of God's communion with his creatures, and that all of creation is the realm by which Christ encounters humans. It is to this positive significance of Luther's *larva*-terminology that we now turn.

Larvae Dei: *Communicating Creation*

If, as we have already developed, the Creator's presence is articulated as a communicative event by the "most active working of God" (*Deus actuossimus*)[106] through the Word[107] in whom creating and preserving are considered identical,[108] then we must simultaneously acknowledge that creation itself is an act of communion,[109] an "address to the creature through the creature."[110] Indeed, acknowledging that the *larva*-terminology encompasses human cooperation,[111] and that indeed God's works in creation are not purely of "instrumental or aesthetic value" but also "expressions of God's intention and will," Niels Henrik Gregersen asserts that "created beings are God's partners with whom God wants to cooperate although God could have created without the help of creatures."[112] Thus, elaborating this positive significance of the *larva*-terminology, let us develop just this claim.

Recognizing creation to be the product of the "most active working" of the Creator, Luther acknowledges that creation no doubt *could* be an *unmediated* matter, that, for instance, God "could give children

---

106. LW 33:233.

107. See LW 1:22: "What else is the entire creation than the Word of God uttered by God, or extended to the outside."

108. LW 4:136.

109. See Bayer, "Creation as History," 253.

110. Bayer, "Angels are Interpreters," 271.

111. Wingren, *Luther on Vocation*, 137.

112. Gregersen, "Natural Events as Crystals of God—Luther's Eucharistic Theology and the Question of Nature's Sacramentality," 147.

without using men and women."[113] Nevertheless, Luther emphasizes—on the matter of procreation/child-rearing—that God "wishes to work only through human cooperation,"[114] that God "joins man and woman so that it appears to be the work of man and woman, and yet [God] does it under the cover of such masks."[115] Or, as Luther illustrates, "What else is all our work to God—whether in the fields, in the garden, in the city, in the house, in war, or in government—but just such a child's performance, by which He wants to give His gifts in the fields, at home, and everywhere else?"[116] Far from setting aside his creation, and specifically, in this case, his creatures, as superfluous to his almighty, "effective presence," instead "they may rather be said to represent Him on the stage where [God] Himself in fact plays the principal part . . . For [God's] creatures are . . . the instruments, the means by which God bestows all things on us."[117] Again, as Schwanke elaborates, "Human creation is grounded in the harmony of divine and human action: on the one hand, in the encounter of . . . Creator and creature . . . on the other hand . . . in the encounter of man and woman, body and soul, and flesh and spirit."[118] This "indivisible wovenness"[119] between Creator and creature is articulated beautifully by Luther when he states

> For God rules us in such a way that He does not want us to be idle. He gives us food and clothing, but in such a way that we should plow, sow, reap, and cook. In addition, He give offspring, which is born and grows because of the blessing of God and must nevertheless be cherished, cared for, brought up, and instructed by the parents. But when we have done what is in us,

---

113. LW 14:114.

114. Schwanke, "Luther on Creation," 7.

115. LW 14:114.

116. Ibid.

117. Watson, *Let God Be God*, 79. So Gustaf Wingren, *Flight from Creation*, 21, eloquently points out, "Underlying the whole of Luther's argument is the conviction that God is the Creator who is still creating life and who, in doing so, uses intercourse between man and woman, the act of birth, suckling one's young, seedtime and harvest, the everyday round" (ibid., 17). Ultimately, then, "Salvation is a deliverance to naturalness, to essentially worldly duties, already given to everyone in the creation but lost by rebellion against God."

118. Schwanke, "Luther on Creation," 5.

119. Ibid., 8.

then we should entrust the rest to God and cast our care on the Lord; for He will take care of us.[120]

Indeed all human work is encompassed "in the three estates (*ordines*) of church (*ecclesia*), family (*oeconomia*) and secular authority (*politia*)" which is thus an acknowledgment "that all human work is embedded in God's comprehensive previous work."[121] But, let us note well on just this point, not only are all the stations and places of humanity which stand within the broad expanse of creation "sanctified by God's address [or, Word,] and bound up with God's own divine action,"[122] but any preconception of a God whose "effective presence" as Creator is depicted unqualifiedly as an "absolute monarch" is countered, according to George Murphy, by a God whose concealment by the masks he uses reveals a God who "is willing to have those [masks] receive the credit."[123] Perhaps we might even say that God is even willing to be considered unnecessary and, therefore, risks being ignored in the process of committing himself to creation in the very process of its creating.[124]

But, obviously, the communicative event of creation is not purely limited to cooperative, human *larvae* through the three estates, but employs the entire realm of creation. Oswald Bayer eloquently addresses this expanded scope of creating via the Creator's "mediated immediacy" when he states that

---

120. LW 8:94, quoted in Schwanke, "Luther on Creation," 8.

121. Holze, "Luther's Concept of Creation," 51. Cf. Bayer, *Living by Faith*, 60, in which Bayer, noting not only the cooperative-creating aspect of the communicative address of the Word, but also its sanctifying reality, notes regarding the three estates that they are the "three basic forms of life into which God's promise has disposed us, the Church, the economy, and the political sphere. Everything natural and everything cultural, the whole world in all the width and depth of its inner and outer nature, all social relationships and our relationship to self, stand under the Word of God that 'sanctifies' these relationships, or institutions." He adds, "These three estates are for Luther the only means by which God sanctifies us in our everyday world." To say the least, much groundbreaking work has recently been written on Luther's articulation of the three estates. A full development of the contours of this research would detain us beyond the scope of the project at hand. For further reading I point the reader to Bayer, "Nature and Institution," 127–25; Schwanke, "Luther on Creation," esp. pp. 10ff.; Westhelle, "Word and Mask," 167–78; LW 2:356, 5:135–39, 37:365, 41:167.

122. Schwanke, "Luther on Creation," 7.

123. Murphy, "Theology of the Cross and God's Work in the World," 225.

124. Ibid.

When present in creation, obviously God does not speak directly. God neither works without mediation nor acts immediately. Although he could, God does not will to do so. God wants to encounter his creatures through creaturely means. Through creaturely means, mediators and messengers, God creates, sustains, guides and leads creation to its consummation. Creation is address to the creature through the creature. *There are no creatures that God cannot use as his messengers*: human beings and stars, animals and elements, a particular succession of notes in a fugue by Bach, Apollo's torso that says to you, "You must change your life," music, the beauty of art, and even the ugly. God can make everything that is created, the visible and the invisible, into his angels.[125]

Essentially, then, God's "effective presence," is not limited to the *larvae* of human cooperation within the three estates of church, family, secular authority, or even to the scope of history[126] and the rise and fall of governments,[127] but encompasses the entirety of creation itself. So Gregersen observes, "Luther never fought against the idea that happenings in the natural world may become a testimony of God in nature

---

125. Bayer, "Angels are Interpreters," 271. Bayer comments, with reference to Luther's Small Catechism petition "Let your holy angel be with me, so that the wicked foe may have no power over me," "Does it not suffice that God is present and has the power to protect? Is it not enough that the heavenly Father has both the power and will to preserve, and to bring creation to its completion? Is anything else needed? The answer is a resounding no! Thus, the subject of the angels of God cannot be about a 'more.' It is not about something that can be added to God's presence or that is to be distinguished from the divine presence. When the talk is of angels, then one speaks about *the concrete ways in which the divine presence is manifest*" (ibid.).

126. For a development of Luther's understanding of history as a *larva Dei*, see Lennart Pinomaa's *Faith Victorious*, 36–43.
Luther asserts, "Hence Nineveh is called a city of God because God gave it increase and His blessing, and because He is concerned about it and governs it. Similarly, trees of God are called those which the Lord made and about which He is concerned, since He supplies rain, sunlight, and winds, from which they derive their increase, even if ungodly men own them. And it is indeed no small comfort that God establishes, maintains, and protects governments, and that they do not, as we generally suppose, either rise or fall by accident. The heathen are not aware of this control; they fancy that governments are established and controlled by their own effort. Hannibal thinks that he is conquering the Romans by reason of the great courage and the extraordinary diligence he possesses. Alexander has greater gifts, which enable him to be successful in all his undertakings. But these are 'masks.' They are the only things we see. But God's control, by which governments are either strengthened or overturned, we do not see" (LW 2:343).

127. LW 26:95.

when and where it pleases God."[128] The one who is justified by faith encounters the Word of God "in the artisan's workshop, in the fruitfulness of a mother's womb, and even see God in the stone of a peach!"[129] Again, as Wingren points out, faith pierces through *die Mummerei* (masquerade), or *das Maskenspiel* (masked ball) in order to recognize nature as God's disguise.[130] He adds, "A fruit tree or rain is a disguise for God. The mother who gives her breast to her child is also a disguise, *eine Maske, eine Mumme*. All the way God is giving life, but he does it disguised."[131] The list extends to "Natural occurrences such as storms and thunder, or sun, or rich harvests [which] are also God's masks, behind which his wrath and his love are hid."[132] Indeed, expounding upon what he terms God's "spiritual presence," or the confession that no corner of creation is bereft of the Creator's presence, and thus free from serving the Creator's purposes,[133] Luther, in his exposition of Jonah 2:4 "lays special stress on the statement that it was God . . . who cast [Jonah] into the sea; that it was not simply the waves of the sea, but God's waves, that encompassed him."[134] As Wingren points out, "For so the troubled conscience looks

---

128. Gregersen, "Natural Events as Crystals of God," 148. Gregersen adds, "An argumentative system of natural theology is one thing, another thing is the sudden experiencing of God, through the Holy Spirit, in and through natural and social events" (ibid.).

129. WA TR 1, 574, quoted by Gregersen, "Natural Events as Crystals of God," 8.

130. Gustaf Wingren, "Doctrine of Creation," 363.

131. Ibid.

132. Wingren, *Luther on Vocation*, 137.

133. LW 19:44–45. "But this must be understood thus: God has two kinds of essence, or presence—the one is natural, the other spiritual. He is present everywhere naturally. Is. 66:1 declares: 'Heaven is my throne, and the earth is My footstool.' Thus God is present also in the midst of hell, death, and sin, as the aforementioned psalm says (Ps 139:8): 'If I make my bed in Sheol, Thou art there.' Therefore no one can escape from Him. But God is present spiritually only where He is spiritually known, Wherever His Word, faith, Spirit, and worship are, there His people are to be found, who alone perceive that God is an almighty and omnipresent God. The ungodly do not feel that; they do not believe and do not know that God is everywhere, even though they hear this said and are able to repeat it. It is therefore possible to flee from God in the sense that we may run off to a place where there is neither Word, faith, and Spirit nor the knowledge of God. In that way Jonah fled from the presence of the Lord, that is, he ran away from the people and the land of Judah, in which God's Word and Spirit and faith and knowledge were present; he fled to the sea among the Gentiles, where there was no faith, Word, and Spirit of God" (ibid.).

134. Wingren, *Luther on Vocation*, 116.

upon everything about him—nature, things, and all creatures ... [as] divine expression[s], God's action and instruments[.]"¹³⁵ So Luther states on this passage: "Jonah does not simply say: 'The waves and the billows passed over me,' but: 'Thy waves and Thy billows, etc.,' for he feels in his conscience that the sea with its waves and billows serve God and His wrath for the punishment of sin ... and that all creatures were in league with God against him."¹³⁶ But it is precisely here that we must segue to our next point.

For if the only God Luther confesses is the One in whom the Redeemer is strictly identified with the Creator, then we may consider the reality that the whole of creation, indeed, is not only a wrapping, or mask, of the Creator (thus serving the Creator's purposes), but certainly a container of Christ, a matrix for encountering the Redeemer's presence.¹³⁷ Therefore if Luther can assert that "all created ordinances are masks or allegories wherewith God depicts his nature; they are meant, as it were, to contain Christ,"¹³⁸ he also expands the scope of this "containing" by asserting that "The whole creation is a face or mask of God."¹³⁹ For if it is an "ever present possibility" of the theologian of the cross to expect "that God wants Godself to be ... found in the miniatures of ordinary life,"¹⁴⁰ then, again, it is only logical from the perspective of the *theologia crucis*, that the whole of creation is a *larva*, and thus a container, for Christ. It is to this point in our development of the *larvae Dei*—with specific attention paid to our development of the presence of Christ's *sub contraria specie* redemption, or "within-redemption"—that we now turn.

---

135. Ibid.

136. LW 19:76.

137. I refer to the reader to what appears to be a little-known gem by Aarne Siirala entitled *Divine Humanness*, for not only a magnificent articulation of this reality, but the articulation of this reality as the essential matter at stake in conflict with Erasmus. See especially 60–81.

138. WA 42:292, 22ff., quoted in Sittler, *Doctrine of the Word*, 66.

139. LW 26:95

140. Gregersen, "Natural Events as Crystals of God," 148.

Creation of Christ

If Luther's radical interpretation of Chalcedon's *communicatio idiomatum*—as we have developed at length—was an expression of the absolute identification of the man Jesus Christ, or the Redeemer, with the Creator's "effective presence," or the "most active working of God" (*Deus actuossimus*), then the result of such an interpretation is nothing less than the "third mode" of Christ's presence. This "third mode" of presence, according to Luther, is articulated in such a wise, according to Luther, that "You must place this existence of Christ, which constitutes him one person with God, far, far beyond things created, as far as God transcends them; and on the other hand, place it as deep in and as near to all created things as God is in them. For he is one indivisible person with God, and wherever God is, he must be also, otherwise our faith is false."[141] Essentially, then, within the logic of Luther's "cruciform theology," or *theologia crucis*, to confess the "third mode" of Christ's presence implies not only the obverse—and simultaneous!—side of the confession that "The whole creation is a face or mask of God,"[142] but indeed is the presupposition upon which such a statement may be made in the first place. On this correspondence between the "third mode" of Christ's

---

141. LW 37:223. Certainly the "third mode" of Christ's presence is no isolated concept, or theological novelty, for Luther. Not only is it the presupposition of Luther's articulation of the *larvae Dei*, but receives explicit elaboration at other points within the same text, as well. Thus Luther can state, "Again, since they do not prove that the right hand of God is a particular place in heaven, the mode of existence of which I have spoken also stands firm, that Christ's body is everywhere because it is at the right hand of God which is everywhere, although we do not know how that occurs. For we also do not know how it occurs that the right hand of God is everywhere. It is certainly not the mode by which we see with our eyes that an object is somewhere, as the fanatics regard the sacrament. But God no doubt has a mode by which it can be somewhere and that's the way it is until the fanatics prove the contrary" (ibid., 213–14). Luther can also state, searching for analogies to this "third mode," "Consider our physical eyes and our power of vision. When we open our eyes, in one moment our sight is five or six miles away, and simultaneously present everywhere within the range of those six miles. Yet this is only a matter of sight, the power of the eye. If physical sight can do this, do you not think that God's power can also find a way by which all creatures can be present and permeable to Christ's body?" (ibid., 217). And again: "Nothing is so small but God is still smaller, nothing so large but God is still larger, nothing so short but God is still shorter, nothing so long but God is still longer, nothing so broad but God is still broader, nothing so narrow but God is still narrower, and so on. He is an inexpressible being, above and beyond all that can be described or imagined" (ibid., 228).

142. LW 26:95.

presence (itself, as has been developed, grounded in God's creating sovereignty) and "mask" Löfgren can state, "It is thus important to be clear on the matter that God, who governs the world through his creatures, his *'larvae'* ... who consequently is the Lord of history without whom nothing occurs—*that for Luther this God is none other than the God revealed in Christ who governs his creation and leads it toward its destiny.*"[143] With this said, let us briefly examine the significance of what it means, on account of Luther's radical interpretation of the *communicatio idiomatum*, and specifically his articulation of the "third mode" of Christ's presence, that the whole of creation is the "mask of God," and thus the "container" of Christ.

If, as Watson avers, "Luther's assertion of the ubiquity of Christ's body ... is fundamentally a defense of his conviction that wheresoever God is at work, He is at work in love,"[144] then the core expression of Luther's doctrine of creation, or the *larvae Dei*, only implies what his Christology makes explicit. In other words, from the perspective of his doctrine of creation, if through the Word the Creator is *Deus actuossimus* throughout the entire scope of creation, then the *larvae Dei* are an expression of the reality that "wheresoever and howsoever He acts, His activity springs from no other source than the love that is revealed in Christ."[145]

Because the divine love which is revealed in, with, and under creation is the same as that which is revealed through the incarnation, not only are the "creatures of God ... so to speak, mirrors of the Divine love that seeketh not its own,"[146] but "everything in creation—except man and the devil—bears open testimony to the constancy and selfless generosity of the Creator's love."[147] As God encountered humans in, with, and under the *involucrum* of the first-century incarnation, so also through the *larvae Dei* "the Divine majesty Himself is [still] actively confronting

---

143. "Es ist auch wichtig, sich klar darüber zu sein, daß der Gott, der durch seine Geschöpfe, seine "larvae" die Welt regiert ... der somit der Herr der Geschichte ist, ohne den nichts geschieht—*daß dieser Got für Luther kein anderer ist, als der in Christus offenbarte Gott, der seine Schöpfung regiert und ihrer Bestimmung entgegenführt.*" Löfgren, *Die Theologie der Schöpfung bei Luther*, 213

144. Watson, *Let God Be God*, 162

145. Ibid., 136.

146. Ibid.

147. Ibid., 137.

men, presenting Himself to them with a 'mediated immediacy.'"[148] For as the *larvae Dei*—whose presupposition is the "third mode" of Christ's presence—are the means by which, and express the dynamic that, the divine love of Christ encounters humans "precisely in the 'material substantial sphere,'"[149] or "in all the circumstances of [the human's] concrete existence"[150] (so much so that through the *larvae Dei* Luther could declare that "God has placed forgiveness of sins in all His creatures"),[151] Watson also observes that, as the essence of the divine love has drawn near, and been revealed, to humanity in the first-century incarnation of the Word, so the *larvae Dei* express the reality that this same presence of divine love has not since ceased being revealed through every corner of creation.[152] But let us also not forget, as Bayer reminds us, hearkening back to our development of the "third mode" of Christ's presence both as the ultimate expression of Luther's *theologia crucis*—through the incarnation God has lowered himself into the scale-pan[153]—and the presupposition of Luther's doctrine of creation as expressed through the *larvae Dei*, "It is not only in the redemption of the world, but already in its creation that God humbles himself, pours himself out, fully and wholly gives himself away. His omnipotence is humble. Creation is God's fully giving himself, as pledge and promise—as establishment and preservation of communion . . ."[154] "Thus," Luther declares of this "down-to-earth" God, "the world is full of God. In every alley, at your door you find Christ; stare not at [the] heavens."[155]

In other words, stated for the purpose of our project, through the *larvae Dei*, which are an expression of, and presuppose, the "third mode" of Christ's presence, there is no aspect of creation which is bereft of Christ's presence of "within-redemption." Thus, countering, on the one hand, those whose "all too human"[156] thoughts prevent them from

148. Ibid., 103.
149. Ibid., 115.
150. Ibid., 80.
151. Quoted in Watson, *Let God Be God*, 116.
152. Watson, *Let God Be God*, 163.
153. LW 41:103–4.
154. Bayer, "Creation as History," 259.
155. WA 20, 514, 27ff., quoted in Westhelle, "Word and Mask: Revisiting the Two-Kingdoms Doctrine," in *Gift of Grace*, 278.
156. LW 33:47.

allowing the "infinite" God to "bear the finite" world of creatureliness, or prevent them from allowing the eternally-begotten Word to completely enter the realm of the flesh,[157] Luther, on the other hand, through his complete identification of the Redeemer with the Creator, subsequently and immediately chastises those who would disavow the presence of this same Redeemer within every present location and circumstance—even the most vile—of this finite creation. On this point, Luther asserts,

> Therefore, a godly mind is not shocked to hear that God is present in death or hell, both of which are more horrible and foul than either a hole or a sewer. Indeed, since Scripture testifies that God is everywhere and fills all things ... a godly mind not only says that He is in those places, but must needs learn and know that he is there. Or are we to suppose that if I am captured by a tyrant and thrown into a prison or sewer ... I am not allowed to call upon God there or to believe that he is present with me, but must wait until I come into some finely furnished church[?][158]

Certainly not. For not only are the "faithful" "able to recognize ... the innumerable ways in which Christ ... *manifests* himself also outside the instituted sacraments,"[159] but indeed they recognize, having pierced the *larvae Dei*, or having "broken through" the "masquerade,"[160] that no aspect of creation can be separated from the Redeemer's presence of "within-redemption." Indeed, though, if this is the case, that the scope of creation—extending all the way to the individual, human tomb itself—is revealed to faith as the presence of the Redeemer's "within-redemption," then we may also assert, according to the criterion of the cross, or the *theologia crucis*, that creation itself, through the "third mode" of Christ's presence, is the cruciform expression of Christ's *sub contraria specie* presence of "within-redemption." It is to this final point that we turn.

Creatio Crucis: Complete "Within-Redemption"

As we have already adduced in the prior sub-section, Luther, in his exposition of Jonah 2:4, lifts up the reality that not only was it God who cast Jonah into the sea, but that the waves themselves served God's ends.

157. Ibid.
158. LW 33:47.
159. Gregersen, "Natural Events as Crystals of God," 150.
160. Wingren, "Doctrine of Creation," 363.

To quote Luther again on this passage: "Jonah does not simply say: 'The waves and billows passed over me,' but 'Thy waves and Thy billows, etc.,' for he feels in his conscience that the sea with its waves and billows serve God and His wrath for the punishment of sin ... and that all creatures were in league with God against him."[161] Luther's textual exposition of Jonah, though, does not end here.

For if it was "Thy waves and Thy billows," and indeed the entirety of "Thy creation" which served God's "wrath for the punishment of sin" with regard to Jonah, ultimately Luther is able to articulate a "reversal" with reference to the "former order of things," that is, "Thy waves and Thy billows" are the *larvae Dei* in which death is harnessed by God "to further life."[162] So, Luther asserts: "What a moment ago served the purpose of death must now serve to further life. The fish who was but recently the tool of death must now be life's implement; it must be a gateway to life, though just a short time before it held Jonah captive and consigned him to death. The ocean, too, must make way for Jonah and give its guest free access to the land. The roots of the mountains no longer hold him; earth's bars are pushed aside; the weeds cover him no more, etc."[163] But, for Luther, it is not simply the *larvae Dei* (or, in accordance with what we have already laid-out regarding the *theologia crucis*, the *opus alienum*) through which death is harnessed to the purpose of life that is of "comfort and confidence for us," but all of this "teaches us to rely on God, with whom life and death are alike. They are both trivial to Him, playthings as it were, as He bestows the one and takes the other, or exchanges one for the other, which God employs to display His power and skill to us ..."[164]

Essentially, then, it is not simply "What" the *larvae Dei* reveal (i.e., death harnessed as an *opus alienum* for the purpose of life), but the "substance,"[165] or the "Who" revealed within the visible realm *sub contraria specie* in, with, and under the *larvae*: the God "with whom life and death are alike." In other words, the *larvae Dei*, or creation, are considered by Luther to be the visible means by which God not

---

161. LW 19:76.
162. Ibid., 82.
163. Ibid., 76.
164. Ibid.,82.
165. LW 9:7.

only drives sinners to recognize "himself a true creator"[166] who is the sole "sufficiency" of humans,[167] but also the means through which his "arm"[168]—or his own invisible, ceaseless, "effective presence" "by which He works without the medium of any creature"[169]—is revealed to the eyes of faith. That is, according to Luther, the presence of this "arm," or "This work[,] is done quietly and in secret, and no one becomes aware of it until all is accomplished; so that this power, or arm, can be known and understood only by faith ... [accomplished] in secret and without the semblance of power."[170]

We can say, then, that creation is the visible mask—God's *opus alienum*—by which sinners are restored, or redeemed—in this age by faith—*to* God's "arm," or invisible presence which is revealed within the masks of creation as the sole-sufficiency, or substance, of that same creation, or the Word alone. And it is the individual human tomb that is the ultimate manifestation of this "arm," or—restated within the conceptual framework of our project—presence of Christ's "within-redemption" (on account of the "third mode" of Christ's presence). In order to unpack this claim, this section will rehearse both the methodology of the *theologia crucis*, now broadened to include the scope of creation and with a particular eye to the significance of "visible things," and the manner in which the visible creation is related by Luther to God's invisible "arm," now developed as the "third mode" of Christ's presence of "within-redemption."

Usus Visibilis

If "*He deserves to be called a theologian ... who comprehends the visible and manifest things of God seen through suffering and the cross*,"[171] then what separates a theologian of the cross from other theologians, especially with reference to creation, is the manner in which she "uses" the "visible things" of creation. That is, as has already been developed (see chapter two), the theologian of glory operates with the presupposition

---

166. LW 21:301.
167. Ibid., 328.
168. Ibid., 339.
169. Ibid.
170. Ibid.
171. LW 31:52.

that the "visible creation yields clues, if not directly at least by analogy, to what is invisible in, to the nature and logic of God."[172] Human reason, according to this theologian, is adroit at transporting one "speculatively into the invisible realm of divine truth."[173] Accordingly, then, in the attempt to directly perceive the invisible things of God, the world becomes "transparent to the human intellect . . .[one presupposes] that one can *see through* what is made and what happens[.]"[174] Ultimately that which is visible, contingent, and particular—and thus "of the world"—is "used," or related, to that which is invisible, and thus infinite ("of God"), as a cipher to a time-less, transcendent realm of ultimate meaning which lingers behind the visible world. Whatever the case, for the theologian of glory, that which is visible militates against, and is mutually exclusive with, the "invisible things of God." The "visible things of the world" are far too contingent and profane to bear the infinite, "invisible things of God." At best they are a cipher for what ultimately lies "behind it all."

But if the real theologian is the one who "comprehends the visible and manifest things of God seen through suffering and the cross," then she puts the "visible things of the world" to another, diametrically opposite, "use."

Far from understanding the visible things of the world as mutually exclusive with the "invisible things of God," theologians of the cross are those "who have eyes only for what is visible, what is actually there to be seen of God, the suffering and despised crucified Jesus."[175] As the theologian of the cross understands that there is no knowledge of the "invisible things of God" given outside of that which is revealed in the man Jesus, so she understands herself as being given permission to focus upon the visible world—creation!—as the realm of divine activity, the realm which is borne by the "invisible things of God"; she is the one who is permitted to discern God's presence visibly hidden *sub contraria specie* in, with, and under creation, thus comprehending that "God is neither to be seen or sought behind creation, nor be inferred from it, but only recognized in and through it."[176]

---

172. Forde, *On Being a Theologian of the Cross*, 73.
173. Williams, *Christian Spirituality*, 146.
174. Forde, *On Being a Theologian of the Cross*, 72.
175. Ibid., 79.
176. Westhelle, *Scandalous God*, 100.

But if the crucified Christ is the "criterion" of proper theology which reveals the Word's "*modus operandi*,"[177] especially with regard to the "visible things of the world," and thus the scope of creation, then we must discern how Luther relates the visible realm—the *larvae Dei*—to the "third mode" of Christ's presence. To do so will take us one step closer to comprehending, ultimately, the manner in which the individual human tomb is considered a *larva*—the ultimate *larva*—of Christ's presence of "within-redemption."

Relating Mask and Third Mode[178]

Acknowledging that Luther's insight regarding the relationship of the revelation of the Word to the liturgical elements—"not because of them, but never without them"[179]—"is exactly what could be said about the visible [world] in general,"[180] Westhelle notes that Luther operates with a distinction between two sets of categories, or "between the visible and the Word, between creature and Creator, the outer and the inner, between what the senses register and reason draws together and what grace reveals to the spirit."[181] Thus, with reference to this project, we may assert that this distinction encompasses the *larva* of creation (visible) and the "third mode" of Christ's presence (Word) which is the "substance," or "invisible arm," of the same *larvae Dei*.

More importantly, between these two sets of categories, the visible world and the Word, or specifically, the *larvae Dei* and the "third mode" of Christ's presence, exists a relationship—essential to Luther's articulation of revelation, now expanded to the scope of creation—comprised of paradox and asymmetry.[182] On the one hand, this relationship be-

---

177. Kolb, "Luther on the Theology of the Cross," 451.

178. This sub-section is simply an expression—expanded to envelope Luther's articulation of the "third mode" of Christ's presence—of Luther's conceptualization of revelation within his *theologia crucis*. Thus, the basic concepts already been developed within this narrower horizon—through the help of Westhelle—in chapter two. The *larvae Dei*, which were narrowly attributed the cross, are now expanded in order to encompass the "third mode." Much of this section will mirror the prior section.

179. WA 19:72–73, quoted in Westhelle, *Scandalous God*, 100.

180. Westhelle, *Scandalous God*, 100.

181. Ibid., 43–4.

182. Again, this dynamic has already been elaborated within a development of Luther's *theologia crucis* in chapter 2. Here, this dynamic is expanded with specific interest laid on the "third mode."

tween the *larvae Dei* and the "third mode" of Christ's presence is "paradoxical" in the sense that that which is visible—the *larvae Dei*—points to the Word—the "third mode" of Christ's presence—but, in the process, is "simultaneously negated or dissimulated."[183] On the other hand, as Westhelle notes, the relationship between the *larvae* and the "third mode" of Christ's presence within the dynamic of revelation is "asymmetrical" in the sense "that what appears to be the case in one set of categories that belong to one of the regimes (spiritual or earthly) is not reflected in the other, but is shaped by it in unexpected ways."[184] By perpetually moving from one set of categories to the other, and back (thus relating the "third mode" of Christ's presence to the *larvae*), Luther—framing his theology of creation within the methodology of his *theologia crucis*—is able to avoid the theologian of glory's method of analogical reasoning by fostering an "ironic destabilizing tone" between the two categories.[185] Therefore, as has been stated earlier, Luther's theology in general—and certainly his theology of creation in particular—consists neither of a complete synthesis nor a separation, yet, as Westhelle observes, it is both in that "it is irony breaking into the realm of analogy. What the mask reveals is the very Word hidden in its cracks."[186] Restated: irony—which conveys "something by using concepts, ideas, and words that suggest the opposite of their literal meaning"—is Luther's intention when he articulates the *larvae Dei* as revelations of Christ *sub contraria specie*.[187] In our case, we may say that the "third mode" of Christ's presence unsettles any direct analogies which might be inferred from the visible mask of creation. For, with reference to the "third mode's" relation the *larva* of creation, "that which seems to be is in fact its opposite."[188]

So, what we have originally stated with regard to our development of the *theologia crucis*, we can now assert with regard to a theology of creation articulated within that same conceptualization of the *theologia crucis*: that the "third mode" of Christ's presence revealed *sub contraria specie* in the *larvae Dei* means that the creation in which theologians

---

183. Westhelle, *Scandalous God*, 44.
184. Ibid.
185. Ibid.
186. Ibid.
187. Ibid.
188. Ibid., 45.

of the cross reside "does not present God to us as simple fact."[189] Thus, with regard to the "third mode" of Christ's presence and his relationship to the *larvae Dei*, "the One who becomes present . . . is simultaneously manifested in God's most radical absence."[190] Ultimately, then, expanding our purview to include the scope of creation, if "What the eyes cannot see, faith brings to vision,"[191] then what faith brings to vision is the "substance" concealed within the *larvae*, or the "third mode" of Christ's presence for whom death not only serves the purpose of life, but for whom "life and death are alike."[192] We may also call this the presence of Christ's "within-redemption," a presence for which even the individual tombs of humanity are mere *larvae*—on account of the "ironic destabilizing tone" created between the two categories, or the Word and the mask—serving the purpose of redeeming humans *to* the sole sufficiency of the Creator's Word alone, or the "third mode" of Christ's presence of "within-redemption."

Articulating Complete "Within-Redemption"

But it must also be developed—in our delineation of Christ's complete "within-redemption" which, it is contended, extends to the location of humanity's individual tombs—that it is this redeeming of humans to the sole sufficiency of the Creator's Word (now articulated as the "third mode' of Christ's presence), according to Luther, which is instantiated both by the life-long recognition of sin, and the existence-encompassing (i.e., including both living and dead human existence) process of its purging, or cleansing. Restated: within Luther's conceptualization of God's *opus alienum* and *opus proprium*, this redeeming of humans to the sufficiency of the Creator's Word is, according to Luther, "God's game"[193] by which the invisible "arm," or "hand of God"—through the mask of God's *opus alienum*—both causes sinners to recognize their sin, and commences in them a complete cleansing from sin which reaches its culmination in the tomb. Or more poignantly: it is within the tomb that the "arm of God," and thus the "ironic destabilizing tone" between

189. Williams, *Christian Spirituality*, 146.
190. Westhelle, *Scandalous God*, 22.
191. Ibid., 52.
192. LW 19:82.
193. LW 7:229.

Word and mask, is made most starkly manifest. Let us finish this section with Luther's development of this matter, or with Luther as an exegete before the biblical text, so-to-speak.

Though once sold into slavery in Egypt by his brothers, Joseph is eventually appointed by Pharaoh to high status in his court with a charge that includes, among other things as "governor over all the land,"[194] protecting the land's integral food supply. It is those same brothers—now experiencing famine in their own land—who are now unknowingly driven into Joseph's court seeking to buy food. And though Joseph recognizes them, and is eventually restored to them as their brother through this series of events ("Even though you intended to do harm to me, God intended it for good, in order to preserve a numerous people, as he is doing today"[195]), we are told in Genesis 42:7 that initially Joseph "treated them like strangers and spoke harshly to them." And, commenting on Genesis 42:7,[196] Luther interprets Joseph's initial harsh treatment of his brothers—with mercy as his ultimate aim—as paradigmatic of the manner by which God both leads the sinner to recognition of her sin, and commences with her the "game"—through his invisible "arm"—of cleansing her completely.

Thus, Luther comments with reference to Joseph's brothers who anticipate their imminent punishment at Joseph's hand, "God afflicts us with various disasters, not to punish us, although this really is a punishment."[197] For though God at first may be experienced as the "devil himself"[198] in one's afflictions, "He takes no pleasure in it,"[199] for these afflictions are worked "in order that you may be led to a knowledge of your sin."[200] And it is through the recognition of this sin—with the simultaneous recognition that God is justified in his judgment—that we "learn to cling to the consolation that although guilt gnaws at our conscience and the goad of the Law and death torments us, yet this is not being done for our destruction but rather for our instruction and cleansing, in order that we may come to a knowledge of ourselves and

---

194. Genesis 41:43.
195. Genesis 50:20.
196. LW 7:224–35.
197. Ibid., 228.
198. Ibid., 226.
199. Ibid., 228.
200. Ibid.

our corruption."[201] Luther then adds, "Therefore let us endure the hand of God, who cleanses us, that is, laughs and plays with us[.]"[202] But what could Luther possibly mean that God "laughs and plays with us"? Is this a sick, divine game? Let us continue developing Luther's thought on just this matter.

It is through the *opus alienum,* or "the conscience [which] is troubled by the Law and by the terrors of sin,"[203] that "God's game begins, not that we may be destroyed, but that He may examine us and lead us to a knowledge of our foulness, yet not in such a way that we despair, but rather that we cry to Him, invoke His mercy, and learn that He shows His mercy wondrously ... For this is what He has meant with His game."[204] For, ultimately, if Luther can assert both that "God's wrath is a sure sign of life,"[205] and that sinners should "learn and accustom [themselves] to endure in trials,"[206] it is only because, according to Luther, faith pierces the masks, perceiving the "Word hidden in their cracks," and is able to confess that "God plays with the saints in this way—not that they may perish, but that they may recognize in Him what He says of Himself in Jeremiah 3:12: 'I am merciful, says the Lord: I will not be angry forever.'"[207] Thus, for Luther, the afflictions, the terror of sin, are "not wrath ... but discipline. It is not disinheritance; it is a purging."[208]

But with this recognition of purging, or cleansing, according to Luther, comes the knowledge that this cleansing—this "game" played by the "arm of God"—encompasses the whole of embodied existence, both living and dead human existence. So, in Luther's words, "it is knowledge characteristic of Christians for a person to know that he was born in sins, that sin clings to the flesh up to the time of death, and that we cannot be perfectly freed and cleansed from it except through death, worms, and the final fire."[209] But, let us be sure to note, "the hour in which [this game] is played does not give [the] appearance [of a "pleas-

201. Ibid.
202. Ibid., 228–29.
203. Ibid., 229.
204. Ibid., 229–30.
205. Ibid., 233.
206. Ibid.
207. Ibid., 232.
208. Ibid., 237.
209. Ibid.

ant delightful game"²¹⁰]. No, this is death itself. At the end of the trial, however, they see the greatest goodwill and love."²¹¹

Commenting on Genesis 45:5, Luther interprets the selling of Joseph into slavery by his brothers as paradigmatic of this "game" of God's—now viewed retrospectively. For it is through Joseph's being sold into slavery through the maliced-laden intentions of his brothers that ironically has afforded him the opportunity to preserve his people. Thus, drawing upon Joseph as a paradigmatic expression of God's *modus operandi* of cleansing sinners, or redeeming them to his sufficiency as Creator, Luther asserts, "This example [of Joseph's being sold], then, teaches that we, too, are not being destroyed when we are afflicted and under a cross, but that we are being saved, provided that we believe."²¹² But this *sub contraria specie* process of being restored, or redeemed, to the sufficiency of the Creator's "arm," or Word, is not merely a matter of one's living existence as a "believer," but indeed is extended to, and encompasses, one's dead existence as an undeniably passive piece of clay in the hand of the Creator, or as a corpse in a crypt. Luther can thus aver, "Holy Scripture speaks in the manner concerning the death and burial of Christ. For Is. 11:10 says: 'His burial, which all men regard as the utmost confusion and wretchedness, is glory before God.'"²¹³ So, now applied to humans lying in their tombs, and on the basis of Christ who is the only expression of this ultimate redemption to the sufficiency of the Creator's Word, for as of yet no other human can retrospectively view the ultimate manifestation of this "game" of "cleansing," Luther declares, "For if we die, we really do not perish. No, we live if we believe His promise. And even though He lets life, goods, wife, and children be torn away . . . what happens? The present life is taken away in order that another and far better life may be restored. For God is able to give, and will undoubtedly give, more than He has ever bestowed."²¹⁴ In other words, on account of the "third mode" of Christ's presence, we may regard the individual tombs of humanity to be the *larvae* of the Word's—the "arm of God"—ongoing presence of "within-redemption."

210. Ibid.
211. Ibid., 237–38.
212. LW 8:35.
213. Ibid.
214. Ibid.

This is a presence for "whom life and death are alike,"[215] or "playthings as it were,"[216] in the process of redeeming humans to the sole sufficiency of the Creator's "effective presence," or Word.

But if the human tomb—on account of the "third mode" of Christ's presence—is the ultimate *larva* of Christ's presence of "within-redemption," then let us be careful to remind ourselves: if "This work [of God's "arm"] is done quietly and in secret, and no one becomes aware of it until all is accomplished,"[217] then verb-tense must be stressed. In other words, if we are unable to "*see through* what is made and what happens so as to peer into the 'invisible things of God,'"[218] and thus live by a faith that only deals with God through *larvae*, or wrappings, which simultaneously both reveal Christ's redeeming presence "while denying to our eyes' sight any evidence of its content,"[219] then for now, Christ's presence of "within-redemption" can only be confessed as an ongoing, *redeeming* presence, a "work in progress." That is, the individual tombs of humanity—and there will be more tomorrow than yesterday!—are the masks of the vigorous, "most active working of God" which, as this is being read, is currently redeeming those humans to the Creator's sufficiency. If "What the eyes cannot see, faith brings to vision,"[220] then on account of the "third mode" of Christ's presence of "within-redemption," the cemetery (a mask!)—no matter its visible condition—is revealed as perhaps the busiest location on earth, overflowing with the Creator's industrious activity, or "effective presence" (Dalferth), of redeeming sinners to the Creator's sole sufficiency. For now, then, there is nothing, for humans, beyond faith.

Summary and Conclusion

If, as we contended in chapter one, Alan Lewis was correct—in his delineation of "within-redemption" on the basis of his "theology of Holy Saturday"—to contend for stressing the *triduum's cordon sanitaire* which allows us to identify a God who resides within the Friday/Saturday nar-

215. LW 19:82.
216. Ibid.
217. LW 21:339.
218. Forde, *On Being a Theologian of the Cross*, 72.
219. Westhelle, *Scandalous God*, 98.
220. Ibid., 52.

rative of Jesus Christ in order to redeem human life "from within," in the process of doing so, he made one major mistake.

Essentially, as we pointed out, he removes the narrative of humanity—which is only manifested in its irreducible, particular, embodied narratives, and as of yet still lie in their tombs—from the presence of "within-redemption" by articulating God's first century presence in Jesus' Saturday sepulcher as a signifier for his presence in all subsequent (and even prior) tombs. Ultimately, although this God of "within-redemption which Lewis has articulated may be able to redeem "from within" Jesus' tomb, his "within-redemption" extends to the individual tombs of humanity only as things "signified." The particular, individual narratives of humanity are essentially removed from the location of God's redeeming presence in Jesus Christ. And all of this has led us to ask: is "redemption through signification" a viable substitute for the redemptive presence of the Redeemer within our very own individual narratives, and thus tombs? Can a "signification" of a once-for-all redeeming presence be a substitute either for his ongoing presence within creation, or our material redemption within that same creation, a redemption of that which is created both as a "psychosomatic unity," and called "very good"? Not only—did it appear—has Lewis reduced the created, "very good" integrity of particular, embodied human narratives to "things signified" by the "signifier" of a "most real" narrative (i.e., Christ's *triduum*), but ultimately—and this perhaps is the most important point—he has accomplished the very thing he has set out not to do: he has allowed the narrative of Jesus Christ so to color *all* of history that *all* particular histories are abandoned! But let us press this point a little further.

If, as we have developed in chapter one, humans are both created "very good," and understood—"nothing more, nothing less"—as being irreducibly embodied, "psychosomatic unities," then an articulation of "within-redemption" is not only necessary with regard to maintaining the integrity of the human (Hall), but it is not to circumvent this same essential humanity in all of its manifestations, even when that which is recognized as human lies "unrecognizable" in the tomb. Does Lewis' articulation of "within-redemption" do justice to this reality? Could it be that an articulation of Christ's resurrection in which his resurrection "signifies the redeeming of our time" performs the same function with regard to individual human narratives that he initially attempted to circumvent with regard to Christ's narrative? or, that is, it makes redemption a *necessary* matter? Ultimately, does he not commit "resurrectionism"?

Although Lewis deftly permitted us to perceive "within-redemption" within the deepest darkness of Jesus' Saturday sepulcher, his rendering of "within-redemption" ultimately became, when applied to the individual narratives of humanity, an "overbearing interpretive instrument" which created the *certainty* of redemption. Though Lewis advanced the discussion of "within-redemption" by powerful, long strides, his articulation of "within-redemption," we have discovered, was not complete. His "within-redemption via signification" created more problems than promises when that redemption was extended to humanity at the location of its irreducible, embodied narratives. And, ultimately, it did not allow for the presence of Christ's "within-redemption" at the location my tomb, and indeed the individual tombs of all of humanity. So we turned to Luther in order to "finish the job" of "within-redemption" which Lewis so eloquently began.

Thus—honoring the irreducible, embodied nature of humanity's narratives—through a development of Luther's *theologia crucis*, and specifically an elaboration of his radical interpretation of the *communicatio idiomatum* which yielded an articulation of the "third mode" of Christ's presence, we were able to involve the individual tombs of humanity—ever increasing in number—as the *loci* of Christ's presence of "within-redemption." Or, within the framework of his *theologia crucis*, the tombs of humanity are, as we speak, *larvae* of the ongoing, redeeming presence of Christ's "within-redemption" of restoring sinners to the sole sufficiency of the Creator's Word.

Ultimately, then, regarding the narratives of those who have gone before us and thus now lie in their tombs, and one day us, let us refuse to seek a "most real" reality of redemption *behind* or *beyond* the creation which God has created—and still creates *ex nihilo*—and "call a thing what it is." That is, let us call their tombs (and one day ours) "masks" of the Real Presence of God's "within-redemption," ultimate expressions that creation exists, and creatures live, by God's sufficiency, or "arm," alone. That "still, small Word"!

We cannot see *through* this history. We can only look *at* it. And dare to hope, on account of what faith continually brings to vision, that it is this history and narrative that God redeems "from within"; that this is the mask of God's *opus proprium*, or work of "within-redemption."

As of yet—to use the narrative framework Lewis so eloquently employed—we are still Friday and Saturday people. We await Sunday.

Waiting and Christ's real presence of "within-redemption" are not mutually exclusive. The confession of the latter emboldens the former.

5

Countering a "High-Pitched" Anthropology
Barth's Communicatio Gratiarum

Introductory Matters

IT IS IMPOSSIBLE TO OVERESTIMATE THE IMPACT OF KARL BARTH UPON both his early contemporaries (both within and without the circle of theologians whose theological program drew such titles as "Theology of Crisis" and "Dialectical Theology," among others), and the discipline of theology in general throughout the twentieth and early twenty-first centuries.

"Few historians of modern theology," asserts James Livingston in what perhaps is the definitive textbook on the history of modern theology, "would reject the judgment that Karl Barth has had a wider and more enduring influence on theology in the twentieth century than any other thinker."[1] Indeed, at a fundamental level, whether one shares or denies Barth's theological proposals, in one way or another one must define themselves in relation to Barth. Livingston evidences this reality, if only in part, when he avers that "[Barth's] influence began in the immediate post-World War I years, and it continues in the current discussions between the so-called 'postliberal' theologians, who share Barth's basic conception of the nature and task of Christian theology, and their critics, who champion one or another form of a "theology of correlation" between the Christian message and modern philosophy and the sciences."[2] Perhaps it should come as no surprise then, as Thomas Torrance has observed, that it is "acknowledged by many in all quarters

---

1. Livingston et al., *Modern Christian Thought*, 109.
2. Ibid.

that Barth must be accorded an honored position among the greatest theologians of the Church—Athanasius, Augustine, Anselm, Aquinas, Luther, and Calvin."[3]

But one cannot attribute greatness to Barth without also acknowledging the price other great theologians paid for Barth's assumption to the inner sanctum of so-called "great theologians." In other words, so Livingston points out, "Part of the greatness and the power of Barth's theology is that it has challenged other positions at their most critical, and often vulnerable points."[4] Indeed, one might argue, the lion's share of Barth's greatness was acquired through challenging the thought of those who stand with him in the pantheon of great Christian thinkers. Yet this fact does not mean that Barth was also *not* influenced by theologians within that same pantheon. For the sake of this project and its context, we must lift up one theologian to whom Barth was indebted in certainly no insubstantial way.

Although the fact that the index volume to the *Church Dogmatics* accords no theologian a longer entry than Martin Luther perhaps suggests little more than that "Barth's engagement with Luther was extensive,"[5] what it does suggest, according to George Hunsinger, is that, with regard to Barth's thinking, Luther was a "towering figure."[6] Hunsinger is even willing to articulate Barth's indebtedness to Luther as "enormous."[7] And though theologians may debate the extent of Barth's indebtedness to Luther, Hunsinger both asserts and delineates the reality, as attested through the course of Barth's writings, that "Indeed, at certain vital points Barth follows Luther not only, broadly speaking, against Calvin and [Barth's own] Reformed tradition, but also against the main lines of the Lutheran tradition. There are points, in other words, where Barth has actually retrieved Luther in order to stand with him not only against modernity, but also against the rest of

---

3. Torrance, *Karl Barth: An Introduction to His Early Thought 1910–1931*, 15. Let the reader note who is missing from Torrance's list: F. D. E. Schleiermacher. It is a curious matter that, with respect to underscoring Barth's impact, Torrance would omit the name of the one theologian against whom Barth constantly matched himself both through his lectures, disputations, and writings throughout the course of his long career.

4. Livingston et al., *Modern Christian Thought*, 109–10.

5. Hunsinger, "What Karl Barth Learned from Martin Luther," 279.

6. Ibid.

7. Ibid., 280.

the Reformation."[8] Hunsinger delineates these "vital points" under the headings of "christocentrism," "theology of the cross," "primacy of the Word of God," "promise and peril... as shaping the life of faith," or the expression of *simul iustus et peccator*, and, finally, the unconditioned nature of grace as it relates to human capacities.[9] But it is where Barth stridently diverges from Luther, indeed at the most fundamental point of Luther's theology (as we have argued in this project), that will be pointed out and developed throughout the course of this chapter.

Essentially, though "vital points" of theological propinquity can be identified between Barth and Luther, and indeed points can be elaborated—as Hunsinger has done—where Barth has actually retrieved Luther against the grain of his own Reformed tradition, it is precisely on that which has been determined to be foundational to Luther's *theologia crucis*, or his radical interpretation of the *communicatio idiomatum*, that Barth most vehemently opposes, and thus diverges from, Luther. Therefore, as will be developed through the course of this chapter, Barth, addressing his theology to the anthropological fixations of the various Protestant, liberal theologies whose vital impulses he has originally identified with the trajectory of F. D. E Schleiermacher's program, both criticizes—with regard to his perception of that fixation—Luther's radical interpretation of the *communicatio idiomatum*, with particular reference to its expression through the *genus maiestaticum*, and, as a counter, articulates in its stead, within the context of his doctrine of election, the *communicatio gratiarum*. If, as this project has developed, Luther was able to articulate the *communicatio idiomatum* in such a manner that expressed the reality that no aspect of creation is bereft of the presence of the whole Jesus Christ, and thus the reality—in our case—that no human tomb is deprived of Christ's presence of "within-redemption," then, for Barth, the *communicatio idiomatum*, especially with reference to its expression through the *genus maistaticum* (the direct communication of the divine *idiomata* to the human *idiomata* within the person of Jesus Christ), again opens wide the door to the theological program identified with the trajectory of Schleiermacher, or

---

8. Hunsinger, "What Karl Barth Learned from Martin Luther," 282.

9. For the development of these five "vital points" which Barth has, according to Hunsinger, "retrieved from Luther, and thus a demonstration of how Barth expresses theological confluence with Luther, see ibid., 283–304.

the fixation of theology—conducted by "absolute man"[10]—to anthropological subject matter.

Though arguments may never abate as to the theological kinship which exists between Luther and Barth, what becomes extraordinarily salient is Barth's critique of, and divergence from, what we have basically argued to be the *sine qua non* of Luther's whole theological program, or the *communicatio idiomatum*. Even more salient with regard to the relationship between these two theologies—it will be demonstrated—are the consequences of such a critique and counter by Barth, especially with reference to what we have developed—above—as "within-redemption." In order to develop this claim, this chapter will proceed through three sections. Let us briefly develop the course of this chapter with an obvious eye to further elaboration.

Although an extraordinary amount of exemplary work has been accomplished both in the delineating the development of Barth's early theology,[11] and in outlining the corpus of his theological program,[12] this chapter will elucidate the development of Barth's Christology—culminating in the *communicatio gratiarum*—from the fundamental perspective of his reaction and response to the program of "absolute man." Drawing upon Barth's signal works in historical theology,[13] the first section will develop this "absolute man" through Barth's own writings,

---

10. The phrase "absolute man" will be developed below.

11. Signal resources, even if only referring to ones published in English, are many. With regard to excellent studies which treat his early theological development, I refer the reader, first and foremost, to both McCormack, *Karl Barth's Critically Realistic Dialectical Theology*, and Jüngel, *Karl Barth*, 53–104. Other sound expositions are Webster, *Barth's Earlier Theology*; Dorrien, *Barthian Revolt in Modern Theology*, 1–130; and Busch, *Karl Barth & the Pietists* and *Karl Barth*, 1–198. An excellent book which places all of Barth's production against the context of current events, thus articulating the reality that Barth was a contextual theologian, is Gorringe, *Karl Barth: Against Hegemony*. This list, by no means, scratches the surface!

12. Perhaps the major work in this regard is Busch, *Great Passion*. Other signal works certainly include von Balthasar, *Theology of Karl Barth*; Berkouwer, *Triumph of Grace in the Theology of Karl Barth*; Torrance, *Karl Barth*; Bromiley, *Introduction to the Theology of Karl Barth*; and certainly—as a hermeneutical proposal—Hunsinger, *How to Read Karl Barth*. Again, this list, by no means, scratches the surface!

13. Especially important here are his *Protestant Theology in the Nineteenth Century*; *Humanity of God*, esp. 11–33; *Theology of Schleiermacher*; and *Theology and Church*. Here it must be noted: As we are developing Barth's *communicatio gratiarum* as theological response, it is Barth's interpretation of theological history that will primarily be the focus of our interest.

particularly as a practitioner of *historical* theology. It will be argued that the *communicatio gratiarum* can only fully be comprehended against the context determined by "absolute man." For it was "absolute man" who, as Barth observed—setting the intellectual stage for the nineteenth century—"discovers his own power and ability, the potentiality dormant in his humanity, that is, his human being as such, and looks upon it as the final, the real and absolute, I mean as something 'detached', self-justifying, with its own authority and power, which he can therefore set in motion in all directions and without any restraint[.]"[14] In the process of developing "absolute man" and his context of influence, we will more deeply understand the one who has most profoundly inherited and appropriated his intellectual agenda. For if Barth can assert that "in the theological field [the nineteenth century] was nevertheless *his* century,"[15] then by "his" Barth is referring to nobody other than Schleiermacher. The second section, then, will be devoted to developing this quintessential expression of "absolute man's" intellectual agenda as it is related to theology, or Schleiermacher. In our delineation of Schleiermacher's appropriation of "absolute man's" intellectual agenda, we will do so with the goal of articulating, for purpose of laying the groundwork for the subsequent section, his conceptualizations of revelation, Christology, and redemption. This, then, will lead us into our third, and final, section. The final section will consist of delineating Barth's articulation of the *communicatio gratiarum* against not only the background of "absolute man" and his quintessential expression in Schleiermacher, but within the context of both Ludwig Feuerbach's "apotheosized man"—that perverted form of "absolute man"—and, perhaps more importantly, the spring from which "apotheosized man" drinks, or the "Lutheran" Christology which ultimately is able to articulate the "ubiquity of Christ's humanity." As will be demonstrated, if, for Barth, the doctrine of election is essentially the "the sum of the Gospel,"[16] and indeed of theology, then the *communicatio gratiarum* is nothing more than the ultimate expression of his doctrine of election. If—we might point out in simplified fashion already—Schleiermacher (in a fashion commensurate with the canon of "absolute man") developed a subjective understanding of redemption in which Christ is only formally and, thus, quantitatively different

14. Barth, *Protestant Theology*, 22.
15. Ibid., 411; italics added for emphasis.
16. CD II/2:10.

than humanity, then it is here that we see Barth fully elaborating that same doctrine in an antithetical manner, that is, through a Christ who is distinguished from humanity not merely materially and qualitatively, but particularly and objectively.

Ultimately, it must be stated, this entire chapter will be subordinated to both developing the *communicatio gratiarum*, and delineating its consequences with regard to what we have developed throughout the course of this project as "within-redemption." This means that this chapter will be limited in its scope to the ends of both articulating Barth's *communicatio gratiarum* according to both its context of development and its theological articulation, and placing the *communicatio gratiarum* within the larger discussion of "within-redemption." With this caveat stated, let us commence our discussion, through Barth's eyes as an historian, of "absolute man."

"Absolute Man"

His Own Emperor

If Barth could ultimately and electrically declare—with no ambiguous implications with regard to the very methodology of theology—in the famous second edition of his *Römerbrief* that "Direct communication from God is no divine communication," thus adding, "If Christianity be not altogether thoroughgoing eschatology, there remains in it no relationship whatever with Christ,"[17] then it must also be acknowledged just *who*, or what kind of theologian, was implicated in this declaration, as well: the theologian who had the audacity to arrogate to herself the capacity for direct communication with God. But, let us ask, is the assumption of possessing this capacity—for direct communication—really a big deal? For Barth, it was what this claim of direct communication presupposed that was ultimately of issue.

What the theologian who claimed direct communication with God was essentially confessing was the *a priori* human capacity to recognize a communication from God whenever encountered by one. But, according to Barth, the theologian who claimed this *human* capacity—that is, of claiming the capacity for a direct communication from God—was really doing nothing more than simultaneously expressing two closely-

---

17. Barth, *Epistle to the Romans*, 314.

related, problematic aspects about themselves. First, such a claim was an admission that one possessed the standard for even recognizing a divine communication when encountered by one. Second, and perhaps most importantly, such a claim was an admission that one was indeed a living descendent of a certain "man's" lineage, and certainly the inheritor of this "man's" confident intellectual capacities. So, we ask, who is this "man"?

If, as Barth has already observed, the "absolute man" of the eighteenth century is the one who has discovered "his own power and ability, the potentiality dormant in his humanity," then certainly this perceived "power and ability" was a manifestation of his previously demonstrated intellectual triumphs, his intellectual ability to pierce the universe with his intellectual prowess. Thus Barth describes this dynamic in detail:

> [Absolute man] was the man who could no longer remain ignorant of the significance of the fact that Copernicus and Galileo were right, that this vast and rich earth of his, the theatre of his deeds was not the centre of the universe, but a grain of dust amid countless others in this universe, and who clearly saw the consequences of all this. What did this really apocalyptic revolution in his picture of the universe mean for man? An unprecedented and boundless humiliation of man? No, said the man of the eighteenth century, who was not the first to gain this knowledge, but certainly the first to realize it fully and completely; no, man is all the greater for this, man is in the centre of all things, in a quite different sense, too, for he was able to discover this revolutionary truth by his own resources and to think abstractly, again to consider and penetrate a world which had expanded overnight into infinity—and without anything else having changed, without his having to pay for it in any way: clearly now the world was even more and properly so *his* world! It is paradoxical and yet it is a fact that the answer to his humiliation was those philosophical systems of rationalism, empiricism and skepticism which made men even more self-confident. The geocentric picture of the universe was replaced as a matter of course by the anthropocentric.[18]

But if this so-called "humiliation" was really nothing more than the revelation of man's intellectual "power," then the consciousness of this power became even more apparent through the consciousness of his power for science, and, certainly, "his power through science." And with

---

18. Barth, *Protestant Theology*, 23–24.

the consciousness of this power came the consciousness that the "authority" to which one should subscribe is nothing other than an internal matter with regard to the self. According to Barth, "The development at the Renaissance, which had been hindered and reduced for almost one hundred and fifty years through the period of religious wars, now began to make immense strides. Once again man, led by a philosophy, which was only apparently disunited but was in essentials united, began to be conscious—and more forcibly than before—*of a capacity for thinking which was responsible to no other authority than himself.*"[19] And it was "the amazing scientific spirit of that time," Barth adds, that "was unquestionably one of the manifestations of all-conquering, absolute man, who expressed himself also and with special effect in this field of human activity."[20] The practical application of science to the material world, and thus the list of "achievements of modern technique" were endless.[21] Indeed not only was this "absolute man" "almost capable of anything,"[22] but certainly "he is the man who no longer has an emperor."[23] But if "absolute man" through science had mastered the material world through his "achievements of modern technique," or his inventions to aid everyday life, Barth also reminds us that "absolute man's" sense of

19. Ibid., 25; italics added for emphasis.

20. Ibid., 25–26.

21. Ibid., 27. Elaborating on the point of the translation of "absolute man's" "scientific spirit" into the field of practical application, and in a manner only a historian of Barth's stature could pull off in a lecture, he states, "Here we may also suitably call to mind the achievements of modern technique which also come from this time. The curve of progress in this field has not yet risen as steeply as it was to do in the nineteenth century. Here are some dates. In 1684 Hooke invented the optical telegraph, in 1690 Papin, a Frenchman, invented the steam cylinder with which, in 1707, he attempted, though without success, to sail a steam-boat on the river Fulda. The invention of springs for coaches in 1706 made the popular activity of traveling more comfortable. In 1714 Fahrenheit constructed his mercury thermometer. In 1718 Lady Mary Wortley Montagu tried to introduce the practice of inoculation for smallpox, and in the same year Leopold von Dessau invented the iron loading-rod for guns. Metal-boring machines appeared in 1720, accurate spinning machines in 1738. The idea of steam heat appears in 1745. In 1747 sugar was produced from beets. In 1751 the Frenchman Chamette invented a gun which was loaded from the rear. in 1764 James Watt invented the steam engine. In 1770 Priestley discovered oxygen. In 1780 Galvani made his decisive discoveries in electricity. In 1782 the brothers Montgolfier offered Paris the sight of the first balloon flight. In 1786 gas for lighting purposes was first made" (ibid.).

22. Barth, *Protestant Theology*, 27.

23. Ibid.

mastery was not limited to the present, material world, but indeed extended to the humans who came before him.

In other words, his perceived mastery over the present, material world via his applied science was extended to his conceptualization of, and thus relationship to, history. So again, Barth (the historian!) offers a profound analysis of "absolute man," this time with reference to his "absolute" relationship to that (or those) which has preceded him, or history itself. He observes that it was during the eighteenth century that "absolute man" "began axiomatically to credit himself with being superior to the past, and assumed a standpoint in relation to it whence he found it possible to set himself up as a judge over past events according to fixed principles, at least as applied by the typical observer of history living at that age, has the inevitable effect of turning that judgment of the past into an extremely radical one."[24] And it is this "yardstick"—whose particular expression will detain us for development when "absolute man" evaluates his theological concerns—that consists, according to Barth, "quite simply [of] the man of the present with his complete trust in his own powers of discernment and judgment, with his feeling for freedom, his desire for intellectual conquest, his urge to form and his supreme moral self-confidence."[25] Thus, from the confident perspective of "absolute man," Barth rhetorically asks, "What historical facts . . . can be true except those which to the man of the age seem psychologically and physiologically probable, or at any rate not improbable?"[26] Indeed, correlated with an external world which was simply perceived as raw material to be formed via applied science, so too, history—according to "absolute man"—was merely the "light and shade" of "absolute man's" "deeds and aspirations."[27] "Absolute man's" application of his "absolute will for form,"[28] driven by his increasing sense of intellectual capacity, knew no bounds. But it is "absolute man's" perceived intellectual capacity—his calculation of that which was "psychologically and physiologically probable"—as it is collectively translated into what Barth calls the

---

24. Ibid., 44.
25. Ibid.
26. Ibid.
27. Ibid., 45.
28. Ibid., 49.

"form of the inner life,"[29] or the "psychological common denominator,"[30] that becomes of vital importance for understanding both "absolute man's" grappling of theological matters, and ultimately lays the conceptual groundwork for a Schleiermacher. Let us briefly develop Barth's observations with reference to "absolute man's" collective "form of the inner life." This will lead us into a discussion of "absolute man" as theologian, and, ultimately, a discussion of who Barth perceives as the quintessential expression of "absolute man-hood," or Schleiermacher himself.

The Inner Masters the Outer

According to Barth "the form of the inner life" is actually "an inner analogue to the form of their outward life."[31] This "inner analogue" is expressed, according to Barth, in several subsequent, notable ways.[32] First, "absolute man" collectively expresses the "naively strong conviction" that the surrounding world is essentially transparent to the human faculties of "apprehension, willing and feeling." His "self-awareness" makes him superior to, and master of, the exterior world.[33] Indeed, corresponding to this "naively strong conviction"[34] is the objective conviction that the external world exists—correspondingly—merely as a canvas for this "expansion" of human self-awareness. "'The world is good,'" Barth observes, only insofar as it is "the object and scene of the deeds of men."[35] Following this "admirable concordance between the inner and the outer world,"[36] "absolute man," Barth observes, "believed . . . in a God who is common lord of both of them, but who of course stands nearer to

---

29. Ibid., 59.
30. Ibid.
31. Ibid.
32. Ibid., 60–62.

33. "It was not for nothing," Barth observes, "that one of the favourite figures in the literature of the time was Robinson Crusoe, the man thrown completely upon his own resources, who in spite of this and for this very reason was able to take care of himself so triumphantly" (Barth, *Protestant Theology*, 60).

34. Ibid.
35. Ibid.
36. Ibid.

man and the human world."[37] With this identification of the divine with the human world, Barth observes, God becomes the "quintessence" of the "wisdom and goodness with which man is confident enough to approach the world, and which clearly meets him in the world."[38] But if God is the "quintessence" of the virtues by which "absolute man" confidently approaches the world, then, according to Barth, God is also not only identified with his motives, but becomes "quietive" with respect to the expression of these same motives. Barth elaborates this dynamic: "God is the highest *motive*—as regards the degree of reasonableness which man and the world can produce, for what is possible in the advancement of knowledge, the extension of the sphere of the will and a deepening of the feelings on man's part, and farther revelations on the part of the universe."[39] Concurrently, Barth adds, "God is the highest *quietive* in respect to the effective limits of human self-consciousness which are to be conceded: these limits are as much a part of it in itself as imposed by the mysteries of the universe which are as yet unsolved or might prove altogether insoluble."[40] With this said, then, "absolute man" operates with the knowledge—at least implicitly acknowledged—that, though his manner of existence is "confused and fragmentary,"[41] nevertheless, man and God are "of the same substance,"[42] that is, they exist in the "same way."[43] Or, as Barth aptly puts it, "God is spirit, man is spirit too. God is mighty and so is man. God is wise and benevolent, and so is man."[44] Subsequently, then, the recognition of God's existence was the proper justification for the "conviction that human self-awareness is superior both in the valiant enthusiasm which is necessary to it and in its equally necessary humble acquiescence."[45] This conviction regarding "absolute man's" superior "self-awareness," then, is founded upon his corresponding conviction regarding God's existence. But it is precisely here, as Barth observes, that the priority of the two convictions, or the

37. Ibid.
38. Ibid.
39. Ibid.
40. Ibid., 60.
41. Ibid., 60–61.
42. Ibid., 60.
43. Ibid., 61.
44. Ibid., 60.
45. Ibid., 61.

question of which is to be subordinated to the other—or their asymmetry, becomes crystal clear. For if—in and of itself—"absolute man's" conviction regarding the existence of God ultimately "does not . . . rest firmly upon anything,"[46] it nevertheless must be reaffirmed if only for the sake of the conviction which "absolute man" has of his own capacities. So Barth expresses this assymetrical dynamic: "The conviction that God exists and holds sway must from time to time be justified and guaranteed anew. How is this to be done? The proof will be conveyed by a renewed confirmation of the existence of this wonderful concordance between man and the world he inhabits. It is by this means that man will once again be fired with a belief in God[.]"[47] Theodicy, then, according to Barth, is nothing other than the theoretical paraphrasing of "absolute man's" experience of this concordance between "absolute man" and the exterior world he inhabits.[48] But what Barth has to say with regard to the "form of the inner life" of "absolute man" comes to a culmination precisely on this question: what does it mean to fulfill the will of God? As surely as "absolute man's" inner world is an analogue of his outer world, both worlds finding their origin in a God whose existence is confirmed by man's superior capacities which have delineated "harmony," Barth avers that "absolute man need only to be told by subjective reason, as the elemental voice within every man, and by objective reason, as the elemental voice speaking to every man . . . He who hears the voice of reason and obeys it is acting virtuously and thus finds the theodicy he was seeking and together with it the anthropodicy he was more truly seeking."[49] With this said, it is precisely here that Barth drives home the critique that will eventually be aimed at that quintessential protégé of "absolute man," or Schleiermacher:

> But has not man in fact asked himself and himself given the answer he apparently really wished to hear from some other source? This is the question of which . . . man in the eighteenth century was not aware. This was the absolution also inherent in his inner attitude to life; he assumed it to be self-evident that in taking himself to account, and himself answering the account, and then acting in obedience to it he was also showing the exis-

46. Ibid.
47. Ibid.
48. Ibid.
49. Ibid., 61–62.

tence of God, justifying and guaranteeing anew his relationship with God and thereby affirming that his own existence was possible. He believed . . . that by virtue of the reality of his own existence he could vouch for God and in so doing for the possible existence of God. This may have been the secret of his inward attitude in outline.[50]

But if this is the case, that by virtue of his own capacities "absolute man" could vouch for the existence of God, then, as Barth observes, perhaps it is in Leibnitz' "teaching of the monad" that we may recognize "absolute man."

Thus, we may say that "absolute man" is the "utterly self-sufficient monad [who] is an emanation, an image, a mirror of God himself and is nowhere limited by things outside it."[51] "Absolute man" is a being, as Barth elaborates, "which has no windows, and changes only by its inner principle, its most peculiar striving; which is always the best it is possible to be, and which can therefore transform itself by the tendency of its own most peculiar nature; but it cannot be destroyed, cannot perish, and is immortal like God himself who created [it.]"[52] Indeed "God"—for "absolute man"—is merely the guarantor of a pre-established harmony with reference to the monad's inner- and outer-worlds, between monads themselves, and between monads and their surrounding, exterior world. In short, "God" is the crown to the monad's "will to form."

But, having developed—sticking with Barth's observations as much as possible—"absolute man," and before we turn to his quintessential nineteenth century protégé in Schleiermacher, let us ask: what was the collective attitude of this "man" with regard to the subject-matter of theology? What we say will set the table for Schleiermacher.

"Absolute Theologian"

Perhaps it is already obvious that the "master of all problems"[53] would fall out of harmony with himself were he not to extend this attitude, and thus perceived "omnipotence of human capability[ies],"[54] to the

50. Ibid., 62.
51. Ibid., 64.
52. Ibid.
53. Ibid., 67.
54. Ibid., 69.

subject-matter of theology! Indeed, as Barth points out, "absolute man" will frame the "question posed to it by Christianity in such a way that it fitted the answer which it . . . could or would give."[55] That is, faith in the omnipotence of human intellectual capacities framed the questions Christianity *should* pose. For Barth this dynamic between "absolute man" and the transformation of the questions of Christianity posed to him was nothing more than the quintessential expression of the "humanization of the problem of theology,"[56] which meant, perhaps, "if not the abolition, at least the incorporation of God into the sphere of sovereign human self-awareness, the transformation of the reality that came and was to be perceived from outside into a reality that was experienced and understood inwardly."[57] Though Barth elaborates this "humanization of the problem of theology" by "absolute man" with reference to 1) the state; 2) morality and the bourgeoisie; 3) science and philosophy; and 4) inwardness and the individual, for our purposes, we will, as concisely as possible, elaborate categories two and four. This will provide a concentrated touchstone for developing the subsequent section.

To understand the attempt at humanization to which Christianity was subjected by "absolute man" is to take note of its collective translation into the categories of "morality" and the "bourgeoisie." To do this, though, according to Barth, was to comprehend this translation "in its sociological sense,"[58] or against the socio-economic context of the era. It is his grasp—and ability to articulate—of this context that, again, reveals Barth as historian *par excellence*:

> [I]n the eighteenth century, active interest in the Church, in religion and Christianity . . . was explicitly a concern of the bourgeoisie who were flourishing again after the terrors of the Thirty Years' War . . . Their interest in possessions and states, their view of life and morality conditioned by their needs and the demands made upon them, the perspectives and ideals of the craftsman and merchant, their aspirations to education, now become increasingly the formative influences which make themselves felt in the religious and ecclesiastical questions which come into their hands. It was typical middle-class ideology that, leaving

---

55. Ibid.
56. Ibid., 71.
57. Ibid., 70.
58. Ibid., 77.

aside their Christian content, gave shape to the liturgies and hymn books, and even the sermons, of the time.[59]

But, completing this picture, Barth notes a turn, a shift, certainly derived from this context, in collective thinking from "theoretical" to "practical": "We can see its sterling, but somewhat limited horizon, its modest but self-centred confidence, its sage compliance with superiors and its condescension towards inferiors, its inclination towards the practical and the tangible and its justified desire for outward peace and inward tranquility, its need to be elevated above the cares of everyday life and its sober disinclination for incomprehensible paradoxes."[60] Ultimately, according to Barth, the effect of this bourgeoisie worldview upon the theology of the eighteenth century expressed itself in very concrete, practical terms. That is, the matter to which theology was to address itself was the problem of shaping, or transforming, life in a visible manner "that could be experienced and established concretely and directly, inwardly and outwardly, accomplished by man in particular thoughts, actions and modes of action. The identification of Christianity with this alteration and shaping of human life is . . . the great attempt of the time at humanizing."[61] And this, for "absolute man," already the self-pronounced and demonstrated master of history, would become the hermeneutic of that same history.

Calling upon his self-awareness' perceived mastery over history, "absolute man" could correct the pasts' perverse mis-interpretations of Christian creeds.[62] According to "absolute man," Christian "man" of previous history reduced the creeds to a mere theoretical level, unfortunately reducing Christianity to a "collection of conflicting doctrines and precepts, dialectic subtleties which merely occupied the mind and heated the head, but left the heart empty and the conscience in perplexity."[63] In short, Christianity had been reduced to "teaching and not . . . life."[64] But if this is the case, then there is a positive side to this discovery, a newly transformed understanding of Christianity and its "usefulness."

59. Ibid.
60. Ibid.
61. Ibid., 77–78.
62. Ibid., 78.
63. Ibid.
64. Ibid., 79.

For that, ultimately, is what determines the worth of Christianity: its usefulness.

If "absolute man" in his adaptation of Christianity to the bourgeoisie life consisted in a "general attack against reasoning, against subtleties, dialectic, the controversy in past theology and the life of the church,"[65] then a practical correction—from a prior theoretical emphasis upon saving facts to a new, moralistic emphasis upon the improvement of life, accompanied by the obvious, visible manifestations of this improvement[66]—to this prior "perverted theoretical understanding"[67] was delineated in its place. But let us note, as Barth observes, this corrective from a theoretically-articulated past to a present spirit of application is not intended as an affront to traditional Church dogma, but simply a demonstration of "absolute man's" capacity to finally pierce the historical accretions of Christianity in order to recognize the real, essential meaning under it all. On this point Barth elaborates that

> . . . through all the pores of orthodoxy there begins to seep the conviction that the change and transformation of life that is so desired is the real meaning of Christianity, the true mystery of revelation, which has only now been understood correctly. For this purpose God was born man in Christ, the Holy Scriptures were given to us as the Word of God, and the Church was founded. In this respect, too, the attempt of [absolute man] at humanization consisted primarily in an embrace from outside, in the application of the self-evident presupposition that Christianity, rightly understood, must necessarily match the needs and hopes of the time . . .[68]

The "text to be read,"[69] for "absolute man," is the "planned transformation of life."[70] This emphasis is then related to the Bible. Ultimately, then, as Barth points out, whether one was a Pietist (who "interpreted the Bible and dogma by means of the leading concept of the improvement of life"[71]) or a rationalist (who "first affirmed and used this concept [of the

---

65. Ibid.
66. Ibid., 83–84.
67. Ibid., 79.
68. Ibid., 80.
69. Ibid.
70. Ibid.
71. Ibid., 84.

improvement of life] as such and later read it into the Bible"[72]), "both Pietists and rationalists were modern men and, more particularly, modern citizens, who applied to traditional Christianity a particular presupposition, namely the presupposition, the idea, the systematic principle that in all circumstances Christianity must serve to improve life."[73] If "absolute man" possessed a driving "will for form," then morality, in its widest possible sense, extending to the expression of culture and civic principles, was its chief manifestation. But, although the effects are culturally and civically instantiated, what this ultimately meant was the reality that Christianity—in the process of theology's "humanizing"— was reduced to a "more *individual*, more *inward* matter."[74] Barth calls this "individualization."

According to Barth, "individualization"—a term which is in many ways a culmination of all that Barth has to say with regard to his articulation of "absolute man"—means that "absolute man" "is given authority to be the secret judge, the secret authority over all things outside God. Individualization means making inward, the making inward of what is external, objective to man, by which it is robbed of its objectivity, so to speak eaten up and digested, made into something within man."[75] The "absolute man" who wants to "have Christianity" will do so, will only take Christianity seriously, only by the criterion which demands that he first take himself with single-minded seriousness. What this means is that Christianity must first be incorporated "into the kingdom of man

72. Ibid.
73. Ibid., 84–85.
74. Ibid., 99.

75. Ibid., 99. It is the "authentic, original Pietist," according to Barth, "who represents the essence of this matter. This Pietist is to be seen as a fighter, a conqueror. The one who fights and conquers here is the man who has discovered himself or in himself that ultimate reality, related to God; who thus knows no object which is not in the first place really within him and which must therefore, if he sets himself against it, be brought in, be made inward, be transposed to where it originally and authentically belongs. The fight here is over Christianity as a Church, a creed, a historical force, as a guide to life, a help in life, a power in life, against the whole possibility of an encounter with God and communion with God, as it now confronts man in Christianity for the first time. The fight of the original Pietist is the fight against this confrontation: he wants to have Christianity . . . but belief—living belief, as he puts it—for him means taking Christianity seriously from the perspective and by the criterion of taking himself seriously . . . The sought-for goal is the appropriation of Christianity, which is regarded as complete when all that is not one's own as such is dissolved and made one's own" (ibid., 100).

... [which] consequently means the interiorization and resultant abolition of the confrontation between man and Christianity."[76] In other words, that which is external and thus "other," for "absolute man," will not be tolerated unless it is "dissolved" and transposed "[into] one's own present."[77] The central data of Christianity, as Barth observes, are commensurately transformed. And, according to Barth, the incarnation of the Word of God in Jesus Christ is the first to suffer this "interiorization" of "absolute man." So Barth avers, "This central fact is intolerable to the individualist, an external object in that it stands over against us in the form of temporal distance, the distance between our time and the period AD 1–30, as an *illic et tunc*."[78] But if this is the case, that "absolute man" possesses the superior capacity in the present moment to mine the vagaries and accidents of the historical past for their essential meaning, thus disqualifying any attribution of authority to a Jesus Christ emanating from the accidents of that same history, then "The real birth of Christ [must be] in our hearts; his real and saving death is that which we see accomplished in ourselves, that which we have to accomplish ourselves; his real resurrection is his triumph in us as those who believe in him."[79] For "absolute man" Christ must be "born again" to accommodate the present moment.

But, in any case, with the intellectual agenda firmly established by "absolute man," this "real birth of Christ" would have to wait a bit longer in order to receive a greater "push," or a more profound elaboration, by a "man" to which "absolute man" himself of the eighteenth century would eventually give birth, or the "man" of the nineteenth century. At the same time, if Barth can assert that "Nineteenth-century theology was burdened with the heritage of the 18th century,"[80] then the close kinship between the two centuries, and thus the indebtedness of the former to the latter, becomes even more explicit when Barth examines nineteenth century theology particularly on the issue of what it means by "faith":

> [T]heir assumptions compelled them to understand faith as the realization of one form of man's spiritual life and self-awareness.

76. Ibid., 100.
77. Ibid.
78. Ibid.
79. Ibid., 101.
80. Barth, *Humanity of God*, 15.

> The more serious they were in this interpretation, the more the Christian faith appeared to be a windowless monad, dependent on human feelings, knowledge, and will. Like these, faith was supposed to be self-nurturing, self-governing, and self-sufficient. A capacity for the infinite within the finite, faith had no ground, object, or content other than itself . . . Faith as the Christian's commerce with God could first and last be only the Christian's commerce with himself.[81]

If one did not know any better, one might think they were simply reading a more developed, mature delineation of what "absolute man" of the eighteenth century had to say on the same subject. And Barth would not disagree. For it is of Schleiermacher that Barth not only called the nineteenth century "his,"[82] but indeed viewed his theological program as the ineluctable *telos* of all that had been initiated by "absolute man" of the previous century. Thus Barth could say that "Positively or negatively we can draw lines from everywhere leading to Schleiermacher; from every point we can come to understand that for his century he was not one among many others, with his theology and philosophy of religion, but that it was possible for him to have the significance of the fullness of time."[83]

If Schleiermacher's significance in the nineteenth century bore the marks of the "fullness of time," then most certainly it not only represented the culmination of the time which preceded it, but, in so doing, "did . . . justice to the best men of his age."[84] Indeed it was the quintessential embodiment of theology's attempt to engage the best of what the "absolute man" of his age had to offer. We now turn to what for Barth is the mature nineteenth century delineation of "absolute man's" theological trajectory, or Schleiermacher.

---

81. Ibid., 26.
82. Barth, *Protestant Theology*, 411.
83. Ibid., 413.
84. Ibid., 414.

"Absolute Man's" Nineteenth Century Protégé

Apology Accepted?

One cannot read Barth's presentation of Schleiermacher's theology—and thus his penetrating criticisms—without simultaneously acknowledging the deep respect which Barth accorded this quintessential expression of "absolute man" (as a theologian). Indeed, we might add, any criticism which Barth directed at Schleiermacher was directed from a profound base of respect and honor. Thus, in the course of his comprehensive and penetrating lectures delivered on this "giant" of nineteenth century theology at Göttingen in the winter semester of 1924, Barth could assert: "I now know better than I did before that he was a great and gifted and pious man, that among all who came after him, whether they followed in his tracks or tried to kick against the pricks, there was and is none to hold a candle to him. Protestantism has not in fact had any greater theologian since the days of the reformers."[85] But, we must add, perhaps in accordance with Barth's method of either following a "No" with a "Yes," or a "Yes" with a "No," there is no encomium that is not followed-up directly with a critique. It is certainly no different for Schleiermacher. The next line Barth writes is this: "But this theologian has led us all into this *dead end*."[86] For, when all was said and done, the differences between these two theologians, according to Barth, lay not in their theological commitments per se, but in the priority given to these theological commitments. Schleiermacher wanted, Barth avers, "in all circumstances to be a modern man as well as a Christian theologian."[87] Not only did Schleiermacher want to be a Christian theologian, "he wanted, come what may, to be a thinking man of his time."[88]

But, when pitting these commitments against each other, both that of being a Christian theologian and that of being a "thinking man of his age," Schleiermacher—like all theologians within the lineage of "absolute man's" program—"went overboard . . . insofar as confrontation with the

---

85. Barth, *Theology of Schleiermacher*, 259.
86. Ibid.
87. Barth, *Protestant Theology*, 419.
88. Ibid., 426.

contemporary age was [his] *decisive* and *primary* concern."[89] The prioritizing of this commitment, according to Barth, meant that he was

> concerned with readers of a certain intellectual make-up and tendency which is accepted from the beginning . . . This is revealed at every turn by the fact that this representation of Christianity systematically removes, or is at all events intended to remove . . . each and every stumbling-block which their own intellectual make-up and tendency might prepare for them in such a representation. Christianity is interpreted in such a way that it acquires room by this way of interpretation, that it acquires room in the kind of thinking which is assumed to be authoritative by Schleiermacher's contemporaries, without causing any friction.[90]

In other words, Schleiermacher is first and foremost an apologist. But what the apologist presupposes is at loggerheads with what Barth regards as the fundamental relationship of the Christian theologian to the subject-matter at hand. That is, in Barth's words, the apologist assumes that she "is the complete master of Christianity, in a position, as it were, to look into it from above just as much as modern cultural awareness is; able to elicit its nature and assess its value."[91] At every turn, then, what Barth calls into question is this fundamental priority which manifests itself in this fundamental relationship to the subject-matter of Christian theology. We might say, using Barth's categories of analysis, that "windowless monad," in the fashion of "absolute man" (now coined the "apologist"), determines the value of all that encounters it from the external world. Or as Daniel Price states the matter, it is "the adequacy of Schleiermacher's mediation between Christian faith and culture [that] Barth calls into question."[92] He adds, "At almost every turn Barth counters Schleiermacher's interpretation of the Christian faith, which, Barth argues, reduced the Christian faith to a culturally accommodating religion expressed in psychological categories."[93] Thus, if Barth could acknowledge that "Protestantism has not in fact had any greater theologian since the days of the reformers," he could also temper

---

89. Barth, *Humanity of God*, 19.
90. Barth, *Protestant Theology*, 432.
91. Ibid.
92. Price, *Karl Barth's Anthropology in Light of Modern Thought*, 63.
93. Ibid., 64.

this assertion with the acknowledgment that Schleiermacher's accommodation of the Christian faith to psychological categories was a far cry from the reformers' appeal to the God who objectively reveals himself through the Word. Thus, according to Barth, if one can reject the fact that Schleiermacher has adequately expressed the reformers' insights, and, indeed, he adds,

> if we cannot find in Schleiermacher a legitimate heir or successor of the reformers, if we cannot see in the indubitable domination of his thinking the gracious guidance of God but the very opposite, a wrathful judgment on Protestantism which invites it to repentance and conversion instead of continuation, then the only possibility that remains—and I do not see how one can avoid this—is obviously that of a *theological revolution*, a basic No to the attempted reconstruction at the *very* point which we have constantly to see him hurry past with astonishing stubbornness, skill, and audacity. Schleiermacher undoubtedly did a good job. It is not enough to know that another job has to be done; what is needed is the ability to do it at least as well as he did his.[94]

With this said, we want to develop Schleiermacher's theological program within the trajectory of "absolute man" developed in the previous section. That is, we will develop Schleiermacher's thought according to, and as an extension of, the moralistic/bourgeoisie and individualistic criteria developed by "absolute man" in his attempt to "humanize the problem of theology." As we will see, this will have tremendous implications for the articulation of "revelation," the significance of Christ, and, ultimately, and understanding of redemption. But let us first develop Schleiermacher within the context of "absolute man's" moralistic/bourgeoisie criteria. As we will see, commensurate with "absolute man" of the eighteenth-century, the inward/individual datum of Schleiermacher's theological program is subordinated to this category.

If "absolute man," in his program of "humanizing the problem of theology," adapted Christianity to the bourgeoisie life in such a manner that a practical correction ensued (i.e., from a theoretical emphasis to

---

94. Barth, *Theology of Schleiermacher*, 259–60, quoted in Price, *Karl Barth's Theology in Light of Modern Thought*, 64. It must be noted that Price's concise outline of Barth's development of Schleiermacher will be used as a model for our own project. Obviously, though, we will diverge from Price's outline at various points for the sake of this project's *telos*, and thus parameters.

a moralistic/practical emphasis upon the advancement of life in all of its cultural expressions), then, commensurate with this agenda, at its core, Schleiermacher articulates the Christian faith "as the root of the active life of the cultured Western European."[95] Acknowledging that Schleiermacher's theology was "cultural theology, a study of religion itself as the exaltation of nineteenth-century European life,"[96] Barth observes of Schleiermacher:

> By birth and upbringing in its innermost sanctuary his theology is cultural theology: in religion itself which is the true object of his theology, it is the exaltation of life in the most comprehensive sense, the exaltation, unfolding, transfiguration, ennobling of the individual and social human life which is at stake. Civilization as the triumph of the spirit over nature is the most peculiar work of Christianity, just as the quality of being a Christian is for its own part the crown of a thoroughly civilized consciousness. The kingdom of God, according to Schleiermacher, is utterly and unequivocally identical with the advance of civilization.[97]

Acknowledging that Schleiermacher "wanted to draw men into the movement of education, the exaltation of life, which at bottom is the religious, the Christian movement,"[98] Barth adds, recognizing the practical commitments of bourgeoisie "man" manifested in Schleiermacher, "I venture to assert that Schleiermacher's entire philosophy of religion, and therefore his entire teaching of the nature of religion and Christianity ... was something ... auxiliary to the consolidation of this true concern of his, the ethical one."[99] Indeed, Barth reminds the reader, not only did Schleiermacher officially subordinate the discipline of theology to the discipline of ethics with regard to academic theory,[100] but he warns us not to overlook paragraph 9 of the introduction to *The Christian Faith*, "where Christianity is suddenly described—contrary to all the expectations the reader acquires form the previous paragraphs—as a

---

95. Price, *Karl Barth's Anthropology in Light of Modern Thought*, 64–65.
96. Ibid., 65.
97. Barth, *Protestant Theology*, 420–21, partially quoted in Price, *Karl Barth's Anthropology in Light of Modern Thought*, 65.
98. Ibid., 422.
99. Ibid.
100. Ibid.

theological religion, one, that is, which is determined in the direction of activity, in which the consciousness of God is entirely related to the sum-total of the states of activity in the idea of a kingdom of God."[101] In other words, paragraphs 3 (the delineation of immediate self-consciousness as the primary datum of theology) and 4 (the delineation of consciousness of absolute dependence as the common element to all expressions of piety)[102] are not to be identified with articulating a species of "mysticism"—far from that—but with delineating a religious consciousness which is nothing other than an "unqualified and direct affirmation of modern cultural consciousness."[103] Thus, as Price points out, the religious consciousness simply provides the major impetus to Schleiermacher's primary motive, or "the movement of civilization."[104] But, let us note, this dynamic has been present in Schleiermacher's theology from the outset.

Indeed, already in his *Speeches* the "advance of European culture"[105] was already intimately linked with—appealing to adherents of the then current romantic movement—religious feelings. So Schleiermacher asserted:

> I have tried as best I could, therefore, to show you what religion really is. Have you found anything therein unworthy of you, nay, of the highest human culture? Must you not rather long all the more for that universal union with the world which is only possible through feeling, the more you are separated and isolated by definite culture and individuality? Have you not often felt this holy longing, as something unknown? Become conscious of the call of your deepest nature and follow it, I conjure you. Banish the false shame of a century which should not determine you *but should be made and determined by you*. Return to what lies so near to you, yes, even to you, the violent separa-

---

101. Barth, *Protestant Theology*, 422. Schleiermacher states in paragraph 9 of *Christian Faith*, 43, "But that figure of a Kingdom of God, which is so important and indeed all-inclusive for Christianity, is simply the general expression of the fact that in Christianity all pain and all joy are religious only in so far as they are related to activity in the Kingdom of God, and that every religious emotion which proceeds from a passive state ends in the consciousness of a transition to activity."

102. Schleiermacher, *Christian Faith*, 5–12.

103. Barth, *Protestant Theology*, 423.

104. Price, *Karl Barth's Anthropology in Light of Modern Thought*, 66.

105. Ibid., 67.

tion from which cannot fail to destroy the most beautiful part of your nature.[106]

And if it was the case that "religious feelings" were harnessed by Schleiermacher for the purpose of activity, or the "advance of European culture," then prayer, too, could be articulated within this bourgeoisie-directed "movement of civilization," and thus this theological program of cultural accommodation.

Having analyzed Schleiermacher's concept of prayer, Barth observes that, for Schleiermacher:

> In seeking and finding God in prayer man reaches, as it were, the watershed between receptivity and self-activity. In reaching it he has already passed beyond it, and he also once again finds himself, now more than ever, upon the ground of is own free, creative activity. In prayer there takes . . . a crystallization of religious life into a particular act of life, which is forthwith dispersed and dissolved again, at the climax of this process, in the communion with God, in which the general act of life can and should take place, and will take place again after this concentration. It is only for the sake of this second state that Schleiermacher describes the first one. *He prays because he wants to work; he is a mystic because without mysticism there could not be any civilization.*[107]

Indeed prayer, for Schleiermacher, parallel with his delineation of "feeling," is important only insofar as it engenders the bourgeoisie bent for "usefulness," and, in Schleiermacher's case, the kingdom of God on earth, a kingdom whose advance bears a strong affinity to the advance of European culture. All matters religious are harnessed to the program of cultural advancement. The whole of Schleiermacher's concept of religion, according to Barth, is nothing other than the "result of the teleological, activistic intention of his theology which affirms civilization."[108] Stated within the larger theme of this project, it is nothing other than a nineteenth-century expression (the quintessential expression!) of "absolute man's"—speaking in the bourgeoisie and moralistic categories Barth has assigned him—presupposition that Christianity "must serve

---

106. Schleiermacher, *On Religion*, 92; italics added for emphasis.
107. Barth, *Protestant Theology*, 423; italics added for emphasis.
108. Ibid., 424.

to improve life."¹⁰⁹ But, having developed Schleiermacher's theology with reference to the bourgeoisie/moralistic categories inherited from "absolute man's" program of "humanizing theology," let us now turn to the category of "inwardness and the individual" as delineated by Schleiermacher in a manner commensurate with his lineage.

Theology's Primary Datum

"What has always interested people about Schleiermacher's *Christian Faith*," Barth observes,

> is the Introduction in which they have found and find—what? a basis for Christianity, a derivation of its truth from universal truth, an *a priori* demonstration which provides a sure foundation for *a posteriori* dogmatizing, in short, a substitute for the last proofs of God and for other proofs of the possibility and truth of the statements of the Bible and the church. It was and is unavoidable that we children of an age whose theology suffers from a chronic lack of objectivity, who do not know what we are talking about when we talk about God, but who still want to talk about him—that we cannot escape the question whether there might not be in these foundations, derivations, and proofs something that can restore a good conscience to us . . . without compelling us to believe in God with that realistic objectivity or to know about as the Middle Ages and the age of the Reformation did. This question, the embarrassed question how one can be a modern man and still be a Christian, is what has made the Introduction to the *Glaubenslehre* interesting, because something like an answer to the question has been obstinately detected in it.¹¹⁰

But if it is here, in the Introduction to the *Glaubenslehre*, that so-called modern man is most drawn, it is specifically with reference to paragraphs 3–6 that we not only enter "the holy of holies of Schleiermacher's theology,"¹¹¹ but indeed encounter the quintessential act, according to the canon of "absolute man's" "humanizing of the problem of theology," of the "interiorizing" of the Word of God. This "interiorizing" act is attributed to "feeling," for Schleiermacher. Indeed, illustrating the

---

109. Barth, *Protestant Theology*, 84.
110. Barth, *Theology of Schleiermacher*, 193.
111. Ibid., 212.

fundamental role "feeling" plays in Schleiermacher's theology, he can ultimately assert in paragraph 15 of his *Glaubenslehre* that "Christian doctrines are accounts of the Christian religion's affections set forth in speech." [112] And it is this "basic datum"[113] of Schleiermacher's theology, or feeling, that we shall now develop.

As Price observes, not only does Schleiermacher's magnum opus, or the *Glaubenslehre*, begin with a discussion of piety, but the matter of piety becomes the "beginning, end, and center of all Schleiermacher's works."[114] And, unlike Barth who articulates the church's theology on the basis of the Word of God, Schleiermacher delineates the church's theology—and more importantly the basis of its communion—on the basis of the believers' common piety.[115] So he states in paragraph 3, "The piety which forms the basis of all ecclesiastical communions is, considered purely in itself, neither a Knowing or a Doing, but a modification of Feeling, or of immediate self-consciousness."[116] And it is when he delineates the relationship between knowing, doing, and feeling that the reader is perhaps better able to grasp what Schleiermacher means by "feeling":

> Now, if the relation of the three elements . . . were anywhere set forth in a universally recognized way, we could simply appeal to that. But, as things are, we must in this place say what is necessary on the subject; though this is to be regarded as simply borrowed from Psychology, and it should be well noted that the truth of the matter (namely, that piety is feeling) remains entirely independent of the correctness of the following discussion. Life, then, is to be conceived as an alternation between an abiding-in-self (*Insichbleiben*) and a passing-beyond-self (*Aussichheraustreten*) on the part of the subject.[117]

Thus, as Schleiermacher elaborates, knowing and feeling—"the two forms of consciousness"—constitute what he terms the "abiding-in-itself," while

---

112. Schleiermacher, *Christian Faith*, 76.
113. Barth, *Theology and Church*, 163.
114. Price, *Barth's Anthropology in Light of Modern Thought*, 73.
115. Ibid.
116. Schleiermacher, *Christian Faith*, 2.
117. Ibid., 7–8.

doing proper is the "passing-beyond-self."[118] Here, though, Schleiermacher makes a further distinction.

Though one can conclude that knowing and feeling stand together in antithesis to doing, ultimately the faculty of knowing, according to Schleiermacher, stands with doing in antithesis to feeling. Schleiermacher develops this dynamic in this manner:

> But while Knowing, in the sense of possessing knowledge, is an abiding-in-self on the part of the subject, nevertheless as the act of knowing, it only becomes real by a passing-beyond-self of the subject, and in its duration as a result of stimulation that it is an abiding-in-self: even as the process of being stimulated, it is not effected by the subject, but simply takes place in the subject, and thus, since it belongs altogether to the realm of receptivity, it is entirely an abiding-in-self; and in this sense it stands alone in antithesis to the other two—Knowing and Doing.[119]

The upshot of this analysis, as Barth points out, is the discernment that, for Schleiermacher, "feeling in itself is the victorious centre between knowledge and action,"[120] being constituted as the "seat"—and thus having priority over—of both knowing and doing.[121] As both knowing and doing are constituted by "pious feeling,"[122] or piety, so piety becomes, for Schleiermacher, the fundamental object of knowledge for the church's theology.[123] So, again, as we already set forth: "Christian doctrines are accounts of the Christian religious affections set forth in speech."[124] But if Schleiermacher can establish "pious feeling" as the fundamental datum of the church's theology, as—commensurate with "absolute man's" canon of the "humanizing of the problem of theology"—"it is itself the true self-awareness, and by virtue of this fact alone is at least the subjective representation of truth,"[125] then Schleiermacher can identify this common element of "pious feeling" at the core of church communion as the "feeling of absolute dependence."

118. Schleiermacher, *Christian Faith*, 8.
119. Ibid.
120. Barth, *Protestant Theology*, 440.
121. Price, *Barth's Anthropology in Light of Modern Thought*, 74.
122. Barth, *Protestant Theology*, 440.
123. Price, *Barth's Anthropology in Light of Modern Thought*, 74.
124. Schleiermacher, *Christian Faith*, 76.
125. Barth, *Protestant Theology*, 440.

According to Schleiermacher in paragraph 4 of the *Glaubenslehre*, "The common element in all howsoever divine expressions of piety, by which these are conjointly distinguished from all other feelings, or, in other words, the self-identical essence of piety, is this: the consciousness of being absolutely dependent, or, which is the same thing, of being in relation with God."[126] And let us note well: not only is this self-consciousness of absolute dependence completely distinguished from, and determined to be mutually exclusive with, a lower animal self-consciousness,[127] but it is indeed reckoned by Schleiermacher as synonymous with one's "being in relation with God." And with regard to the self-consciousness' "being in relation with God," and therefore being determined by an Other, Schleiermacher asserts that not only is this "Other" elusive, but it is also certainly no matter of primary concentration. So he states the matter:

> Thus in every self-consciousness there are two elements, which we might call respectively a self-caused element (*ein Sichselbsetzen*) and a non-self-caused element (*ein Sichselbstnichtsogesetzhaben*); or a Being and a Having-by-some-means-come-to-be (*ein Sein und ein Irgenwiegewordensein*). The latter of these presupposes for every self-consciousness another factor besides the Ego, a factor which is the source of the particular determination, and without which the self-consciousness would not be precisely what it is. *But this Other is not objectively present in the immediate self-consciousness with which we alone are here concerned*. For though, of course, the double constitution of self-consciousness causes us always to look objectively for an Other to which we can trace the origin of our particular state, *yet this search is a separate act with which we are not at present concerned*.[128]

Not only, then, is it self-evident for Schleiermacher that the feeling of absolute dependence does not emanate from any earthly source (for such a point of origination would create feelings of relative dependence and relative freedom),[129] but he presumes to have identified the source of all religious consciousness. Indeed he supposes that he has bridged

---

126. Schleiermacher, *Christian Faith*, 12.

127. Price, *Karl Barth's Anthropology in Light of Modern Thought*, 74. See also Schleiermacher, *Christian Faith*, 20ff.

128. Schleiermacher, *Christian Faith*, 13; italics added for emphasis.

129. See also ibid., 15ff.

the gap between God and human, creating a "theology of encounter" between the two.[130] Barth has another analysis of the matter.

Mere Anthropology!

The "feeling" that Schleiermacher has delineated, according to Barth, "as pious feeling is man's feeling of utter dependence, i.e., the feeling of his connexion with God, Schleiermacher's theology is the theology of feeling, or to put it more exactly, the theology of pious feeling, or the theology of awareness, or to put it more exactly, the theology of pious self-awareness."[131] According to Schleiermacher's program, if what it is that a theologian is to preach from the pulpit is simply the "determination of a feeling," thus subordinating the Word to a secondary level of importance, then Schleiermacher—for Barth—has proven himself to be the quintessential manifestation of "absolute man's" hubris. That is, in his proclamation of God he is doing nothing more than proclaiming his own individual, inward piety.[132] But this individual, inward piety has extensive reach for Schleiermacher, leaving its fingerprints on every aspect of his church theology.

"Schleiermacher's real and serious opinion," according to Barth, "was that all theological pronouncements were strictly theological to the extent that they were intended and meant to be received as pronouncements of religious feeling, referring to this feeling itself and to nothing else."[133] But certainly Schleiermacher is not ambiguous on this point when he asserts in paragraph 30 of his *Glaubenslehre* that "All propositions which the system of Christian doctrine has to establish can be regarded either as descriptions of human states, or as conceptions of divine attributes and modes of action, or as utterances regarding the constitution of the world; and all three forms have always subsisted alongside of each other."[134] Even more explicitly regarding the main datum of theology, which in turn directly relates to his conceptualization of revelation, Schleiermacher can assert that "All attributes which we ascribe to God are to be taken as denoting not something

130. Price, *Karl Barth's Anthropology in Light of Modern Thought*, 74–75.
131. Barth, *Protestant Theology*, 440.
132. Ibid.
133. Barth, *Protestant Theology*, 441.
134. Schleiermacher, *Christian Faith*, 125.

special in God, but only something special in the manner in which the feeling of absolute dependence is to be related to Him."[135] But, no matter how wide the scope of theology's pronouncements are extended for Schleiermacher, according to Barth, on the matter of his conceptualization of revelation—from which all else is derived—"The great X which Schleiermacher had in mind was not so much the Christian revelation as the modern pagan feeling for life."[136] Stating the matter of Schleiermacher's articulation of revelation perhaps even more critically, Barth asserts that "the formula concerning the feeling of utter dependence can at the same time be understood as a formula for God himself."[137] Revelation has, according to Barth's analysis, become a matter of complete inward, individual subjectivity. But Schleiermacher is simply showing his roots.

If Barth could articulate nineteenth-century theology's collective understanding of faith—consistent with its lineage traced back to "absolute man"—as one which was "the realization of one form of man's spiritual life and self-awareness,"[138] adding that "The more serious they were in this interpretation, the more the Christian faith appeared to be a windowless monad, dependent on human feelings,"[139] then Barth can assert regarding this quintessential "absolute man" of the nineteenth-century that "Christian pious self-awareness [simply] contemplates and describes itself: that is in principle the be-all and end-all of this theology.[140] Indeed, Barth presses the point of Schleiermacher's relation to his lineage to "absolute man," that "windowless, Leibnitzian monad" and "measure of all things,"[141] even further by maintaining—in sympathetic form!—that "What interests [Schleiermacher] is the question of man's action in regard to God. We must not condemn him for this out of hand. If we call to mind the entire situation of theology in the modern world then we shall find it understandable that it fasted upon the point which had come to the centre of the entire thought of

135. Ibid., 194.
136. Barth, *Church and Theology*, 191.
137. Barth, *Protestant Theology*, 442.
138. Barth, *Humanity of God*, 26.
139. Ibid.
140. Barth, *Protestant Theology*, 443.
141. Barth, *Humanity of God*, 26.

modern man. This point was simply man himself."¹⁴² But, Barth adds, "This shifting of interest did not necessarily have to mean man without God, man in is own world."¹⁴³ Ultimately Barth may be sympathetic of Schleiermacher, but he will never offer excuses. For, according to Barth, in Schleiermacher's attempt—in the lineage of "absolute man"—to be a modern theologian speaking to modern man his theology became "anthropocentric" without remainder.¹⁴⁴ Where the reformers, with regard to the matter of revelation, would have said "Christ," Barth avers, Schleiermacher now says "religion or piety."¹⁴⁵ But precisely at this point we need to pause for a moment in order to survey what, for Barth, are the concrete consequences of Schleiermacher's "humanization of the problem of theology." These consequences, as we will see, not only implicate fundamental categories of theology, but indeed implicate the concrete world his theological inheritors would inhabit.

If Schleiermacher's appropriation of "absolute man's" categories of "morality"/"bourgeoisie" ultimately created a "culturally accommodating" Christianity which both exalted the nineteenth-century European civilization, and directed its forward advance, it also contained within itself the seeds of that same civilization's destruction. According to Barth in a retrospective piece written from the mid-1950's, when, according to "absolute man's" canon of religious anthropocentrism, "the Christian gospel was changed into a statement, a religion, about Christian self-awareness, the God was lost sight of who in His sovereignty confronts man, calling him to account, and dealing with him as Lord. This loss also blurred the sight horizontally. The Christian was condemned to uncritical and irresponsible subservience to the patterns, forces, and movements of human history and civilization. Man's inner experience did not provide a firm enough ground for resistance to these phenomena. Deprived of a guiding principle man could turn anywhere."¹⁴⁶ Indeed the reduction of theology's primary datum to the religious self-consciousness, or "piety," stripped theology—especially in time of national crisis—of the capacity to give the church "an objective basis

---

142. Barth, *Protestant Theology*, 445.
143. Ibid.
144. Ibid., 446.
145. Ibid., 444.
146. Barth, *Humanity of God*, 27.

on which to judge the surrounding culture."¹⁴⁷ And so it went, Barth notably asserts, that, on one day in early August, 1914, "Ninety-three German intellectuals impressed public opinion by their proclamation in support of the war policy of Wilhelm II and his counselors."¹⁴⁸ Barth adds, "Among these intellectuals I discovered to my horror almost all of my theological teachers whom I had greatly venerated. In despair over what this indicated about the signs of the time I suddenly realized that I could no longer follow either their ethics and dogmatics or their understanding of the Bible and of history. For me ... the 19th-century theology no longer held any future."¹⁴⁹ The nineteenth century, anthropocentric theology—quintessentially articulated by Schleiermacher—provided no vantage-point by which to transcend the culture in which it existed in order to pronounce judgment upon that same culture.

But if Schleiermacher's appropriation of "absolute man's" bourgeoisie-accommodating emphasis drew Barth's ire, it was his appropriation of "absolute man's" penchant for "interiorization" that drew out Barth's theological ink in waves. More than this, if it was the analysis that Schleiermacher's delineation of revelation was simply synonymous with the expression of the monad's "piety" that caught Barth's undivided scrutiny, then the matter of *how* that revelation was translated into the categories of redemption and Christology only intensified Barth's criticism and constructive reaction. We shall briefly develop these two points before we move to Barth's articulation of "real man" in contradistinction to "absolute man," especially as he is articulated by Schleiermacher.

Where It Matters the Most!

One cannot comprehend the category of "redemption," as Schleiermacher develops it, without acknowledging the fundamental datum of which it is an application, and thus to which it is intimately connected. For Schleiermacher, in other words, as Price observes, "the connection between feeling (*Gefühl*) and redemption (*Erlösung*) is so integral that redemption nearly represents an unfolding of feeling." At the same time, to understand the condition of redemption intended for humans means

---

147. Price, *Karl Barth's Anthropology in Light of Modern Thought*, 69.
148. Barth, *Humanity of God*, 14.
149. Ibid.

that one necessarily grasp the "evil condition"[150] which obstructs the condition of redemption.

Although, as Schleiermacher observes, the word "redemption" is employed by Christians "with perhaps different meanings," there is a "common element which they all have in mind."[151] "The term itself," according to Schleiermacher in paragraph 11 of his *Glaubenslehre*, is "merely figurative, and signifies in general a passage from an evil condition, which is represented as a state of captivity or constraint, into a better condition—this is the passive side of it."[152] This state of "captivity or constraint," for Schleiermacher, is the "evil condition" from which one passes to the condition of redemption. But, with Schleiermacher's fundamental datum in mind, the category which determines the content of complete redemption should become obvious: absolute "God-consciousness." More explicitly, Schleiermacher states that "the evil condition can only consist in an obstruction or arrest of the vitality of the higher self-consciousness, so that there comes to be little or no union of it with the various determinations of the sensible self-consciousness, and thus little or no religious life. We may give to this condition, in its most extreme form, the name of *God-lessness*, or, better, *God-forgetfulness*."[153]

Redemption, then, for Schleiermacher, is a process in which God-consciousness progresses from a worse state—God-forgetfulness—to a better state of consciousness.[154] "Sin," for Schleiermacher, is delineated in commensurate fashion in paragraph 63 of the *Glaubenslehre* when he describes it as the "bondage of the feeling of absolute dependence."[155] But here, as Barth notes, Schleiermacher views "sin" simply as a "derangement of human nature but no more."[156] Indeed, having delineated Schleiermacher's development of redemption, Price observes that one is not only left with the "inevitable conclusion that Schleiermacher's doctrine of redemption does not represent anything coming *to* hu-

---

150. Schleiermacher, *Christian Faith*, 54.
151. Ibid.
152. Ibid.
153. Ibid.
154. Price, *Karl Barth's Anthropology in Light of Modern Thought*, 77.
155. Schleiermacher, *Christian Faith*, 263.
156. CD III/3: 320; cited in Price, *Karl Barth's Anthropology in Light of Modern Thought*, 78.

manity from a transcendent source,"¹⁵⁷ but that indeed also "sin seems more akin to a mental derangement than an infraction committed against a transcendent and holy God."¹⁵⁸ And, finally, it is Barth, indeed recognizing the parameters which Schleiermacher has set for himself in complementing nineteenth-century European culture with Christianity according to the canon of "absolute man's" "humanizing of the problem of theology," who asserts, regarding the "history" embraced by Schleiermacher's articulation of "redemption," that "In this history it is a question of the "redemption" of human nature. This redemption, however, is at the same time its fulfillment. It is a question of the furtherance of [human nature's] "higher life," of its gradual ascent from the sensory to the spiritual state, from a dim to a powerful consciousness of God."¹⁵⁹ "Redemption," for Schleiermacher, is the capstone to "absolute man's" nineteenth-century bourgeoisie impulses. But, let us ask, where does Jesus Christ—especially with regard to his peculiarity—fit into this scheme of "redemption-as-fulfillment-of-human-nature"?

Ultimately (and obviously!), according to Barth, it is the "problem of Christology"¹⁶⁰ which is essentially at stake for Schleiermacher. Recognizing both Schleiermacher's articulation of Christology and the context in which he articulated Christology, he states,

> It can be asked whether what he wanted to say about the relation of God and man could possibly be said also in the form of Christology. And it can, moreover, be asked whether Christology can possibly serve as the form for what Schleiermacher wanted to say. The Christology is the great disturbing element in Schleiermacher's doctrine of faith, not a very effective disturbance, perhaps, but a disturbance all the same. What he wanted to say might perhaps have been said better, more lucidly and more concisely, if he had been able to say it in the form of a circle with one centre, instead of as an ellipse with two foci. But Schleiermacher could not avoid this element of disturbance.¹⁶¹

As a churchman for whom being "modern" was on level-footing with being a "theologian," Schleiermacher "could not present his views in any

157. Price, *Karl Barth's Anthropology in Light of Modern Thought*, 77.
158. Ibid., 78.
159. Barth, *Protestant Theology*, 450.
160. Ibid., 417.
161. Ibid., 417–18.

other way; he had to present them [according to his canon of "absolute man"] as he did."[162] The ultimate expression of these theological priorities, as Barth observes, is the reality that "Jesus of Nazareth fits desperately badly into this theology of the historical 'composite life' of humanity, a 'composite life' which is really after all fundamentally self-sufficient."[163] One might even be tempted to think, Barth avers, that "he is *simply* there."[164] But let us develop Barth's analysis, and thus arrival, at this point.

Analyzing Schleiermacher's *Glaubenslehre*, but certainly also entertaining his readings of the early *Speeches* and his novella entitled the *Christmas Celebration*, Barth observes that the "dignity of Christ consists in a consciousness of God which is utterly powerful, which precludes all sin, and which is posited together with Christ's self-consciousness."[165] And it is this God-consciousness of his, of which he is "the single, original seat,"[166] that is "identical with the existence of God in him[.]"[167] As the "archetypal image"[168] of Schleiermacher's original datum, or piety, Christ's work consists of "imparting to others the power of his God-consciousness, of his untroubled blessedness."[169] Indeed, as Barth elaborates, if it is (according to paragraph 100 of the *Glaubenslehre*) "The Redeemer [who] assumes believers into the power of His God-consciousness, and this is His redemptive activity,"[170] then it is in the Christian's life that the "activity of the Redeemer has become the Christian's own activity, the furtherance of his own higher life."[171] Essentially, then, religious consciousness can be said to be Christian consciousness only insofar as it can be said to refer to the archetypal manifestation of that God-consciousness, or revelation of Christ, of

162. Ibid., 418.
163. Ibid.
164. Ibid.
165. Ibid., 451.
166. Barth, *Theology and Church*, 188.
167. Ibid. In paragraph 94 of *Christian Faith* Schleiermacher asserts, "The Redeemer, then, is like all men in virtue of the identity of human nature, but distinguished from them all by the constant potency of His God-consciousness, which was a veritable existence of God in Him."
168. Barth, *Protestant Theology*, 456.
169. Barth, *Theology and Church*, 187.
170. Schleiermacher, *Christian Faith*, 425.
171. Barth, *Theology and Church*, 186.

which the community is now both a mediator and expression.¹⁷² And let us be mindful at just this point regarding the priority of community.

As Barth observes, though, for Schleiermacher, the impulse of God-consciousness which proceeds from Christ "imparts to Christianity colour and tone, historical breadth and the possibility for its existence," it is the church community which is both the primary mediator and context of this redemption.¹⁷³ Thus, when the communal aspect of redemption is developed, according to Barth, the *relative* function of Christ receives, perhaps, even greater clarity. "Consequently," Barth asserts, "it is still doubtful whether the methodological point of departure, the exalted humanity of Christ, is not really the original, and whether Christ himself is not the derivative destined to vanish. Under redemption, Schleiermacher in the last analysis understood only an empowering, and under Redeemer only a strong helper or a helping power. Therefore there could not be any word of a founding of communion in the strict sense, but only of confirming it and of continuing the fulfillment of an already existing communion."¹⁷⁴

But, when all is said and done, whether we are mindful of the communion for which Schleiermacher did his Christian theology, or the datum (piety) by which he did Christian theology, that which, for Barth, is most distinctive of Christian theology, or Christology, had "as its summit [only] the indication of a quantitative superiority . . . in Christ as opposed to our own Christianity."¹⁷⁵ He adds: "This is as much as to say that just because the point with Christ is that he has only an incomparably greater quantity of that which we see in ourselves as our Christianity, this indication is ultimately linked with the assertion, the self-assertion, of our own Christianity."¹⁷⁶ But perhaps the most devastating critique Barth can level at Schleiermacher—recognized by one who is familiar with Barth in even the most cursory manner—is simply (after devouring and dissecting Schleiermacher's theology) the posing of these four words in his direction: "why Christ in particular?"¹⁷⁷

---

172. Barth, *Protestant Theology*, 451.
173. Ibid., 456. Cf. paragraphs 87/88 in Schleiermacher, *Christian Faith*, 358–65.
174. Barth, *Theology and Church*, 189.
175. Barth, *Protestant Theology*, 457.
176. Ibid.
177. Ibid., 456.

Summation and Segue

Though Barth's criticisms of Schleiermacher, especially on the matter of Christology, could be downright devastating—even when launched from a responsibly sympathetic and respecting stance (i.e., "*Jesus of Nazareth fits desperately badly into this theology* . . ."!), let us not forget that, for Barth, Schleiermacher is merely the quintessential expression of a theological program which had commenced well before his own time. It is safe to say, based upon a reading of Barth as both church *historian* and theologian, that "absolute man," or that "windowless," "Leibnitzian monad" who is the "measure of all things," thus manifesting his "will for form" through his program of "humanizing the problem of theology," is certainly the indirect recipient of whatever salvo of criticism Barth launches directly at his nineteenth-century sibling, or Schleiermacher. Schleiermacher, though, was the head of "absolute man's" household, for Barth, and thus received the most intense scrutiny. Though Barth the historian was sympathetic of Schleiermacher, he made no theological apologies for his penetrating criticisms.

And it would be Schleiermacher's appropriation of "absolute man's" theological categories, especially with regard to the "interiorizing" of that which had been traditionally an exterior matter for Christianity, or his subjectivizing of revelation, that would—at least initially—fire Barth's re-construction of the theological task, especially as it pertains to its central, defining subject-matter, or Christology. But to say that Barth, especially with regard to his re-construction of Christology, was simply countering the agenda of "absolute man" according to his Schleiermacherian expression would be a narrow analysis of the dangerous landscape of influences that could dictate the priorities which affected one's Christology. But, to adumbrate the matter, let us remember that Barth had no problem attacking his own brethren in the theological pantheon. The more the merrier, it might seem.

Not only did Barth ultimately consider "absolute man"—most notably in his Schleiermacherian expression—to be a "godless man,"[178] but it was the logical outcome of such a theological agenda that horrified Barth. That is, if Ludwig Feuerbach could articulate a God—as subject—who was simply determined by human-derived predicates,[179]

---

178. Cf. Busch, *Great Passion*, 82ff.
179. Barth, *Theology and Church*, 226.

then, for Barth, theology—as manifested by Feuerbach's pressing of "absolute man's" agenda to its logical conclusion—had become unadulterated anthropology.[180] Indeed in his famous *The Essence of Christianity* it was Feuerbach who ultimately pronounced that

> We have shown that the substance and object of religion is altogether human; we have shown that divine wisdom is human wisdom; that the secret of theology is anthropology; that the absolute mind is the so-called finite subjective mind. But religion is not conscious that its elements are human; on the contrary, it places itself in opposition to the human, or at least it does not admit that its elements are human. The necessary turning-point of history is therefore the open confession, that the consciousness of God is nothing else than the consciousness of the species; that man can and should raise himself only above the limits of his individuality, and not above the laws, the positive essential conditions of his species; that there is no other essence which man can think, dream of, imagine, feel, believe in, wish for, love and adore as the *absolute*, than the essence of human nature itself . . . Religion is the first form of self-consciousness. Religions are sacred because they are the traditions of the primitive self-consciousness. But that which in religion holds the first place—namely, God—is, as we have shown, in itself and according to truth, the second, for it is only the nature of man regarded objectively; and that which to religion is the second—namely, man—must therefore be constituted and declared the first.[181]

But if Schleiermacher's program of subjectivism, as ultimately articulated by Feuerbach, could result in a complete "turning [of] theology into anthropology,"[182] and thus an "inversion of Christology into anthropology,"[183] then the only logical matter left to be articulated by "absolute man" in his "triumph of subjectivity"[184] was "man's apotheosis,"[185] or "the final absorption of theology's object (namely, God) by the human subject"[186] as the primary datum of theology. And indeed Feuerbach had accomplished just this, according to Barth, putting the finishing

180. Forde, *Preached God*, 69.
181. Feuerbach, *Essence of Christianity*, 270–71.
182. Forde, *Preached God*, 70.
183. Ibid., 74.
184. Ibid.
185. Barth, *Protestant Theology*, 522.
186. Forde, *Preached God*, 69.

touches on this complete inversion of the theological task. But in order to articulate "man's apotheosis," according to Barth, Feuerbach needed an influence to supplement Schleiermacher's. According to Barth, we need only turn to Luther and his Christology. Indeed it was Feuerbach "who was brash enough to call himself Luther II."[187]

And with regard to Luther (in the context of his analysis of Feuerbach's inversion) Barth asserts that

> With ingenious overemphasis Luther himself urged us to seek deity not in heaven but on earth, in man, man, the man Jesus; and for him the bread of the Lord's Supper had to *be* the glorified body of the Exalted One . . . With great elation people triumphantly turned away (and are still turning away) from the Reformed *finitum non capax infiniti* . . . All this clearly suggests the possibility of an inversion of above and below, of heaven and earth, of God and man—the possibility of forgetting the eschatological limit. Indeed, Hegel (by his own confession) showed himself perhaps only too good a Lutheran in his exploitation of this possibility. It is certain that Luther and the old-Lutherans with their heaven-storming Christology have left their followers in a somewhat exposed and defenseless situation, in face of the speculative anthropological consequences that have irresistibly developed.[188]

And was it not Feuerbach, breathing in the atmosphere of both Schleiermacher's expression of "absolute man," and Luther's "heaven-storming Christology," who, "as a keen-eyed spy," finally "let out the esoteric secret of this whole priesthood"[189] of which other theologians of his time were not aware? that is, has not theology become nothing other than anthropology? and thus the divinization of man? So Barth asks:

> How does it happen that they seem to have been blind to the obvious possibility of continuing on their own line of thought until they reached Feuerbach's trivial conclusion? Why were they incapable of guarding themselves against this outcome? Why did they not speak at some decisive place in such a way that Feuerbach's question could not concern them in the least; so that the slander could not have arisen at all? If the eyes of that

---

187. Ibid.

188. Barth, "Introductory Essay," xxiii, quoted in Forde, *Preached God*, 74. Emphases are Forde's.

189. Forde, *Preached God*, 75.

> generation were closed, would we find the same blindness in the generation of their disciples, in those who continue their work ... ? Or will that generation of theologians, in whose midst this spy lived, at least become aware of the threatening danger, will they therefore take pains to work in a direction that would not expose them to that mean insinuation? And if Feuerbach and his question were hidden from his contemporaries, or remained without effect—as certainly can happen—what will the following generation do, whose leading or most characteristic figure will be Albrecht Ritschl?[190]

If a generation of theologians were unaware of Feuerbach's insinuations, one can certainly attribute this to an unquestioned *Weltanschauung* inherited from "absolute man" and quintessentially expressed by Schleiermacher. But perhaps, for Barth, "absolute man's" agenda was only intensified in its insidiousness, magnified in its inversion, by the influence and appropriation of Luther's "heaven-storming Christology."

Ultimately for Barth, with the criticisms complete, the task of re-constructing Christology, then, did not merely consist of countering "absolute," or "godless man," with an objective Immanuel, or "God-with-us," who could not be reduced to an "interiorized" datum of the monad's experience, or simply subjectivism, but indeed of articulating a "God-with-us" without incurring the expense of apotheosizing of "us." To do this, Barth would have to objectively delineate both "real man" and "God-with-us." But, most importantly, he would have to insure that "man," in his formulation of Christology, was prevented from be being apotheosized at all costs. Though the subsequent section will briefly develop the first two points, the matter at issue is the third. Within the context of our project, this means that Luther, and specifically his radical interpretation of the *communicatio idiomatum*, is placed directly in Barth's crosshairs.

Ultimately, as we segue to the next section, it is only appropriate to adduce a portion from the *Church Dogmatics* in which Barth, in a manner evincing his love/hate relationship with Schleiermacher, can both critique yet subsequently employ Schleiermacher as a springboard for expressing the preliminary criteria of his own, mature Christological proposal, especially with reference to the role of the human subject. So he states:

---

190. Barth, "Introductory Essay," xxi-xxii, quoted by Forde, *Preached God*, 75.

In the theology of Schleiermacher and his more or less loyal and consistent followers, this last theme [the Christian being "enlightened in hope," or the domesticating of the Christian hope to human experience] was the first, and it also became the last because on their presupposition there could not be any other. Theology in general and with it the doctrine of the atonement could only be the self-interpretation of the pious Christian self-consciousness as such, of the homo *religiosus in curvatus in se*. In this way Schleiermacher's genius was to bring to its logical conclusion the truncating tendency in the older Protestantism to which we have already alluded ... We do not intend to avoid the problem of the *homo religiosus* or *christianus*. In the final development of the doctrine of reconciliation we shall have to treat very seriously of the special question of the *homo christianus*, of the Christian and what makes him a Christian, of his understanding of himself. It is, in fact, "self-understood" that he must occupy a special place in dogmatics, and undoubtedly in the analysis of the concepts faith, love and hope we have to do with a *conditio sine qua non* of the whole ... But faith and love and hope are relative concepts. The being of the Christian indicated by them is a being in relation. Faith lives by its object, love by its basis, hope by its surety. Jesus Christ by the Holy Spirit is this object and basis and surety. And faith and love and hope in this relation to Jesus Christ are all primarily His work, and His work first in the community of God, and only then His work in individual Christians. We must not confuse the *conditio sine qua non* of the knowledge of the atonement with its *ratio essendi*. The doctrine of reconciliation must end where it began. We shall speak correctly of the faith and love and hope of the individual Christian only when it remains clear and constantly becomes clear that, although, we are dealing with our existence, we are dealing with our existence in Jesus Christ as our true existence, that we are therefore dealing with Him and not with us, and with us only in so far as absolutely and exclusively with Him.[191]

---

191. CD IV/1: 153–54.

Countering "Absolute" and "Apotheosized Man": Karl Barth and the Communicatio Gratiarum

All Aboard . . . the Lutheran "train of thought"?!

If, as has been demonstrated in the course of this project, Luther's radical interpretation of the *communicatio idiomatum* can be applied—specifically with reference to the ubiquity of Christ's humanity, or the *genus maiestaticum* (the direct communication of the divine *idiomata* to the human *idiomata*)—for the purpose of delineating a complete "within-redemption" which cannot be abstracted from the embodied, particular narratives—and ultimately tombs!—of humanity, then, according to Barth, the implications of such a radical interpretation are far less amicable for the task of theology. That is, for Barth, the "Lutheran" *communicatio idiomatum*, particularly with reference to its expression through the *genus maiestaticum* (allowing for the articulation of the "ubiquity of Christ's humanity") simply leaves the door open to an anthropological, or "inverted," subject matter for theology culminating in the danger of crowning "absolute man" by divinizing, or apotheosizing, him. But let us already ask: could not Barth appeal for justification of his criticism to folks like Feuerbach—already inhaling Schleiermacher's air—who both not only were more than happy to walk through this door, but did so while claiming a helpful "nudge" from Luther and his Christology in the process? Let us continue with Barth's analysis of the matter.

With Luther and his followers, too, as he was with Schleiermacher, Barth could both give a sympathetic hearing—in this case with reference to the ubiquity of Christ's humanity through the *communicatio idiomatum*—while granting no apologies for his theological criticisms. And certainly Barth makes it known that he is fully aware of the "Lutheran" intentions expressed in the ubiquity of Christ's humanity. So he addresses the matter: "What is the real meaning and intention of this remarkable train of thought?" He elaborates that

> We have to realize that for all its curious and alien features the reality of the high grace of the reconciliation of the world with God, the perfection of the fellowship established between God and man, and the presence and efficacy of God in our human sphere, are all taken with final and total seriousness. An attempt is made to think out to the very last the fact and extent that all this did and does take place in Jesus Christ the one Son of God

> and Son of Man. If we, too, take this seriously, if we, too, think it out to the end, and if we are clear that the decisive word must be spoken in Christology, and particularly in an understanding of the humanity of Jesus Christ, *we cannot keep our distance from at least the intention of this theologoumenon*, which is so closely akin to the distinctive Eastern Christology and soteriology of the Greek fathers.[192]

But for all of Barth's sympathetic circumspection regarding this "remarkable train of thought," he adds: "But when all this has been said, it has also to be perceived and said that this intention cannot be executed as attempted along these lines."[193] Essentially, for Barth, this "train of thought," though certainly holding the "humanity of Christ" in high esteem, only reinforces the impulses of "absolute man"—that "individualist" and "interiorizer"—to abrogate the temporal distance "between our time and the period AD 1–30,"[194] thus rounding-off the accidents of history—and in this case the objective, particular revelation of Jesus of Nazareth—in order to place the "real birth of Christ in our hearts"[195] in the present, individual moment of experience, or piety. Something to counter "absolute man's" agenda of subjectivism is needed. Hence, Barth could immediately state in his *Church Dogmatics*, re-asserting his agenda—countering that of "absolute man"—of maintaining Christ as an objective datum,

> But does not a recognition of the reality of the atonement as it has taken place in Jesus Christ, of the perfection of the new fellowship established in Him between God and man, and of the presence and efficacy of God in the human sphere as guaranteed by Him, imply that the look which we direct at Him, and at the act of God which has taken place in Him, should be not merely openly but totally directed at Him and Him alone, as a look at the Victor and His victory, to use our earlier expression, or at His giving and our corresponding receiving, at the history as such takes place between God and man in Jesus Christ?[196]

---

192. CD IV/2:78–9; italics added for emphasis.
193. Ibid., 79.
194. Barth, *Protestant Theology*, 100.
195. Ibid.
196. CD IV/2:79.

The "Lutheran" articulation of the *communicatio idiomatum*, especially as manifested in the ubiquity of Christ's humanity, detracted from "the history . . . which takes place between God and man in Jesus Christ" *illic et tunc*, thus playing into the hands of "absolute man's" agenda of "humanizing the problem of theology." It is along the lines of this logic that Barth issues several objections to the "Lutherans":

> did they look only at the given happening as such, the victory which took place in the history, looking away from the event of the divine giving and human receiving to what is given to the human essence of Jesus Christ in this event, to a status mediated to Him in this event? What is really meant by the humanity of Jesus Christ as it is appropriated and illuminated and inter-penetrated by His deity, because participant in all its attributes? The objection can obviously be brought at once against this view that it is a strange deity which can suddenly become the predicate of human essence, and a strange humanity to which all the divine predicates can suddenly be ascribed as subject. Does not this compromise both the true deity and the true humanity of Jesus Christ? Does it not involve either a deification of the creature, or a humanization of the Creator, or both?[197]

But if Barth's objections to the "Lutheran" "train of thought" "acquire their full weight" when placed within the concern for maintaining the integrity of the objective history—*illic et tunc*—of Jesus Christ, an objective history of revelation from which, as Barth perceives, the "Lutherans" have "abstracted" his "humanity,"[198] indeed it is the specter of something much more sinister that brings Barth's criticisms of the "Lutherans" beyond those which could be merely categorized with the garden-variety fouls of "absolute man" so eloquently expressed by Schleiermacher. That is, Barth's criticism of the "Lutherans" reaches crescendo-level pitch when he perceives, through his analysis of the "Lutheran" *genus maiestaticum*, the prospects for affirming the complete "inversion" of theology's task which he had so clearly exposed in Feuerbach, or the "apotheosis" of man. Thus, with regard to the ubiquity of Christ's humanity of which the "Lutherans" speak, Barth asserts, "[W]hen it speaks of a divinization of human essence in Jesus Christ, and when this divinization of the flesh of Jesus Christ is understood as the supreme and final purpose of the incarnation . . . a highly equivocal

197. Ibid., 79.
198. Ibid., 80.

situation is created."[199] So now we turn to Barth's analysis of this "highly equivocal situation" which—Barth perceives—advances the theological "front" beyond the original battle-line of "absolute man" to the no-man's land of "divinized humanity."

Although Barth seemingly (and sympathetically) recognizes that this aspect—the ubiquity of Christ's humanity—of the *communicatio idiomatum* is articulated only within the sphere of Christology, and thus with reference only to the humanity of Christ, he still asks—pressing the horizon of danger with Feuerbach in his rear-view mirror, "But how are we to guard against a deduction which is very near the surface, which once it is seen is extremely tempting, and once accepted very easy to draw, but which can compromise at a single stroke nothing less than the whole of Christology?"[200] Barth elaborates: "For after all, is not the humanity of Jesus Christ, by definition, that of all men? And even if it is said only of Him, does not this mean that the essence of all men . . . is capable of divinization?"[201] For were this to be asserted, and taken to its logical conclusion, according to Barth, ". . . in Christology a door is left wide open . . . from the very heart of the Christian faith"[202] itself. For the way "through this door" of the "Lutherans'" *communicatio idiomatum* leads, with specific reference to the *genus maiestaticum*,

> smoothly and directly to anthropology: and not to a dull naturalistic and moralistic anthropology, but to a 'high-pitched' anthropology; to the doctrine of a humanity which is not only capable of deification, but already deified, or at any rate on the point of apotheosis or deification. If the supreme achievement of Christology, its final word, is the apotheosized flesh of Jesus Christ, omnipotent, omnipresent and omniscient, deserving of our worship, is it not merely a hard shell which conceals the sweet kernel of the divinity of humanity as a whole and as such, a shell which we can confidently discard and throw away once it has performed this service?[203]

Restated within the context of our project: if Luther's radical interpretation of the *communicatio idiomatum* lends itself, with reference to all of

199. Ibid., 81.
200. Ibid.
201. Ibid.
202. Ibid.
203. Ibid., 81–82.

humanity's embodied, particular narratives, to the articulation of the complete—and completely historicized—presence of Christ's "within-redemption," then Barth could only view the "Lutheran" *communicatio idiomatum*, with specific reference to its expression through the *genus maiestaticum*, through the lens of his own Reformed theological tradition (*finitum non capax finiti!*) and his analysis of both "absolute man" (ultimately manifested by Schleiermacher) and "apotheosized man" (ultimately and brazenly manifested by Feuerbach). Thus, for Barth, the *communicatio idiomatum*—with specific reference to the *genus maiestaticum*—was not only an "open door" to the very theology which once reduced God's revelation of Jesus Christ, according to the canon of "absolute man," to a datum of inward experience, or piety, but indeed a super-highway to a theology which conducted a complete inversion of its proper subject matter; a theology which not only divested its proclamation of the ability of rendering judgment upon humanity's attempt to "absolute-tion," but indeed apotheosized that humanity in the process. What, then, shall we ask, did Barth call for in lieu of the *communicatio idiomatum*? In providing an answer, we will essentially be delineating the ultimate expression of the primary datum, and thus parameters, by which Barth re-constructed his Christology in response to "absolute man's" "humanizing of the problem of theology." Indeed, let us remember, if "absolute man" is essentially "godless man" according to Barth, then "godless man" is to be reminded that he essentially exists within a primary relationship. It is this dynamic which will subsequently be developed.

Another Framework

Acknowledging that the manner of thought which ultimately deified human nature has "already been weighed and rejected," Barth asserted that a new answer to the Christological question "must move strictly within the framework of . . . mutual participation."[204] Instead of delineating a direct exchange of *idiomata*, or even an indirect exchange of *idiomata*, Barth called for a *communicatio gratiarum*, or

> the effective confrontation, not only of the divine with the human, but also of the human with the divine essence, and there-

---

204. Ibid., 87.

fore the determination of the relationship [of the natures within the person of Jesus Christ] of the one to the other which, without altering its essence, takes place in this confrontation. Each of [the natures] is determined in a way peculiar and not arbitrarily ascribed to it: the divine in such a way . . . that it remains the divine; and the human in such a way that it remains the human, but is as such confronted with the divine in the One who as the Son of Man is also primarily the Son of God.[205]

Stated concisely, the *communicatio gratiarum* is the expression of "the total and exclusive determination of the human nature of Jesus Christ by the grace of God."[206] With this adduced, though, it is the context of this "confrontation" that provides no doubt as to "who" Barth is combating through his articulation of the *communicatio gratiarum*; that "man" possesses nothing "absolute" in and of himself, that indeed he is not a self-standing, self-determining entity. In Barth's words, "This confrontation with divine essence takes place in the fact that it pleased God in His grace to condescend to it, Himself to become man in His Son, to become this particular man, and therefore to unite His divine with human essence, to give this *telos* and form to His divine essence for the sake of man."[207] What this means, Barth elaborates, is that "there is no other subject apart from the Son of God which can give even partially a different determination or character to human essence. The Son of Man exists only in his identity with the Son of God, and His human essence only in its confrontation with His divine."[208] This, according to Barth, of which the *communicatio gratiarum* expresses with regard to delineating the role/place of the humanity of Christ, is "the electing grace of God"[209] which thus demonstrates the reality that the Son of God alone—through the en- anhypostatic union[210]—is the Son of Man's "first but also its last and total and exclusive determination."[211] Again: "The existence of the man Jesus Christ is an event by and in the existence of the Son of God, i.e., by and in the event of the divine act of reconciliation, by and in

205. Ibid., 88.
206. Ibid. Cf. Busch, *Great Passion*, 100ff.; and Gorringe, *Karl Barth: Against Hegemony*, 149ff.
207. Ibid.
208. Ibid.
209. Ibid.
210. Ibid., 91.
211. Ibid., 88.

the electing grace of God."[212] Indeed, we may say, the en-anhypostatic union is the eternal event of the "electing grace of God.[213] But to speak of the humanity of Christ as an "event by and in the existence of the Son God," and thus as a "determination" of God's "electing grace," means simultaneously to speak of the exaltation of the human essence in the one Jesus Christ. But what does Barth mean by "exaltation"? "Exaltation to what?"[214]

Answering his own question regarding the meaning of "human exaltation," Barth asserts:

> To that harmony with the divine will, that service of the divine act, that correspondence to the divine grace, that state of thankfulness, which is the only possibility in view of the fact that this man is determined by this divine will and act alone, and by them brought in His existence into not merely indirect but direct and indestructible confrontation with the divine essence. We may indeed say that the grace of the origin of Jesus Christ means the basic exaltation of His human freedom to its truth, i.e., *to the obedience in whose exercise it is not superhuman but true human freedom*.[215]

And this "obedience," according to Barth, means that "In [the en-anhypostatic union] there is given to human essence the human power fully to attest His divine power, to serve it in a way commensurate with it, effectively to execute its act and acts."[216] Indeed, according to Barth, the *communicatio gratiarum* expresses the concurrent reality through the en-anhypostatic union that, not only does the Son of God venture into the "far country" of human disobedience, suffering, humiliation, and

---

212. Ibid., 90.

213. Ibid., 91. For a development of the background of Barth's employment of the en-anhypostatic union, see McCormack, *Karl Barth's Critically Realistic Dialectical Theology*, 358–67. As McCormack points out, the en-anhypostatic union is retrieved by Barth in order to articulate, within his dialectic of veiling/unveiling, the objective possibility of revelation. Indeed, expressing the reality that human nature in the incarnation subsists only within the "Logos of God," the en-anhypostatic union, simultaneously avoiding adoptionism, articulates the dynamic that, "To be sure, revelation is *in* history in such a way as to be withdrawn from all intuitability" (ibid., 363). See also Barth, *The Göttingen Dogmatics: Instruction in the Christian Religion*, 152–67.

214. Ibid.

215. Ibid., 92.

216. Ibid., 97.

death[217] as a "satisfactory offering before God for the men of all times and places,"[218] and thus as the true revelation "human ... fellowship with the divine,"[219] but indeed, in doing so,

> the Son of Man ... returns home. And what He brings with Him—we might almost say as the spoils of the divine mercy—from that far country, what He places in the closest proximity to God from the greatest distance, is the human essence assumed by Him. As He adopts it, making it His own existence in His divine nature, He does not deify it, but He exalts it into the *consortium divinitatis*, into an inward and indestructible fellowship with His Godhead, which He does not in any degree surrender or forfeit, but supremely maintains, when He becomes man. Already in the eternal will and decree of God He was not to be, nor did He will to be, God only, but Emmanuel, God with man, and, in fulfillment of this "with," according to the free choice of His grace, this man, Jesus of Nazareth. And in the act of God in time which corresponds to this eternal decree, when the Son of God became this man, He ceased to all eternity to be God only, receiving and having and maintaining to all eternity human essence as well. Thus the human essence of Jesus Christ, without becoming divine, in its very creatureliness, is placed at the side of the Creator ... It is a clothing which He does not put off.[220]

Essentially then, through the event of the en- anhypostatic union, not only does Barth provide a Christological counter to "god-less man," simultaneously countering both "absolute man" (through the asymmetrical "confrontation," and thus "determination," of attributes in the person of Jesus Christ) and "apotheosized man" (through the articulation of the union in such a manner that the divine attributes remain "divine," and the human attributes remain "human"), but indeed eliminates any manner of delineating a "man-less god" (i.e, "... He ceased from all eternity to be God only ...").[221]

And not only is the connection between God and man in the en-anhypostatic union unassailable, but indeed the establishment of this

---

217. Cf. ibid., 290ff, 310ff.
218. Ibid., 142.
219. Ibid., 107.
220. Ibid., 100–101.
221. For a development of this simultaneous elaboration, see Busch, *Great Passion*, 82–105.

unassailable connection, or fellowship, extends to humanity in general. Thus:

> The electing grace of God addressed to this essence in the one Jesus Christ consists in the fact that there is established, and will never cease, a connexion between God and Him and therefore between Him (and in Him ourselves) and God. And the direct and practical significance of a knowledge of this grace is that we cannot have to do with God without at once, *eo ipso*, having to do also with His human essence (our own), with the flesh of His Son (and in Him our own flesh). There is, therefore, no knowledge of God, no calling upon Him ... which on any pretext or in any way can escape His humanity (and therefore our own), or in which the Father and the Spirit can be sought except in and by Him.[222]

Not only, then, can Barth declare that "God is God [only] in His connexion with the human essence of Jesus Christ (and therefore our own) as it has taken place in Him and is indissoluble in His existence,"[223] but indeed, the *communicatio gratiarum* is nothing other than an expression for that which "comes to all flesh in His flesh, the exaltation of human essence to fellowship with the [divine nature]."[224]

But for all that has been said with regard to the *communicatio gratiarum*, for all of the theological technicality with regard to delineating the asymmetrical determination of the God-man relationship within the en- anhypostatic union, the *communicatio gratiarum* is really, essentially, the triumphal culmination—the *Eschatos!*—to a Christological reconstruction conducted in the face of "absolute man's" original program of "humanizing the problem of theology." Indeed, the *communicatio gratiarum* articulates, contra "absolute man's" perceived self-determining "will-to-form," "the true nature behind our corrupted nature,"[225] and thus human nature "in its original and basic form."[226] Simply, the *communicatio gratiarum* delineates—in a fashion antithetical to "absolute man's" self-perceptions—"true man." So Barth can assert, "God has created human beings for Himself, and so 'real man' is for God and not the

---

222. CD IV/2:101.
223. Ibid.
224. Ibid., 103.
225. CD III/2:43
226. Ibid., 52.

reverse. He is the covenant-partner of God. He is determined by God for life with God."²²⁷ Thus, to be a "true man," according to Barth, is to be "man" completely determined by God to live in fellowship, or covenant, with God. Indeed, to live in covenant relationship with God is "man's" only ontological possibility. Let us briefly elaborate just this point.

Barth's Satis Est

The covenantal relationship between God and man, a relationship ultimately coined as a "covenant ontology,"²²⁸ thus articulating the sole parameters within which "true man" is determined, is articulated by Barth on the basis of one, particular, objective datum. In Barth's words (certainly with his analysis of "absolute man" placed front and center!):

> The ontological determination of humanity is grounded in the fact that one man among all others is the man Jesus. So long as we select any other starting point for our study, we shall reach only the phenomena of the human. We are condemned to abstractions so long as our attention is riveted as it were on other men, or rather on man in general, as if we could learn about real man from a study of man in general, and in abstraction from the fact that the one man among all others is the man Jesus. In this case we miss the one Archimedean point given us beyond humanity, and therefore the one possibility of discovering the ontological determination of man. Theological anthropology has no choice in this matter. It is not yet or no longer theological anthropology if it tries to pose and answer the question of the true being of man from any other angle.²²⁹

If it is the covenantal fellowship with God as revealed in the en- anhypostatic union of the person Jesus Christ that both reveals both "true man's" determination, and—in a complete manner which cannot

---

227. Ibid., 203.
228. McCormack, "Grace and being," 99.
229. CD III/2:132; also cited at length in Price, *Karl Barth's Anthropology in Light of Modern Thought*, 125. Barth observes, "The question of anything preceding our being apart from the divine summons can arise only if we try to explain ourselves by ourselves instead of by our concrete confrontation with God." He adds, "Perhaps the fundamental mistake in all erroneous thinking of man about himself is that he tries to equate himself with God and therefore to proceed on the assumption that he can regard himself as the presupposition of his own being. The presupposition of man is God in His Word" (ibid., 151).

be augmented or superseded[230]—applies to the "men of all times and places,"[231] it must be necessarily noted that, for Barth, this "election of grace is the sum of the Gospel . . . the Gospel *in nuce*."[232] Indeed, as God simultaneously reveals in the en- anhypostatic union both that he is God only as "God with us,"[233] and that "real man" is man determined purely within this covenantal relationship (articulated by the *communicatio gratiarum*), so also this "election of grace," this electing of "man" through the Son of God—the *objectivissmus*—is "grounded and determined in the fact that God is the God of the eternal election of His grace. In the light of this election the whole of the Gospel is light."[234] "Who" God "is" is ultimately who God has eternally committed himself to be in the "election of grace," or the election of "true man" into covenantal fellowship with him.[235] The en- anhypostatic union of Jesus Christ is the non-augmentable, complete revelation of this covenantal fellowship. Indeed, Barth's delineation of "reconciliation" is formed against the background of this eternal election of "real man" into covenantal fellowship.[236] Indeed, as Barth asserts regarding Jesus Christ, "He is the atonement as the fulfillment of the covenant. In Him that turning of God to man and the conversion of man to God is actuality in the appointed order of the mutual interrelationship, and therefore in such a way that the former aims at the latter and the latter is grounded in the former. In Him both are in this order the one whole event of reconciliation."[237] With regard to the "completeness" of this reconciliation, or the eternal election of "man" into "mutual interrelationship" with God, or covenantal fellowship, Barth asserts,

> The being of Jesus Christ was and is perfect and complete in itself in His history as the true Son of God and Son of Man. It does not need to be transcended or augmented by new qualities or further developments. The humiliation of God and the exaltation of man as they took place in Him are the completed

---

230. CD IV/2:142.
231. Ibid.
232. CD II/2:13–14.
233. CD IV/1:6.
234. CD II/2:14.
235. Cf. McCormack, "Grace and being," 93–101.
236. CD IV/1:22.
237. Ibid., 122.

> fulfilment of the covenant, the completed reconciliation of the world with God. His being as such... was and is the end of the old and the beginning of the new form of this world even without His resurrection and ascension. He did not and does not lack anything in Himself. What was lacking was only the men to see and hear it as the work and Word of God—the praise and thanksgiving and obedience of their thoughts and words and works.[238]

The upshot of all of this, then, is "the removal of antitheses; the antitheses between God and man."[239] For if in Jesus Christ the covenant between God and man is perfectly fulfilled, with "true man" being determined through the *communicatio gratiarum* of the en- anhypostatic union of Jesus Christ, then not only is God's "history" revealed to be only a "history in partnership,"[240] but that, indeed, it is in this partnership, "and not therefore the history of an isolated individual... [that it is revealed that] God was never solitary." Barth adds, "Therefore the thought of a solitary man [read: "absolute man"] and his history can only be the aberration of a thinking which is either godless or occupied with that alien God which is properly death. God was always a Partner. The Father was the Partner of the Son, and the Son of the Father."[241] But if "reconciliation" means the abrogation of the "antitheses between God and man, and "reconciliation" is "complete" through their restoration within the covenant—with "absolute man" giving way to "man" determined by the *communicatio gratiarum*—then what role, may we ask, does Barth assign such events as the "resurrection" and "ascension" of Jesus Christ?

Ultimately Barth is unambiguously clear as to the roles which "resurrection" and "ascension" play in his *Dogmatics*. Indeed they are subordinated to the primary activity of sealing the eternally-determined covenant between God and man in the en- anhypostatic union. He states accordingly:

> Thus the resurrection and ascension add to what He was and is and to what took place in Him [in the en- anhypostatic union]—they add to what was to be seen in Him—only the new fact that in this event He was to be seen and was actually seen

---

238. Ibid., 133.
239. Ibid., 314.
240. Ibid., 344.
241. Ibid.

as the One He was and is . . . His resurrection and ascension were simply the authentic communication and proclamation of the perfect act of redemption once for all accomplished in His previous existence and history, of the Word of salvation once for all spoken in Him.²⁴²

And again, regarding the objective, particular event of the resurrection of Jesus Christ itself, Barth asserts: "The event of Easter Day is the removing of the barrier between His life in His time and their life in their times, the initiation of His lordship as the Lord of all time. What He has done in His time He has done as the Representative of all other men, as the elect man, for them. In His resurrection it is fixed that what He did in His time He did in their time for and to them."²⁴³ Indeed, it is the resurrection that connects en- anhypostatic union of Jesus Christ with the rest of history without submerging that particular, objective revelation into the vagaries of history, or allowing it to be swallowed into an individually-determined subjectivism.²⁴⁴ Ultimately, for Barth, if in the en- anhypostatic union the "godlessness" and "opposition" and "hostility" of both "absolute" and "apotheosized man" "are not only denied but removed and replaced by His perfect fellowship with God . . . [and] In him the homecoming of the Son of Man has already taken place . . . [and] The true man [read: *communicatio gratiarum*] . . . is already present,"²⁴⁵ then "redemption" has reached its proper *telos*. "We are there."²⁴⁶ And if

242. Ibid., 133.
243. Ibid., 316.
244. Ibid., 313ff.
245. Ibid., 117.

246. Ibid., 307. So Barth can concisely state in 1956 in an address entitled "Humanity of God," 46–47, "Certainly in *Jesus Christ*, as He is attested in Holy Scripture, we are not dealing with man in the abstract: not with the man who is able with his modicum of religion and religious morality to be sufficient unto himself without God and thus himself to be God. But neither are we dealing with *God* in the abstract: not with one who in His deity exists only separated from man, distant and strange and thus a nonhuman if not indeed an inhuman God. In Jesus Christ there is no isolation of man from God or of God from man. Rather, in Him we encounter the history, the dialogue, in which God and man meet together and are together, the reality of the covenant *mutually* contracted, preserved, and fulfilled by them. Jesus Christ is in His one Person, as true God, *man's* loyal partner, and as true *man*, *God's* He is the Lord humbled for communion with man and likewise the Servant exalted to communion with God. He is the Word spoken from the loftiest, most luminous transcendence and likewise the Word heard in the deepest, darkest immanence. He is both, without their being confused but also without their being divided; He is wholly the one and wholly the other. Thus in this oneness Jesus Christ is the Mediator, the Reconciler, between God and man."

this is the case, "absolute man"—whether he admits it or not—no longer "is." Indeed, perhaps, the great upshot of this entire Christological reconstruction is the comfort that, for Barth, "Godlessness is not, therefore, a possibility, but an ontological impossibility for man."[247] Now it is just a matter of proclaiming the knowledge of this completed, perfect reality.

Summation and Conclusion

If, for the sake of this project, Luther's radical interpretation of the *communicatio idiomatum*—ultimately expressing itself through the "third mode" of Christ's bodily presence—could be employed in order to articulate the redeeming presence of the Word within the manifold, particular, embodied narratives of humanity—and ultimately within its very own tombs, thus lending itself to funding a presence of *complete* "within-redemption," then Barth could condemn this same "Lutheran" *communicatio idiomatum*—specifically as expressed in the *genus maiestaticum*—on behalf of upholding the same integrity of the "human."[248]

---

247. CD III/2:135.

248. Barth asserts in a rather sizable footnote—and one which develops even further his logic against the *communicatio idiomatum*—that: "If justice is to be done to the *communicatio idiomatum*, the *unio natuarum* and the *unio hypostatica*, what the human nature has received must consist—beyond the grace and its gifts addressed to it—in the impartation and appropriation of the distinctive qualities of the divine nature to the human, and therefore in its divinsation. *It is hard to see where this necessity arises. It is hard to see why its total and exclusive determination by the grace of God [communicatio gratiarum] is not enough. It is hard to see why this should not be the absolute distinction and empowering which has come in it to the one Son of Man who is also and primarily the Son of God.*" He elaborates, by referencing Colossians 2:9, "Is temple or dwelling—a dwelling which is certainly filled with Godhead and totally and exclusively claimed and sanctified, but still a dwelling—not really enough to describe what we have to say of human essence in relation to Jesus Christ and the history which took place in Him? Do we have to deify this temple, this dwelling as such, in order that the dwelling of Godhead in it may be a real one? If it is deified, does it not cease to be His temple? Or, to abandon the metaphor, does not a deified human essence cease to be our human essence, usable as such for the work of the Son of God for us and to us, and accessible and recognizable to us as such? If the human essence of Jesus Christ is deified, can He really be the Mediator between God and us? He is totally unlike even the most saintly among us in the fact that His human essence alone is fully, because from the very outset, determined by the grace of God. This is the qualitatively different determination of His human essence, and of His alone as that of the One who as the Son of Man is also and primarily the Son of God. But He is like us in the fact that His human essence determined in this way is in fact the same as ours. In this, even as the

Countering a "High-Pitched" Anthropology   253

Not only did Barth discern within the *communicatio idiomatum* a collapsing of the objective, particular Word of God into the de-historicized, abstract realm of subjectivism (as per the canon of "absolute man"), but indeed, for Barth, the *communicatio idiomatum* "opened the door" to the "high-pitched anthropology" which he ultimately exposed in Feuerbach, that quintessential "apotheosized man." In the place of the "Lutheran" *communicatio idiomatum* Barth delineated, as the ultimate manifestation of "real man" revealed in the en- anhypostatic union in the person of Jesus Christ, or the eternally-determined "election of grace," or the eternally-instantiated-in-Jesus Christ covenant fellowship between God and man, the *communicatio gratiarum*. In short, the *communicatio gratiarum* expresses the "real man," as he was eternally elected to be, that is, as a true covenant partner existing in, and completely determined by, his covenant fellowship—and thus covenant obedience—with God; a fellowship initiated, determined, and fulfilled by God. Thus, contrary to what "enlightener" "absolute men" might think, they have never either been "godless" or not "true men."

And within the scope of this project—the delineation of the redeeming presence of complete "within-redemption" through the application of Luther's "third mode" of Christ's bodily presence—we cannot say that Barth did not explicitly annunciate "within-redemption" as a primary matter in his construction of his covenant ontology. He did. For as Barth asserts,

> This is undoubtedly the mystery of the divine mercy. God acted in this way because He grieved over His people, because He did not will to abandon the world in its unreconciled state and therefore on the way which leads to destruction, because He willed to show to it an unmerited faithfulness as the Creator, because in His own inconceivable way He loved it. But in this respect it

---

exalted Son of Man, He is still our Brother, and as such accessible and recognizable and able to be the first-born among many brethren, our Head. But it does not alter the human essence that it becomes the recipient, the only and exclusive recipient, of the electing grace of God. The likeness between the Son of Man, Jesus Christ, and us is not broken by the fact that He confronts us in this unlikeness. On the contrary, as the recipient of the electing grace of God, His human essence is proved by its exaltation to be the true essence of all men. It is genuinely human in the deepest sense to live by the electing grace of God addressed to man. This is how Jesus Christ lives as the Son of Man. In this He is the Mediator between God and us men in the power of his identity with the Son of God and therefore in the power of His divinity" (CD IV/2:89); italics added for emphasis.

> is as well to be clear that the mystery of His mercy is also the mystery of His righteousness. He did not take the unreconciled state of the world lightly, but in all seriousness. *He did not will to overcome and remove it from without, but from within.*[249]

Again: "What we are He Himself willed to become, in order to take and *transform it from within.*"[250] Barth recognizes that to counter "absolute man" through his Christological re-construction, he has to be countered, or "transformed," *from within.*

And neither can one unqualifiedly assert that Barth is not able to place the Son of God within the Fridays and Saturdays (to use Alan Lewis' parlance) and, ultimately, the tomb of the "man" he has elected from all eternity for covenant fellowship. He does. And he does so eloquently:

> For if God Himself became man, this man, what else can this mean but that He declared Himself guilty of the contradiction against Himself in which man was involved; that He submitted Himself to the law of creation by which such a contradiction could be accompanied only by loss and destruction; that He made Himself the object of the wrath and judgment to which man had brought himself; that He took upon Himself the rejection which man had deserved; that He tasted Himself the damnation, death and hell which ought to have been the portion of fallen man? What did God choose of glory or of joy or of triumph when in Jesus Christ He elected man? What could this election bring except something of which God is free in Himself and for which He cannot truly have any desire: darkness, and the impossibility of our existence before Him as sinners, as those who have fallen victim to his penalties? *If we would know what it was that God elected for Himself when He elected fellowship with man, then we can answer only that He elected our rejection. He made it His own. He bore it and suffered it with all its most bitter consequences. For the sake of this choice and for the sake of man He hazarded Himself wholly and utterly. He elected our suffering . . . He elected it as His own suffering. This is the extent to which His election is an election of grace, and election of love, an election to give Himself, an election to empty and abase Himself for the sake of the elect. Judas who betrays Him He elects as an apostle. The sentence of Pilate He elects as a revelation of His judgment on the world. He elects the cross of Golgotha as His*

249. CD IV/1:237.
250. Ibid., 242.

> kingly throne. He elects the tomb in the garden as the scene of His being as the living God.[251]

But what Barth gives with his right hand regarding his commitments to "within-redemption" and the redeeming presence of the Word of God within, ultimately, the human tomb, he takes away with the left hand of his theological priorities with regard to these same commitments.

That is, although Barth not only conveys both the necessity, and thus priority, of "within-redemption" and the need for articulating the presence of the Son of God within—ultimately—the human tomb itself, in addition to delineating (in a fashion reminiscent of Luther's risen Christ) the eternally simultaneous states of *exinanitio* and *exaltatio* within the en- anhypostatic union,[252] ultimately we may press no farther. The act of redemption has been completed according to the parameters within which it has been placed and articulated. If fulfillment of the covenant fellowship in response to "absolute man" and his program of "humanizing the problem of theology" is the goal, then—logically!—the "work" that has been accomplished through the en- anhypostatic union cannot, and should not, be superseded. If this is the case, then Barth is justified in his line of rhetorical questioning regarding the sufficiency of the work of this en- anhypostatic union, or the person of Jesus Christ:

> How can that which God did in Jesus Christ yesterday not be His act to-day and to-morrow? How can it be present and future only as the significance or influence of His then act? For all its "then-ness," is it not once-for-all, and therefore His act to-day, which cannot and need not be continued or augmented or superseded? And will it not be the same to-morrow? Again, if we continue: "He is and will be," how can this present and future being—our question is now reversed—be anything other than His present and future as the One who exists and acts and speaks and suffers and conquers in that completed history, His being in the outlines of His then form? Is there any reason, then, to understand His being after that "He was," after that completed history, the continuation of His being beyond that given time, as a present and future being in a second and different history which we obviously do not know? Was He not in the history of that time altogether and once for all the Son of God and Son of Man, humiliated and exalted as such, and therefore the Reconciler of

---

251. CD IV/1:164–65; italics added for emphasis.
252. CD IV/2:110, 292ff.

the world with God? Can His being in that accomplished history—as though it were not His perfect being in that "then," that yesterday—be dissolved or augmented or superseded by any other history? Can it find its continuation in any other history? Can it continue to-day and to-morrow except as His then history, and therefore in such a way that His then history takes place also to-day and will take place also to-morrow?[253]

Although Barth is correct within the line of rhetorical questioning he has posed, he is ultimately hand-cuffed in the scope of his articulation of redemption by his own theological starting-point and goal: "absolute man" (and all the manifestations of his program of "humanizing the problem of theology") and his replacement by "real man," or the Son of Man who is expressed in the particular, objective en- anhypostatic union through the *communicatio gratiarum*. And though Barth is able to speak of a God eternally identified with the crucified Christ,[254] and therefore a Jesus Christ who exists, identified with his people, in a simultaneous state of *exinanitio* and *exaltatio*, all of this is trumped—in countering the inward, re-present-ing program of "absolute man"—for the sake of protecting the particular, objective, *illic et tunc* event of the crucifixion. So Barth states:

> The crucifixion and death of Jesus Christ took place once. As this happening once it stands eternally before God and it is the basis and truth of the alteration of the human situation willed and brought about by God: from sin to righteousness, from captivity to freedom, from lying to truth, from death to life, our conversion to Him. For that reason the crucifixion and death of Jesus Christ does not ever take place again. But the life of the Resurrected as the life of the Crucified, as it began in that Easter period, and needs no new beginning, is an eternal life, a life which is also continuous in time. And that means that God, and we too, have to do with the Crucified only as the Resurrected, with the one event of His death only as it has the continuing form of His life. There is no Crucified *in abstracto*. There is no preaching of the cross or faith in the cross *in abstracto* . . . There is no going back behind Easter morning. To the extent that they may contain or express such a going back, all theologies or

---

253. Ibid., 111.
254. CD IV/1:185ff.

pieties or exercises or aesthetics which centre on the cross . . . must be repudiated at once.[255]

He adds, pressing the point of the sufficiency of the objective, particularity of "man's" redemption in the en- anhypostatic union, or Jesus Christ:

> We must understand clearly what such a going back involves. It involves going back to the night of Golgaotha as not yet lit up by the light of Easter Day. It involves going back and into the event of judgment not yet proclaimed and revealed as that of salvation. It involves going back into the sphere where the divine Yes to man which He Himself alone can reveal is still inaccessibly concealed under His No. It involves going back into the death in which all flesh is hope-lessly put to death in and with the Son of God. As though we could find Jesus Christ in any other place, as though we could expect to be with Him in any other way, than in the wholeness of His history as it took place according to the witness of the New Testament! As though we had to begin again at the place where He made an end for us and of us! As though He had not done this once and for all for us all![256]

Although his words are triumphal and eloquent, we must be reminded with regard to what Barth means by "*in abstracto*," especially as it relates to a delineation of the crucified Christ: anything that is conceptualized outside of the particular, objective en- anhypostatic union which has already been instantiated "once-for-all" is "*in abstracto*." But let us indeed, again, be reminded of Barth's intentions regarding the re-construction of Christology, especially as he delineated them over and against that quintessential "absolute man," or Schleiermacher: "[W]e are dealing with our existence in Jesus Christ as our true existence, that we are therefore dealing with Him and not with us, and with us only in so far as absolutely and exclusively with Him."[257] That is, although Jesus Christ exists—identified with, and "for," the "men of all times and places"— simultaneously *exinanitio* and *exaltatio*, it is an eternally self-contained simultaneity, for the manifold particular, embodied narratives of suffering and dead humanity are to be considered as "*in abstracto*" to the most-real, completed narrative of redemption: the restoring of "disobe-

255. Ibid., 343–44.
256. Ibid., 344.
257. Ibid., 154.

dient man" to covenant fellowship with God in the en- anhypostatic union. But let us press our point a little further.

If Luther in his articulation of the two-natures within the *communicatio idiomatum* (see chapter three) could describe the human *idiomata* within the natural, created and creaturely manner of "dying, suffering, weeping, speaking, laughing, eating, drinking, sleeping, sorrowing, rejoicing, being born, having a mother, suckling the breast, walking, standing, working, sitting, lying down . . ."[258] then Barth's human *idiomata*, shaped within his aforementioned starting-point and parameters, are primarily paired-down to reflecting most prominently a single-lane expression of obedience within an asymmetrically-determined, covenantal relationship between God and man. A "covenant of grace." And if Luther's conceptualization of redemption was—from the beginning—articulated within the scope of the Creator's creating Word,[259] indeed ultimately articulating a Redeemer whose presence—"third mode"—permeates the scope of that same ongoing work of creation (a creation simultaneously created/preserved *ex nihilo* at all moments), then Barth's articulation of creation is merely an advertisement for his original theological starting-point. Indeed creation itself is subordinated to, and is an expression of, the priority of the establishment of this *illic et tunc*, particular, objective, completed covenant. Creation, indeed, is articulated by Barth as the "External Basis of the Covenant."[260] Most importantly, the covenant is articulated as the "Internal Basis of Creation."[261] If, as Colin Gunton has pointed-out with reference to creation, "Everything important seems already to have happened,"[262] it is only because Barth's Christological re-construction, organized by the establishment—and completion—of the covenant between God and man and driven by the revealing of that same knowledge, ultimately amounts—when juxtaposed with Schleiermacher's primary "datum"—

258. LW 41:100.
259. LW 1:56ff.
260. CD III/2:94–227.
261. Ibid., 228–329.
262. Gunton, *Christ and Ceation*, 95. I also refer the reader to Prenter's critique—through the lens of the EST!—of Barth's attempt to harmonize creation and redemption through Christ in his "Die Einheit von Schöpfung und Erlösung," 161–86. On the nature of redemption—and questions of its scope as Barth articulates it, with particular attention to "representation," I refer the reader to Sauter's "Why Is Karl Barth's Church Dogmatics Not a 'Theology of Hope'?" 407–29.

to a rearranged anthropocentricity.²⁶³ Indeed, it is Barth's *communicatio gratiarum* that is the ultimate expression of a theology that not only betrays speculative tendencies, but is driven the by the disgust, or "repugnance awakened by an intimacy that has gone too far,"²⁶⁴ or the complete entry of God into creation. But, finally, let us be clear about the implication of Barth's re-construction of Christology, ultimately expressed through his articulation of the *communicatio gratiarum*, as it is juxtaposed with our development of Luther's radical interpretation of the *communicatio idiomatum* for the sake of this project.

If Luther's radical interpretation of the *communicatio idiomatum* lent itself, ultimately, to the ability to comprehend the manifold, particular tombs—eventually our tombs!—as *larvae Dei* of the real presence of God's "still, small voice," or Word of "within-redemption," then, for Barth, the concrete tombs of humanity are nothing but transparencies to an *illic et tunc* narrative of "most-real-redemption" which is located elsewhere. This much he declares explicitly:

> ... for there is no *theologia crucis* which does not have its complement in the *theologia gloriae*. Of course, there is no Easter without Good Friday, but equally certainly there is no Good Friday without Easter! Too much tribulation and sullenness are too easily wrought into Christianity. But if the Cross is the Cross of Jesus Christ and not a speculation on the Cross, which fundamentally any heathen might also have, then it cannot for one second be forgotten or overlooked that the Crucified rose again from the dead the third day. We shall in that case celebrate Good Friday quite differently, and perhaps it would be well not to sing on Good Friday the doleful, sad Passion hymns, but to begin to sing Easter hymns. It is not a sad and miserable business that took place on Good Friday; for He rose again. I wanted to say this first, that you are not to take abstractly what we have to say about the death and the Passion of Christ, *but already to look beyond it to the place where His glory is revealed*.²⁶⁵

Regardless of his employment of the phrase "*theologia crucis*," is this not simply the "triumphant"²⁶⁶ God of "classical theism" (Lewis) whose

263. Cf. Wingren, "Doctrine of Creation," 95, and *Theology in Conflict*, 23–44.
264. Wingren, *Living Word*, 211.
265. Barth, *Dogmatics in Outline*, 114–15; italics added for emphasis.
266. For this critique, see Hall, *Hope against Hope*, 40–43, and Berkhouwer, *Triumph of Grace in the Theology of Karl Barth*, 18–19. "Barth's theology must from its incep-

presence remains only the presence of "power" above and beyond the decomposition of humanity's particular tombs? tombs that are still sealed?

Though Barth is to be congratulated for his steering of the primary of datum of theology, and ultimately Christology, away from "absolute man's" inward, subjective datum, or "piety," it is his re-construction of Christology that perhaps both teaches a lesson regarding the parameters within which theology is conducted, and the implications for the narrowing of these parameters. That is, though Barth ultimately shifts the primary datum of theology—countering "absolute man"—to the triumphant narrative of the *illic et tunc*, en- anhypostatic union, or the covenant of grace which is ultimately manifested—as expressed through the *communicatio gratiarum*—by the true, obedient "man," essentially, in the process, he has allowed (again, to borrow Lewis' phrase) the narrative of Jesus Christ so to color *all* of history that *all* particular histories—and narratives—are either abandoned or rendered superfluous in relation to a completed, "most real" narrative of redemption. The problem is not that Barth did not correctly perceive and evaluate the manner in which "absolute man" absorbed revelation into his context. He did. And he was correct in the vehemence by which he addressed it. But his theology was limited in the scope of its development and application to the context—and agenda—created by the "man" he was confronting, or "absolute man." In this way, perhaps Barth may be viewed as perhaps one of the most contextually-attuned, timely theologians ever.

Ultimately, though, no amount of Christological reconstruction, or subtle distinctions or delineations of the "irreducible complexities" regarding the "unity of time and eternity" within the primary datum of Barth's theology[267] can re-direct humanity from the narratives—living

---

tion be characterized as triumphant theology which aims to testify to the overcoming power of grace. We do not find in it a transition from crisis to grace, or from disjunction between God and man to fellowship between these polarities which Barth was concerned to set forth in varying emphases and accents (ibid., 37).

267. Cf. George Hunsinger, *How To Read Karl Barth*, 14–23. Hunsinger, analyzing various critiques of Barth's theology, specifically lifts up Robert W. Jenson's interpretation of Barth's theology in that, "What Jenson sees in contrast to all the Berkouwers is that Jesus Christ in Barth's theology *is* the unity of time and eternity. Eternity is not to be understood in abstraction from Jesus of Nazareth. However difficult the resulting conceptuality might turn out to be . . . eternity is *defined* as inseparable from the particular temporality of Jesus, as ontologically filled and shaped by it" (ibid., 16–17). Hunsinger adds, "There is neither a general divine nor a general human temporality

and dead—existing in the flesh. Only a theology whose primary datum was not the objective, creating Word of the first article would settle for such abstractions. And no completed "triumph" somewhere else can remove the reality that our Fridays are still being suffered and our Saturday stone sepulchers are still sealed, not to mention the Saturday grief which remains over those same, as of yet, perpetually-sealed sepulchers. To seek a redemption—completed!—in a location outside of this narrative's history is to abrogate both the integrity of what God has created—*and continually creates*—to be "very good" in its embodied particularity, and the sovereignty of the God Immanuel who is able—in his own way as a God of "resumption beyond rupture" (Lewis)—to redeem that same narrative's history completely "from within" that same embodied particularity.

Regarding the narratives of those who have gone before us and thus now lie in their tombs, and one day us, let us refuse to seek—or make apologies for—a reality behind, before, or beyond the creation (and creation's history) which the Creator has created—and still creates—

---

which takes ontological precedence over the particular temporality of Jesus. No general divine or human temporality has ever occurred in abstraction from his" (Ibid., 17). Indeed, beyond the observation of time and eternity's unification in the particular man Jesus, Hunsinger notes, "Veiled behind Barth's appeal to the particularity of Jesus . . . is the extent to which all dimensions of 'temporality' are subjected to radical reinterpretation according to christological and Trinitarian modes of thought. Barth knew what he meant when he appealed to the particularity of Jesus, but what he meant remained at least partially intuitive and therefore did not become fully explicit in statement. The procedure of particularism and its basis in the uniqueness of Jesus Christ was being brought into play in a way which only served to perplex Berkouwer and many other readers as well" (ibid., 14–15). Not only is Hunsinger's appeal to a "Barth-behind-the-text" fascinating, but indeed his appeal to Berkouwer's (et. al.) "misunderstanding" is also quite interesting. Could it be that Berkouwer (et. al.) does "understand?" That is, that it is the particularity of creation in all of its manifestations, and the Creator's primary commitment to the thoroughing-going contextuality of that same creation, that is preeminent? that the first article comes before the second? More importantly, could it be that Barth both convinced himself and others that his theological program transcended all contextuality? Regardless, what Hunsinger does understand completely is that Barth stresses the particularity of Jesus of Nazareth to such an extent that both "eternity" and "temporal humanity" are subsumed into his particularity; a particularity that strangely becomes "generality." They are devoured and flattened-out in the process. "Eternity," which ultimately buttresses the gospel proclamation, is flattened-out into "time," and "temporal humanity"—in all of its ongoing and thorough-going contextuality—is devoured by the *in illo tempore* meta-narrative of the en- anhypostatic union. Perhaps the question is this: did Barth understand the consequences of subordinating everything to the "particularity" of Jesus?

and "call a thing what it is." That is, let us call the tombs of humanity "masks"—not transparencies!—of Christ's presence of "within-redemption." We cannot see *through* this history. As Friday and Saturday people we can only look *at* it. And dare to hope that it is this history and these concrete narratives which God redeems "from-within"; that this is the mask of God's *opus proprium*, or work of "within-redemption."

Conclusion

Summation

IF, AS DOUGLAS JOHN HALL ASSERTED AT THE OUTSET OF OUR PROJECT, the most appropriate expression of the gospel's meaning for contemporary humanity consists of the declaration that "You are free to be a creature ... [that indeed] You are liberated for creaturehood,"[1] then—as we have developed through the course of this project—both "creaturehood" and "redemption" must necessarily be articulated in a commensurate, corresponding fashion.

With regard to "creaturehood": if we are permitted to be human beings, "nothing more, nothing less," then the theologian— countering timeworn dualistic tendencies—must not avoid completely delineating the "human"—as a "thorough-going psychosomatic" entity—according to "creaturely" categories befitting its irreducible, embodied "creatureliness." But, as has also been pointed-out, if the theologian is free to describe the "human" entirely on the basis of its irreducible, embodied nature, then the description of what is "human" must necessarily entail that which is ultimately unrecognizable as "human." That is, to be "human" not only encompasses the vitalities of life, but also both suffering and the decomposing stench of death and the tomb.

With regard to "redemption": if, within the context of the *theologia crucis*, discussion regarding human redemption is to reflect God's "abiding commitment" to the "human," then redemption is to be delineated in such a manner that it entails the restoration—not the annihilation—of the "human" in the process of redeeming it. What this means, according to the *theologia crucis*, is that Emmanuel's "with" must "press on toward 'within.'"[2] For it is "only from within [that] the destructive, annihilating power of creaturely ambiguity and estrangement [can] be overcome

---

1. Hall, *Professing the Faith*, 340.
2. Ibid., 59.

without destroying creation as such."³ Redemption, according to the *theologia crucis*, entails the presence of "transformative solidarity," or the presence of "within-redemption."

But, as Hall has pointed out, if "within-redemption" reflects God's "abiding commitment" to the "human," then it must also reflect the thorough-going contextuality of the "human." This means the dismissal of a "theoretical humanity" for the sake of a "human" who is only manifested through particular, embodied "human beings in their private and social reality, generation after generation; male and female human beings; adults and children; healthy, sick, dying, and dead people."⁴ The "within-redemption" of the *theologia crucis*, then, is an expression of the "ongoingness" of God's commitment to the redemption of a humanity in all of its embodied particularity. But if this is the case, then it is precisely the presence of this "ongoingness" of "within-redemption" that cannot be compromised.

That is, we asked, how can we apply the triumph, the finality, of Christ's resurrection to the "within-redemption" of humanity without nullifying the "ongoingness" of human existence in all of its contextuality and embodied particularity? without lapsing into "resurrectionism," or the failure to apply the incarnation—the presence of "within-redemption"—to the ongoing contextuality of humanity in all of its forms? Or as we asked with Hall, "[I]n view of [Christ's] indisputably biblical affirmation of triumph, is it possible to prevent the Bible's equally indisputable acknowledgment of the reality of evil, death, and decay from being swallowed up and rendered unreal or illusory by the triumph?"⁵ If "within-redemption" is to address God's ongoing commitment to the complete contextuality of the embodied, particular "human" in all of its forms, then how may we delineate "within-redemption" in such a fashion that it "takes place" even at the location where the human form may be most unrecognizable, or the human tomb? Though we may shout "Hallelujah, Christ is Risen!" the Saturday tombs of our loved-ones still remain sealed. Responding to this line of inquiry, it was Alan Lewis who funded the first steps to our answer. Let us briefly rehearse his response and our critique.

---

3. Ibid., 67.
4. Ibid., 529.
5. Hall, *Lighten Our Darkness*, 137.

Lewis, in his delineation of "within-redemption," eloquently articulated the *cordon sanitaire* of the *triduum* which affords us the ability to identify a God who abides—in his "expansive creativity of self-limitation"—in the Friday/Saturday narrative of Jesus Christ in order to redeem *his* life "from within." But, in the process of doing so, he removed the particular, embodied narratives of humanity from the presence of that same "within-redemption" by articulating God's first-century presence in Jesus' Saturday sepulcher as a signifier for his presence in all subsequent (and prior) tombs. Although, as we pointed-out, this God may be able to redeem "from within" Jesus' tomb, his "within-redemption" extends to the location of humanity's particular tombs only as "things signified." This forced us to inquire: is "redemption via signification" even a viable substitute for the redeeming presence of the Answerer—the incarnate presence of "transformative solidarity" (Hall)—within the location of our very own particular, embodied narratives? Lewis did advance our discussion of "within-redemption" by long strides. But, in the process, not only did he—through his articulation of "within-redemption"—reduce the created, "very good" integrity of humanity's particular, embodied narratives to "things signified" by the "signifier" of a "most real" narrative (i.e., Christ's *triduum*), but he ultimately accomplished the very thing which he set out not to do: he has allowed the narrative of Jesus Christ so to color *all* of history that *all* particular histories are either abandoned or rendered superfluous in relation to a "most real" narrative of "within-redemption." Although providing a fine framework within which to delineate "within-redemption," especially with regard to the framework of human narrative, it was revealed that we needed a fuller development of "within-redemption," one that extends to the "within-locations" of all particular, embodied human narratives.

In the context of juxtaposing his articulation of the *communicatio gratiarum* with Luther's radical interpretation of the *communicatio idiomatum*, we also turned to Karl Barth, that giant of twentieth-century theology, to provide us an answer with regard to our question of "within-redemption." Though Barth could certainly speak of "within-redemption" and Christ's redeeming presence ultimately extending to the human tomb itself, he was ultimately handcuffed by the very starting point and parameters of his own theology. Though, as we pointed out, Barth is certainly to be congratulated for his ability to steer the primary datum of theology, and ultimately Christology, away from "absolute man's" inward, subjective datum, or "piety," we are ultimately reminded that, according to Barth, "[W]e are dealing with our existence in Jesus Christ as our true existence, that we are dealing with Him and not with us, and with us only in so far as absolutely and exclusively with Him"[6] That is, the particular, embodied narratives of suffering and dead humanity are considered by Barth as "*in abstracto*" to the most-real narrative of redemption: the restoring of "disobedient," or "absolute man" to covenant fellowship with God in the en- anhypostatic union. "Man" has reached his *telos* through the *communicatio gratiarum*, or the complete determination—and resultant obedience—of the Son of Man by the Son of God within the en- anhypostatic union itself. Indeed, the *communicatio gratiarum* is the ultimate expression of "real man," or the "man"—despite the protestations of "absolute man"—who has eternally through Jesus Christ never existed as "godless." Subsequently, as we discovered, the resurrection and ascension were articulated, and thus subordinated, in a fashion to facilitate the recognition of this primary datum; the resurrection and ascension were relegated to a noetic function. Though he could ultimately shift the primary datum of theology to the objective narrative of the datum of the *illic et tunc*, en- anhypostatic union which ultimately expresses—through the *communicatio gratiarum*—the "real man," Barth has—like Lewis—allowed the narrative of Jesus Christ (the event of the en- anhypostatic union) so to color *all* of history that *all* particular histories—and narratives—are either abandoned or rendered superfluous in relation to a "most real" narrative of redemption. In the process of countering "absolute man," Barth's re-construction of Christology was unable to account for, and apply "within-redemption" to, the "ongoingness" of human existence in all of its embodied particularity.

Ultimately, in order to articulate "within-redemption" in such a fashion as to account for both God's abiding commitment to humanity in all of its embodied particularity, and the ongoingness of that commitment within all the permutations of human contextuality, we turned to Luther's *theologia crucis*. As we demonstrated, if we are to understand the *theologia crucis*—as Hall has pointed out—as a complete redemption "from within," and thus ultimately not removed from particular, embodied human narratives to a "once-for-all" location (committing

---

6. CD IV/1:154

"resurrectionism"), then this can only be accomplished through the delineation of that which is foundational to Luther's *theologia crucis*, or his radical interpretation of the *communicatio idiomatum*. Through Luther's application of the *communicatio idiomatum* we were able to avoid "resurrectionism" by applying the Incarnate One to the ongoing contextuality of humanity in all of its material forms. Specifically, as we developed, it is only through what Luther has termed the "third mode" of Christ's bodily presence that we were not only able to locate the presence and work of redemption within the particular, embodied narratives of humanity, even when that humanity no longer is recognized as "human," but indeed—recognizing that Luther's doctrine of redemption is framed within his conceptualization of the creating Word—we were able to recognize this presence and work of redemption as an *ongoing* one. Restated: if the "third mode" of Christ's presence affords us the ability to extend the presence of "within-redemption" to the scope of creation, then the *larvae Dei* are the means by which that "within-redemption" is localized for the sake of ongoing, individual, embodied narratives. Indeed, through a delineation of Luther's application of his *theologia crucis* to the scope of creation, we were able to declare that the manifold tombs of humanity—far from being transparencies to a "once-for-all" redemption—are *larvae* of Christ's ongoing presence of "within-redemption."

Analysis and Application

> What dare we hope? We may hope that God will be faithful to those who are created anew in Christ. The fact that many will be lying deep under the earth and long will have decayed (Luther cannot paint it drastically enough)—this need not dismay God. He is the God who creates life out of death, in that he swallows up death—as surely as God is God. The God who awakened Jesus Christ from the dead is the God of the living, not of the dead. Yet this does not mean an exclusion of the dead.[7]

If, in our attempt to delineate within the framework of the *theologia crucis* a complete presence of "within-redemption," or One that could be extended as a presence of "within-redemption" to all particular, embodied human narratives, we discovered that it was only through

7. Sauter, "Luther on the Resurrection," 211.

Luther's radical interpretation of the *communicatio idiomatum*—and his resultant articulation of the "third mode" of Christ's presence—that God's presence of "within-redemption" could be conceptualized within the locations of all human narratives, then we must also understand that such an all-encompassing claim of "presence" will never stand within the majority of theological assent. Concisely: if the *theologia crucis* is represented by a "thin tradition,"[8] then we may say that the "third mode" of Christ's presence, developed within that "thin tradition," is represented by a "trickle tradition."

It is precisely the matter of God's presence—not to mention the presence of God's ubiquitous humanity!—which perennially is omitted from popular theological press. For instance, if with Luther we could articulate the present ubiquity of Christ's humanity, we must also be reminded that a theologian such as Michael Welker criticizes even the positing of the omnipresence of the Creator's agency—"in every point of space-time"—due to both the lack of biblical support, and—in its place—the influence of popular philosophical opinion.[9] Indeed, we might also add, if an "era-defining" theologian such as Jürgen Moltmann could assert in his early *Theology of Hope* that "The God of the exodus and of the resurrection 'is' not eternal presence, but he *promises his presence and nearness* to him who follows the path on which he is sent into the *future*,"[10] that indeed the "*parousia* of Christ . . . is conceived in the New Testament only in categories of expectation, so that it means not *praesentia Christi* but *adventus Christi*,"[11] then, thirty years later, with reference to the scope of creation—taking the discussion even further than Welker, he could more fully elaborate the logic of an eschatologically-reserved presence of God by combining the Jewish concept of *Shekinah* with his future-directed eschatology. So he asserted in his later work on eschatology:

> The history of God's indwellings in people and temple, in Christ and in the Holy Spirit, point forward to their completion: 'The whole earth is full of his glory (Isa. 6.3). Through the historical process of indwelling and its eschatological completion, the

---

8. Hall, *Lighten Our Darkness*, 108. Tracy, *Form and Fragment*, also refers to the *theologia crucis* as a "marginal tradition" within the history of Christian theology.

9. Welker, *Creation and Reality*, 86.

10. Moltmann, *Theology of Hope*, 30; italics added for emphasis.

11. Ibid., 31.

distanced contraposition of the Creator *towards* his creation becomes the inner presence of God *in* his creation. To the external presence of God *above it* is added the inner presence of God *within it*. To the transcendence of the Creator towards his creation is added the immanence of his indwelling in his creation. With this the whole creation becomes the *house of God*, the *temple* in which God can dwell, the *home country* in which God can rest. All created beings participate directly and without mediation in his indwelling glory, and in it are themselves glorified. They participate in his divine life, and in it live eternally. Once God finds his dwelling place in creation, creation loses its space outside God and attains to its place in God. Just as at the beginning the Creator made himself the living space for his creation, so at the end his new creation will be his living space. A mutual indwelling of the world in God and God in the world will come into being.[12]

Essentially, during the course of history, according to Moltmann, God is not "in" creation, but "over against it" until the moment of new creation ensues. Then the universe will be the presence of God's universal *perichoresis*.[13] But, until the *eschaton* "Only God can be the space of the world . . . [but] the world cannot be God's space."[14] And, following Moltmann, the litany of theologians who, for various reasons, defer the present presence of God, either with reference to his agency as Creator in general, or with reference to his agency as Redeemer in particular, is long.[15]

But, it must also be noted, even when Christ's presence is affirmed within the tradition of Luther—with direct appeal to Luther!—there is an ecumenically-driven tendency to remove the elaboration of Christ's presence from Luther's framework of the first article, or the creating Word, in order to articulate that same presence in an individually-focused manner under the category of sanctification, or *theosis*. If Luther's delineation of Christ's presence of "within-redemption" afforded us the ability to articulate Christ's presence as one which redeems humans to the sufficiency of the Creator's Word, thus delineating "redemption"

12. Moltmann, *Coming of God*, 307.
13. Cf. Fiddes, *Promised End*, 250ff.
14. Moltmann, *Coming of God*, 306, quoted in Fiddes, *Promised End*, 252.
15. To give just a small sampling of influential titles, the reader may refer to Hodgson, *Jesus—Word and Presence*; Ritschl, *Memory and Hope*; Stroup, *Before God*; and Boulton, "Forsaking God."

within the sweeping scope of a doctrine of creation, then the purveyors of *theosis* reduce "Christ's presence" to the category of individual sanctification. Concisely, "presence" is articulated *narrowly* as both the "*favor* of God (forgiveness of sins, atonement, abolition of wrath) and gift (*donum*), God himself present [in faith]." For, as Tuomo Mannermaa, adds, "Faith means justification precisely on the basis of Christ's person being present in it as favor and gift. *In ipsa fide Christus adest*: in faith itself Christ is present, and so the whole of salvation."[16] But, for the one who not only follows the "thin tradition" of the *theologia crucis*, but the "trickle tradition" inside that "thin tradition," or the "third mode" of Christ's presence, she will discover an appropriation, a wider *vista* of hope, that embraces not just the scope of creation, but indeed the breadth of human history—even when that which is human is not recognized as "human"—within that creation, as well. We shall finish this project of delineating complete "within-redemption" with just such an elaboration.

In 1954 Joseph Sittler advocated for "fresh work on Christology"[17] on the basis that

> Christology remains formally imprisoned in categories which are felt by the initiated to be inadequate and by the uninitiated to be irrelevant. This inadequacy and this irrelevancy are made the more painful because we recognize that the classical Christology of the Creeds perpetuates formulations which operate with a way of speaking about God which is incongruent with our time and its ways of thinking.[18]

This "incongruency," according to Sittler is evidenced by the fact that the "Classical terms were expressive of bodies; ours must be expressive of functions. Nicaea operated with the discourse of *statics*; contemporary discourse is permeated through and through with a world view which is dynamic. For us, *persons* are not bodies, but units of force and will; all things are not bodies, but aims, means, and creations of these units. The classical relationship between bodies was positional; our understanding of relationship is functional. Christology is therefore called upon to transpose an entire theological vocabulary to conform with a

---

16. Mannermaa, "Why Is Luther So Fascinating? Modern Finnish Luther Research," 14–15; see also Mannermaa, *Christ Present in Faith*.

17. Sittler, "Christology of Function," 122.

18. Ibid.

thoroughly functionalized understanding."[19] But if Christology—which "is meaningful only when it swings within the larger orbit of a doctrine of creation"[20]—is to be conformed to a "functionalized understanding of the human," then Sittler could supplement and expand upon this assertion seven years later by stating that "Unless the reference and the power of the redemptive act includes the whole of man's experience and environment, straight out to its farthest horizon ... [otherwise] the redemption is incomplete."[21] But if the farthest horizon of human "experience and environment" which Christology, and thus the redemptive act of Christ, is called to embrace is the human tomb which is bereft of the units of "force" and "will," then the "third mode" of Christ's presence of "within-redemption" can re-direct the focus of one of the most "theologically significant controversies of [the twentieth] century."[22] Let us briefly elaborate this controversy.

In 1937 the German-Jewish philosopher Walter Benjamin published an essay in a journal edited by his friend Max Horkheimer entitled *Zeitschrift für Sozial Forschung*. In that essay Benjamin wrote that "The work of the past is *not closed* for the historical materialist. He cannot see the work of an epoch, or any part of it, as reified, as literally placed in one's lap."[23] Horkheimer, however, responded sharply and critically to Benjamin by writing: "The supposition of the *unclosed past* is idealist ... Past injustice has occurred and [history] is *closed*. Those who were slain in it were truly slain ... In the end, your statements are *theological*."[24] Benjamin, in turn, responded: "The corrective for this sort of thinking lies in the reflection that history is not simply a science but a form of empathetic memory [*Eingedenken*]. What science has "settled," empathetic memory can modify. It can transform the unclosed (happiness) into something closed and the closed (suffering) into something unclosed. That is theology, certainly, but in empathetic memory we

---

19. Ibid., 122–23.

20. Sittler, "Called to Unity," 178.

21. Ibid., 179.

22. Peukert, *Science, Action, and Fundamental Theology*, 206. As this controversy is cited in Peukert (ibid., 206–8), I give full credit to my doctoral advisor, Dr. Vítor Westhelle, for bringing this controversy to my attention. It is cited by him in an unpublished lecture titled "*Usus Crucis*," delivered November, 2006.

23. Peukert, *Science, Action, and Fundamental Theology*, 206; italics added for emphasis.

24. Ibid., 206–7; italics added for emphasis.

have an experience that prohibits us from conceiving history completely non-theologically."[25] But—in light of this controversy—having expanded, with Sittler, "the redemptive act to include the whole of man's experience and environment," and thinking "theologically" with Luther strictly according to the presence of the humanity of God, the matter at stake between Benjamin and Horkheimer receives new direction. That is, on the matter of whether or not those "who were slain . . . [eternally remain] truly slain," it is not essentially a matter of whether history is "open" or "closed." For, ultimately, far beyond the inherent machinations of history and the horizon of empathetic memory, when all those who harbor such a heart for past history have become dust, the issue becomes—thinking *theologically!*—one of *presence* or *non-presence*; of whether or not Christ's presence of "within-redemption" not only "is," but "is" in such a fashion to encompass both creation and the slain of history. But such a presence comes with a present price tag.

Far from standing in the manufactured light of "resurrectionism," or a realized eschatology where all is "placed in one's lap," to look out over the vista of creation and history—and history's dead—through the lens of Christ's ongoing presence of "within-redemption"—especially with regard to the possibility of discerning "ultimate meaning"—hurls one into the seemingly "deep undecidability" (to borrow a phrase from the philosopher John Caputo) [26] of history's terrifying darkness and accompanying silence. It is the darkness and silence of a faith which cannot break through to the *understanding* of a "meaning behind it all" in order to—in a fashion commensurate with this "meaning"—*logically* anticipate a *telos pro nobis* (or even delineate a "proleptic" one!). For, according to Theresa Sanders, it is the terrifying silence of an eschatology that *cannot* be logically "realized" according to any sense of discerning "ultimate meaning" that "raises the deeply frightening, deeply troubling possibility that the meaning we think we find in life is simply *one* meaning, one meaning among thousands of other potential meanings."[27] She adds, "It raises the possibility that in the end there is really no meaning at all. It raises the possibility that, if we are honest with ourselves, we have no way of knowing if the grave is the final word or if there is

---

25. Ibid., 207.

26 Caputo, *More Radical Hermeneutics*, 237; cited in Sanders, *Tenebrae*, 154.

27. Sanders, *Tenebrae*, 154.

reason to hope that even there we are of concern to God. We simply do not know."[28] Sanders is correct, perhaps, with two modifications.

We *do* have reason to hope that even in the grave we are a concern of God. But it is not a question which can either be reduced to a possible discernment of "meaning," or of whether or not the grave is the final Word. It is a question, instead, of whether or not the grave is the location of the presence of the Creator's first and final Word of "within-redemption." It is a hope born of the faith which crucifies all attempts to *see through* history and its material tombs in order to get behind it to the meaning of it all; a faith which acknowledges that it can only *look at* history, at the material tombs of history, and dare to hope that it is this history and these material tombs that are the location—and thus contain the presence—of Christ's "within-redemption."

As for the ultimate "meaning behind it all"?

Perhaps even when God is "all in all" (1 Corinthians 15:28) and humans have the ability to understand God's ways by the "light of glory,"[29] this may still be a presumptuous matter for human creatures to entertain. Even *then* the distinction between Creator and creature will remain. Even *then*, perhaps, as the prophet declares, God's "ways" will still be higher than human "ways" and God's "thoughts" will be higher than human "thoughts" (Isaiah 55:9). Perhaps the eternal, overwhelming joy of being reunited with the beloved dead of history—including, among others, both the slayers and the slain—may quench our creaturely thirst to know the Creator's mind.

---

28. Ibid.

29. LW 33:292. "Let us take it that there are three lights—the light of nature, the light of grace, and the light of glory, to use the common and valid distinction. By the light of nature it is an insoluble problem how it can be just that a good man should suffer and a bad man prosper; but this problem is solved by the light of grace. By the light of grace it is an insoluble problem how God can damn one who is unable by any power of his own to do anything but sin and be guilty. Here both the light of nature and the light of grace tell us that it is not the fault of the unhappy man, but of an unjust God; for they cannot judge otherwise of a God who crowns one ungodly man freely and apart from merits, yet damns another who may well be less, or at least not more, ungodly. But the light of glory tells us differently, and it will show us hereafter that the God whose judgment here is one of incomprehensible righteousness is a God of most perfect and manifest righteousness. In the meantime, we can only *believe* this, being admonished and confirmed by the example of the light of grace, which performs a similar miracle in relation to the light of nature" (ibid.).

Regardless, for the time (and place!) being, we dare to hope that the tomb is the wrapping of a Presence of "within-redemption." We dare to wait for the unwrapping of this Presence. We hope that it truly is a *larva* that we are looking at. To confess this is the great victory of faith.

It is only appropriate, then, to conclude our project with the words of the early Barth, words indicating a reality which, for the time (and place!) being, joyfully cannot be superseded:

> Redemption is that which cannot be seen, the inaccessible, the impossible, which confronts us as hope. Can we wish to be anything other and better than men of hope, or anything additional?[30]

---

30. "Erlösung ist das Unanschauliche, Unzugängliche, Unmögliche, das als *Hoffnung* uns begegnet. Können wir etwas Anderes, Besseres sein wollen als Hoffende oder etwas anderes *daneben*?" Karl Barth, *Der Römerbrief*, Zweite Fassung, 325.

Appendix

Douglas John Hall and Complete "Within-Redemption"

THIS PROJECT'S INDEBTEDNESS TO HALL'S CONCEPTUALIZATION OF THE *theologia crucis* is obvious. Through Hall's delineation of the *theologia crucis* we have been able both to identify the fundamental significance of "within-redemption," and create the framework for articulating complete "within-redemption." Indeed the phrase "within-redemption" has been commandeered—with a few significant twists—from his writings. This project is a fuller, more complete elaboration of Hall's original impulses with regard to developing "within-redemption." With this stated, it is necessary that a few words be said with regard to Hall's fundamental inconsistency with regard to delineating "within-redemption"; an inconsistency which further prompted—in addition to Alan E. Lewis's delineation of "within-redemption"—a fuller elaboration of "within-redemption" via Luther's "third mode" of Christ's presence.

At its core, according to Hall, the *theologia crucis* is both about "*God's abiding commitment to the world*,"[1] and the recognition that "Creaturehood is so very good that the biblical God intends not only to save it, provide for it, clothe it—but to repeat it."[2] The significance of a "very good" creaturehood produces the reality—with regard to the redemption—that it is "only from within [that] the destructive, annihilating power of creaturely ambiguity and estrangement [can] be overcome without destroying creation as such."[3] Complementing this, the significance of "God's abiding commitment to the world" results in the reality that God's "transformative solidarity" with creation, and thus

1. Hall, *Thinking the Faith*, 25.
2. Hall, *Professing the Faith*, 340.
3. Ibid., 67.

his "real involvement in the life of the world,"[4] eschews any recourse to a "theoretical humanity."[5] God's "transformative solidarity" (read: "within-redemption), according to Hall, is committed to "an existing, living, breathing, interacting humanity, alive within the web of the universe—in fact, not even 'humanity' at all, since so such universal actually exists, but human beings in their private and social reality, generation after generation; male and female human beings; adults and children; healthy, sick, dying, and dead people. In short, the actual condition of humankind describes and determines the condition under which God may be 'with' it."[6] "Within-redemption" is a redemption, according to Hall, of nothing other than individual, embodied human beings, a humanity which is only manifested in its manifold particularity. God's "transformative solidarity" responds appropriately to this particularity. Indeed, "*Unless God's act in Christ is a credible participation in our very mundane lives, the redemptive import of it is lost to us.*"[7] To fail to allow for this complete participation "within" the particularity of humanity—the "ongoingness" of human existence—results, according to Hall, in the committing the error of "resurrectionism." "Resurrectionism," in short, is the inability to commit God's "transformative solidarity" to the profound, ongoing contextuality of humanity.[8] "Resurrectionism," as we have pointed-out, is the articulation of a "realized eschatology" in which the work of redemption—disregarding the ongoing, embodied contextuality humanity's narratives—is completed, needing only to be applied to the manifold narratives of humanity. But for all of Hall's ability to both identify the necessity of "within-redemption" and the pitfall of "resurrectionism," ultimately he commits the same error as Lewis. Let us briefly develop this point.

It is when Hall finally arrives at the matter of "representation"—perhaps what might entail the ultimate manifestation of the original impulses regarding "transformative solidarity"—that a fundamental inconsistency is revealed. Specifically, it is on the matter of relating Christ's humanity, and the representational aspect of that humanity, to

---

4. Hall, *Thinking the Faith*, 101.
5. Ibid., 238.
6. Hall, *Professing the Faith*, 529.
7. Hall, *Thinking the Faith*, 330–31.
8. Hall, *Professing the Faith*, 528–30.

the individual narratives of humanity, that Hall comes up short in his delineation of "within-redemption." Thus Hall states,

> But we may and must consider the question of Jesus' humanity also from the perspective of his representation of our humanity before God. We have said that it is his unique relationship with God that propels him toward solidarity with humanity, and that it is this solidarity with us which must then be understood as the prerequisite of his representation of us before God. How then may we think about Jesus' representation of *our* humanity?—the humanity whose content, positive and negative, is defined or at least highly conditioned by the realities of our context? In what ways can we see the moment of Jesus' appearing before God in Gethsemane, "the crucifixion before the cross," as incorporating also our historical moment? Does he bring us, with all the particularity of our contemporary life, as far as possible toward this encounter?[9]

He adds, "The point is that unless we, too, can know ourselves brought forward at least a little way toward the place of encounter, we shall not be able to consider ourselves among those who, in turn, are being brought to live, with and in Jesus, his mediatorial life in the world."[10] But here is where Hall's inability—acknowledging the significance of Christ's humanity in relationship to the question of representation, especially regarding the representation of a profoundly contextual humanity ("Jesus must not only 'be' human—this in itself would mean little; he must participate in our humanity"[11])—to articulate this "encounter" in a concrete manner, addressing the "ongoingness" human contextuality, becomes evident. Acknowledging the limitations of his conceptualization of Christ's humanity, he struggles to find a contact-point regarding humanity's representation by Christ. Representation ultimately comes at the level of meaning. The "transformative solidarity" of God quickly shifts from the concreteness of a humanity only manifested in its embodied particularity (as he develops in theory) to the level of meaning culled from the "spirit of our context." So he asserts, "Accordingly, it has been our decision that the dominant spirit of our context is one of a repressed but increasingly conspicuous disillusionment over the loss of

---

9. Hall, *Professing the Faith*, 541.
10. Ibid.
11. Hall, Professing the Faith, 542.

the meaning that profoundly shaped our earlier New World history."[12] He quickly adds, "If and insofar as this truly does represent our contemporary North American humanity, it is precisely this humanity that, as Christians, we must understand Jesus to represent before God."[13]

And though "We shall never penetrate to the heart of his representation of us before God,"[14] what we can affirm is that "In entering into full solidarity with us as God's anointed one, Jesus carries our humanity with him to the encounter with God, our Creator."[15] But it is merely the "spirit of our context" that Jesus carries with him in this encounter of representation. But if this "encounter" is watered-down from its concreteness by Hall's recourse to "meaning," (derived from the collective "spirit of our context"), the rationale for this recourse to "meaning," according to Hall, is necessitated by the increasingly widened gap created between Jesus' first century humanity and our own ongoing humanity. Ultimately Hall asserts,

> We must . . . confront the most difficult problem, theologically speaking—perhaps existentially speaking as well. Granted that faith may profess that Jesus has done this—that what Jesus has done includes "our" particular quarrel with life—how shall we understand and speak about this representation as involving us? When I am being represented by a lawyer in a court of law, I know perfectly well that I am involved. But we are speaking of an event some two thousand years ago, and one, besides, that lacks the specificity of most of the acts of representation that are part of daily life today. How does anyone come to understand that Jesus carries our humanity forward into the presence of the eternal, pleading our cause, voicing our questions and our forsakenness?[16]

He answers by adding: "There is no universally applicable answer to this."[17] "Moreover," Hall asserts,

> no doctrinal answer can do justice to the mystery of the answers that are given it existentially. We may only say what it seems to

---

12. Ibid.
13. Ibid.
14. Ibid., 543.
15. Ibid.
16. Hall, *Professing the Faith*, 545.
17. Ibid.

> have usually entailed in the experience of the disciple community. To begin with, it certainly entails hearing: that is, the sense of our involvement—that *we* are being represented by this "high priest"—can only occur if we are told of this event . . . There must be a bridge between then and now. Jesus must become for us in some sense our contemporary (Kierkegaard). This is why we have elaborated his representation of our humanity . . . in terms of the crisis of meaning.[18]

If the humanity of the Word, which for Hall is obviously bound to Christ's representative function, is limited by time and location, then, according to Hall, our contemporary "crisis of meaning" is the means both by which "then and now" is bridged, and "humanity" is collectively represented. The dynamics of "then and now" prevent the "then" humanity of Jesus Christ from being involved in the complete "within-redemption" of "now" humanity.

Though we could engage Hall in a further, expanded discussion on the issue of articulating complete "within-redemption," and no doubt this would require a conversation that would move well beyond the scope of this project, we can ultimately assist him in correction on three points, the first two of which being provided on his own terms. First, one could simply remind Hall to reconsider the nature of Emmanuel's complete, abiding commitment to a profoundly contextual humanity, a commitment which is determined, as he points out, not by God's limitations, but by the demands of humanity's thorough-going, contextual, concrete particularity. Second, recognizing that Hall delineates "representation" under the rubric of Christ as the "high priest" (and thus within the *munus triplex*), one could remind Hall of his own words: "This is not the only schema under which it is possible to discuss the work of the Christ, or soteriology."[19] Could it be that "representation" could also be delineated against the backdrop of a wider vista, perhaps of the Creed's first article? Third, recognizing the significance of Christ's humanity with regard to humanity's humanity on the point of representation, perhaps Hall could articulate a more thorough identification of the humanity of Christ with the Creator's agency through the Word? Is this not the same Word? Would this not bridge the "time gap" (and location gap!) between the Jesus of the first century and the humans

---

18. Ibid., 545–46.
19. Hall, *Professing the Faith*, 405.

who live now? Or is the recourse to "meaning" the only means by which the "gap" is bridged?

On this final point we cannot ask Hall to be the stripe of theologian he is not. He may represent the "thin tradition" of the *theologia crucis*. But to represent the "trickle tradition" of the "third mode" of Christ's presence—a representational presence nonetheless!—may be asking too much. But, as we have argued, this "trickle tradition" is foundational to Luther's *theologia crucis*.

Bibliography

Alison, James. *Living in the End Times: The Last Things Re-imagined*. New York: Crossroad, 1996.

———. *Raising Abel: The Recovery of the Eschatological Imagination*. New York: Crossroad, 1996.

Allen, Diogenes. "Theological Reflection on the Natural World." *Theology Today* 25 (1969) 435–45.

Althaus, Paul. *The Theology of Martin Luther*. Translated by Robert C. Schultz. Philadelphia: Fortress, 1966.

Altmann, Walter. *Luther and Liberation: A Latin American Perspective*. Translated by Mary M. Solberg. Minneapolis: Fortress, 1992.

Anderson, Ray S. "On Being Human: The Spiritual Saga of a Creaturely Soul." In *Whatever Happened to the Soul? Scientific and Theological Portraits of Human Nature*, edited by Warren S. Brown, Nancey Murphy, and H. Newton Malony, 175–94. Minneapolis: Fortress, 1998.

Balthasar, Hans Urs von. *The Theology of Karl Barth: Exposition and Interpretation*. Translated by Edward T. Oakes, SJ. San Francisco: Ignatius, 1992.

———. *Mysterium Paschale: The Mystery of Easter*. Translated with an Introduction by Aidan Nichols. San Francisco: Ignatius, 1990.

Barth, Karl. *Christ and Adam: Man and Humanity in Romans 5*. Translated by T. A. Smail. Introduction by Wilhelm Pauck. New York: Macmillan, 1968.

———. *Church Dogmatics* I/1–IV/4. Edited by Geoffrey W. Bromiley and T. F. Torrance. Edinburgh: T. & T. Clark, 1936–1977.

———. *Dogmatics in Outline*. Translated by G. T. Thomson. London: SCM, 1949.

———. *The Epistle to the Romans*. Translated from the 6th edition by Edwyn C. Hoskyns. Oxford: Oxford University Press, 1968.

———. *The Göttingen Dogmatics: Instruction in the Christian Religion*. Vol. 1. Translated by Geoffrey W. Bromiley. Edited by Hannelotte Reifen. Grand Rapids: Eerdmans, 1991.

———. *The Humanity of God*. Richmond, VA: John Knox, 1960.

———. *Protestant Theology in the Nineteenth Century: Its Background and History*. New ed. Translated by Brian Cozens and John Bowden. Grand Rapids: Eerdmans, 2002.

———. *The Resurrection of the Dead*. Translated by H. J. Stenning. 1933. Reprint, Eugene, OR: Wipf & Stock, 2003.

———. *Theology and Church: Shorter Writings 1920-28*. Translated by Louise Pettibone Smith. With an introduction by T. F. Torrance. New York: Harper & Row, 1962.

———. *The Theology of Schleiermacher: Lectures at Gottingen, Winter Semester of 1923/24*. Translated by Geoffrey W. Bromiley. Edited by Dietrich Ritschl. Grand Rapids: Eerdmans, 1982.

———. *The Word of God and the Word of Man*. Translated with a new foreword by Douglas Horton. Gloucester, MA: Peter Smith, 1978.

Basch, Michael Franz. *Understanding Psychotherapy: The Science Behind the Art*. New York: Basic Books, 1988.

Bayer, Oswald. "Angels are Interpreters." *Lutheran Quarterly* 13 (1999) 271–84.

———. "The Being of Christ in Faith." *Lutheran Quarterly* 10 (1996) 135–50.

———. "Creation as History." In *Gift of Grace: The Future of Lutheran Theology*, edited by Niels Henrik Gregersen, Bo Holm, Ted Peters, and Peter Widmann, 253–63. Minneapolis: Fortress, 2005.

———. *Creator est Creatura: Luthers Christologie als Lehre von der Idiomenkommunikation*. Herausgegeben von Oswald Bayer und Benjamin Gleede. Berlin: de Gruyter, 2007.

———. "I Believe That God Has Created Me With All That Exists. An Example of Catechetical-Systematics." *Lutheran Quarterly* 8 (1994) 129–61.

———. *Justification and Sanctification*. Lutheran Quarterly Books. Translated by Geoffrey W. Bromiley. Grand Rapids: Eerdmans, 2003.

———. "Justification as Basis and Boundary of Theology." *Lutheran Quarterly* 15 (2001) 273–92.

———. "Nature and Institution: Luther's Doctrine of the Three Orders." *Lutheran Quarterly* 12 (1998) 125–59.

———. "Rupture of Times: Luther's Relevance for Today." *Lutheran Quarterly* 13 (1999) 35–49.

———. *Theology the Lutheran Way*. Lutheran Quarterly Books. Edited and translated by Jeffrey G. Silcock and Mark C. Mattes. Grand Rapids: Eerdmans, 2007.

Beker, J. Christiaan. *Paul the Apostle: The Triumph of God in Life and Thought*. Philadelphia: Fortress, 1980.

Benjamin, Walter. *Illuminations: Essays and Reflections*. Translated by Harry Zohn. Edited with an introduction by Hannah Arendt. New York: Schocken, 1968.

Berkhouwer, G. C. *The Triumph of Grace in the Theology of Karl Barth: An Introduction and Critical Appraisal*. Grand Rapids: Eerdmans, 1956.

Boff, Leonardo. *Jesus Christ Liberator: A Critical Christology for Our Time*. Translated by Patrick Hughes. Maryknoll, NY: Orbis, 1978.

Bonhoeffer, Dietrich. *Christology*. The Fontana Library Theology and Philosophy. Translated by John Bowden. Introduced by Edwin H. Robertson. New York: Harper & Row, 1966.

———. *Creation and Fall / Temptation: Two Biblical Studies*. Translated by John C. Fletcher and Kathleen Downham. New York: Macmillan, 1983.

———. *Letters and Papers from Prison*. Enlarged edition. Edited by Eberhard Bethge. New York: Macmillan, 1971.

Boulton, Matthew. "Forsaking God: A Theological Argument for Christian Lamentation." *Scottish Journal of Theology* 55 (2002) 58–78.

Braaten, Carl E. *Justification: The Article by Which the Church Stands or Falls*. Minneapolis: Fortress, 1990.

Braaten, Carl E., and Robert W. Jenson, editors. *Christian Dogmatics*. 2 vols. Philadelphia: Fortress, 1984.

———. *Union with Christ: The New Finnish Interpretation of Luther*. Grand Rapids: Eerdmans, 1998.
Brecht, Martin. *Martin Luther: His Road to Reformation, 1483–1521*. Translated by James L. Schaaf. Minneapolis: Fortress, 1985.
Bromiley, Geoffrey W. *Introduction to the Theology of Karl Barth*. Edinburgh: T. & T. Clark, 1991.
Brown, Alexandra. *The Cross and Human Transformation: Paul's Apocalyptic Word in I Corinthians*. Minneapolis: Fortress, 1995.
Brown, Peter. *The Body and Society: Men, Women, and Sexual Renunciation in Early Christianity*. New York: Columbia University Press, 1988.
Brown, Warren S., Nancey Murphy, and H. Newton Malony, editors. *Whatever Happened to the Soul? Scientific and Theological Portraits of Human Nature*. Minneapolis: Fortress, 1998.
Brueggemann, Walter. *The Prophetic Imagination*. Minneapolis: Fortress, 1978.
Bultmann, Rudolf. *Theology of the New Testament*. Vol. 1. Translated by Kendrick Grobel. New York: Scribner, 1951.
Busch, Eberhard. *The Great Passion: An Introduction to Karl Barth's Theology*. Translated by Geoffrey W. Bromiley. Edited and annotated by Darrell L. Guder and Judith J. Guder. Grand Rapids: Eerdmans, 2004.
———. *Karl Barth: His Life from Letters and Autobiographical Texts*. Translated by John Bowden. Grand Rapids: Eerdmans, 1976.
———. *Karl Barth & the Pietists: The Young Karl Barth's Critique of Pietism and Its Response*. Translated by Daniel W. Bloesch. Downers Grove, IL: InterVarsity, 2004.
Bynum, Caroline Walker. *The Resurrection of the Body in Western Christianity, 200–1336*. New York: Columbia University Press, 1995.
Caputo, John. *More Radical Hermeneutics: On Not Knowing Who We Are*. Bloomington: Indiana University Press, 2000.
Cullmann, Oscar. *Christ and Time: The Primitive Christian Conception of Time and History*. Translated by Floyd V. Filson. Philadelphia: Westminster, 1949.
———. *Immortality of the Soul or Resurrection of the Dead? The Witness of the New Testament*. 1964. Reprint, Eugene, OR: Wipf & Stock, 2000.
Daley, Brian. "A Hope for Worms: Early Christian Hope." In *Resurrection: Theological and Scientific Assessments*, edited by Ted Peters, Robert John Russell, and Michael Welker, 136–64. Grand Rapids: Eerdmans, 2002.
Dalferth, Ingolf Ulrich. *Becoming Present: An Inquiry into the Christian Sense of the Presence of God*. Studies in Philosophical Theology. Leuven: Peeters, 2006.
———. "Creation—Style of the World." Translated by Douglas Knight. *International Journal of Systematic Theology* 1 (1999) 119–37.
Damasio, Antonio. *Descartes' Error: Emotion, Reason, and the Human Brain*. New York: Quill, 1994.
Descartes, Rene. "Meditations on First Philosophy in which the Existence of God and the Distinction of the Soul from the Body are Demonstrated." In *Discourse on Method and Meditations on First Philosophy*. Translated by Donald A. Cress, 89–100. Indianapolis: Hackett, 1980.
———. *The Passions of the Soul*. Translated and Annotated by Stephen Voss. Indianapolis: Hackett, 1989.

Dorrien, Gary. *The Barthian Revolt in Modern Theology: Theology without Weapons.* Louisville: Westminster John Knox, 2000.
Ebeling, Gerhard. *Luther: An Introduction to His Thought.* Translated by R. A. Wilson. Philadelphia: Fortress, 1970.
Edwards, Mark U., Jr. *Luther and the False Brethren.* Stanford: Stanford University Press, 1975.
———. *Luther's Last Battles: Politics and Polemics, 1531–1546.* 1983. Reprinted, Minneapolis: Fortress, 2004.
Feuerbach, Ludwig. *The Essence of Christianity.* Translated by George Eliot. New York: Harper & Row, 1957.
Fiddes, Paul. *Past Event and Present Salvation: The Christian Idea of Atonement.* Louisville: Westminster John Knox, 1989.
———. *The Promised End: Eschatology in Theology and Literature.* Oxford: Blackwell, 2000.
Flanagan, Owen. *The Problem of the Soul: Two Visions of Mind and How to Reconcile Them.* New York: Basic Books, 2002.
Forde, Gerhard O. *Justification by Faith: A Matter of Death and Life.* Philadelphia: Fortress, 1982.
———. *On Being a Theologian of the Cross: Reflections on Luther's Heidelberg Disputation, 1518.* Grand Rapids: Eerdmans, 1997.
———. *The Preached God: Proclamation in Word and Sacrament.* Edited by Mark C. Mattes and Steven D. Paulson. Lutheran Quarterly Books. Grand Rapids: Eerdmans, 2007.
———. "Robert Jenson's Soteriology." *Trinity, Time, and Church: A Response to the Theology of Robert W. Jenson,* edited by Colin E. Gunton, 126–38. Grand Rapids: Eerdmans, 2000.
———. "The Christian Life." In *Christian Dogmatics.* Vol. 2. Edited by Carl E. Braaten and Robert W. Jenson. Philadelphia: Fortress, 1984.
———. *Theology is for Proclamation.* Minneapolis: Fortress, 1990.
———. *Where God Meets Man: Luther's Down-to-Earth Approach to the Gospel.* Minneapolis: Augsburg, 1972.
Forell, George. "Justification and Eschatology in Luther's Thought." Supplement Series 2. *Word & World* (1994) 37–47.
Forstman, H. Jackson. "A Beggar's Faith." *Interpretation* 30 (1976) 262–70.
Gerrish, Brian. "'To the Unknown God': Luther and Calvin on the Hiddenness of God." In *The Old Protestantism and the New: Essays on the Reformation Heritage,* 131–49. Chicago: University of Chicago Press, 1982.
Giddens, Anthony. *Modernity and Self-Identity: Self and Society in the Late Modern Age.* Stanford: Stanford University Press, 1991.
Gillman, Neil. *The Death of Death: Resurrection and Immortality in Jewish Thought.* Woodstock, VT: Jewish Lights, 1997.
Gorringe, Timothy J. *Karl Barth: Against Hegemony.* New York: Oxford University Press, 1999.
Grane, Leif. *The Augsburg Confession: A Commentary.* Translated by John H. Rasmussen. Minneapolis: Augsburg, 1987.
Green, Joel. "Bodies—That Is, Human Lives": A Re-Examination of Human Nature in the Bible." In *Whatever Happened to the Soul? Scientific and Theological Portraits*

of Human Nature, edited by Warren S. Brown, Nancey Murphy, and H. Newton Malony, 149–73. Minneapolis: Fortress, 1998.

Gregersen, Niels Henrik. "Ten Theses on the Future of Lutheran Theology." In *Gift of Grace: The Future of Lutheran Theology*, edited by Niels Henrik Gregersen, Bo Holm, Ted Peters, and Peter Widmann, 1–16. Minneapolis: Fortress, 2005.

———. "Natural Events as Crystals of God—Luther's Eucharistic Theology and the Question of Nature's Sacramentality." In *Concern for Creation: Voices on the Theology of Creation*, edited by Viggo Mortensen, 143–57. Uppsala: Svenska kyrkans forskningsråd, 1995.

Gunton, Colin. *Christ and Creation: The Didsbury Lectures, 1990*. 1992. Reprint, Eugene, OR: Wipf & Stock, 2005.

Haikola, Lauri. "A Comparison of Melanchthon's and Luther's Doctrine of Justification." *Dialog* 11 (Winter 1963) 32–39.

Hall, Douglas John. *The Cross in Our Context: Jesus and the Suffering World*. Minneapolis: Fortress, 2003.

———. *God and Human Suffering: An Exercise in the Theology of the Cross*. Minneapolis: Augsburg, 1986.

———. *Hope against Hope: Towards an Indigenous Theology of the Cross*. WSCF Books 1, no. 3. Geneva: World Student Christian Federation, 1971.

———. *Lighten Our Darkness: Towards an Indigenous Theology of the Cross*. Rev. ed. Foreword by David J. Monge. Lima, OH: Academic Renewal Press, 2001.

———. *Professing the Faith: Christian Theology in a North American Context*. Minneapolis: Fortress, 1993.

———. *Thinking the Faith: Christian Theology in a North American Context*. Minneapolis: Fortress, 1991.

Harnack, Adolf von. *What Is Christianity? Fortress Texts in Modern Theology*. Translated by Thomas Bailey Saunders. Introduction by Rudolf Bultmann. Minneapolis: Fortress, 1986.

Harrison, Edward. *Masks of the Universe: Changing Ideas on the Nature of the Cosmos*. 2nd ed. Cambridge: Cambridge University Press, 2003.

Hendel, Kurt. "Luther's Theology of the Cross." *Currents in Theology and Mission* 24 (1997) 223–31.

———. "The Material as a Vehicle of the Divine." *Currents in Theology and Mission* 28 (2001) 326–34.

Hendry, George S. "Eclipse of Creation." *Theology Today* 28 (1972) 406–25.

Hendrix, Scott H. *Luther and the Papacy: Stages in a Reformation Conflict*. Philadelphia: Fortress, 1981.

Heyward, Isabel Carter. *The Redemption of God: A Theology of Mutual Relation*. 1982. Reprint, Eugene, OR: Wipf & Stock, 2010.

Hinkson, Craig. "Luther and Kierkegaard: Theologians of the Cross." *International Journal of Systematic Theology* 3 (2001) 27–45.

Hodgson, Peter C. *Jesus—Word and Presence: An Essay in Christology*. Philadelphia: Fortress, 1971.

Hoffman, Bengt R. *Luther and the Mystics: A Re-examination of Luther's Spiritual Experience and His Relationship to the Mystics*. Minneapolis: Augsburg, 1976.

———. *Theology of the Heart: The Role of Mysticism in the Theology of Martin Luther*. Minneapolis: Kirk House, 1998.

Holze, Heinrich. "Luther's Concept of Creation: Five remarks on his interpretation of the first article in the large catechism (1529)." In *Concern for Creation: Voices on the Theology of Creation*, edited by Viggo Mortensen, 49-53. Uppsala: Svenska kyrkans forskningsråd, 1995.

Hordern, William. *Experience and Faith: The Significance of Luther for Understanding Today's Experiential Religion*. Minneapolis: Augsburg, 1983.

Hovland, C. Warren. "Anfechtung in Luther's Biblical Exegesis." *Reformation Studies: Essays in Honor of Roland H. Bainton*, edited by Franklin H. Littell, 46-60. Richmond, VA: John Knox, 1962.

Hunsinger, George. *Disruptive Grace: Studies in the Theology of Karl Barth*. Grand Rapids: Eerdmans, 2000.

———. *How To Read Karl Barth: The Shape of His Theology*. New York: Oxford University Press, 1991.

Inge, John. *A Christian Theology of Place*. Explorations in Practical, Pastoral and Empirical Theology. Burlington, VT: Ashgate, 2003.

Iwand, Hans Joachim. *Luther's Theologie*. Mit einer Einführung von Karl Gerhard Steck. Fünfter Band. *Nachgelassene Werke*. Herausgegeben von Johann Haar. Gütersloh: Guterslöher, 2000.

———. "Um den rechten Glauben." In *Gesammelte Aufsätze*, 87-109. Munich: Kaiser, 1959.

Jüngel, Eberhard. "The Christian Understanding of Suffering." *Journal of Theology for Southern Africa* 65 (December 1988) 3-13.

———. *God as the Mystery of the World: On the Foundation of the Theology of the Crucified One in the Dispute between Theism and Atheism*. Translated by Darrell L. Guder. Grand Rapids: Eerdmans, 1983.

———. *Karl Barth: A Theological Legacy*. Translated by Garrett E. Paul. Philadelphia: Westminster, 1986.

———. "The Relationship between 'Economic' and 'Immanent' Trinity." *Theology Digest* 24.2 (1976) 179-84.

Kant, Immanuel. *Critique of Practical Reason*. Translated by Werner S. Pluhar. Introduction by Stephen Engstrom. Indianapolis: Hackett, 2002.

Käsemann, Ernst. "On the Subject of Primitive Christian Apocalyptic." In *New Testament Questions of Today*, 108-37. Translated by W. J. Montague. New York: SCM, 1969.

———. "The Pauline Theology of the Cross." *Interpretation* 24 (1970) 151-77.

———. "The Saving Significance of the Death of Jesus." In *Perspectives on Paul*, 32-59. Translated by Margaret Kohl. Philadelphia: Fortress, 1969.

Kelly, J. N. D. *Early Christian Doctrines*. Rev. ed. San Francisco: Harper, 1978.

Kolb, Robert. "Luther on the Theology of the Cross." *Lutheran Quarterly* 16 (2002) 443-66.

Kortner, Ulrich H. J. *The End of the World: A Theological Interpretation*. Translated by Douglas W. Stott. Louisville: Westminster John Knox, 1995.

Lane, Dermot. *Keeping Hope Alive: Stirrings in Christian Theology*. New York: Paulist, 1996.

Latour, Bruno. *We Have Never Been Modern*. Translated by Catherine Porter. Cambridge: Harvard University Press, 1993.

Leith, John H., editor. *Creeds of the Churches: A Reader in Christian Doctrine from the Bible to the Present*. 3rd ed. Louisville: Westminster John Knox, 1982.

Lessing, Gotthold Ephraim. *Lessing's Theological Writings*. Selected and translated by Henry Chadwick. Stanford: Stanford University Press, 1956.

Lewis, Alan E. *Between Cross and Resurrection: A Theology of Holy Saturday*. Foreword by John Alsup. Grand Rapids: Eerdmans, 2001.

———. "The Burial of God: Rupture and Resumption as the Story of Salvation." In *Scottish Journal of Theology* 40 (1987) 335–62.

Lienhard, Marc. *Luther: Witness to Jesus Christ: Stages and Themes of the Reformer's Christology*. Translated by Edwin H. Robertson. Minneapolis: Augsburg, 1982.

Livingston, James, et al. *Modern Christian Thought: The Twentieth Century*. Vol. 2. 2nd ed. Minneapolis: Fortress, 2006.

Loewenich, Walter von. *Luther's Theology of the Cross*. Translated by Herbert J. A. Bouman. Minneapolis: Augsburg, 1976.

Löfgren, David. *Die Theologie der Schöpfung bei Luther*. Göttingen: Vandenhoek & Ruprecht, 1960.

Lohse, Bernhard. *Martin Luther: An Introduction to His Life and Work*. Translated by Martin C. Schultz. Philadelphia: Fortress, 1986.

———. *Martin Luther's Theology: Its Historical and Systematic Development*. Translated by Roy A. Harrisville. Minneapolis: Fortress, 1999.

Luther, Martin. *Luther's Works*. 55 vols. Edited by Jaroslav Pelikan and Helmut T. Lehman. Philadelphia: Fortress; St. Louis: Concordia, 1955–1986.

Mannermaa, Tuomo. *Christ Present in Faith: Luther's View of Justification*. Edited and introduced by Kirsi Stjerna. Minneapolis: Fortress, 2005.

Mattes, Mark. *The Role of Justification in Contemporary Theology*. Grand Rapids: Eerdmans, 2004.

McClendon, James W. *Ethics: Systematic Theology*. Vol. 1. Rev. 2nd ed. Nashville: Abingdon, 2002.

McCormack, Bruce L. "Grace and being: The Role of God's Gracious Election in Karl Barth's Theological Ontology." In *The Cambridge Companion to Karl Barth*, edited by John Webster, 92–110. Cambridge: Cambridge University Press, 2000.

———. *Karl Barth's Critically Realistic Dialectical Theology: Its Genesis and Development 1909–1936*. New York: Oxford University Press, 1995.

McGill, Arthur C. *Death and Life: An American Theology*. Edited by Charles A. Wilson and Per M. Anderson. Philadelphia: Fortress, 1987.

———. *Suffering: A Test of Theological Method*. Foreword by Paul Ramsey and Paul F. May. Philadelphia: Westminster, 1982.

McGrath, Alister E. *Luther's Theology of the Cross: Martin Luther's Theological Breakthrough*. Cambridge, MA: Blackwell, 1985.

Madsen, Anna M. *The Theology of the Cross in Historical Perspective*. Distinguished Dissertations in Christian Theology. Eugene, OR: Pickwick, 2007.

Martyn, J. Louis. "Epistemology at the Turn of the Ages." In *Theological Issues in the Letters of Paul*, 269–287. Edinburgh: T. & T. Clark, 1997.

Metz, Johann Baptist. *Faith in History and Society: Toward a Practical Fundamental Theology*. Translated and Edited by J. Matthew Ashley with Study Guide. New York: Crossroad, 2007.

Mildenberger, Friedrich. *Theology of the Lutheran Confessions*. Translated by Erwin L. Lueker. Edited by Robert C. Schultz. Philadelphia: Fortress, 1986.

Moltmann, Jürgen. *The Coming of God: Christian Eschatology*. Translated by Margaret Kohl. Minneapolis: Fortress, 1996.

---. "The 'Crucified God': A Trinitarian Theology of the Cross." *Interpretation* 26 (1972): 278–99.

---. *The Crucified God: The Cross of Christ as the Foundation and Criticism of Christian Theology*. New York: SCM, 1974.

---. *Theology of Hope: On the Ground and the Implications of a Christian Eschatology*. Translated by James W. Leitch. New York: Harper & Row, 1967.

Murphy, George L. "The Theology of the Cross and God's Work in the World." *Zygon* 33 (1998) 221–31.

Murphy, Nancey. *Bodies and Souls, or Spirited Bodies?* Cambridge: Cambridge University Press, 2006.

---. "Human Nature: Historical, Scientific, and Religious Issues." In *Whatever Happened to the Soul? Scientific and Theological Portraits of Human Nature*, edited by Warren S. Brown, Nancey Murphy, and H. Newton Malony, 1–29. Minneapolis: Fortress, 1998.

---. "The Resurrection and Personal Identity: Possibilities and Limits of Eschatological Knowledge." In *Resurrection: Theological and Scientific Assessments*, edited by Ted Peters, Robert John Russell, and Michael Welker, 202–18. Grand Rapids: Eerdmans, 2002.

Nestingen, James Arne. "Luther's Heidelberg Disputation: An Analysis of the Argument." Supplement Series 1. *Word & World* (1992) 147–53.

Ngien, Dennis. *The Suffering of God according to Martin Luther's 'Theologia Crucis.'* Series VII, American University Studies. New York: Lang, 1995.

Niebuhr, Reinhold. *The Nature and Destiny of Man*. Introduction by Robin W. Lovin. 2 vols. Louisville: Westminster John Knox, 1996.

Nilsson, Kjell Ove. *Simul: Das Miteinander von Göttlichem und Menschlichem in Luthers Theologie*. Göttingen: Vandenhoeck & Ruprecht, 1966.

Oberman, Heiko A. *The Dawn of the Reformation: Essays in Late Medieval and Early Reformation Thought*. Grand Rapids: Eerdmans, 1992.

---. *The Harvest of Medieval Theology: Gabriel Biel and Late Medieval Nominalism*. Durham, NC: Labyrinth, 1983.

---. *The Impact of the Reformation*. Grand Rapids: Eerdmans, 1994.

---. *The Reformation: Roots and Ramifications*. Translated by Andrew Colin Gow. Grand Rapids: Eerdmans, 1994.

Panksepp, Jaak. *Affective Neuroscience: The Foundations of Human and Animal Emotions*. New York: Oxford University Press, 1998.

Pannenberg, Wolfhart. *Jesus—God and Man*. 2nd ed. Translated by Lewis L. Wilkins and Duane A. Priebe. Philadelphia: Westminster, 1977.

Paulson, Steven D. "The Wrath of God." *Dialog* 33 (Fall 1994) 245–51.

Pelikan, Jaroslav. *The Emergence of the Catholic Tradition (100–600)*. Vol. 1 of *The Christian Tradition: A History of the Development of Doctrine*. Chicago: University of Chicago Press, 1971.

Peukert, Helmut. *Science, Action, and Fundamental Theology: Toward a Theology of Communicative Action*. Cambridge, MA: MIT Press, 1984.

Pinomaa, Lennart. *Faith Victorious: An Introduction to Luther's Theology*. Translated by Walter J. Kukkonen. Philadelphia: Fortress, 1963.

Placher, William C. *The Domestication of Transcendence: How Modern Thinking about God Went Wrong*. Louisville: Westminster John Knox, 1996.

Plato. "Phaedo," in *Plato: The Collected Dialogues Including the Letters*, edited by Edith Hamilton and Huntington Cairns, 40–98. Bollingen Series LXXI. Princeton: Princeton University Press, 1989.

Polkinghorne, John. "Eschatological Credibility," in *Resurrection: Theological and Scientific Assessments*, edited by Ted Peters, Robert John Russell and Michael Welker, 43–55. Grand Rapids: Eerdmans, 2002.

———. *The God of Hope and the End of the World*. Yale Nota Bene Edition. New Haven: Yale University Press, 2002.

Polkinghorne, John, and Michael Welker, editors. *The End of the World and the Ends of God: Science and Theology on Eschatology*. Harrisburg, PA: Trinity, 2000.

Prenter, Regin. *Creation and Redemption*. Translated by Theodor I. Jensen. Philadelphia: Fortress, 1967.

———. Die Einheit von Schöpfung und Erlösung. Zur Schöpfungslehre Karl Barths. *Theologische Zeitschrift* 2 (May/June 1946) 161–86.

———. *Luther's Theology of the Cross*. Philadelphia: Fortress, 1971.

———. *Spiritus Creator: Luther's Concept of the Holy Spirit*. Translated by John M. Jensen. Philadelphia: Fortress, 1953.

Price, Daniel. *Karl Barth's Anthropology in Light of Modern Thought*. Grand Rapids, MI: Eerdmans, 2002.

Ritschl, Dietrich. *Memory and Hope: An Inquiry Concerning the Presence of Christ*. New York: Macmillan, 1967.

Russell, William R. *Luther's Theological Testament: The Schmalkald Articles*. Minneapolis: Fortress, 1995.

Sanders, Theresa. *Tenebrae: Holy Week after the Holocaust*. Maryknoll, NY: Orbis, 2006.

Sasse, Hermann. *This Is My Body: Luther's Contention for the Real Presence in the Sacrament of the Altar*. Minneapolis: Augsburg, 1959.

———. *We Confess Anthology*. Translated by Norman Nagel. St. Louis: Concordia, 1999.

Sauter, Gerhard. "Eschatological Rationality." *Dialog* 38 (Winter 1999) 10–14.

———. "Luther on the Resurrection." *Lutheran Quarterly* 15 (2001) 195–216.

———. "Our Reasons for Hope." In *The End of the World and the Ends of God: Science and Theology on Eschatology*, edited by John Polkinghorne and Michael Welker, 209–21. Harrisburg, PA: Trinity, 2000.

———. *What Dare We Hope? Reconsidering Eschatology*. Theology for the 21st Century. Harrisburg, PA: Trinity, 1999.

———. "Why Is Karl Barth's *Church Dogmatics* Not a 'Theology of Hope'? Some Observations on Barth's Understanding of Eschatology." *Scottish Journal of Theology* 52 (1999) 407–29.

Schleiermacher, Friedrich Daniel Ernst. *On Religion: Speeches to Its Cultured Despisers*. Translated by John Oman. Foreword by Jack Forstman. Louisville: Westminster John Knox, 1994.

———. *The Christian Faith*. English translation of the second German edition. Edited by H. R. Mackintosh and J. S. Stewart. Philadelphia: Fortress, 1976.

Schmid, Heinrich. *The Doctrinal Theology of the Evangelical Lutheran Church*. 3rd ed., revised. Translated by Charles H. Hay and Henry E. Jacobs. Minneapolis: Augsburg, 1899.

Schwanke, Johannes. "Luther on Creation." *Lutheran Quarterly* 16 (2002) 1–20.

Schwarz, Hans. *Eschatology*. Grand Rapids: Eerdmans, 2000.

———. *On the Way to the Future: A Christian View of Eschatology in the Light of Current Trends in Religion, Philosophy, and Science*. Minneapolis: Augsburg, 1979.

Schwarzwäller, Klaus. "The Lutheran Tradition and its Obligation." *Lutheran Quarterly* 1 (1987) 170–83.

———. "Theology as Unfolding the Article of Justification." *Logia: A Journal of Lutheran Theology* 16 (Eastertide 2007) 37–42.

Siggins, Ian K. *Martin Luther's Doctrine of Christ*. New Haven: Yale University Press, 1970.

Siirala, Aarne. *Divine Humanness: Towards an Empirical Theology in the Light of the Controversy between Luther and Erasmus*. Translated by T. A. Kantonen. Philadelphia: Fortress, 1970.

Sittler, Joseph. "Called to Unity." *Ecumenical Review* 14 (1962) 177–87.

———. "A Christology of Function." *Lutheran Quarterly* 6 (1954) 122–31.

———. *The Doctrine of the Word in the Structure of Lutheran Theology*. Philadelphia: Muhlenberg, 1948.

———. "The Presence and Acts of the Triune God in Creation and History." In *The Gospel and Human Destiny*, edited by Vilmos Vajta, 90–136. Augsburg, 1971.

———. "The Scope of Christological Reflection." *Interpretation* 26 (1972) 328–37.

Sobrino, Jon. *Christology at the Crossroads: A Latin American Approach*. Translated by John Drury. Maryknoll, NY: Orbis, 1978.

———. *The True Church and the Poor*. Translated by Matthew J. O'Connell. Maryknoll, NY: Orbis, 1984.

Solberg, Mary. "All That Matters: What an Epistemology of the Cross is Good for." In *Cross Examinations: Readings on the Meaning of the Cross Today*, edited by Marit Trelstad, 139–50. Minneapolis: Fortress, 2006.

———. *Compelling Knowledge: A Feminist Proposal for an Epistemology of the Cross*. Albany, NY: State University of New York Press, 1997.

Sölle, Dorothee. *Suffering*. Translated by Everett R. Kalin. Philadelphia: Fortress Press, 1975.

Soulen, R. Kendall, and Linda Woodhead, editor. *God and Human Dignity*. Grand Rapids: Eerdmans, 2006.

Steiger, Johann Anselm. *Fünf Zentralthemen der Theologie Luthers und seiner Erben: Communicatio-Imago-Figura-Maria-Exempla. Mit Edition zweier christologischer Frühschriften John Gerhards*. Studies in the History of Christian Thought 104. Leiden: Brill, 2002.

———. "The *Communicatio Idiomatum* as the Axle and Motor of Luther's Theology." *Lutheran Quarterly* 14 (2000) 125–58.

Stroup, George. *Before God*. Grand Rapids: Eerdmans, 2004.

Sturm, Richard E. "Defining the Word 'Apocalyptic.'" In *Apocalyptic and the New Testament: Essays in Honor of J. Louis Martyn*, edited by Joel Marcus and Marion Soards, 17–48. Journal for the Study of the New Testament Supplement Series 24. Sheffield: JSOT Press, 1989.

Tanner, Kathryn. *God and Creation in Christian Theology: Tyranny or Empowerment?* Minneapolis: Fortress, 1988.

Tappert, Theodore G., trans. and ed. *The Book of Concord: The Confessions of the Evangelical Lutheran Church*. Philadelphia: Fortress, 1959.

Thompson, Deanna. A. *Crossing the Divide: Luther, Feminism, and the Cross*. Minneapolis: Fortress, 2004.

Thunberg, Lars. "The Cosmological and Anthropological Significance of Christ's Redeeming Work." In *The Gospel and Human Destiny*, edited by Vilmos Vajta, 64–89. Minneapolis: Augsburg, 1971.

Tillich, Paul. *Biblical Religion and the Search for Ultimate Reality*. The James W. Richard Lectures in the Christian Religion, University of Virginian 1951-52. Chicago: University of Chicago Press, 1955.

Torrance, Thomas F. *Karl Barth: An Introduction to His Early Thought 1910–1931*. Edinburgh: T. & T. Clark, 2000.

Tracy, David. "The Hidden God: The Divine Other of Liberation." *Cross Currents* 46 (Spring 1996) 5–16.

———. *Form and Fragment: The Recovery of the Hidden and Incomprehensible God*. Center for Theological Inquiry (22 March 2002) online: www.ctinquiry.or/publications/reflections_volume_3/tracy.htm.

Troeltsch, Ernst. *The Christian Faith: Based on Lectures delivered at the University of Heidelberg in 1912 and 1913*. Translated by Garrett E. Paul, edited by Gertrud von le Fort. Foreword by Marta Troeltsch. Fortress Texts in Modern Theology. Minneapolis: Fortress, 1991.

Vajta, Vilmos, editor. *The Gospel and Human Destiny*. Minneapolis: Augsburg, 1971.

Vercruysse, Joseph E. "Luther's Theology of the Cross at the Time of the Heidelberg Disputation." *Gregorianum* 57 (1976) 523–46.

———. "Luther's Theology of the Cross and its Ecclesiological and Ecumenical Implications." Edited by Kenneth Hagen. *Luther Digest: An Annual Abridgment of Luther Studies* 13 (2005) 78–80.

Watson, Philip. *Let God Be God: An Interpretation of the Theology of Martin Luther*. With a checklist of Luther's writings in English by George S. Robbert. Philadelphia: Fortress, 1970.

Webster, John. "Atonement, History and Narrative." In *Theologische Zeitschrift* 42 (1986) 115–31.

———. *Barth's Earlier Theology: Four Studies*. Edinburgh: T. & T. Clark, 2006.

Wengert, Timothy. "'PEACE, PEACE . . . CROSS, CROSS': Reflections on How Martin Luther Relates the Theology of the Cross to Suffering." *Theology Today* 59 (2002) 190–205.

Westhelle, Vítor. "Cross, Creation, and Ecology: The Meeting Point between the Theology of the Cross and Creation Theology in Luther." In *Concern for Creation: Voices on the Theology of Creation*, edited by Viggo Mortensen, 159–67. Uppsala: Svenska kyrkans forskningsråd, 1995.

———. *The Scandalous God: The Use and Abuse of the Cross*. Minneapolis: Fortress, 2006.

———. "The Way the World Ends: An Essay on Cross and Eschatology." *Currents in Theology and Mission* 27 (2000) 358–80.

———. "The Word and the Mask: Revisiting the Two-Kingdoms Doctrine." In *The Gift of Grace: The Future of Lutheran Theology*, edited by Niels Henrik Gregersen, Bo Holm, Ted Peters, and Peter Widmann, 167–78. Minneapolis: Fortress, 2005.

———. "Wrappings of the Divine: Location and Vocation in Theological Perspective." *Currents in Theology and Mission* 31 (2004) 368–80.

Williams, Rowan. *Christian Spirituality: A Theological History from the New Testament to Luther and St. John of the Cross*. Atlanta: John Knox, 1979.

Wingren, Gustaf. "The Doctrine of Creation: Not an Appendix but the First Article." *Word & World* 4 (1984) 353–71.

———. *The Flight from Creation*. Minneapolis: Augsburg, 1971.

———. *The Living Word: A Theological Study of Preaching and the Church*. Translated by Victor C. Pogue. Philadelphia: Fortress, 1960.

———. *Luther on Vocation*. Translated by Carl C. Rasmussen. Evansville, IN: Ballast, 1994.

———. *Theology in Conflict: Nygren—Barth—Bultmann*. Translated by Eric H. Wahlstrom. Philadelphia: Muhlenberg, 1958.

Yeago, David S. "The Catholic Luther." In *The Catholicity of the Reformation*, edited by Carl E. Braaten and Robert W. Jenson, 13–34. Grand Rapids: Eerdmans, 1996.

Name Index

Alison, James, 143, 281
Althaus, Paul, 55, 82, 90, 91, 106, 118, 137–39, 281
Altmann, Walter, 119, 120, 281
Anderson, Ray S., 11, 12, 281

Balthasar, Hans Urs von, 25, 28, 33, 200, 281
Barth, Karl, xi, xx, 2, 9, 96, 117, 197–262, 274, 281, 282
   and ascension, 250–51
   and Christology, restructuring of Christology (see *communicatio gratiarum*)
   and *communicatio gratiarum*, 239–48
   and critique of *communicatio gratiarum* from perspective of *communicatio idiomatum* and "resurrectionism," 258–62
   and criticism of *communicatio idiomatum*, 117, 239–43
   and critique of F. D. E. Schleiermacher, 216–38
   and embodied selfhood, 2
   and en- anhypostatic union, 244, 245, 246, 247, 248, 249, 250, 251, 253, 255, 256, 257, 258, 260, 261, 266
   and his conceptualization of "absolute man," 202–15
   and his conceptualization of "apotheosized man," xx, 201, 239, 243, 246, 251, 253
   and resurrection, 250–51
   and "within-redemption," 254–55
Basch, Michael Franz, 19, 20, 282
Bayer, Oswald, 43, 44, 45, 57, 58, 80, 119, 120, 122, 126, 133, 139, 140, 151, 161, 165, 166, 167, 174, 176, 177, 182, 282
Beker, J. Christiann, 46, 47, 282
Benjamim, Walter, 271, 272
Berkhouwer, G. C., 200, 259, 282
Boff, Leonardo, 116, 282
Bonhoeffer, Dietrich, 2, 9, 21, 282
Braaten, Carl E., 67, 114, 120, 282, 284, 292
Brecht, Martin, 55, 283
Bromiley, Geoffrey W., 200, 281, 282, 283
Brown, Alexandra, 46, 47, 48, 283
Brown, Peter, 15, 283
Brueggemann, Walter, 78, 283
Bultmann, Rudolf, 2, 3, 9, 283, 285, 292
Busch, Eberhard, 200, 234, 244, 246, 283
Bynum, Caroline Walker, 15, 16, 17, 283

Caputo, John, 272, 283
Cullmann, Oscar, 3, 8, 9, 283

Daley, Brian, 14, 15, 283
Dalferth, Ingolf U., 144, 152, 156–59, 161, 162, 165, 193, 283
Damasio, Antonio, 18, 19, 283
Descartes, Rene, 5, 283

Ebeling, Gerhard, 52, 53, 55, 68, 82, 85, 284

Feuerbach, Ludwig, xx, 201, 234, 235, 236, 237, 239, 241, 242, 243, 253, 284
Fiddes, Paul, 37, 284
Flanagan, Owen, 5, 284
Forde, Gerhard O., 29, 56, 63, 66, 68, 78, 81, 82, 83, 84, 94, 95, 96, 97, 98, 99, 101, 103, 186, 193, 235, 236, 237, 284
Forstman, H. Jackson, 67, 83, 284, 289

Gerrish, Brian, 95, 96, 97, 284
Gillman, Neil, 8, 284
Gorringe, Timothy J., 200, 244, 284
Green, Joel, 10, 11, 12, 284
Gregersen, Niels Henrik, 95, 174, 177, 178, 179, 183, 282, 285, 291
Gunton, Colin, 258, 284, 285

Haikola, Lauri, 63, 285
Hall, Douglas John, xvii, xviii, xix, xx, xxi, 1, 9, 12, 13, 18, 23, 24, 25, 26, 29, 38, 39, 40, 50, 102, 103, 106, 107, 115, 194, 259, 263, 264, 265, 268, 275–80, 285
Harnack, Adolf von, 6, 7, 285
Harrison, Edward, 158, 159, 285
Hendel, Kurt, 55, 56, 88, 285
Hendrix, Scott H., 55, 285
Heyward, Isabel Carter, 116, 285
Hinkson, Craig, 53, 90, 285
Hoffman, Bengt R., 55, 285
Holze, Heinrich, 142, 150, 151, 152, 160, 161, 162, 163, 165, 167, 176, 286
Hordern, William, 101, 286
Horkheimer, Max, 271, 272

Hunsinger, George, 198, 199, 200, 260, 261, 286

Iwand, Hans Joachim, 55, 66, 98, 109, 286

Jüngel, Eberhard, 25, 200, 286

Kant, Immanuel, 6, 7, 286
Käsemann, Ernst, 47, 48, 50, 286
Kelly, J. N. D., 114, 286
Kolb, Robert, 22, 53, 55, 85, 104, 151, 155, 187, 286

Lane, Dermot, 7, 8, 286
Latour, Bruno, 133, 286
Leith, John H., 114, 115, 286
Lessing, G. E., 5, 287
Lewis, Alan E., xviii, xix, 27, 28, 29, 30, 31, 32, 33, 34, 35, 36, 37, 42, 43, 45, 49, 50, 104, 128, 135, 136, 137, 149, 151, 157, 193, 194, 195, 196, 254, 259, 260, 261, 264, 265, 266, 275, 276, 287
Lienhard, Marc, 108, 109, 110, 112, 120, 122, 123, 125, 126, 146, 147, 287
Livingston, James, 197, 198, 287
Loewenich, Walter von, 55, 56, 81, 88, 90, 97, 98, 287
Löfgren, David, 138, 141, 142, 144, 162, 181, 287
Luther, Martin, ix, x, xi, xviii, xix, xx, 22, 23, 33, 43, 44, 50, 51, 52–105, 106–53, 154–96, 198, 199, 200, 236, 237, 239, 242, 252, 253, 255, 258, 259, 265, 266, 267, 268, 269, 272, 280 (see also *theologia crucis*, *communicatio idiomatum*, justification by faith, *larvae Dei*, "Within-redemption")

Luther, Martin (cont.),
  Against the Heavenly Prophets in the Matter of Images and Sacraments (1525), 100, 110
  Heidelberg Disputation (1518), 52, 53, 54, 55, 56, 57, 58, 68, 74, 75, 76, 77, 78, 79, 86, 107, 152
  On the Councils and the Church (1539), 129–35
Madsen, Anna M., 52, 55, 85, 88, 92, 287
Mannermaa, Tuomo, 270, 287
Martyn, J. Louis, 46, 47, 48, 49, 287, 290
McClendon, James W., 3, 4, 8, 9, 287
McCormack, Bruce L., 200, 245, 248, 249, 287
McGrath, Alister E., 55, 56, 58, 68, 70, 71, 72, 73, 74, 75, 76, 84, 88, 92, 97, 287
Moltmann, Jürgen, 52, 117, 118, 268, 269, 287
Murphy, George L., 176, 288
Murphy, Nancey, 3, 5, 8, 9, 10, 17, 18, 19, 20, 21, 281, 283, 285, 288

Nestingen, James Arne, 56, 77, 288
Ngien, Dennis, 55, 56, 67, 80, 84, 288
Niebuhr, Reinhold, 2, 9, 288
Nilsson, Kjell O., 122, 123, 124, 126, 127, 142, 146, 288

Oberman, Heiko, 55, 88, 288

Panksepp, Jaak, 19, 288
Pannenberg, Wolfhart, 116, 288
Pelikan, Jaroslav, 114, 287, 288
Pinomaa, Lennart, 55, 137, 177, 288
Plato, 3, 4, 14, 117, 289
Polkinghorne, John, 1, 4, 6, 12, 13, 14, 24, 289

Prenter, Regin, 148, 163, 164, 258, 289
Price, Daniel, 217, 218, 219, 220, 223, 224, 225, 226, 229, 230, 231, 248, 289

Russell, William R., 59, 289

Sanders, Theresa, 41, 42, 272, 273, 289
Sauter, Gerhard, 45, 258, 267, 289
Schleiermacher, F. D. E., xi, xx, 199, 201–43, 289
  as a theological expression of "absolute man," 216–38
Schwanke, Johannes, 140, 161, 162, 170, 171, 175, 176, 289
Schwarz, Hans, 5, 290
Schwarzwäller, Klaus, 149, 155, 166, 290
Siggins, Ian K., 118, 119, 290
Siirala, Aarne, 179, 290
Sittler, Joseph, 154, 155, 168, 169, 179, 270, 271, 272, 290
Sobrino, Jon, 90, 115, 290
Solberg, Mary, 53, 54, 68, 72, 76, 281, 290
Sölle, Dorothee, 41, 290
Steiger, Johann Anselm, 113, 117, 122, 123, 126, 127, 149, 290

Thompson, Deanna, 53, 55, 77, 82, 84, 98, 155, 291
Thunberg, Lars, 126, 291
Torrance, Thomas F., 197, 198, 200, 281, 291
Tracy, David, xvii, 95, 96, 268, 291
Troeltsch, Ernst, 7, 291

Vercruysse, Joseph E., 53, 56, 77, 78, 79, 85, 89, 155, 291

Watson, Philip, 109, 126, 168, 169, 170, 171, 181, 182, 175, 291

Webster, John, 200, 287, 291
Welker, Michael, 268, 283, 288, 289,
Wengert, Timothy, 41, 291
Westhelle, Vítor, ix, 68, 69, 70, 74,
  75, 79, 80, 85, 86, 88, 91, 92,
  94, 95, 96, 97, 145, 146, 149,
  150, 152, 156, 161, 168, 171,
  172, 176, 182, 186, 187, 188,
  189, 193, 271, 291
Williams, Rowan, 81, 82, 83, 87,
  100, 102, 186, 189, 292
Wingren, Gustaf, 93, 99, 121, 122,
  124, 133, 170, 173, 174, 175,
  178, 183, 259, 292

Subject Index

Anthropological dualism, 4–12
Apocalyptic, 46, 47
  apocalyptic as epistemology, 48–50

Communicatio idiomatum, ix, x, xviii, xix, xx, 52, 54, 56, 57, 86, 87, 105, 106–53, 154, 164, 180, 181, 195, 199, 200, 237, 239, 241, 242, 243, 252, 253, 258, 259, 265, 267, 268, 290
  and "Third mode" of Christ's Presence, ix, x, xi, xiii, xviii, xix, xx, xxi, 128, 135, 137–53, 154, 155, 157, 164, 180, 181, 182, 183, 185, 187, 188, 189, 192, 193, 195, 252, 253, 258, 267, 268, 270, 271, 275, 280
  and "Within-Redemption," 56, 57, 107, 112, 119, 121, 128, 129, 135, 136, 137, 147, 150, 151, 152, 153, 154–96, 200, 202, 252, 253, 255, 259, 262, 267, 268, 269, 270, 271, 272, 273, 274

Embodied humanity, *see* Psychosomatic unity

Formula of Chalcedon, ix, x, 105, 107, 113, 114, 115, 116, 117, 119, 120, 122, 126, 128, 129, 180

Hidden God, xvii, 95, 96, 97, 98

Immortal soul, *see* Anthropological dualism

Justification by Faith, 58, 138, 162, 165, 166 (*see also Theologia Crucis*)

larvae Dei, 86, 87
  as an expression of the *communicatio idiomatum*: xix, xx, xxi, 153, 154–96, 259, 267, 274

Narrative, *see Triduum*
Natural theology of glory, 43, 45, 46, 49

"Psychosomatic unity," xix, 1–3, 9, 11, 12, 16, 263
  as expressed through the work of "within-redemption," 36, 46, 50, 194

Realized eschatology (*see also* Resurrectionism), 40, 272, 276
Resurrectionism, 40, 195, 264, 267, 272, 276
Revelation, *see Theologia Crucis*

Theologia Crucis, xvii, xviii, xix, xx, 1, 22, 28, 42, 43, 51, 52–105, 106, 107, 111, 112, 113, 117, 120, 122, 126, 127, 128, 132, 136, 156, 163, 164, 169, 171, 179, 180, 184, 185, 187 (FN

Theologia Crucis (cont.),
    178 and 182), 188, 195, 259, 263, 268, 270
    modus operandi of, xix, 22, 23, 24, 25, 34, 53, 54, 65, 80, 85, 103, 108, 111, 122, 148, 153, 155
    and "third mode," 152, 187–89
    as criterion for creation, xix, 156, 167, 183
    and "Within-Redemption," xvii–xix, 22–51, 263, 264, 266, 267, 275–80
    and complete "Within-Redemption," 189–93
    Theologia crucis as a theology of justification, 59–80
    Theologia crucis as a theology of revelation, 80–88
    Theologia crucis as a theology of faith, 88–99
    Theologia crucis as a theology for creation, 100–103

Communicatio idiomatum as an expression of *Theologia Crucis*, 113–35, 147, 151–55, 182, 183, 195, 199, 267

Theolgia Crucis Naturalis, 42-45
    as expressed by a signifier-signified framework, xvii, 36, 41, 43, 49, 50, 104, 128, 136, 194, 265 (*see also* Resurrectionism)

Triduum
    as reference point for "within-redemption," 34, 35, 36, 43, 45, 49, 50, 135, 193, 194, 265

"Within-Redemption," xvii, xviii, xix, xx, xxi, 1, 9 (FN 23), 22, 26, 27, 29, 30, 35, 36, 37, 39, 42–45, 49, 53, 104, 105, 264–66, 275, 276, 277, 279

Scripture Index

Genesis

1:26	143
1:31	136
45:45	192
42:7	190
41:43	190
50:20	190

Exodus

33:20	82, 106
33:23	83

Isiaiah

55:9	273
53:11	75

Galatians

1:3	119

www.ingramcontent.com/pod-product-compliance
Lightning Source LLC
Chambersburg PA
CBHW050621300426
44112CB00012B/1601